BIGGER THAN LIFE

BIGGER THAN LIFE

[The Close-Up and Scale in the Cinema]

Mary Ann Doane

DUKE UNIVERSITY PRESS   DURHAM AND LONDON   2021

© 2021 Duke University Press
All rights reserved
Designed by Aimee C. Harrison and Matthew Tauch
Typeset in Garamond Premier Pro and Univers LT Std
by Westchester Publishing Services

Library of Congress Cataloging-in-Publication Data
Names: Doane, Mary Ann, author.
Title: Bigger than life : the close-up and scale in the cinema /
Mary Ann Doane.
Description: Durham : Duke University Press, 2021. |
Includes bibliographical references and index.
Identifiers: LCCN 2021011901 (print)
LCCN 2021011902 (ebook)
ISBN 9781478013563 (hardcover)
ISBN 9781478014485 (paperback)
ISBN 9781478021780 (ebook)
Subjects: LCSH: Cinematography—History. | Digital
cinematography. | Motion picture audiences—Psychology. | Space in
motion pictures. | Place (Philosophy) in motion pictures. |
Participatory theater. | BISAC: PERFORMING ARTS / Film / History
& Criticism | SOCIAL SCIENCE / Gender Studies
Classification: LCC TR848 .D63 2021 (print) | LCC TR848 (ebook) |
DDC 777—dc23
LC record available at https:// lccn.loc.gov/2021011901
LC ebook record available at https:// lccn.loc.gov/2021011902

Cover art: Cary Grant and Eva Marie Saint in *North by
Northwest* (1959). MGM/Photofest. © MGM.

In memory of my sister, Janice Louise Doane

(1950–2018)

and

For my daughter, Hannah Doane Rosen

Contents

Acknowledgments

It has become conventional in the genre of acknowledgments to confess how long it has taken to write the book (always longer than one thought it would be). I will not attempt to resist or undermine this generic convention since *this* book has taken even longer than longer. It began life as a short book on the filmic strategy of the close-up and has expanded exponentially to address more extensive issues of scale and media (it has been "scaled up," one might say). Even more than is typical, I feel that the writing of this book could have been prolonged into infinity. But the time has come to stop. Due to the *longue durée* of the work on the manuscript, this list of acknowledgments will inevitably be incomplete. My profound apologies in advance to anyone whom I may have inadvertently omitted.

I have many people to thank for their support, guidance, ideas, and encouragement. I am grateful to Bernhard Siegert and Lorenz Engell at the Internationales Kolleg für Kulturtechnikforschung und Medienphilosophie in Weimar, Germany, for a fellowship in the fall of 2011 that allowed me not only time to think and write but also the opportunity to inhabit a stimulating and provocative environment for those involved in deep analysis of the media. During the fall of 2016, I was privileged to be awarded an Anna-Maria Kellen Fellowship at the American Academy of Berlin. The camaraderie and support offered by the Academy and other fellows were incomparable in further developing my manuscript. Work on the project "Face of Terror: The Social and Cultural Agency of Media in Globalized Environments" with Anne Gjelsvik has been especially illuminating in thinking about the international politics of the represented face. Many of the chapters in this book emerged from invited lectures at a wide range of places—Nanjing, Melbourne, Zurich, Chicago, Vancouver, Beijing, Shanghai, Irvine, Berlin, Seoul, Copenhagen, São Paulo, to name a few. I am exceedingly grateful to the organizers of these symposia and conferences and to the audiences who challenged me with both difficult questions and suggested paths. The form and conceptualization of this project have benefited enormously from being tested in teaching at both the undergraduate and graduate level at UC Berkeley. My students' gregariousness, openness, and insight have been continually invigorating. The university has provided me with research support and the Townsend Humanities Center with a stimulating forum in which to present my work.

I have been privileged to have some *amazing* graduate research assistants at both Brown University and UC Berkeley. Another indicator of the duration of my work on this book is the fact that a number of them have gone on to become excellent scholars in their own right with a substantial impact on the field of media studies. My heartfelt thanks and admiration to Genie Brinkema, Jennifer Pranolo, Anna Fisher, Dolores McElroy, Jonathan Mackris, and Nicholas Gutierrez. Their dedication and commitment to the project, as well as their insight, sheer intelligence, and precision, nurture optimism for the future of media studies. My colleagues in the Department of Film and Media at UC Berkeley have been a constant source of support, humor, inventiveness, and joy. Colin Brant, the department's media technology specialist, patiently and meticulously helped me with the film stills. I also received professional assistance in locating and viewing silent films from the British Film Institute and the Library of Congress. I would like to single out Mutahara Mobashar at the LOC for her aid and support during the difficult period when the library closed due to the COVID-19 pandemic. Thanks as well to Paul Hogroian at the LOC for his digital photography of images from early films.

Earlier versions of the first section of chapter 6 appeared in Portuguese in *Cinema Transversais*, ed. Patricia Moran (São Paulo: Editora Iluminuras Ltda., 2016); in Italian in *Filmidee*, no. 12 (October 7, 2014); and in *Ends of Cinema*, ed. Richard Grusin and Jocelyn Szczepaniak-Gillece (Minneapolis: University of Minnesota Press, 2020). Different sections of chapter 4 were published in *Gender and Chinese Cinema*, trans. into Chinese by Li Shuling, ed. He Chengzhou and Wang Lingzhen (Nanjing: Nanjing University Press, 2012); *The Question of Gender: Joan Scott's Critical Feminism*, ed. Elizabeth Weed and Judith Butler (Bloomington: Indiana University Press, 2011); and in Italian in *La Valle dell'Eden*, no. 19 (July–December 2007). Sections of chapter 2 appeared in *Realism and the Audiovisual Media*, ed. Lucia Nagib and Cecilia Antakly de Mello (Hampshire: Palgrave Macmillan, 2009); and in *NTU (National Taiwan University) Studies in Language and Literature*, no. 20 (December 2008). An earlier version of a section of chapter 5 was published in *The Art of Projection*, ed. Stan Douglas and Christopher Eamon (Stuttgart: Hatje Cantz, 2009); and in Chinese in *Chung-wai Literary Quarterly*, no. 423 (December 2008). An earlier version of a section of chapter 3 appeared in *New German Critique* 122 (Summer 2014); and a primitive version of chapter 1 was published in *differences: A Journal of Feminist Cultural Studies* 14, no. 3 (Fall 2003).

I would also like to thank my editor at Duke University Press, Courtney Berger, for her openness and generosity, and her assistant editor, Sandra Korn, for her efficiency and attention to detail. Mark Sandberg, John Belton, Maggie Hennefeld, Tim Corrigan, and two anonymous readers gave the manuscript a rigorous reading and offered invaluable suggestions. A massive number of people over the years have contributed to helping me refine and improve this book. I am sure I will forget some of them, but I will begin by expressing gratitude to Esra Akcan, Weihong Bao, Beth Bird, Harry Burson, Erica Carter, Michel Chion, Wendy Chun, Barbara Creed, Corey Creekmur, Florian Dombois, Thomas Elsaesser, Oliver Gaycken, Tom Gunning, Jan Holmberg, Laura Mulvey, Veronica Pravadelli, Philip Rosen, Joan Scott, Margrit Tröhler, Lingzhen Wang, Elizabeth Weed, Kristen Whissel, Linda Williams, and Damon Young.

My daughter, Hannah Doane Rosen, has been an unending source of comfort and delight and my most faithful ally and confidante.

This book is dedicated to the memory of my sister, Janice Louise Doane. She was a stolid and uncompromising feminist and my best friend since childhood, a bulwark against the four brothers. She was certainly critical of me but was also the only one who could make me laugh for hours on end. Despite the fact that Jan and I had a lot in common in our work—an interest in feminist theory, an interest in language and form—we did not talk very often about our intellectual interests or our writing. I guess I didn't want her to be a figurative sister, of which I have many, but a literal sister, of which I have/had one. Jan sustained and supported me in ways that neither she nor I understood. I know that I don't even know now how very much I miss her.

Introduction

Scale, the Cinematic Image,
and the Negotiation of Space

The sites in films are not to be located or trusted. All is out of proportion.
Scale inflates or deflates into uneasy dimensions. We wander between the
towering and the bottomless. We are lost between the abyss within us and
the boundless horizons outside us. Any film wraps us in uncertainty.
—ROBERT SMITHSON, "A Cinematic Atopia"

The history of film theory is inundated with speculation about the effects of
various scales of shots, but by far the most heavily discussed scale is that of
the close-up. From Jean Epstein's rapture when confronted with the magnification of the human face to Béla Balázs's and Gilles Deleuze's insistence that
the close-up of the face absorbs all space within itself and no longer acts as
metonymy pointing to a larger whole, the close-up has been accompanied by
an excessive discourse or, at the very least, a discourse about excess.[1] It is as
though scale had gone awry. In comparison, the medium shot and the long
shot appear to be of "normal" scale. "Normal" or "proper" scale is generally
measured in relation to the human body. It is difficult for us to imagine the
impact of enlarged, detached faces or even objects seemingly distorted in size
on the screen in the early cinema. For Sergei Eisenstein, tearing the object
from the real, the close-up introduced "absolute changes in the dimensions of

I.1 Georges Méliès's *The Man with a Rubber Head* (*L'homme à la tête de caoutchouc*; 1901).

bodies and objects on the screen."[2] The ordinary rules of classical perspective no longer obtain: "The laws of cinematographic perspective are such that a cockroach filmed in close-up appears on the screen one hundred times more formidable than a hundred elephants in medium-long shot."[3] Because the close-up exaggerates a perceived distortion of scale that, in fact, characterizes any projected image of film, it has been the subject of a film theoretical obsession. The close-up carries the threat of a certain monstrosity, a face or object filling the screen and annihilating all sense of scale.

In practice, cinema has always exploited the structuring ambiguity of shot size in the cinema—the ambiguity of scale versus distance. Is the close-up larger or closer? Despite the demand for life-size images of human beings in journalistic discourses about early cinema and a certain anxiety about cutting up the body, very early films often played intensively with the relations, contradictions, and potential misreadings of the interplay between scale and distance. In Georges Méliès's *The Man with a Rubber Head* (*L'homme à la tête de caoutchouc*; 1901), a chemist (played by Méliès) produces a close-up within the diegesis (narrative space) by placing his own head on a table and then pumping it with air (fig. I.1). Méliès generated the illusion by superimposing in the open space under an arch a view of his enlarging head obtained by having the director roll on a trolley on an inclined plane toward the camera. The effect in the image is not that of a decreasing distance between the head and the camera/spectator position but that of a head growing larger and larger as it is pumped full of air. The precariousness and instability of such a perversion of magnitude, of bodily scale, are underlined by the catastrophic explosion at the end of the film. Méliès's play with scale, his ironic and hyperbolic exploitation of the "larger than life" quality of the cinema, is consistent with a more widespread interrogation of the aesthetic feasibility of the close-up in early cinema.

Both in threatening a "proper" scale and in its dangerous proximity, the close-up poses the problem of the threshold, of the surface or screen as limit, as barrier. The screen presents itself as a boundary between two territories— that of the "world" of the film and that of the space of the spectator. The specter of the close-up is raised whenever an object or person moves toward the camera, potentially putting into crisis the distance between screen and spectator, threatening to bridge the abyss of representation. Perhaps the most extreme of these early filmic ruminations on that threshold is *The Big Swallow* (aka *Interviewee Swallows Camera*, James A. Williamson, 1901). As the film catalog tells us, a gentleman reading is interrupted by a cameraman threatening to take his picture. The gentleman objects vociferously, shouting, "I

I.2 *The Big Swallow* (aka *Interviewee Swallows Camera*, James A. Williamson, 1901).

won't, I won't, I'll eat the camera first!" Then, shouting and gesticulating, he approaches the camera until he is in extreme close-up, opening his mouth to reveal a black void (fig. I.2). There is then a cut to the cameraman and his camera indeed toppling over the edge of a parapet and disappearing. The gentleman retreats from the close-up, munching and smacking his lips in satisfaction. The film dramatizes in raw form the implications of the extreme close-up, of occupying a space that is too proximate, a kind of no-man's-land of representation. For it is not only the cameraman who is incorporated, absorbed within the diegesis, but also the figure of the spectator, who succumbs, if only momentarily, to the enveloping nothingness of the screen. There is an ironic play here on the inextricability of proximity and size in relation to the camera. The gentleman has only to move closer to the camera to become large enough to swallow it. As Noël Burch has pointed out with respect to *The Big Swallow* in the context of early cinema, "It is one of a series of battering rams beating on the 'invisible barrier' that maintains the spectator in a state of externality."[4]

The close-up of early cinema seems more acutely to evoke the possibility of breaching the limit of the screen, the protective barrier of representation. These two films signify by putting into play and exploiting the cinema's ability to shatter conventional scale, its tendency to produce (or, in these instances, to thrive on) disorientation and dislocation, to construct a space and a world to its own measure. In these examples, the problematic of scale and its distortion in cinema is performed. This distortion is not limited to the close-up, which is perhaps its best example, but is endemic to every shot size. With the rise of the classical Hollywood narrative and its continuity editing, the spectator was positioned to be less aware of the ambiguity. Preserving the unity and homogeneity of space, this style transmuted the perception of scale—that is, calling attention to the size of the screen, that of the image, and aspect ratio (representational space)—into the perception of distance within the diegesis (represented space). This technique effects a displacement or amelioration of the threat of large scale, disproportion, and a disturbing monumentality by translating scale (the logic of large and small) into distance (closer or farther). Throughout this book, I will be discussing the effects of this abstraction and distortion of scale in the cinema and the way they cannot be confined to the floundering of an early cinema coming to grips with (and even commenting upon) its own unfamiliarity. Indeed, this scalar abstraction is endemic to the form, and it suffuses media to the present day, informing the work of IMAX, virtual reality, "immersive" sound systems, and Global Positioning Systems (GPS) that seek to dislocate and relocate the spectator/user in the production of an *other* experience.

There is an anomaly in the history of scalar effects in cinematic classical narrative—the zoom. In general, the zoom has been derided as a cheap and easy (or even facile) technique, one often associated with the "lesser" medium of television (the "small" screen). Serge Daney refers to it as having the reputation of an "automatic reflex" and as bearing the connotations of rape, penetration.[5] The zoom is of course the attempt to combine all cinematic scales—from the telephoto view to the extreme wide-angle view—in a single, continuous shot. Unlike the tracking shot, which because it is the result of an actual camera movement appears to transport the spectator along with the camera through a physical space with depth and varying perspectives, the zoom, as a mechanical movement changing the focal length of the lens, flattens and abstracts space. It is not a *real* movement. As John Belton points out, "In a tracking shot, the camera moves bodily through space, producing a two-dimensional image through a three-dimensional filming process which endows that image with an illusion of depth (via parallax and changes in perspective)." In contrast, in the zoom, movement through space is itself illusory and "a zoom lens produces the illusion of movement *optically* through continuous changes in the focal length of the lens, rather than through the actual movement of the camera, creating an image which progressively alters the original space being photographed and which subverts the illusion of depth."[6] There is always something uncanny or explicitly artificial about a zoom, which manufactures scale so blatantly and without shame, annihilating any physical space that the spectator might inhabit. The zoom makes visible the *abstraction* of space and scale that is usually concealed in classical cinema, and this is perhaps why it is derided. For we tend to take cinematic scale for granted, as a reasonable measure in relation to the human body—of both the character and the spectator. But it is far more than that.

The word and the concept of scale have many different meanings that are worth pausing to consider. In geometry, scale is a relatively straightforward concept linked to proportion and ratio. Scale refers to the relation between the representation of an object (or a territory on a map) and the object itself. In the *Oxford English Dictionary*, scale is "a system of representing or reproducing objects in a smaller or larger size proportionately in every part. *to scale*: with exactly proportional representation of each part of the model."[7] But the term can also refer to a range (of exposures or colors in photography or of notes in music). Scale is in addition a standard of measure or calculation (as "on a global scale" or "the scale of the catastrophe"). In the plural, it can be an attribute of the body: scales as "membranous or horny outgrowths or modifications of the skin in many fishes and reptiles and some mammals" or, as a disease, one of the layers of the epidermis that can become separated.[8] In another somewhat remote sense, scales can be a cause of blindness or lack of knowledge—"to remove the scales from one's eyes" means to become enlightened and binds knowledge to the visible. Scale is also a measure of weight, as in "the scales of justice" (although here the judge is blindfolded), one of the most potent symbols of democracies.

In the late 1990s and early 2000s, the discipline of geography witnessed a transition in the understanding of scale whereby it was no longer taken for granted and instead became a shifting epistemological (and ideological) tool. In recent years there have been vigorous debates about the concept of scale in human geography, cultural geography, and radical geography. The project of geographers has aimed at the de-ontologization of scale and its understanding as a social and hence variable construction. Although there is widespread acceptance of a methodological division between the local, the urban, the regional, the nation-state, and the global, the relations between these scales (and sometimes the usefulness of the divisions themselves) are subject to great dispute—are these relations nesting, hierarchical, dialectical? Where does one end and the other begin? Andrew Kirby echoes David Harvey in claiming that globalization itself is a concept displacing the more politically charged concepts of imperialism and neocolonialism.[9] Marxist radical geographers tend to see capitalism as the driver of scale and through accumulation fostering a greater and greater expansion.[10] This position is substantiated by a relatively recent twist in the understanding of scale by corporations that use the term "as shorthand for '*scale* up' ('to grow or expand in a proportional and usually profitable way') and as a noun that means 'proportional growth especially of production or profit' and/or 'a large market position.'"[11] Feminist geographers often claim that the emphasis upon production has suppressed an understanding of the scale of realms of reproduction and the domestic usually associated with women.[12] Taken further, this position claims that the global-over-local hierarchy "underwrites the problematic view that social processes can be detached from the grounded sites where people and objects concretely reside and social practices take place (e.g. in streets, bedrooms, boardrooms)."[13] Larger scales (the nation-state, the global), in their absolute abstraction, should be dismissed in favor of human, experiential scales. This, in turn, poses a number of problems linked to its polarization of the abstract and the concrete, assuming, for instance, that nationalism and globalization are not "lived," or do not have very real effects, and that the "experiential" is not infused with abstraction. But this is a recurring problem in discourses about scale that almost always calibrate themselves in relation to a particular conceptualization of the "human."

A number of scholars have insisted upon a distinction between scale and size. Joan Kee and Emanuele Lugli initially proffer a definition whereby size refers to "absolute dimension" and scale to "proportions," but then go on to claim that "the production of scale often depends on various articulations of size which themselves are far from stable."[14] Yet Anne Wagner invokes the assumption of stability in size in her claim that "scale is not the same as size. On the contrary, scale is the appearance of size" and therefore scale can be "deceptive."[15] Size is here linked to scientific exactitude and secure, unshifting knowledge. However, measurement (of size) itself is a cultural (and often political) phenomenon, and its units are variable or variably grounded across history. If scale is understood as the perception of size, it would seem to be chained to individual subjectivity and call for a phenomenological reading. Scale is ineluctably linked to size, but it cannot be reduced to individual perception (as is particularly visible in the geographic determinations of local, national, and global). Nor is size the effect of a secure and unwavering system. As Emanuele Lugli points out in his book on measurement, "Size standards are not mere objects, but objects that come with assumptions, desires, and projections."[16] Measurement is the ceaseless and historically grounded attempt to connect the material and the abstract in an unquestionable way—an attempt destined to fail. Perhaps this is why much of its history is illustrated by the role of the human body as measure, a human body that seems to be the most assured, unchanging support—at least until the meter.

For instance, in Robert Tavernor's vast intellectual history of the various systems of measurement devised by cultures over the last two millennia, *Smoot's Ear: The Measure of Humanity*, the practice of calculating size in relation to the human body as ultimate standard (the foot, the cubit) is displaced historically by the search for a universal system ultimately based on the abstract and dehumanized (if not antihuman) meter.[17] For Tavernor, this development constitutes a great loss, a denial of human experience or human scale, both determined by the body. Hence, the narrative of Oliver R. Smoot acts not simply as an amusing anecdote but as a hyperbolic confirmation of Tavernor's call for a greater humanization of scale. Smoot, the shortest initiate (pledge) in a fraternity at the Massachusetts Institute of Technology (MIT) in 1958, was chosen as the subject and tool of a prank revolving around measurement. The initiates were given the task of measuring the length of the Harvard bridge using Smoot's height as the determinate unit (five feet seven inches). They found that the bridge was 364.4 smoots, plus or minus one ear. Here, the body is quite literally used as a form of measurement. For Tavernor, Smoot's ear represents the leftover, the plus or minus, the inevitable impossibility of truly accurate measurement, and hence the confirmation of the persistence of the human—here encapsulated as the fallible—in all measuring systems.[18] In addition, the humor of the prank hinges on the knowledge that Smoot's height has no generalizability but is one of the specific features of individuality, given the very large range of human sizes. The MIT prank is an ironic conflation of the scientistic and the humanistic.

And yet scale is associated with the corporeal in another way, as the flakes or laminates of skin that can be peeled away, as traces of the body, lost to the body—a pathological phenomenon. In this sense, scale is entangled with a vision of mechanical reproduction as a peeling off and circulation of the forms/skins of bodies or objects. In the June 1859 issue of the *Atlantic Monthly*, Oliver Wendell Holmes wrote that photography, and specifically stereography, divorced form from matter and hence deprived matter of the value of its visuality: "There is only one Coliseum or Pantheon; but how many millions of potential negatives have they shed—representatives of billions of pictures—since they were erected! . . . Every conceivable object of Nature and Art will soon scale off its surface for us. Men will hunt all curious, beautiful, grand objects, as they hunt the cattle in South America, for their skins, and leave the carcasses as of little worth."[19] Holmes was concerned with the impact of this for the archive—how to store and make accessible the resulting huge numbers of scales or skins of objects? But the detachability of these forms in photography and their later projection in the cinema also dissolved any concept of scale that could be soldered to the spectator's body, occasioning an anxiety that manifested itself in the early cinema as a demand for "life-size" images and "grandeur naturelle" in early press commentary on moving pictures.[20] The close-up in particular was perceived as aesthetically offensive in extreme ways—as monstrous or grotesque, even castrating, an excessive display of disproportion in scale and a violence to the human body. The residue of this hysteria can be seen in the hyperbolic language of early film theorists such as Epstein and Balázs.

The continuing and compensatory effects of this anxiety about representation and scale can still be seen in the concept of "actual size" or "actual scale" often used in advertising photographs. "Actual scale" is a paradox insofar as it is an attempt to annihilate representation, to authenticate the image by denying its scalelessness; yet it is an admission of the scalar instabilities of visual representation (for, like television and liveness, where the graphic "Live" is required to authenticate the temporality of the image, one always has to be told, with a caption, that this *is* the actual scale of an object). There is an exception whose exceptionality is a function of its indexicality, its physical adherence to its object—the nature print, a physical imprint of a plant specimen, which Jeremy Blatter has named the "zero degree of scale." However, as he points out, this scalar fidelity sacrifices other attributes of the object, including its three-dimensionality.[21] The cinema, even in films like Man Ray's rayograms, in which pins and nails are scattered across the surface of the celluloid to exploit their direct imprint, has no access to this zero degree of scale because the images are projected on a screen and hence enlarged (unpredictably, given the variation in theatrical "throws").

The concept of "actual size" or the "zero degree of scale" is hyperbolized and ironized in Jorge Luis Borges's famous short essay "Of Exactitude in Science." Jean Baudrillard's well-known reading of this essay emphasizes the ludic nature of a map the size of the territory it represents and deploys Borges's essay to shed light on his own concept of simulation and the destruction of the real. But what is lost in his reading is Borges's ironic critique of science and his invention of a mythical cartography as an absurd instantiation of scientific exactitude:

> In that Empire, the craft of Cartography attained such Perfection that the Map of a Single province covered the space of an entire City, and the Map of the Empire itself an entire Province. In the course of Time, these

Extensive maps were found somehow wanting, and so the College of Cartographers evolved a Map of the Empire that was of the same Scale as the Empire and that coincided with it point for point. Less attentive to the Study of Cartography, succeeding generations came to judge a map of such Magnitude cumbersome, and, not without Irreverence, they abandoned it to the Rigours of sun and Rain. In the western Deserts, tattered fragments of the Map are still to be found, Sheltering an occasional Beast or beggar; in the whole Nation, no other relic is left of the Discipline of Geography.

From *Travels of Praiseworthy Men* (1658) by J. A. Suarez Miranda

"Of Exactitude in Science" appears in a collection of Borges's short essays titled *A Universal History of Infamy* and takes the form of a literary forgery—attributed to a fictional J. A. Suarez Miranda and allegedly written centuries ago.[22] The appeal to historicity is redoubled by the inconsistent use of capital letters as signs of an aged and historical writing. The historical loss emerges as that of the "Discipline of Geography" (whose tool, cartography, has evolved from a craft to a college, study, and finally a discipline). Why do we find this characterization of cartography and the ideal map so absurd? Maps are supposed to be utilitarian, and their utility hinges upon their reduced scale and hence portability. A map usually carries within it its own explanation/illustration of the scale it uses (e.g., one inch = five miles). But here the "perfection" of cartography entails its own annihilation, the erasure of proportion as an instrument of representation, the very rejection of representation so that the map merges with its territory. Scientific exactitude avoids the possibility of inaccuracy by invoking a scale of 1 to 1, or "point for point." Nostalgia for the "Discipline of Geography" is here nostalgia for the scale of the real. The cinema is the antithesis of this Borgesian "perfect cartography."

The cinema in its earliest years had barely started to generate a hysteria about scale deviating from the scale of the human body when it began to exploit the scalar instabilities of the projected image through the use of the scale model, one of the first "special effects." In 1898, E. H. Lumet used miniature ships in a tank to film *Battle of Santiago Bay*. And Fred Dobson used a scale model of San Francisco burning in order to film the earthquake of 1906. The use of the scale model takes advantage of the illegibility of scale in the cinema, the spectator's inability to locate herself spatially in relation to the image (fig. I.3). The comparability required to acquire a sense of scale resides only within the image, where perspective and distance can

I.3 On the set of *Blade Runner* (Ridley Scott, 1982).

be manufactured independently of any "real" space.[23] The unreality of this space is accompanied by a necessary derealization of time when the object is moving (a ship on the ocean, a gigantic monster roaming a city, large rocks crushing a small-scale model of a house). In the 1920s and 1930s, film technicians noticed that a small-scale car filmed at the usual frame rate (where the rate of the film moving through the camera equals that through the projector) will appear to the spectator as a toy car. This is linked to the inextricability of expectations about size, mass, and movement. Filming at a higher speed produces a more plausible movement of a gigantic figure when projected at normal speed. Hence, the manipulability of size and the production of scalar illusion are dependent upon a manipulation of frame rate and hence represented temporality. The artifice of space/size is wedded to an artifice of time.[24]

Robert Smithson's sense of dislocation in the cinema, of proportion out of control, leads him to label the cinema an "atopia" (no place).[25] The scale model depends upon and instantiates what could be seen as two (not unrelated) failures of the classical theatrical cinema: (1) the inability of the spectator to orient herself or to measure scale in relation to her own body, thus producing a fundamental dislocation; and (2) the failure of the cinema to provide the precision and control of a scientific instrument due to its scalar instability (both spatially and temporally; this was Étienne-Jules Marey's reason for dismissing film as a viable tool of scientific method).[26] There is a sense in which cinema exposes the impossibilities of scale as it has been conceived in relation to both the realm of the human and the realm of abstract science.

The scale model deployed in the early years of cinema can be linked to a long history of magic and illusion, including Étienne-Gaspard Robertson's phantasmagoria of the 1790s, based on the magic lantern but distinguished from it by the concealing of both lantern and screen, so that the dark space of the auditorium was illegible to and unnavigable by the audience, making them vulnerable to the fear and anxiety of ghostlike apparitions.[27] In the nineteenth century, the very popular "Pepper's Ghost" used a partially reflective mirror to produce the illusion of a bodiless actor or ghost (the mirror image) on the stage, again concealing the means of production. In the European film industry in the mid-1920s, Eugen Schüfftan invented a process using mirrors to generate illusory scales that came to be known as the Schüfftan process.[28] This widely used process was economical, allowing the extensive use of small-scale models in place of large, expensive sets (fig. I.4). A mirror, part of whose reflective surface has been removed, is placed at a forty-five-degree angle in front of the camera, and the small-scale model is situated to the side of the camera. The live action of the scene appears in the nonreflective part of the mirror, seemingly surrounded by the environment provided by the model reflected in the mirror. The Schüfftan process was used in two of Fritz Lang's films—*Die Nibelungen: Siegfried* (1924) and *Metropolis* (1927).[29] As Katharina Loew points out, the Schüfftan process was associated with "Gulliver" effects—that is, "the rendition of extreme size differences between living things."[30] Special effects in this case are based on the meticulous confusion of virtual and "real" images in order to produce effects of scale. The use of

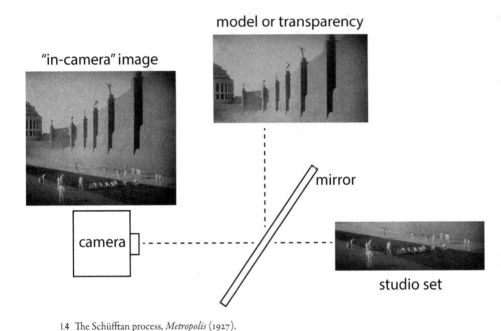

model or transparency

"in-camera" image

mirror

camera

studio set

I.4 The Schüfftan process, *Metropolis* (1927).

scale models contributes to the growing dissociation of scale and the human body (here, the body of the spectator) as measure.

The critique of the abstract metric scale in evidence in Tavernor's work was shared by Le Corbusier, who conceived of architecture first and foremost as a space designed *for* the human body, one that humans must inhabit and, therefore, one whose proportions must accommodate that body. In the 1942 treatise *The Modulor*, he applauded units of measure based on parts of the human body: elbow (cubit), finger (digit), thumb (inch), foot, pace, and so on, and disdained the move to the metric system, which was abstract and "indifferent to the stature of man."[31] Organic units were superior to the metric units because they grounded mathematics in the human body rather than in a cold, scientific, and inorganic system; in addition, they partook of the elegance and harmony of that body.[32] Despite, or perhaps because of, the nostalgia for "man [not woman] as the measure of all things," the anthropometric system was problematic. It evinced a desire to naturalize and ground the concept of scale, to repudiate its resolute denial of an absolute and its consequent embeddedness in the process of comparison. And, as Christopher Lukinbeal has argued, "Anthropometric measures are attributes of power and class struggle, they are symbolic and built on the 'process of social conditions in which the idea of "just measures" becomes a symbol of "just man," of justice as such, and of just human relations,'" hence the scales in the figure of a blind justice.[33]

While the development of the metric system was allegedly an attempt to produce and enforce a universal mode of measurement, grounded in scientific principles, it simply incarnated a shift from the human body as regulator of scale to a globe that had become ever more definitive of experience, whose symbolic pressure was increasingly felt. In the late eighteenth century, well into the era of colonialism, there were two schools of thought about the definition of a standard unit of measurement, one based on the duration of the swing of a pendulum (ultimately rejected due to perturbations caused by gravity) and the other advocating the definition of the meter as one ten-millionth (1/10,000,000) of the length of the distance from the equator to the North Pole. The approach based on the measurement of the circumference of the earth was the historical victor, at least temporarily. In 1889, the first General Conference of Weights and Measures established an international prototype meter bar, which is still housed in Sèvres, France.[34] Its original ground of authority was the measurement of the globe (an enterprise that was increasingly perceived as problematic, since the earth is not a perfect sphere).

The globe, according to Peter Sloterdijk, has constituted the imaginary image of location at least from the time of the circumnavigation of the world in the sixteenth century and is hence a product of the colonial enterprise: "Discovery aims for acquisition: this gave cartography its world-historical function. Maps are the universal instrument for securing what has been discovered, in so far as it is meant to be recorded 'on the globe' and given as a secure find."[35] Contemporary discourses of globalization as a new phenomenon are blind to the fact that the concept of space in relation to a world conceived as a sphere (and hence as conquerable) are effectively much older than these discourses admit. The apprehension of the world as a globe coincided with the concept of discovery and control of new territory, with colonialist and imperialist discourses. From the outset, globalization presupposed that any point on the globe was equidistant from the center and hence, in terms of measurement at any rate, equivalent to any other location, a homogenization of space that continued to accelerate into the twentieth century and beyond.

The cinema participated in this early discourse of globalization in a number of ways. It is not coincidental that the prototype meter bar came to incarnate

I.5 Esperanto poster stamp for 1913 international congress.

a universal measurement at the same time that the cinema emerged with the claim that it was a universal language, readable across national and linguistic borders, accompanying the concurrent cult surrounding Esperanto. The promotion of Esperanto as a universal language in stamps and posters for conferences invoked the globe as an imprimatur, blessing its worldwide aspirations (fig. I.5). Echoing this exploitation of the trope, an early 1909 advertisement in the journal *Moving Picture World* situates a globe as background framed on the bottom by two supportive film reels (fig. I.6), and RKO's logo presents a transmission tower straddling the top of the globe. On the occasion of its hundred-year anniversary, a reprise of the history of the Universal Studios logo displays the insistence of the globe as trope in the cinematic imaginary.

But, in addition, the cinema was an arena for a certain play with scale, an alignment of scales of shots that produced an imaginary space in which the idea of the spectator's "location" was repressed and reconfigured. The iconography of cinema often colluded with this discourse on scale and its malleability. Scale models go hand in hand with tales of enormous scalar disproportion between monsters and human beings—monsters whose spectacular size is often a result of world disaster, of atomic catastrophe, whose effects are perceived in relation to seemingly unimaginable sizes, both small and large. Mothra (in the 1961 film of that title produced by Toho Studios)

I.6 Ad in *Moving Picture World* 4, no. 24 (June 12, 1909).

is a gigantic egg, then caterpillar, then moth whose disproportion is directly linked to atomic testing on the island where she resides (fig. I.7). The island in general is inhabited by fantastic forms of both plants and animals and two women, only twelve inches tall, who act as Mothra's priestesses and are able to summon her after they are captured to be put on display in Japan. As miniatures, they are carnival-like attractions who prove to be the fascinating scalar counterpart of the enormous Mothra. Godzilla, in the original film of that name (*Gojira* [*Godzilla* is the Americanization], Ishirō Honda, 1954), is both a metaphor for and a product of nuclear holocaust (fig. I.8). In his immensity and unstoppability, Godzilla is the atomic bomb itself (Honda, the director, said years after the film, "I wanted to make radiation visible").[36] For the threat of the atom bomb lies not so much in its materiality or even its tremendous energy but in the devastation and scale of its lasting effects. A prominent paleontologist in the film inspects a giant radioactive footprint and hypothesizes that Godzilla is a creature from the Jurassic period whose dormancy was broken by American testing of the H-bomb. Godzilla breathes radioactive fire.

Unable to afford the stop-motion techniques of *King Kong*, Toho Studios borrowed from traditional Kabuki and Bunraku drama and portrayed

1.7 On the set of *Mothra* (Ishirō Honda, 1961).

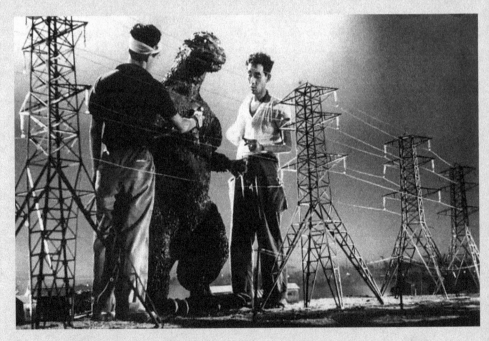

1.8 On the set of *Godzilla* (Ishirō Honda, 1954).

Godzilla by having an actor wear a latex costume. The scale of the miniature sets ranged from a ratio of 1/25 to one of 1/33, the logic being that Godzilla must be able to see over what were the largest buildings in Tokyo at that time.[37] In films of the ensuing series, Godzilla was rescaled to keep pace with the new skyscrapers of Tokyo. Godzilla's size is directly linked to visibility and invisibility—Gareth Edwards made his 2014 Godzilla larger than any previous incarnation (350 feet high) in order to make "the monster . . . so big as to be seen from anywhere in the city, but not too big that he couldn't be obscured," allowing the capitalization of fear and anxiety associated with invisibility in the classic horror film.[38] Giganticism in this genre, including Godzilla, Mothra, and King Kong, is accompanied by a number of tropes: the utter destruction of urban architecture—bridges, skyscrapers, and so forth; the ineffectivity of armies, missile systems, or any known defensive weapons in battling the monster; the awakening of a contained monster often associated with a primitive culture and the resulting havoc it wreaks upon civilized societies. The tropes of discovery and conquest are pervasive. King Kong is "discovered" by a film crew and stolen from his primitive and even prehistoric surroundings in order to be put on display in New York.[39] The Empire State Building, because its scale is widely known, can ironically act as the measure of both empire and its conquest, King Kong. These pathologies of scale accompany the aggressive incursion/penetration into new spaces on the globe. The proof of this exploration of the new, other, alien is the creature whose scale is unimaginable, inhuman.

For Sloterdijk, the globe became "the central medium of the new homogenizing approach to location," and its "monopoly on complete views of the earth's surface" was only broken late in the twentieth century by satellite photography.[40] A sense of the world as globe ruptured the experience of location as potentially separate, isolated, and protected. No place was immune from the knowledge that there was more, outside, that one is caught within a global network. Location, for Sloterdijk, is "not a blind spot in a field, but rather a place in which one sees that one is seen" as a consequence of globalization.[41] In this sense, cinema is compensatory. For in the theater, the spectator sees that they are not seen; the credibility of the film's space depends upon it. The delocalization of the spectator (not necessarily their disembodiment) is the precondition for the intense production of location that is a crucial component of cinema.

It is strange that film theory historically has not been more attentive to scale. It is a crucial component of the cinema's representation of space in a quite specific way that cannot be duplicated in theater or literature, the usual arts invoked in early discussions of cinematic specificity. While the scale model is perhaps the most overt and obvious incarnation of the cinema's ability to exploit the illegibility of scale, that tendency can be seen in the less ostentatious realms of the scale of shots (close-up, medium shot, long shot), the aspect ratio and scale of the screen, perspectival relations, and the very fact of projection (a small frame becomes a dauntingly large projected image). The management of scale in the cinema is a fundamental aspect of its production of a space that resides nowhere else but in the cinema (hence its characterization as "atopia")—a space that could, perhaps, be characterized as both unreadable and overly readable, illusorily navigable and fundamentally disorienting.

The two parts of this book, each containing three chapters, address two aspects of scale in the cinema: first, shot size, with an emphasis on the scale that has dominated film theoretical discourse—the close-up; and, second, larger questions of scale concerning perspective, projection, the screen as surface, and the size of the screen. Chapter 1 traces the vicissitudes of the close-up in the history of film theory and the way in which it uneasily navigates the oppositions between miniature and gigantic, size and distance, interiority and exteriority, detail and totality. Virtually every film theorist, from Hugo Münsterberg to Gilles Deleuze, situates the close-up as vital to their analysis. In part, this is due to the fact that the close-up stands out as the most easily isolable and decipherable unit of filmic technique in an otherwise seemingly continuous and unbroken imagistic flow. In a semiotic form that strikes early observers as objective and without need of human intervention—the machine that writes itself—the close-up also functions to reactivate the domain of the human through its love affair with the face. That face, in its magnitude, elicits panic and delight, both responses hyperbolic, disproportionate. The scale of the close-up stimulates an insistent discourse about its despatialization. It seems to many theorists to extract the face from any recognizable diegetic space, to in effect make it spaceless. This is one of the earliest recognitions of the cinema's potential for a derangement of scale and the construction of a space that has no referent.

Chapter 2 addresses the historical vicissitudes of the close-up, its contradictory reception, and the way in which its scale has been correlated with that of the human body, whether abstractly or concretely conceived. In the early years of the cinema, the close-up was the source of both an anxiety linked to its perceived monstrosity and adulation for its ability to reveal a character's "interiority." The monumental close-up (often referred to as "close view" or "large view" in journalistic discourse), particularly of the face, was regarded as grotesque, often horrifying, while its violent fragmentation of the body was made equivalent to a form of castration. *The Big Swallow*, discussed earlier, gave witness to an implicit grasp of the close-up's aberrant relation to space, its annihilation of depth, and its testing of the screen as surface and border between the spectator and the diegetic world. The close-up could be *too close*, threatening to invade the space of the viewer, demolishing the otherness of the depicted space. Later, as in IMAX and surround sound, discussed in chapter 6, the expansion of the realm of the diegesis into the auditorium would be celebrated. But here, in the early cinema, the close-up's annihilation of depth, of the existence of a vanishing point so adamantly asserted by the train tracks in the popular films depicting the arrival of a train, was the uneasy sign of a confounding of size and distance and a potential breaching of the demarcation between two incommensurable spaces. Yet the integrity of the diegetic space was bolstered by an alignment of the close-up with characterization. Domesticated by narrative, the close-up could expose the interiority of a character through its magnification of detail and expression. There is a displacement of the depth of the perspectival vanishing point to the depth of interiority, signaled by the face. In this way, the close-up could be subjected to the spatial logic of the narrative. Nevertheless, this domestication of the scalar instability of the close-up was always fragile, tenuous, and threatened to disturb spatial equilibrium, even within classical narrative.

The historical predilection of the close-up for the face is the condition of possibility of yet another implementation of scale in the cinema. The foregrounding of the face in narrative film for purposes of characterization is based upon the assumption of its transparency, its general legibility. Chapter 3 explores early discourses about the readability of facial expression in film and their alignment, whether conscious or unconscious, with the concept of a universal language. The silent cinema as a whole had been equated with a universal language, easily understandable globally, and hence available for worldwide marketing. The alleged transparency of the face anchored the universal language trope in a humanism that seemingly repressed all difference. However, the claims for this legibility relied on the pseudoscience of physiognomy, a discourse that was saturated with assumptions about racial difference and its relation to facial configurations. The concept of a universal language and, indeed, the very concept of the universal were responses to the colonial encounter with difference/otherness. In addition, the perceived necessity of physiognomic guidelines for reading faces also emerged from the increasing confrontations with strangers in modern urban milieux. Film was seen as a kind of training ground for dealing with the explosive expansion of the world, and its ostensibly easy access to a global scale reconfirmed its modernity.

Part II shifts the focus from the close-up as an isolable unit and the most visible marker of scale within the film to relations between scale and the screen itself. The perception of the cinema as a universal language collaborated with the desire to disseminate it on a worldwide scale, as a global commodity. Chapter 4 details the special contribution of the image of the woman to this economy of scale and the transnational binding of her image to the technology of the screen as a support of this logic of commodification. In this process, the female face is bound to the surface of the screen and annihilates the legibility so crucial to the conceptualization of the cinema as a universal language, producing contradictions that are only precariously resolved. My approach here involves investigating forms of cinema other than the classical Hollywood film (forms that are nonetheless inextricable from thinking about modernity), including the historical avant-garde of the 1920s (Richter and Eggeling, Man Ray, Fernand Léger, Marcel Duchamp) and the avant-garde of the 1960s and 1970s (Andy Warhol and Jean-Luc Godard). These two avant-gardes manifested an intense fascination with light, projection, and the location of the image, and this project was intimately linked to the image of the "modern" woman and her very close relation to the screen. In another register, Shanghai cinema of the 1930s and 1940s deployed the figure of the woman (as did much of Western cinema at the time) as the privileged exemplar of modernity and of the urban reordering of space and its negotiability. This transcultural obsession helps to illuminate the very concept of modernity and the debate about a singular modernity versus multiple modernities.

Projection has historically been integral to the cinema and one of the elements of its specificity. It enables scalar alteration and destabilization—the maneuvering of the large and the small. Chapter 5 analyzes the relationship between projection, perspective, and the scale of the image, as well as the way in which these strategies/structures are linked to the question of location— the location of both the viewer and the image itself. In the history of the generation of moving images, the cinema was preceded by the optical toy, whose image was tangible, localized. Here, I trace the movement from the optical toy, where the illusion of movement is diminutive and holdable as a possession, to the emergence of a publicly viewable cinema, where scale becomes variable and erratic through projection and the dematerialization of the image. In cinematic projection, the distance of the image is a measure of this dispossession, its intangibility a sign of the increasing abstraction of a consumer economy and the rise of the spectacle. Projection is integral to the cinema but rarely foregrounded in its analysis. In psychoanalysis, it is intimately linked to a confusion between the interior and the exterior and names a fundamental disorientation, a spatiopsychical instability. In the avant-garde of the 1960s and 1970s, projection becomes a technology that is disengaged from any content of the image in flicker films and the work of Anthony McCall (for instance, in *Line Describing a Cone*, 1973).

Projection, in its geometric signification, refers to a plotting of points to produce a two-dimensional representation of a three-dimensional space—hence its strong affiliation with not only the cinema but also mapping, the translation of a sphere, the globe, onto a flat surface. Cartography is about location, navigation, and the generation of space as homogeneous and rational. Renaissance perspective shares a history with mapping and also produces a space that is systematic and homogeneous. Both are about location, position, "knowing where one is." The grids of latitude and longitude in mapping and the network of orthogonals and transversals in perspective situate both places and viewers in a stable and knowable site. In the work of Albrecht Dürer and others, perspective is inseparable from the idea of bodily proportion—both are concerned with achieving "harmony" and "correctness," one in relation to space, the other in relation to the human body. In this context, the female body resists and is instead allied with a fundamental *disproportion*, destabilizing the homogeneous space of perspective and suggesting the conundrums of its concepts of the vanishing point and infinity. A number of artworks—including Dürer's famous illustration of the production of perspective using a grid, *Draughtsman Making a Perspective Drawing of a Reclining Woman* (ca. 1600); Gustave Courbet's *Origin of the World*; and Marcel Duchamp's *Étant donnés*—give witness to this difficulty of thinking the spatiality of the female body in relation to the coherence and homogeneity of perspective.

Perspective is often situated as a technology that has been superseded in the current era by the pervasiveness and apparent inescapability of the aerial view and what has been labeled its "vertical perspective." Drones, surveillance cameras, military aerial photography, and the zooming and floating vision facilitated by Google Earth obliterate the power of the horizon in vertical perspective and situate the spectator in an unstable place—suspended, hovering. Ironically, GPS, which provides perhaps the vertical perspective par excellence, is designed to orient the viewer and pinpoint location. It increases exponentially the scale of our access to any part of the earth. Yet, as the image becomes a heterogeneous collection of data only mimicking wholeness, the viewer's orientation is based upon a profound disorientation. While perspective strove to guarantee a stable position of vision, to make the world available for representation, the aerial view bestows upon the spectator a military, strategic, and probing comprehension and a perpetually shifting perception.

The satellite view and the zoom of Google Earth escalate the stakes of scale. On a more "local" level, this can be seen in the proliferation of different sizes of screens from mobile phones to IMAX. IMAX in a sense competes with these modes of viewing, exploiting the zoom through space of Google Earth in its attempt to "immerse" the spectator in an ever-expanding world/diegesis. From its emergence in the world fairs and expos of the 1970s to its later transformation into a mainstream narrative format, IMAX has always been about large scale, sheer magnitude. Like widescreen processes before it, IMAX attempted to expand the space of the diegesis to more intensely engage the spectator in its "world." Together with surround sound processes such as Dolby Atmos, it strives to eliminate the frame, invading spectatorial space. Chapter 6 dissects these two technologies and their relation to the concept of "immersion," an idea that goes beyond the realism and absorption of classical film and is defined primarily as a relation between the body and space. The rhetoric of immersion, deployed within both IMAX advertising and critical discourse, is symptomatic of a crisis of location in technologically mediated space—a despatialization, a reconceptualization of position, scale, and infinity that undergird the mechanisms of late capitalism and its incessant expansion of commodification. Immersion is always about the provision of an elsewhere designed as a lure, so much so that it is often portrayed as an inevitable end point of media history. The vicissitudes of scale discussed throughout this book in relation to cinema constitute early stages of a reconfiguration and abstraction of space and its corollary dislocation of the spectator.

Scale is always comparative, relational—a ratio—and it can only be understood as produced for a particular viewpoint or subjectivity, a perspective. Most frequently, this perspective exhibits an anthropocentric and hence humanist bias. As outlined in chapter 2, this bias is deeply inscribed in the analytical classification of types of shots (close-up, medium shot, long shot) and their various gradations—medium long shot, medium close-up, and even *plan américain*, all defined in relation to the human body. In the reception of early cinema, the demand for "life-size" representation of objects and human beings was a demand for a ratio of one-to-one, of a complete mimesis of the scale of everyday life. Once the anxiety attached to the close-up of the human face was allayed, the rationalization of shot size continued to append itself to the human body. As Pascal Bonitzer has pointed out, if the entire body of a cockroach fills the frame, we call it a close-up or an extreme close-up. If the frame encompasses the entire body of a human being, we call it a medium shot, or medium long shot (*plan général*). The close-up originally responded to a narrative requirement for representation of the intensity and differentiation of emotions—"It is therefore, retroactively, in relation to the close-up, that the difference of shots (the sizes of shots) takes on meaning" and "The cinematographic impression of reality is sustained by human stature and reciprocally."[42] Modern cinema (e.g., Godard and Syberberg), according to Bonitzer, negates or at least represses this anthropocentrism and opens up a dimension that is "nonhuman, infrahuman, or extrahuman: that of the gods and the quarks [subatomic particles]."[43]

This desire to exceed or surpass the scale of the human has been allied historically with film theory insofar as the camera lens is understood as inhuman, "objective," independent of authorial perspective. For André Bazin, the painter's work was "always in fee to an inescapable subjectivity," and photography and cinema satisfy our desire for realism with "a mechanical reproduction in the making of which man plays no part."[44] For Jean Epstein, *photogénie*, the essence of cinema, is "the taste of things . . . the human eye cannot discover it directly . . . a lens zeroes in on it, drains it, distilling *photogénie* between its focal planes."[45] The documentary movement of cinema verité was sustained by the assumption of the detachment and impartiality of the lens whose only function was to observe, independently of the human eye. In terms of scale, one of the earliest uses of film was for the scientific recording of microscopic images of cells and structures invisible to human beings.

From a somewhat different perspective, this desire to transcend or surpass the human has been espoused by certain trends in contemporary theory, including "new materialism," posthumanism, and thing theory, and often these discourses invoke the concept of scale.[46] Karen Barad, for instance, insists that distinctive scales such as the local, the national, and the global do not have "nesting relations" in which one is simply included as a miniature (or larger) version of the other. Rather, "this 'connectedness' should be understood not as linkages among preexisting nested scales but as the agential enfolding of different scales through one another . . . intra-actively produced through one another."[47] The "agential realism" she espouses returns agency to matter so that determination becomes an intricately entangled dance of different factors, only part of which is the human (which is highly overrated in her theory): "In my agential realist account, intelligibility is an ontological performance of the world in its ongoing articulation. It is not a human-dependent characteristic but a feature of the world in its differential becoming. The world articulates itself differently."[48] Zachary Horton pursues the implications of Barad's approach in his impressive and incisive analysis of the mediation of scale. Horton advocates a "trans-scalar ecology" that would honor the "difference that is immanent to matter itself." Citing Barad, he claims that "matter differentiates itself, and thus meaning arises as a material rather than mental process."[49] This is a far cry from the linguistic and semiotic understanding of difference as the central mechanism of language and underlines the degree to which the new materialisms constitute a rejection of structuralism and poststructuralism. Scale achieves an ontological status in this approach—for Horton, "scalar difference is real and ontologically prior to our encounter with objects at other scales," and "we make scales, but scale bites back."[50] Scale is presented as a subject, as an already given environment, with different scales providing different logics and determinations incompatible with other scales.

I share Horton's leeriness of anthropocentric scales that are calibrated in relation to the human, particularly the human body. But I also believe that the concept of scale is inevitably one that is produced through human discourse (a discourse that can be anthropocentric or not). It has no ontology. To the extent that scale is always comparative (even in the metric system), it is a ratio, a word whose etymology is traceable to *logos* in ancient Greek and reason/the rational in Latin. The scales of the interplanetary and the microscopic are certainly alien to the space and scale of human encounter, but they are accessible to us and made knowable through scientific and social technologies. One could go further and claim that precisely as scales they are generated by human discourse (although this term is redundant). Microscopic realms are diminutive not for the beings/things that inhabit these realms but for those who label them. The technological/medial generation of scales perceived as "other," that is, mind-bogglingly large or staggeringly small, no doubt produces anxiety about the fragile, precarious, and potentially meaningless domain of the human (which is not equatable with humanism as an ideology). This anxiety is reinforced by climate change, the glut of information/data made possible by computers, the technological compression of space and time and corresponding annihilation of distance, and the illusory dematerialization of the digital. There seem to be two responses to this predicament. The first would be a form of abdication of analysis/interpretation and a corresponding celebration of the posthuman and the ontological agency of matter—that is, new materialism (or a kind of rematerialization in the wake of the digital). In its rhetorical embrace of rhizomes, material flows, intensities, and dynamics, as well as irreducible complexity, this approach ironically resigns itself to an unending description as methodology and the (unacknowledged) renunciation of a political position of analysis. The second response to this anxiety is the resuscitation of a nostalgia for the "life-size," human scale, the antitechnological. This nostalgia is manifested in the work of, among others, Jonathan Crary, Peter Sloterdijk, and Paul Virilio.[51]

Virilio, for instance, distinguishes between a "small-scale optics," that is, a geometric optics of Renaissance perspective (an optics "which, in the end, only covers man's immediate proximity"), and a "large-scale optics," the "active optics of the time of the speed of light," an optics that "disregards the traditional notion of a horizon." Here, scale refers to a way of inhabiting space and time. The concept of a large-scale optics emerges in relation to phenomena such as teleconferencing and the digital more broadly, which are made possible by real-time emission and instantaneous reception of audiovisual signals. Its scale is that of time and instantaneity, and it crushes the optics of perspective, the horizon, and the vanishing point. In teleconferencing, the "now" outweighs the "here" of the meeting room and the meeting, in fact, takes place nowhere. While perspectival small-scale optics preserves the concepts of extension and duration and hence geography, large-scale optics "dissolves the scale of the human environment." What is lost in this transition is the quality of the "life-size." But, in fact, there are a series of associated losses for Virilio—the horizon, optical density, physical proximity, depth of field (everything is flattened)—and ultimately what is risked is the loss of "our own world." There is a slippage in Virilio's argument between the here and now of our everyday life, of our apprehension of time and space, and a perspectival optics, which is not the optics of everyday life but that of representation, mediation. This becomes most evident when he laments the loss of the horizon and a perspective "that previously allowed us to recognize ourselves here and now."[52] Perspective as a representational strategy is indeed about position and location, but it does not mirror the position and location of everyday life. As has been extensively argued in film theory and elsewhere, perspective *constructs and rationalizes* a position for the spectator. In this sense, it has been viewed as stabilizing, especially in comparison with the realm of the digital. Virilio is not the only theorist who makes this claim. Hito Steyerl, for instance, has argued that the vertical perspective of contemporary digital media (of drones and satellite imaging), in contrast with the stable horizon of perspective, induces a sense of floating and free fall in the spectator, producing both a new set of ideological constraints and new forms of political possibility in art.[53]

Nevertheless, I think it is crucial to understand how the vicissitudes of scale in the cinema act as a kind of premonition of the placelessness of new technologies and allow it in its own way to disturb the "here and now" of the spectator. Cinema's deployment of differently scaled shots, its use of the scale model and especially the close-up constitute a derangement of scale that upends classical notions of location and orientation. As Susan Stewart has extensively demonstrated, the cultural fascination with the miniature and the gigantic predates the cinema by centuries. But the cinema builds into its representation or deployment of scale a position or location for the spectator in relation to its world. As Robert Bird has maintained in another context, film "animates a subjectivity that is capable of viewing it," of absorbing its scalar logic.[54] In the cinema, the miniature and the gigantic do not inhabit the world of ordinary proportions, where the astonishment/shock of their difference constitutes a great deal of their pleasure. The cinema, through the very fact of projection, produces a world of imaginary proportions and interpolates the spectator within it. The here and now of the spectator's location in the theater disappears as location is dynamically produced. It is not "large-scale optics," in Virilio's terms, that initiates the process of dissolving "the scale of the human environment," but the cinema before it which activates another scalar logic.

PART I
CLOSE-UP
/FACE

Chapter 1

The Delirium of a Minimal Unit

The history of thinking about film and its effects is heavily shaped by a particular filmic technique, the close-up. Next to montage, the close-up has received perhaps the most sustained attention. Because it is easily identifiable as a delimitable unit and as specific to the medium of film as opposed to the theater, the filmmakers, aestheticians, and psychologists who grappled with defining and describing the new form often singled out and celebrated the close-up. Hugo Münsterberg, the German American Harvard psychologist who was a protégé of William James, exemplifies this tendency. *The Photoplay: A Psychological Study* (1916), his book-length analysis of the cinema, is one of the first extensive and coherent attempts to explain the cinema using an elaborated theoretical approach, in this case, experimental psychology (at that time, a young discipline in its own right). Münsterberg, who has been variously described as a Kantian, an advocate of Schopenhauer's idealist aesthetics, and the founder of psychotechnics or psychotechnology, was also an admirer of Frederick Winslow Taylor and interested in applied and industrial psychology.[1] But his attraction to the cinema, like that of many early film theorists, was thoroughly imbricated with his desire to prove that it was an art and hence isolated from the functionality of everyday life. I begin this consideration of the close-up in film theory with Münsterberg not because he was the "first" or earliest of its analysts (he was not) but because the aesthetics that grounds his understanding of the close-up yokes it to a reconfiguration of space and scale that is peculiar to the cinema and haunts film theory throughout its course, even up to the work of Gilles Deleuze.

Münsterberg's experimental psychology approach led him to emphasize the way in which the cinema mimics the processes of the mind. The close-up, from this perspective, is analogous to the mental act of attention (the flash-back to memory, the flash-forward to imagination, etc.). Comparing the cinema with the theater in order to demonstrate that it is not just a copy or mechanical recording of the latter, Münsterberg fastens on the close-up as a specific and unique ability of the film. In the cinema, there are ways of focusing the attention of the spectator on a small detail—a hand holding a gun, for instance.[2] Münsterberg writes, "It is as if this one hand were during this pulse beat of events the whole scene and everything else had faded away. On the stage this is impossible; there nothing can really fade away. That dramatic hand must remain, after all, only the ten thousandth part of the space of the whole stage; it must remain a little detail."[3] The theater, unlike the cinema, is incapable of actually transforming the space and scale of the scene:

> Here begins the art of the photoplay. That one nervous hand which fever-ishly grasps the deadly weapon can suddenly for the space of a breath or two become enlarged and be alone visible on the screen, while everything else has really faded into darkness. The act of attention which goes on in our mind has remodeled the surrounding itself. The detail which is being watched has suddenly become the whole content of the performance, and everything which our mind wants to disregard has been suddenly ban-ished from our sight and has disappeared.[4]

Fundamental to Münsterberg's argument is the insistence that mental pro-cesses such as attention, memory, and imagination are externalized or objec-tified by film. While it is clear that our attention has not remodeled the space of the film as Münsterberg here contends (the film itself does this) and that there are flaws with his analogy between mind and film, I am more interested here in the way in which he describes the work of the close-up. It is essential to its operation that the detail becomes the whole, that the space of the scene is annihilated in favor of the object whose scale is enlarged to the extent that it becomes the entirety of the visible. Elsewhere, Münsterberg claims that the close-up is "a scheme by which a particular part of the picture, perhaps only the face of the hero or his hand or only a ring on his finger, is greatly enlarged and replaces for an instant the whole stage."[5] The close-up is not metonymic here; it is a replacement, a substitution that becomes the whole. Its work is characterized by a loss of the diegesis. It is abstracted (removed, extracted) from space and becomes, in a sense, an abstraction (a de-ontologized concept).

Within the larger context of Münsterberg's film theory and attempt to demonstrate that film is an art, the close-up plays a crucial role. It is far more central to his argument than the other techniques he discusses—the flashback, the flash-forward, the perception of depth and movement. In fact, the close-up reveals in microcosm the very essence and goal of art in general. Like Rudolf Arnheim in his book *Film as Art* (1932), Münsterberg believed that film could be an art only to the extent that it deviated from the real (and, like Arnheim, Münsterberg was opposed to sound cinema). Mechanical imitation could not be its function. Art was characterized by its isolation of the particular from the everyday forms of space, time, and causality. Its role was the opposite of that which he associated with scholarly work and science—to demonstrate the connections of an object to that which is outside it within a larger system. Art, on the contrary, detaches, dissociates: "*The work of art shows us the things and events perfectly complete in themselves, freed from all connections which lead beyond their own limits, that is, in perfect isolation.*"[6] Münsterberg repeats time and again that both art and the photoplay "free us from" or even "overcome" space, time, and causality—"*the massive outer world has lost its weight.*"[7] The close-up, in isolating objects from their connections to the external universe and its laws, in transforming the particular detail into its own world, in despatializing the object, incarnates the fundamental nature of art in general. For Münsterberg, it is not simply another technique in the cinema's repertoire.

Arnheim's discussion of the close-up is similar to that of Münsterberg insofar as Arnheim sees it as one of the defining characteristics of film as opposed to theater. For Arnheim, for whom the frame and its delimitation constitute the fundamental ground of film's status as an art, the close-up's significance lies in its ability to enlarge details, create suspense by increasing the amount of off-screen space, and grant objects symbolic status. But the extremity of the close-up's delimitation of space also leads Arnheim to be wary of its powers of delocalization and despatialization:

> The close-up, however, has one serious drawback. It easily leaves the spectator in the dark as to the surroundings of the object or part of the object. This is especially true in a film where there are too many close-ups, where hardly any long shots are given, as for instance in Dreyer's *The Passion of Joan of Arc*, or in a number of Russian films. The close-up shows a human

head, but one cannot tell where the man is to whom the head belongs, whether he is indoors or outdoors, and how he is placed in regard to other people—whether close or distant, turning toward them or away from them, in the same room with them or somewhere else. A superabundance of close-ups very easily leads to the spectators having a tiresome sense of uncertainty and dislocation.[8]

The close-up hence constitutes a potential danger, the foreclosure of the spectator's spatial orientation, the annihilation of the rationality of place. If the close-up subsumes all space, the systematic interconnections within the diegesis are broken. The close-up's work of isolation and disconnection, celebrated by Münsterberg and feared by Arnheim, is a persistent theme in the history of film theory. The close-up is both an object of apprehension and a site of praise, and even of delirious fascination.

Another of the earliest attempts to produce film theory, that of the French Impressionists in the 1920s, generated a concept, *photogénie*, which is usually considered to be theoretically incoherent. No doubt this is due to the fact that photogénie is designed to account for that which is inarticulable, that which exceeds language and hence points to the very essence of cinematic specificity. Photogénie names a supplementarity, an enhancement, that which is added to an object in the process of its subjection to a photographic medium.[9] For Jean Epstein, it is inextricably bound up with an ethics: "I would describe as photogenic any aspect of things, beings or souls whose moral character is enhanced by filmic reproduction."[10] The close-up is the privileged site for this experience of photogénie, and Epstein often labored to produce a language that would be adequate to this experience. Witness, for instance, the linguistic contortions in his description of the close-up of a face breaking into a smile:

> I will never find the way to say how I love American close-ups. Point blank. A head suddenly appears on screen and drama, now face to face, seems to address me personally and swells with an extraordinary intensity. I am hypnotized. Now the tragedy is anatomical. The décor of the fifth act is this corner of a cheek torn by a smile. . . . The orography of the face vacillates. Seismic shocks begin. Capillary wrinkles try to split the fault. A wave carries them away. Crescendo. A muscle bridles. The lip is laced with tics like a theater curtain. Everything is movement, imbalance, crisis. Crack. The mouth gives way, like a ripe fruit splitting open. As if slit by a scalpel, a keyboard-like smile cuts laterally into the corner of the lips.[11]

The description verges on the obscene, perhaps because it transforms the face, usually reserved as the very locus of subjectivity, into a harsh and alien object (a geographic site, a wave, a theater curtain, a piece of fruit, a keyboard). The excessiveness of Epstein's language is consistent with the inescapably hyperbolic nature of the close-up (the title of Epstein's article is "Magnification"). The intensifying properties of the close-up were linked by Epstein directly to its size, to its capacity for magnification, and called up metaphors of orality, of incorporation: "It's not even true that there is air between us; I consume it. It is in me like a sacrament."[12] It was the magnified face that particularly struck Epstein and drove his discourse to almost delirious paroxysms of adulation: "I can see love. It half lowers its eyelids, raises the arc of the eyebrows laterally, inscribes itself on the taut forehead, swells the masseters, hardens the tuft of the chin, flickers on the mouth and at the edge of the nostrils."[13] But, in addition, Epstein's prose extracts and abstracts the close-up from the scene, from the body, from the spatiotemporal coordinates of the narrative, performing, in effect, its monstrosity. Any viewer is invited to examine its gigantic detail, its contingencies, its idiosyncrasies. The close-up is always, at some level, an autonomous entity, a fragment, a "for-itself."

Epstein's writing about the close-up always seems to entail an element of violence: "An eye that occupies the entire screen suddenly reveals itself to be a monster: a wet and shiny beast with its own movements like those of any animal; which, with its shadowy mouth, projects a force unlike any other form of life; which unveils itself and hides itself, in between two tremulous valves, planted with a long and graceful vegetation of curved darts whose venom we cannot fathom."[14] When eyelashes become darts harboring venom, the image of an eye loses any concept of referentiality in order to become something entirely different, ominous, filled with unease. Epstein habitually refers to this as the surrealization of objects or appearances. A capacity for surrealism is "inherent to the apparatus itself."[15] Beyond any reference to the contemporary movement of surrealism, Epstein seems to be invoking here a supplement—something beyond the real, something that can be grasped only by the cinema. While it is true that he sees this inherent surrealism in other filmic techniques, especially slow motion and reversibility of movement, it is the close-up and its scale, especially when presenting the human face as an otherworldly object, that appear most horrifying.

The close-up has inspired fascination, love, horror, empathy, pain, unease. It has been seen as the vehicle of the star, the privileged receptacle of affect, of passion, the guarantee of the cinema's status as a universal language, one of the most (if not *the* most) recognizable units of cinematic discourse, yet simultaneously extraordinarily difficult to define. (At what distance from the object or tightness of the frame does it begin? At what point does the medium shot become a medium close-up and the medium close-up give way to the pure close-up?) For Walter Benjamin, the close-up was one of the significant entrance points to the optical unconscious, making visible what in daily life went unseen.

Echoing Arnheim's anxiety, Epstein's extravagant language, perhaps unconsciously and certainly despite the invocation of morality, delineates the close-up as a lurking danger, a potential semiotic threat to the unity and coherence of the filmic discourse. The most heavily used close-up, that of the face, fragments the body, decapitating it (bringing to mind the perhaps apocryphal story in which Griffith's producer, confronted with the close-up, complains, "We pay for the whole actor, Mr. Griffith. We want to see *all* of him.")[16] The close-up in general is disengaged from the mise-en-scène, freighted with an inherent separability or isolation, a "for-itself" that inevitably escapes, to some degree, the tactics of continuity editing that strive to make it "whole" again. Space is "used up" by the face or object, and the time of the moment, the time of Epstein's contemplation, is expanded at the expense of the linear time of narrative. The close-up embodies the pure fact of presentation, of manifestation, of showing—a "here it is."

Also writing in the 1920s and 1930s, Béla Balázs approached the cinema influenced by his teachers, Georg Simmel and Henri Bergson, and heavily invested in the Romantic categories of subjectivity and expression.[17] The dilemma, for Balázs and for a host of other theorists after him, was how to situate the close-up of the face in relation to space, time, and visibility. For the face purportedly makes visible that which is of neither a visual nor a spatiotemporal order—emotions, moods, intentions, thoughts. The visible is necessary, but insufficient. Similarly, there is a sense in which the face is radically separable from the very notions of space and time. Unlike a hand, which is never dissociable from both the body and the surroundings of which it is a part, a face constitutes its own self-sufficient, autonomous unity—it becomes the only domain.[18] Balázs writes, "When Griffith's genius and daring first projected gigantic 'severed heads' on to the cinema screen, he not only brought the human face closer to us in space, he also transposed it from space into another dimension."[19] That other dimension is labeled variously "expression" or "physiognomy" (or sometimes "microphysiognomy"). The privileged epistemological position of the face in Balázs's theory is signaled by its possession of its very own dimension, by its unique status in the realm of representation, by its flirtation, in fact, with the unrepresentable but nevertheless knowable: "The facial expression on a face is complete and comprehensible in itself and therefore we need not think of it as existing in space and time."[20] The close-up severs all relation with the establishing shot of which it might at first appear to be merely a fragment. Balázs claims that even if we have seen in long shot the crowd of which this face is a part, the close-up effects a dramatic shift in significance—"We would still feel that we have suddenly been left alone with this one face to the exclusion of the rest of the world. . . . Facing an isolated face takes us out of space."[21] Gilles Deleuze, allying himself explicitly with Balázs, claims that "the close-up does *not* tear away its object from a set of which it would form part, of which it would be a part, but on the contrary *it abstracts it from all spatio-temporal co-ordinates*, that is to say it raises it to the state of Entity."[22] Of all the different types of shots, it is the close-up that is most fully associated with the screen as surface, with the annihilation of a sense of depth and its corresponding rules of perspectival realism. The image becomes, once more, an image rather than a threshold onto a world. Or, rather, the world is reduced to this face, this object.

Perhaps this status as potential semiotic threat can help to explain the pivotal role of the close-up in film history and theory. An intensive and persistent search for the earliest incarnation of the close-up has characterized many historical accounts, and candidates range from Edison's kinetoscopic record of a sneeze to the close shot of a bank robber shooting his gun toward the audience in Edwin S. Porter's *The Great Train Robbery* (1903) to Griffith's early melodramas.[23] It is as though assigning the close-up a definitive and determinant chronology limited its threat. With respect to these discourses, Pascal Bonitzer raises the question, "Why does the first appearance of the close-up in cinematographic space always seem to be contemporaneous with the first stammerings of a 'cinematographic language'?"[24] The close-up, together with an editing that penetrates space and is at least partially rationalized by that close-up, seems to mark the moment of the very emergence of film as a discourse, as an art.

For Béla Balázs, the close-up was "the technical condition of the art of film."[25] Epstein described the close-up as the "soul of the cinema."[26] Despite the fact that Münsterberg defined the close-up in relation to isolation and release from the categories of space, time, and causality, there is a sense in which he naturalized the close-up, reducing its potential danger, by aligning it with the mental act of attention; film was simply a simulation of the human mind, its techniques the technological embodiment of that mind's capacities.[27] Over and against Münsterberg's domestication and rationalization, the close-up has more frequently appeared as the mark of cinematic difference and specificity, as in Epstein's photogénie—the invocation of an otherwise unknown dimension, a radically defamiliarized alterity. Sergei Eisenstein, for instance, argued for the disengagement of the close-up from reality, criticizing Griffith for his inability to abstract, to get beyond the "narrowly representational."[28] The function of the close-up in the Soviet cinema was "not so much to *show* or to *present* as to *signify*, to *give meaning*, to *designate*."[29] As a crucial element of montage, the close-up was the support of an intellectual, critical cinema. Tearing the object from the real, the close-up introduced "absolute changes in the dimensions of bodies and objects on the screen."[30]

As Eisenstein and others have pointed out, the concept is inflected differently through its varying nomenclature in different languages. In Russian and in French, the term for close-up denotes largeness or large scale (e.g., *gros plan* in French), while in English, it is nearness or proximity that is at stake. The close-up hence invokes two different binary oppositions—proximity versus distance and the large versus the small. In the American context, it is conceptualized in terms of point of view, perspective, the relation between spectator and image, the spectator's *place* in the scene, assuming an identification between viewer and camera. In the Soviet and French context, it is thought as a quality of the image, as extensiveness, scale, an imposing stature, the awe of the gigantic as opposed to the charm of the miniature. In his discussion of capitalism, the commodity, and the mechanically reproduced image, Walter Benjamin delineates the defining desire of the masses in a capitalist society as a desire for a closeness that is also a leveling of difference, a desire, in effect, for the close-up. He refers to "the desire of contemporary masses to bring things 'closer' spatially and humanly, which is just as ardent as their bent toward overcoming the uniqueness of every reality by accepting its reproduction. Every day the urge grows stronger to get hold of an object at very close range by way of its likeness, its reproduction."[31] The decay of the aura, insofar as it is predicated upon distance, finds its perfect embodiment in the close-up (despite its association with the false aura of the star). Here, closeness is allied with possession, possessiveness, the desire to "get hold of an object" by, somewhat ironically, making moot the question of ownership. In contrast, the Russian and French terms reject possession in favor of transcendence (the image is truly "larger than life"), a scale that guarantees unattainability. I will return to this issue later in arguing that the close-up performs the inextricability of these two seemingly opposed formulations, simultaneously posing as both microcosm and macrocosm, detail and whole. The exorbitance, even hysteria, of much of film theory's discourse on the close-up is symptomatic of a strongly felt loss specific to modernity. Faced with an accelerating rationalization, specialization, and disintegration of the sense of a social totality, the subject clings to the hope of simulacra of wholeness. The close-up, with its contradictory status (as both detail of a larger scene and totality in its own right—a spectacle of scale with its own integrity), responds to this need.

With the linguistic turn of film theory in the 1970s and the quasi-scientific approach of a scholar like Christian Metz, the elation and insistence upon evaluation characteristic of early film theory's approach to the close-up disappear. Yet the close-up remains a pivotal figure. In attempting to demonstrate why there is no unit in the cinema that corresponds to the word in language (and hence why the cinema is always speech—*parole* versus *langage* in Saussure's terms), Metz invokes the close-up as exemplary:

> The image is *always actualized*. Moreover, even the image—fairly rare, incidentally—that might, because of its content, correspond to a "word" is still a sentence: This is a particular case, and a particularly revealing one. A close-up of a revolver does not mean "revolver" (a purely virtual lexical unit), but at the very least, and without speaking of the connotations, it signifies "Here is a revolver!" It carries with it a kind of *here* (a word which André Martinet rightly considers to be a pure index of actualization).[32]

The close-up, more than other types of shots, demonstrates the deictic nature of the cinematic image, its inevitable indexicality. Mimicking the pointing finger, it requires no language and is not comparable to it. With the gesture of presenting its contents (making them actual), it supports the cinema's aspiration to be the vehicle of presence.

And yet the most strident of analyses of the close-up insist upon its alliance with a quite particular content, one that is indeed presented as indissociable from the very mechanism of the technique: the human face. The face is that bodily part not accessible to the subject's own gaze (or accessible only as a virtual image in a mirror), and simultaneously it is the site that is *seen* and read by the other—hence its overrepresentation as *the* instance of subjectivity. The scale of the close-up transforms the face into an instance of the gigantic, the monstrous: it overwhelms. The face, usually the mark of individuality, becomes tantamount to a theorem in its generalizability. In the close-up, it is truly bigger than life.

For Balázs, the close-up, whether of objects or the human face, is inherently anthropomorphic: "When the film close-up strips the veil of our imperceptiveness and insensitivity from the hidden little things and shows us the face of objects, it still shows us man, for what makes objects expressive are the human expressions projected on to them. The objects only reflect our own selves."[33] And yet something of the object contaminates the face in close-up as well: "This most subjective and individual of human manifestations is rendered objective in the close-up."[34] The close-up underwrites a critical breakdown in the opposition between subject and object. This is particularly true in the silent film, where both were mute and where "both man and object were equally pictures, photographs, their homogeneous material . . . projected on to the same screen."[35] According to Jacques Aumont in *Du visage au cinéma*, Balázs did not quite understand the radical consequences of his own theory—that a face "filmed intensively," even one in long shot, is always in close-up, and that a close-up always represents a face, whether a human face or the face of an object. The close-up and face are hence equivalent, interchangeable, and what they have in common, according to Aumont, is "the operation which produces a surface that is sensible and legible at the same time, which produces, as Deleuze says, an Entity."[36] The close-up transforms whatever it films into a quasi-tangible thing, producing an intense phenomenological experience of presence, and yet, simultaneously, that deeply experienced entity becomes a sign, a text, a surface that demands to be read. This is, inside or outside of the cinema, the inevitable operation of the face as well.

Deleuze's formulation is even more extreme: "As for the face itself, we will not say that the close-up deals with [*traite*] it or subjects it to some kind of treatment: there is no close-up *of* the face, the face is itself close-up, the close-up is by itself face and both are affect, affection image."[37] This analysis hinges upon a quite precise definition of the face (which coincides with Bergson's definition of affect) and a hypothetical history in which the significance of the face is, in effect, *compensatory*. The face's function as a privileged site of meaning makes up for a loss or lack. According to this quasi-evolutionary history, in order to become the location of the organs of reception (sight, hearing, taste, smell), the face had to "sacrifice most of its motoricity."[38] Upon this largely immobile surface, the features were then capable only of micro-movements, but extraordinarily intense ones that conjoin to make up what we call "expression." This history produces, for Deleuze, a definition of "face": "Each time we discover these two poles in something—reflecting surface and intensive micro-movements—we can say that this thing has been treated as a face [*visage*]: it has been 'envisaged' or rather 'faceified' [*visagéifiée*], and in turn it stares at us [*dévisage*], it looks at us . . . even if it does not resemble a face."[39] I will return later to the way in which the gaze emerges as a crucial component at the heart of Deleuze's description of "faceification."[40] But here, it is objects that, in the manner of Lacan, look back at us and objects that, like the face, have expressions, and are therefore capable of being "facialized."

This understanding of the face requires that it be completely detached from ordinary notions about its social semiotics. Traditionally, according to Deleuze, the face has been given three roles:

1. as the privileged site of individualization (it embodies each person's uniqueness);
2. as the manifestation of social role or social type;
3. as the primary tool of intersubjectivity, of relation to or communication with the other (this also refers to an adequate, mimetic relation, within the individual, between face and character or role).

Although the face, as traditionally understood, embodies these three roles both inside the cinema (when it appears in medium or long shots) and outside of it, the close-up effectively strips the face of all three: "There is no close-up of the face. The close-up is the face, but the face precisely in so far as it has destroyed its triple function—a nudity of the face much greater than that of the body, an inhumanity much greater than that of animals."[41] The close-up pushes us beyond the realm of individuation, of social role, and of the exchange that underlies intersubjectivity. This is why the face is indissociably linked with the process of *effacement*, a move beyond codification, and why Deleuze's discourse at some points seems to rejoin the ecstasy of Epstein's photogénie.

In Deleuze's discourse, a particular filmic technique, the close-up, is equated with a broad cultural signifying phenomenon—that encapsulated in the term "face." Jacques Aumont, in a similar fashion, expounds upon the global significance of the face (which is, again, equivalent to the close-up in the cinema, both producing a surface that is simultaneously sensible and legible). The face is the very origin of representation insofar as it is founded upon resemblance and identity. When we say that someone resembles or does not resemble someone else (or oneself, for that matter), we are referring, above all, to the face. According to Aumont:

All representation is really inaugurated by the desire of man to figure himself as face. In addition, the phrase "it resembles" is the first experience of representation. . . .

What we call representation is nothing other than the more or less complicated history of that resemblance, of its hesitation between two poles, that of appearances, of the visible, of the phenomenon, of representative analogy, and that of interiority, of the invisible or of the beyond-the-visible, of the being, of expressive analogy. The face is the point of departure and the point of anchorage of this entire history. It is not possible to represent without representing the face of man.[42]

Almost all theories of the face come to terms in some way with this opposition between surface and depth, exteriority and interiority. There is always something *beyond* and it is this sense of the beyond that fuels the hystericization of film theory when confronted with the close-up. The close-up in the cinema classically exploits the cultural and epistemological susceptibility to this binary opposition. Dreyer's *Joan of Arc*, a chain of close-ups that seem to constitute the very revelation of the soul, is the epitome of the genre. It is barely possible to see a close-up of a face without asking, What is this person thinking, feeling, suffering? What is happening beyond what I can see? Or, in Balázs's terms, the close-up of the face allows us to understand that "we can see that there is something there that we cannot see."[43]

Hence are born all the metaphors of textuality, of the face as book, of reading and legibility. The face is the intensification of a locus of signification. For Balázs, the spectator must be able to "read between the lines."[44] In the natural order of things, the face constitutes a kind of universal language, and Balázs refers to the "universal comprehensibility of facial expression and gesture."[45] However, the discovery of printing displaced the site of intensive reading from the face to paper, providing so much to read that it "gradually rendered illegible the faces of man."[46] The mission of the cinema, for Balázs, must be that of retraining us to decipher the face. According to Susan Stewart, "The face is a type of 'deep' text, a text whose meaning is complicated by change and by a constant series of alterations between a reader and an author who is strangely disembodied, neither present nor absent, found in neither part nor whole, but, in fact, *created* by this reading. Because of this convention of interpretation, it is not surprising that we find that one of the great *topoi* of Western literature has been the notion of the face as book."[47]

In laying out the terms of this history of the analysis of the cinematic close-up, I have been attempting to emphasize not only its frequent recourse to hyperbolic rhetoric but also its insistence (outside of the case of Eisenstein) upon treating the close-up synchronically rather than diachronically, as stasis, as resistance to narrative linearity, as the vertical gateway to an almost irrecoverable depth behind the image. The discourse seems to exemplify a desire to stop the film, to grab hold of something that can be taken away, to transfer the relentless temporality of the narrative's unfolding to a more manageable temporality of contemplation. However, the theory is more adequate to the memory of the film than to its experience. In memory, it is possible to believe that the gaze of the face in close-up is directed at *me*, whereas in reality, given the strictures of the classical cinema, it is more often caught in a network of other gazes. The remembered close-up effects the reappearance of Benjamin's aura (investing the object with "the ability to look at us in return").[48] But it does so in a form that seems to embrace rather than resist technical reproducibility.[49] Yet there is simultaneously a strong denial that cinematic specificity is at work here—the face and the close-up are equated in the arguments of Deleuze, Aumont, and even Balázs. Inevitably these analyses (particularly those of Epstein and Balázs) produce nostalgia for the silent cinema, since it is the face that speaks there, and speaks to us (rather than to other characters) so much more eloquently when mute.

The close-up has historically constituted a moment of stoppage or stasis within a medium renowned for its ability to represent movement and time. It elicits a protracted stare, brings the forward linear movement of the narrative to a standstill, coagulates time. Laura Mulvey's influential distinction between spectacle and narrative aligns the close-up with the atemporal, with the attempt to localize desire, fantasy, and longing in a timeless time, outside contingency.[50] The insistent historical association of the close-up with the face of the woman—preeminently the star—posits its smooth, pore-less, wrinkle-free surface as a protection against time and its inevitable corruption. This is why memories of the cinema so often take the form of the close-up, the graspable and memorable instant. The archival desire manifested here is an attempt to halt the vertiginous movement of mechanical and electronic reproduction. Consistent with processes of commodification, close-ups reduce the corrupting, dismantling work of time to an instant that can be seized and circulated. As Michael Chanan has pointed out, "It is this fixing of our experience of time that constitutes the dominant ideological form of time in commoditized society."[51]

But does the close-up really produce the effects that are assigned to it? Does it look at us? Does the close-up extract its object from all spatiotemporal coordinates? Does it constitute a momentous pause in the temporal

1.1–1.4 *The Cheat* (Cecil B. DeMille, 1915).

unfolding of the narrative? It is instructive to examine a few examples. Sessue Hayakawa, for instance, was a crucial figure for Epstein because of his relative restraint as an actor of the silent cinema, rejecting the histrionics usually associated with the era. Given the stony immobility of his face, a slight twitch of an eyebrow could convey extraordinary significance. In Cecil B. DeMille's *The Cheat* (1915), a film deeply marked by Orientalism, Hayakawa plays a nefarious Japanese businessman who lends money to a socialite (played by Fannie Ward) who has borrowed and lost charity funds in a bad Wall Street investment. Hayakawa, who has amorous designs, refuses to allow her to pay him back (holding her to their deal, which involved the exchange of sex for the money), and instead brands her as a sign of his sexual ownership. She shoots him, injuring him in the shoulder, and her husband takes the blame. At the trial, tension is produced as an accumulation of close-ups, connected by gazes saturated with affect. When asked the question, "Who fired that shot?," Hayakawa glances down and to his left, angling his head just slightly so that he can see around the lawyer and hold Ward in his gaze. The following close-up of her highlights her anxiety, eyes wide open, lower lip trembling (fig. 1.1). In response, his close-up gives evidence of only a slight narrowing of the eyes before he asserts that it was the husband who shot him (fig. 1.2). When the husband is on the stand, close-ups of Ward's hyperbolic anxiety (fig. 1.3) are contrasted with those of Hayakawa's barely mobile smug complacency (fig. 1.4). The eyeline matches are quite precise, suggesting that both a space and an affective logic link the various close-ups.

1.5 *Queen Christina* (Rouben Mamoulian, 1933).

The second example is from *Queen Christina* (Rouben Mamoulian, 1933), the film Roland Barthes mentions in "The Face of Garbo," an essay in *Mythologies*.[52] After Christina forfeits her throne and leaves her country in order to marry her lover, the lover is shot in a duel. The final shot of the film is a slow track in to an extremely tight close-up of Garbo that is held for an unexpectedly long time. Although Garbo's face here seems to constitute a veritable zero degree of expression, its blankness nevertheless is forced into legibility by the pressure of the narrative culminating in that moment (fig. 1.5).

Finally, in a frequently cited scene from Alfred Hitchcock's *Sabotage* (1936), Sylvia Sidney (Mrs. Verloc) appears to kill Oscar Homolka (Mr. Verloc), but the stabbing itself takes place off-screen and is saturated with a certain undecidability. Sidney has just learned that Homolka, using her younger brother to carry a bomb, has caused his death and that of an entire busload of people. At the dinner table, as Sidney carves the meat, she becomes fascinated by her own fascination with the knife as a potential murder weapon

and is alternately attracted and repelled by it. At one point, the camera tracks in to a close-up of Sidney as she looks across the table at Homolka (fig. 1.6). The next shot is a tight close-up of Homolka's quizzical expression (fig. 1.7) followed by a close-up of the knife, fork, and potatoes, Sidney's hands wavering hesitantly above them, one hand reaching out to the knife but quickly withdrawing (fig. 1.8). A series of glance-object cuts establishes, first, her own guilty and murderous desire and, second, the gradual recognition by Homolka of that desire.

The legibility of all three instances of the close-up is intimately linked to their very *lack* of autonomy. This is most visible in *Sabotage*, where the struggle between Sidney's desire and her resistance to that desire is produced *between* the shots of her anxious face, the knife and potatoes, Homolka's face, and her brother's empty chair, all of which signify through a relay of gazes. According to Epstein, the close-up provides "the mimetic décor in which the look suddenly appears as a character."[53] As Bonitzer points out, the face in close-up brings with

1.6–1.8 *Sabotage* (Alfred Hitchcock, 1936).

it a "specific terror (that of the gaze). . . . Without the close-up, without the face, no suspense, no terror, domains so crucial to the cinema that it is almost identified with them."[54] Hitchcock and, differently, Luis Buñuel, understood well the limit of that terror as an attack on the eyes themselves—note the close-up of the cutting of the eye in *Un Chien Andalou* (1929), the bloody eye sockets in *The Birds* (1963), or the hollow eyes of the mother's skeleton in *Psycho* (1960). In the first example, *The Cheat*, Hayakawa's impassive face would be a complete cipher without its implantation *between* the shots of a hysterical Ward, her fearful husband, and the voyeuristic courtroom spectators, all mediated, again, by the lines of force of the gaze. In *Queen Christina*, the close-up seems most extractable, most autonomous (and hence seems to invite Barthes's nostalgia): "Garbo still belongs to that moment in cinema

when capturing the human face still plunged audiences into the deepest ecstasy, when one literally lost oneself in a human image as one would in a
philtre, when the face represented a kind of absolute state of the flesh, which
could be neither reached nor renounced."[55] Yet Garbo's completely expressionless face invites a reading that is indissociable from the narrative's
adamant production of overwhelming loss. Behind the perfect, seamless face,
the unwavering stare, it is impossible not to project thought and emotion,
although the face itself gives no indication of either.

However, I am not confirming here the banal argument that the close-up
must always be read in context and that therefore film theory's espousal of
the idea of its autonomy, its unavoidable despatialization, is simply wrong.
Indeed, I would agree that there is always a residue of separability, an uncontainable excess, attached to the close-up. But the question remains: Why the
marked discrepancy between theory's excessive concentration on the close-
up's extractability from all spatiotemporal coordinates, its production of a
hitherto unknown dimension, and its practice within specific films? Why is
the memory of and desire for the close-up as an autonomous entity so over-
whelmingly strong? I would argue that it has a great deal to do with an implicit politics of cinematic scale, most visibly incarnated in the close-up. The
experience of photogénie, of a cinephilia intimately bound up with the practice of the close-up, is indissociable from the experience of the big screen, the
"larger than life" phenomenon of the cinema.

A number of theorists attempt to elaborate a politics of the close-up or
a politics of the face, but rarely is it formulated in relation to scale. According to Gilles Deleuze and Félix Guattari in *A Thousand Plateaus*, "The face
is a politics. . . . *Certain assemblages of power require the production of a face,*
others do not. . . . The reason is simple. The face is not a universal. It is not
even that of the white man; it is White Man himself, with his broad white
cheeks and the black hole of his eyes."[56] In this text, the face is determined by a
white wall/black hole system—the white wall of *signifiance* or the field of play
of the signifier and the black hole of subjectivity, of passion, consciousness, the
illusion of a depth. In such a system, the face becomes the screen upon which
the signifier is inscribed, reaffirming the role of the face as text, accessible to a
reading that fixes meaning. Simultaneously, the "black hole" allows access to
an assumed interiority where passions and affects reside. The societies that do
not require the production of a face are (predictably enough) primitive societies, ones that are "collective, polyvocal, and corporeal" as opposed to signifying and subjective. They operate not through the face but through the body,

bringing into play heterogeneous forms and substances. The semiotic of capitalism, of what Deleuze and Guattari call modern White Men, requires the face as a mixed semiotic of significance and subjectivity, both of which work to annihilate, or at a minimum constrain, polyvocality. In this argument, the face is not preeminently human, as has been claimed so often, but inhuman, and the solution is to work toward defacialization, not in order to rehumanize the face but to dismantle it as the pathway to the soul, to make it opaque and hence allow human beings to become "imperceptible," "clandestine."[57]

For Aumont, on the other hand, the face has operated as the very location of the human since it, together with the voice, allows us a privileged access to the humanity of the other. The "ordinary face," which is that of the classical sound cinema where speech disciplines and dominates, is "an attribute of a free and equal subject with rights like all the others but which must ceaselessly exercise its liberty and equality in confronting that of other free and equal subjects. The ordinary face of the cinema is also that of Western democracy, that is to say, American and capitalist. It is a trait of imperialism, its ordinariness is an order."[58] The face in the cinema inherits certain tendencies of the portrait in its reflection/production of the concept of the bourgeois subject, but it is the shot/reverse shot that consolidates that humanity as an aspect of intersubjectivity. For Aumont, the promise of the face lies in its ineradicable link to what is human, beyond any utilitarian function of communication or signification. In that sense, he inherits some of the tendencies of 1920s film theory in its embrace of the close-up of the face as supplement.

Godard and Jean-Pierre Gorin's film *Letter to Jane* (1972; discussed more fully in chapter 4) subjects Jane Fonda's expression in a photograph taken of her in North Vietnam (the photo that earned her the nickname "Hanoi Jane") to an intense and frequently misogynist interrogation. In their analysis, her face is simply an "expression of an expression," a copy of a long line of cinematic faces, including her own in *Klute* (Pakula, 1971) and *Tout va bien* (Godard, 1972) and her father's in *The Grapes of Wrath* (Ford, 1940) and *Young Mr. Lincoln* (Ford, 1939). It is an expression of vague liberal concern, "borrowed principle and interest from Roosevelt's New Deal," and "says nothing more than how much it knows." It is the recapitulation of a quasi-Cartesian stance inflected by the requirements of a media-saturated society: "I am film, therefore I think, at least I think of the fact that I am being filmed." Godard and Gorin's semiotic analysis of the photograph attempts to demonstrate that, despite Fonda's pose of listening to the North Vietnamese, the photo speaks too much, drowning out the discourse of the North Vietnamese. Through framing and focus, the photo represents a face that represents only its own status as a star and refuses listening, refuses the possibility of a reverse shot.

The only film theorist who situates the politics of the close-up in relation to the question of scale is Eisenstein, with his emphasis upon the superiority of the Russian term (large scale or large shot) to that of the English— close-up. It is the very possibility cinema has of representing disproportion, of interrogating and displacing realism, that opens up a space for political critique. But, for Eisenstein with his cockroaches and elephants, the close-up is most significantly the close-up of objects, not of the human face: "The representation of objects in the actual (absolute) proportions proper to them is, of course, merely a tribute to orthodox formal logic. A subordination to an inviolable order of things. . . . Absolute realism is by no means the correct form of perception. It is simply the function of a certain form of social structure."[59] As opposed to the American cinema's use of the close-up to suggest proximity, intimacy, and knowledge of interiority, Eisenstein argues for a disproportion that transforms the image into a conduit for thought, an epistemological tool, undermining identification, and hence empowering the spectator as analyst of, rather than vessel for, meaning.

However, the close-up in the classical Hollywood film has never simply connoted closeness and interiority. Rather, its legibility has always been allied with its scale and its status as a form of magnification. More than other types of shots, the close-up exploits the expanse of the screen—the face or the object filmed covers the screen, using up, exhausting all space. At least in part, this explains the theoretical fascination with the diegetic autonomy of the close-up, the repeated assertion that it escapes the spatiotemporal coordinates of the narrative. The film is "larger than life," but it is most visibly larger than life in the close-up, seemingly promising an expanded cognition and recognition. From this point of view, the semiotic status of the close-up seems to bear within itself a structuring contradiction. Is the close-up a detail, a part of a larger whole, or is it instead its own whole, its own totality? Balázs claims, "A multitude of close-ups can show us the very instant in which the general is transformed into the particular."[60] Benjamin's notion of the optical unconscious or the many discourses in film theory about the defamiliarizing properties of the close-up, its ability to force us to see those minute aspects of life otherwise lost, buttress the idea that the close-up is, indeed, a detail. On the other hand, Balázs, who embraces the defamiliarization argument, also argues that the close-up is not a detail because there is no whole from which it is extracted. The space of the narrative, the diegesis, is constructed by a multiplicity of shots that vary in terms of both size and angle—hence it exists nowhere; there is no totality of which the close-up could be a part. And certainly, if one accepts the theories of the close-up's despatialization, it cannot be defined as a detail, since it occupies the only space there is, constituting itself as its own whole or totality, abolishing off-screen space. Is the close-up the bearer, the image of the small, the minute, or the producer of the monumental, the gigantic, the spectacular? This confusion and the apparent collapse of the oppositions between detail and totality, part and whole, microcosm and macrocosm, the miniature and the gigantic, are crucial to the ideological operation of the close-up, that which makes it one of our most potent memories of the cinema.

Of course, it is possible to argue that there really is no contradiction here, since the status of the image as detail or totality depends upon whether it resides in one or the other of the two worlds/spaces involved in the cinema— the space of the narrative (the diegesis) or the space of the spectator. In the diegesis, that fictional space produced by the film, the close-up, despite Balázs's denial, will always constitute a detail, a part. Yet, in the spectator's space, that of the theater, the close-up will, even if only momentarily, constitute itself as the totality, the only entity there to be seen. Three decades of film theory have insisted that the classical cinematic text works to annihilate this space— that of the spectator—to suggest that the only world is that on the screen. Hence, the embrace of the close-up as autonomous entity by Balázs, Deleuze, and especially Epstein is an attempt to salvage spectatorial space, to reaffirm its existence and its relevance in the face of the closed, seamless space of the film. Because scale as a concept has been traditionally understood through its reference to the human body, it is also an attempt to reassert the corporeality of the classically disembodied spectator.

In order to do so, however, one must effectively stop the film, deny it mobility and temporality, and, in addition, deny that the detail, the miniature also inhabits the gigantic, the spectacular, the space of the big screen. It is, ironically, to transform grandeur, largeness, and hence the spectacle into an ideologically subversive tactic, whereas we know this is not necessarily the case. As Susan Stewart argues, preindustrial culture located the gigantic in nature, as the origin of the formations of landscape, but industrial capitalism allies the gigantic with consumerism, an exchange economy, and the commodity (on billboards, in advertising in general, and in the cinema).[61] Guy Debord claims that spectacle, the most striking instantiation of the gigantic in contemporary culture, is a substitution for the loss of unity in the world—it "expresses the totality of this loss."[62] For Stewart, the movie star exemplifies the commodification of the gigantic: "The fact that such subjects are 'larger than life' is not a result of their historical acts so much as it is a matter of their medium of presentation. . . . And that formation, that generation of sign by means of sign, provides the aesthetic corollary for the generative capacity of commodity relations."[63]

The miniature, on the other hand, relates to the commodity system as well, but in a different way. For Stewart, the miniature represents "closure, interiority, the domestic, and the overly cultural. . . . It is a metaphor for the interior space and time of the bourgeois subject."[64] The miniature can be held in the hand, possessed, and hence imparts an illusion of mastery, the imprimatur of the subject. The close-up is an object of vision, not touch, but it nevertheless provokes a sense of the tangible, the intimate. This is Benjamin's desire of the masses to bring things closer, to sacrifice uniqueness for reproduction. Epstein writes, "The close-up modifies the drama by the impact of proximity. Pain is within reach. If I stretch out my arm I touch you, and that is intimacy. I can count the eyelashes of this suffering. I would be able to taste the tears."[65] In the close-up, there is a curious mixture of the small and the large, the miniature and the gigantic, the detail and the monument. As Stewart points out, while the miniature is usually associated with the private and the domestic, the gigantic is aligned with the public and highly visible: "The gigantic represents infinity, exteriority, the public, and the overly natural."[66]

In an essay on sculpture, Robert Morris also sees small-scale and large-scale objects as linked, respectively, to the intimate and the monumental:

> In the perception of relative size the human body enters into the total continuum of sizes and establishes itself as a constant on that scale. One knows immediately what is smaller and what is larger than himself. . . . The quality of intimacy is attached to an object in a fairly direct proportion as its size diminishes in relation to oneself. The quality of publicness is attached in proportion as the size increases in relation to oneself. This holds true so long as one is regarding the whole of a large thing and not a part. The qualities of publicness and privateness are imposed on things. . . . Most ornaments from the past, Egyptian glassware, Romanesque ivories, etc., consciously exploit the intimate mode by highly resolved surface incident. The awareness that surface incident is always attended to in small objects allows for the elaboration of fine detail to sustain itself.[67]

Small-scale objects or miniatures in the intimate mode are "closed" and "spaceless." In contrast, according to Morris, monumental objects not only exhibit or call attention to the very quality of size as size but also activate the space around them. Because scale is comprehended through the register of the body, the distance between subject and object becomes crucial, and "space does not exist for intimate objects."[68] Monumental objects, on the other hand, literally require a certain distance to be seen properly and inscribe that space as a part of their relation to the viewer. He continues: "The smaller the object the closer one approaches it and, therefore, it has correspondingly less of a spatial field in which to exist for the viewer. It is this necessary greater distance of the object in space from our bodies, in order that it be seen at all, that structures the non-personal or public mode."[69] This activation of an extensive space surrounding the object calls for physical participation on the part of the viewer, who must adopt, in succession, different points of view.

Morris is, of course, describing sculpture, and this kinesthetic demand is necessarily inapplicable to the cinematic spectator of the classical period, who is defined by immobility. Yet this discussion of scale has some intriguing implications for the analysis of the close-up, which combines and perhaps confounds aspects of both types of dimension. The cinematic image, projected in a theatrical space, is indeed a monumental object whose visibility is a function of a certain distance from the image (by Noël Burch's calculation, the perfect position for the spectator is a centered one, at a distance from the screen of two and a half times the width of the image).[70] Sitting too close to the image entails the loss of its legibility. But, in addition, the close-up makes available the detail, either of a larger scene or of a human face with its pores, eyelashes, wrinkles, tears. In the intimacy with which it reaches out to the audience and in the self-enclosure and radical separability described by theorists from Béla Balázs to Gilles Deleuze, it shares the "spacelessness" of Morris's small-scale object with its "resolved surface incident." Existing in the modes of both the miniature and the gigantic, the close-up continues to trouble cinematic space.

The close-up, as an isolable entity, can be taken and held within memory, as residual trace of the film's commodification of time. As simultaneously microcosm and macrocosm, the miniature and the gigantic, the close-up acts as a nodal point linking the ideologies of intimacy and interiority to public space and the authority of the monumental. In the close-up, the cinema plays simultaneously with the desire for totalization and its impossibility. The cinematic spectator clings to the fragment of a partial reality—a fragment that mimics the effect of a self-sufficient totality. The classical close-up assures us that we can indeed see and grasp the whole, in a moment rich with meaning and affect.

The close-up can be seen in terms of proximity (as "close" or "near" to the spectator) rather than in terms of scale (as "large") only by conferring upon it the attribute of depth, of perspective—in other words, that which it resolutely denies in its embrace of the screen as surface. Proximity is, in this sense, only a figurative reading of size or grandeur, but it is a reading that the classical cinema regularly asks us to make. Because the close-up fills the frame with its content and hence annuls any depth of field, it carries with it a loss—that of the interior of the image, of its perspectival space. The screen becomes most visibly a surface in these moments. The predilection of the close-up for the human face in the classical cinema can be seen as a displacement of this missing depth and interiority. For the face is designated as that part of the body most suited to the expression of an interiority, of a depth of character legible in its every movement.

It has often been said that we live in an age of the image, in a society saturated by images. But, if this is so, that image (with the exception, perhaps, of virtual reality) always requires a support, a screen, hence the equal aptness of noting that we also live in an era of the proliferation of screens. Contemporary culture is witness to an exaggeration of the two extremes of screen size. While the screen becomes smaller and smaller in personal computers, laptops, notepads, and cell phones, the television screen is becoming larger and larger in competition with the construction of cinemas with stadium seating and mammoth screens. The screen haunts both private and public realms and, indeed, envisages the potential collapse of this opposition. Miniaturized, the image it bears can now literally be held in the hand, sustaining the illusion of its possession. Made gigantic in IMAX theaters, it presents the spectator with a vision of impossible totality, of modern transcendence.

The excessiveness and exuberance of the historical discourse on the close-up can, perhaps, help us to understand what is at stake in this contemporary schizophrenia of scale. The French Impressionist concept of photogénie was fashioned to evoke that which was inarticulable yet specific to the filmic experience. Its unspeakability is no doubt linked to the desire to make it a corporeal experience, a matter of touching, feeling, tasting, as well as seeing. Yet the historical trajectory of classical cinema was to defeat that body by annihilating its space, its ability to act as a measure of scale. Photogénie is usually referred to as one of the earliest examples of cinephilia, a love of the cinema that insists upon its uniqueness and its ability to induce a form of incomparable ecstasy. Such an ecstasy seemed to celebrate, but actually resisted, the lure of absorption into the image, of losing oneself in a cinematic space. Today, the gigantic screens of IMAX theaters work to reassert, to reconfirm that possibility of absorption, which has played such an important role in the history of cinema. In other words, it seems necessary today to exaggerate, to hyperbolize the cinema in order to be assured that it works. Yet the possibility of its failure is also allayed by the proliferation of miniature screens so that it could be said that the screen is not simply enormous, it is everywhere. The inevitable limit to its magnitude is compensated for by its proliferation. Focusing on the close-up, the discourse of photogénie elaborated the way in which detail and enormity, miniature and gigantic, are inextricable in the cinema. It is the cinema understood in this way that laid the groundwork for a future cultural logic of the screen, a logic that continues to exploit the delocalizing effects of scale.

Chapter 2

The Cinematic Manufacture of Scale, or Historical Vicissitudes of the Close-Up

Now I want to smash The Vitascope. The name of the thing is in itself a horror, but that may pass. Its manifestations are worse. The Vitascope, be it known, is a sort of magic lantern which reproduces movement. Whole scenes are enacted on its screen. La Loie dances, elevated trains come and go, and the thing is mechanically ingenious, and a pretty toy for that great child, the public. Its managers were not satisfied with this, however, and they bravely set out to eclipse in vulgarity all previous theatrical attempts.

In a recent play called *The Widow Jones* you may remember a famous kiss which Miss May Irwin bestowed on a certain John C. Rice, and vice versa. Neither participant is physically attractive, and the spectacle of their prolonged pasturing on each other's lips was hard to bear. When only life-size it was pronounced beastly. But that was nothing to the present sight. Magnified to Gargantuan proportions and repeated three times over it is absolutely disgusting.

—"Notes," *The Chap-Book*, 1896

The problem with novels is that they actually tell you what the character is thinking.
—DAVID BORDWELL, in conversation, circa 1981

The problem with theatre is that the people are too small.
—DAVID BORDWELL, email, April 2017

Lauded today as providing one of the first examples of a close-up in the cinema, *The Kiss* (Thomas Edison, 1896) was received in very different ways. It was popular and often produced hysterical laughter. According to one reviewer in the *Boston Herald*, the film was "absolutely 'too funny' for anything."[1] But as the first epigraph to this chapter demonstrates, for others it was the very incarnation of the vulgarity and degeneration of the new invention, especially given its scale and repetition—it is "absolutely disgusting." In both cases, it represents an "absolute," whether positive or negative. This theme of the absolute, the excessive, the immoderate will accompany discourse about the close-up throughout its history and reveals the extent to which the social sense of scale impacted its reception and, conversely, the way in which it impacted the social sense of scale. Writing almost one hundred years later, in a special issue of *Revue belge du cinéma*, Philippe Dubois comments on this film and especially the *Chap-Book* review. He refers to the object of the film, the kiss, and its filming (looped, in close-up) as constituting for its public a "double obscenity." But it is above all "the excessiveness [of the close-up] (Gargantuan) which is finally intolerable."[2]

In the introduction, I discussed two films that are particularly striking in their canny performance of the ambiguities of the close-up in its relation to scale, space, and legibility before the close-up (or even the shot) was recognized as an entity—Méliès's *The Man with a Rubber Head* (1901) and Williamson's *The Big Swallow* (1901). The latter continues *The Kiss's* thematics of excessive orality. Dubois sees *The Big Swallow* as exemplary of the affective power of the close-up. This moving, inexorable close-up, with its "dark and deep circle of the open mouth" echoing the lens of the camera, is the very figure of "menace and anguish: it is the fear in front of the becoming-monstrous of the face (its disfiguration, its obscenity, its immoderation, its loss of identity through excessive proximity) . . . it is the fantasy of castration, of swallowing of devouring ('the big swallow')."[3] The tension is fictively resolved, according to Dubois, by the transformation of a threat (the "absolute of the close-up") into a humorous joke, a trick that discharges the accumulated affect.[4] The excessiveness of Dubois's own rhetoric is reminiscent of that of Epstein and Balázs, but here dystopian rather than utopian.

In the earliest cinema, the large scale of the "close view" is not yet domesticated and disciplined through the construction of a homogeneous space detached from that of the spectator. This is a period of play, of humor (often manifesting traces of the influence of vaudeville), of exploration of the capabilities of a new medium. In the genre of "facial expression films" (discussed more extensively in chapter 3), the close view is used to display a series of meaningless, exaggerated, or grotesque facial expressions (examples include Edison's *Facial Expressions* [1902] and *Goo Goo Eyes* [1903]; *Anna Held* [American Mutoscope and Biograph Co. (AM&B), 1902]; George Albert Smith's *Comic Faces* [1898]; Cecil Hepworth's *The Comic Grimacer* [1901]; *Wrinkles Removed* [AM&B, 1902]; and *The Rose* [AM&B, 1903]). In line with Tom Gunning's "cinema of attractions," these faces directly confront the spectator; they display the rich contingency, multiplicity, and mobility of the cinematic image.[5] As a performance or display of the sheer capabilities of the new technology, the close-up was in itself an attraction, a demonstration of the cinema's potential for disproportion and the play of scale. In these films, the close-up is the site of a hysterical performance of faciality, of exaggerated expressions and hyperbolic affects. The monstrosity of its scale is rationalized, in effect, by the monstrosity/grotesqueness of the facial expressions that exceed all expected norms, reinscribing disproportion at a different level. It is only in the later years of the silent cinema that the face is sutured to revelation of character in the service of narrative.

Nevertheless, the vicissitudes of scale, even in the earliest years of the cinema, registered a threat, or at least a problem that must be contained. One way of effecting this containment was to situate a technology of vision such as the microscope, telescope, or even reading glass as the motivation for the insertion of a close view. In *Grandma's Reading Glass* (George Albert Smith, 1900), a young boy uses his grandmother's looking glass to examine various objects—a bird, a watch, a newspaper, and Grandma's roving eye—which appear in inserts at close range with an iris banishing the surroundings to blackness. A spin-off, *Grandpa's Reading Glass* (AM&B, 1902), similarly centers on two young girls who use their grandfather's reading glass to examine various objects, including their mother's eye. In *As Seen through a Telescope* (George Albert Smith, 1900), an older man uses his telescope to fetishistically view a young woman's ankle as her shoe is tied by her beau. The technologies of vision invoked here help to rationalize a drastic change in scale.[6] For

Jan Holmberg, getting "near" the object is simultaneous with maintaining a distance, and the significance of these technologies is aligned with a peculiarly modern experience of distance and proximity that is Heideggerian in its dialectic of remoteness and nearness—the world becomes closer "according to Heidegger not by simply approaching it, but *negatively*, by making the distance disappear, by distancing distance."[7] The use of an iris in these films not only focuses the gaze but also consigns the space around the object to darkness. Above all, the technologies in these films serve to internalize and mobilize a shift in size; they provide a diegetic excuse for the close view.

Even in early narrative films, the close-up is used judiciously, often banished from the diegesis to the edges of the film. The most famous example of this is the close-up of the outlaw firing a gun at the camera in Edwin S. Porter's *The Great Train Robbery* (1903). Whether the close-up appeared at the beginning of the film or the end was left to the discretion of the projectionist, but in either case, it was separated from the diegesis. In *The Widow and the Only Man* (AM&B, 1904), the two main characters are introduced at the beginning of the film through close-ups labeled "the only man" and "the widow." He smokes a pipe while she glances at the camera, smiles, and makes faces in the manner of the earlier facial expression films. And perhaps one of the most intriguing instances of this tendency is located in the opening shot of the AM&B film *The Village Cut-Up* (1906), in which the title figure, in close-up, moves and fidgets, twisting his facial features, while posing for a photograph. Behind his head is an anachronistic photography brace, used to stabilize and offer support for the human body for the long duration required for the early daguerreotype—here, its function successfully evaded by the perpetual movement of the protagonist (fig. 2.1). In an extremely rare invocation of off-screen space, two hands emerge from the right of the frame, attempting to still or steady the village cut-up (fig. 2.2). The body of the film traces the pranks of a figure whose social marginality is marked, who cannot be contained. The obsessive attempt to still this figure in the introductory shot, to immobilize him for representation, is a reiteration of and response to the instability of scale embodied in the close-up. In these examples, the use of the close-up is emblematic, haunting the edges of the film body "proper," evicted from the narrative space itself. To segregate the close-up as an alien entity, as extradiegetic and therefore more legible as a *sign*, is one way of attempting to contain the trauma of scale associated with it. Through this strategy, the close-up's legibility is no longer spatial; hence, the disturbance of excessive scale is reduced. The success of this tactic seems

2.1 & 2.2 *The Village Cut-Up* (AM&B, 1906). Courtesy of the Library of Congress.

to be demonstrated by the fact that the avid criticism of the monstrosity of the close-up is most prevalent during the period in which narrative becomes the dominant cinematic mode and the close-up is incorporated within the diegesis—the years from 1907 to 1913.

Another means of reducing the menace of scalar instability in the use of the close-up as narrative takes hold might be seen as transitional. The close-up is integrated within the diegesis at the end of the film but is associated with hysteria or the catastrophic, borrowing from the excessive faciality of the earlier films.[8] In *The Curtain Pole* (AM&B, 1909), a man breaks his friend's curtain rod as he attempts to help hang it over the window. The body of the film traces his attempts to return with a new pole, which continually escapes his control, hitting passersby and objects as he walks, then takes a carriage. By the time he returns, the friend has already replaced the pole and everyone in the gathering ignores the protagonist. His hysterical and seemingly irrational response is to bite into the pole in close-up (fig. 2.3). But this close-up is incorporated within the diegesis when there is a cut back to a medium shot in which the protagonist ultimately throws the pole down on the floor. This shot is a final instance of the way in which the pole is used throughout the

2.3 *The Curtain Pole* (AM&B, 1909). Courtesy of the Library of Congress.

film as a humorous device to test the limits of the frame and film space, to work out, in comic form, the spatial possibilities of the screened image.

The apprehensiveness surrounding the close-up is in evidence in the period in journalistic tirades against its violation of the integrity of the human body and in the perception of a certain "grotesqueness" in such a large-scale representation. The sheer magnitude of the projected image seemed to undermine the indexical guarantee of a realistic effect.[9] And the castrating tendencies of the close-up, in its automatic fragmentation of the body, instilled an incipient anxiety that found an outlet in the frequent rehearsal of scenarios of decapitation or explosions resulting in the proliferation of separated body parts (examples include *Mary Jane's Mishap* [George Albert Smith, 1903] and *Explosion of a Motor Car* [Cecil Hepworth, 1900]). The close-up posed incessantly the problem of a castration, of a radical violence to the body, to its integrity and its anchoring function as the image of psychic wholeness and identity. On the other hand, it generated an anxiety of scale, of monstrosity, giganticism, and disproportion, and consequently of a perversion of space. While the development of continuity editing allayed that anxiety to some extent by suturing the close-up to the diegetic space, the close-up continued to harbor within it the danger of a radical incommensurability with that space. Both in threatening a "proper" scale (scale as measured by one's own body) and in its dangerous proximity, the close-up poses the problem of the threshold, of the surface or screen as limit, as barrier. This may help to explain the persistence of the stories of early film audiences fleeing in terror as the locomotive approaches in a Lumière brothers film of a train arriving at a station, despite the inability of film historians to substantiate this claim. The spectator of this story may be naive but nevertheless embodies a deeper knowledge of the close-up's ontological instability, its absolute discordance, its heterogeneity. From the depths of the perspectival image, the train approaches a space that is a non-space, the figure of a void—an absolute surface with no volume or thickness. As things approach this non-space, they implode. This is what the early silent cinema knew. The anxiety surrounding the close-up in the early years of film is progressively managed through conventions of editing, internalization and psychologization of the gaze, point of view, and eyeline matching so that the close-up is sutured to the space of the diegesis, becoming a detail or part of a homogeneous whole, rarely acknowledging its location on the brink or its deictic status—the "here it is" it incessantly presents to the spectator.[10] Yet its scale continues to pose the possibility of a rupture, of a barely contained disproportion endemic to cinematic signification.

Journalistic discourses discussing the close-up in the early years saw it imperiling the establishment of the scale of the human body as norm and the way in which the photoplay, unlike the earlier hand-cranked Edison kinetoscope image, was able to provide that scale. In 1895, Thomas Edison referred to projected kinetoscope images as "life size," and, as John Belton points out with respect to the Lumières Cinématographe projections in London in 1896, "In comparison with peepshow images, a 5-to-6 foot projected image would clearly be perceived as 'life-size,' rendering human figures on a scale closer to their actual size."[11] Jan Holmberg has extensively documented the demand for "life-size" images and "grandeur naturelle" in early press commentary on moving pictures.[12] The clearest violation of this norm was the close-up, an object of anxiety and hostility in much of the journalistic discourse of the early period. The close-up presented two threats to the norm of the mimetic body: first, it was perceived as aesthetically offensive in extreme ways—as monstrous or grotesque, an excessive display of disproportion in scale; and, second, as an untenable fragmentation of the human body. One particularly adamant rejection of the close shot was written by an author with the pseudonym Yhcam in a 1912 issue of *Ciné-Journal*:

> Now we have reached what could be called *the age of the legless cripple*. For three-quarters of the time, the actors in a scene are projected in close shot, cut off at the knees; from the artistic point of view, the effect produced is highly disagreeable and shocking. . . . I have seen a film where an actor and a horse, placed side by side, were both partially cut off at the knees; then when the man mounted the horse, he found himself suddenly decapitated. To pass instantaneously from being legless to being headless is really pushing things a bit far.[13]

Here, the frame itself is perceived as aggressive, capable even of decapitation. Off-screen space does not exist or, at least, has no aesthetic function. Yhcam also strongly criticizes the "unnatural grandeur" of the close shot and the tendency to move quickly between shots of different scales, disorienting the spectator.

In a 1912 article entitled "Cutting Off the Feet," in *Moving Picture World*, H. F. Hoffman complains about the widespread tendency to cut off the feet, then the knees, then the legs of actors in motion pictures. He derides the overvaluation of facial expression at the expense of the more aesthetic landscape and composition of the image: "The picture is *all* facial expression and nothing else."[14] His claim is that motion pictures are not the appropriate venue for the portrait or character studies. Ironically, this resistance to the close-up emerges in a period when narrative is becoming the dominant mode and many directors are exploiting the possibility of facial expression and its greater legibility in the close-up. Here, the anxiety is aligned with the castrating powers (disguised as unaesthetic) associated with this shot—"An arrangement with the feet cut off is not a complete and harmonious whole. There is something lacking."[15] Others cite disproportion and large scale as the main drawbacks of the close shot. The "life-size" stature of figures on the screen becomes the standard that must be preserved at all costs, and writers often cite the theater as a norm for the representation of actors. In "Too Near the Camera" (*Moving Picture World*, 1911), the editors claim, "There are very many moving pictures nowadays, even by reputable makers, in which the figures are too near the camera: that is to say, they assume unnecessarily large and, therefore, grotesque proportions."[16] They praise Porter for maintaining the proper distance between camera and characters, avoiding "abnormality of size" and expressing "the proper sensuous impression of size. . . . the fundamental rule to be observed in this matter is that no figure should appear larger than life-size to the eye."[17] The distinction between the normal and the abnormal circulates around the scale of the human body, which must be protected and defended assiduously.

Although Harry Furniss in "Those Awful Cinematograph Faces" (*Motography*, 1913), seems to accept the close-up as a form of access to facial expression, he is dismayed by the accompanying tendency "to stretch one's mouth open to the extreme limit of cavernous expansion, to twist and distort every muscle in the facial area and to goggle one's eyes to a seemingly perilous extent."[18] He sees this as due, in part, to the enlarging of the image and imagines a scenario that is uncannily close to that of *The Big Swallow*: "There would seem to be no escape from this aggressive grin that spreads and spreads until one feels in imminent danger of disappearing into the vast, grinning mouth."[19] Large dimensions in both cases are equated with a devouring or engulfing movement, an oral incorporation that threatens to reach out of the screen and obliterate the spectator. The horror of the large is that of invading the space of the spectator. The variability and unpredictability of scale in the motion picture is also a target of derision in an editorial in *Moving Picture World* in 1909, "The Factor of Uniformity."[20] Here the editors complain about the movement from an image that was so large that the audience members were led to believe the story was being enacted by "a race of giants or giantesses" to an image taken at a greater distance from the camera in which the figures were "less monstrous to the eye" to another image taken so far from the camera that the figures appeared to be "their natural size [the correct scale, according to the writers]."[21] The variation in scales ("between Brobdignagian monstrosity and Lilliputian pigmies") is disorienting to the spectator and suggests that the motion picture has access to an infinite number of sizes.[22] The editors compare this mobility of scale negatively to vaudeville and theater where "figures of human beings do not expand or contract irrationally or eccentrically; they remain the same size."[23] Constancy, predictability, and human stature are the norms.

However, this is a period of transition in which these writings coexist side by side with others that laud the close-up's ability to display facial expression (whether subtle or not) as well as its affinity with the growing establishment of a star system and its assurance of recognition (and hence profits).[24] Yet the vehemence in the language of the discourses described here (the use of terms such as "monstrous," "grotesque," "gigantic," "abnormal," "contortion," "degeneration," "irrationality," and "eccentricity") indicates the trepidation that characterized the confrontation with the potential of shifting scales in the early cinema. That anxiety continues to infect discourses on the close-up in both early and later cinema. Philippe Carcassonne, discussing the use of the close-up in the American thriller, claims that it functions as an "exorbitant abnormality . . . calling into question the scene in which it is inscribed."[25] Taking pornography as exemplary of the potential of the close-up as insert, he writes, "The insert, in allowing the anatomical detail to invade the totality of the field [on-screen space], transforms . . . its relation to the real, and ends by *détourning* its meaning from the 'truths' that it pretends to show; reality is no longer demonstrated, but simply engulfed by the shot, which regurgitates it without any mediation, without any coordination, a fortiori without any dialectical construction. The result is a quasi-unhealthy disarticulation, an 'autism' of the image."[26] The close-up in pornography is so telling for Carcassonne because pornography itself is an "autistic genre," a kind of "zero-degree of cinema," paring down elements such as narrative, characterization, and dialogue to reveal the specific effect of cinematic technique. His use of the term *détournement* is clearly a nod to the Situationist International, but he activates the concept in a somewhat different way. For the situationists, détournement refers to the upending or negation of conventional notions of artistic value and the artworks aligned with them; it involves a clash between but nevertheless a coexistence of the old and the new significations in a work that has been *détourned*. Its aim is the negation of preexisting cultural values.[27] For Carcassonne, it is the close-up itself that is détourned; rather than acting as a part of the whole, it itself becomes the whole, evacuating meaning from the scene from which it is extracted. In pornography, desire and the erotic are reduced to the precise details of pubic hair, sweat, semen, blood. He argues that the détournement effected by the close-up produces a *supplement* of meaning, an ironic result of its work of fragmentation. The close-up reverses the logical construction of meaning—rather than determining the set beginning from the element, the element itself plays the central role. This has consequences for the legibility of space. Although the close-up destroys depth of field, shrinking the space of the scene to the detail alone, it ironically enables the invasion of the on-screen space of the close-up by off-screen space ("precisely because it [off-screen space] has been excluded in the most radical fashion").[28] At the same time, it *détourns* the fictional or narrative emphasis by abruptly presenting, designating, the object that was previously masked or hidden as supervisible, as all-invasive and overpresent.

Dubois, on his part, reverses Carcassonne's analysis: in the close-up, on-screen space is not invaded by off-screen space— the reverse is true. He locates the exorbitance of the close-up in one of the earliest and most iconic of films—Auguste and Louis Lumière's *L'arrivée d'un train en gare de La Ciotat* (1895). He cites Georges Sadoul's contention that this early film contains all the scales of shots in use in the current cinema. Beginning with a long shot of the train, a mere point, at the horizon, the film ends with what is effectively a close-up of both train and travelers (figs. 2.4– 2.6). But Dubois contests the fact that these "shots" are actually shots, since there is no cutting, no articulation, no rupture of the continuity of the film, and hence no scale of shots conceived as an a priori optical-technical system.[29]

2.4–2.6 *L'arrivée d'un train en gare de La Ciotat* (Auguste and Louis Lumière, 1895).

He nevertheless claims that the close-up is at work in *L'arrivée,* but not as a fixed unit, not as an element taken from an optically fixed scale, but rather as "a movement, a force, an effect, a stake . . . a conceptually complex entity."[30] What this means for Dubois is that the close-up is not a shot. Just as pornography is central for Carcassonne as the exemplary field of play of the close-up, the realm in which it exhibits its essential traits, Dubois focuses on *L'arrivée* as a proto-typical instance of the astonishing force of the close-up. Whether or not the persistent story about spectators fleeing in horror as the Lumières' train approached is verifiable, its strength and longevity is explained by Dubois in relation to the work of the close-up, which threatens to break through the screen and hence invade the space of the spectator.[31] The space of the close-up is "absolutely heterogeneous . . . it completely escapes the anthropo-logical references of canonical scale."[32] It destroys the scale of shots and "it is this which generates fear."[33] As in *The Big Swallow,* the close-up is always a devouring close-up. It breaks the rule of proxemics that dictates the "good distance"; it is *too close.* For Dubois, "it is not for nothing that the cinema has experienced difficulty in integrating the close-up."[34] It is crucial that the trajectory of *L'arrivée* is that of a *movement* from background to foreground. For the film plays out a passage from the moment at which the train, rivet-ing the spectator's attention, is only a dot, a stain on the horizon, appearing to emerge out of the vanishing point indicated by the perspectival lines of the rails, to the moment at which it reaches another limit point, that of the surface of the screen. Both are unrepresentable; both point to the ultimate off-screen space, whether the unknowable infinity of the depth of the image or the beyond of the surface of the screen, too close, menacing the space of the spectator.

However, there is another "story" (*histoire*) of the close-up in the film, according to Dubois, one that mitigates the first. Rather than the movement of the train across the depth of field, this movement is largely lateral and scalable. On the train platform, human figures move back and forth, with smaller, more discrete movements than that of the train, at times approach-ing the camera and exiting toward the bottom of the frame. But they never function to put pressure on the surface of the screen, instead establishing the spectator as a more or less distant observer, outside of the scene, unin-volved. The impending collision of the train with the space of the spectator is displaced by both the arresting of the train's movement and the bustling circulation of the people on the platform, who attract the interest of a now detached spectator. In the first histoire, the spectator is the target of the inexorable and relentless movement of a machine; in the second, the spectator is confronted with "a multitude of small, irregular and discontinuous movements" that are primarily lateral, calming, and familiar, prompting an amused and detached curiosity.[35] The distance from the filmed object is here irreducible, and the "good distance" of proxemics is maintained. Whereas the subject can only lose itself in the face of the train's assault on representation, here the subject refinds and reconstitutes its identity in the crowd of the "humanist close-up."[36] The camera is at eye level, human height, and anthropocentric scale is regained, in contradistinction to the assault on scale launched by the train and its onslaught. The force of the machine has been tamed, and it becomes mere background for the human drama. This process, for Dubois, is that of the détournement of the critically unrepresentable theoretical end point of the extreme close-up—that of off-screen space itself.[37] It is subject to a recuperation or detour into the familiar space of human representation. It is necessary to "render *fictional*" the possibility of this breach of the screen's surface, this inexorable threat that is nevertheless the source of the film's emotional power. Dubois goes so far as to claim that all of the history of film can be found summarized in this movement from the

> *machinic* close-up (that of movement, of continuity and of infinity; that of the drive, of terror and of devouring; that of the desert, of the void and of loss; that of negative depth and the death of the subject) to the *humanist* close-up (that of scale, of moderation [*mesure*], of the scene; that of system, of closure, of reassurance; that of possession, knowledge and power; . . . that of the very constitution of the identity of the subject). One more time—it is all of the cinema that is at play here.[38]

As has often been pointed out, the French word for "story" coincides with that for "history"—*histoire*. Dubois finds two histories of the close-up embedded in this unassuming short film of the Lumières. One of these histories posits a danger, an unease always associated, more or less explicitly, with the close-up, that of breaching the surface of the screen. The fear of the train barreling toward off-screen space is not that it will hit the spectator but that it will demolish the otherness of the world of the film, that it will expand exorbitantly its space, that it will break the line that separates the diegesis from the spectator. In this early instance, that interpenetration of spaces induces horror and anxiety. Later, in chapter 6, I will describe how this fear has morphed into a desire to extend or even transgress the limits of representation, to promote the leakage of representational space (in systems like IMAX, 3D, virtual reality, and surround sound). But here, at the moment of the emergence of cinema as an institution, the uncanniness of film in its relation to space, time, and movement is particularly marked. Dubois insists that the close-up in this first history is not about scale and is not a matter of an isolable unit but rather of a trajectory. Nevertheless, he situates it time and again as "outside of scale," in other words, in a relation to scale even if that relation is one of going beyond, of transcending. This close-up is not calculable in relation to any system of scale or measurement because it absorbs in itself all the space of the image. This scalelessness is a part of its terror/threat. Dubois refers to the two universes whose demarcation is endangered (that of the film, that of the spectator) as "incommensurable." Here, incommensurable means not only incompatible but *without common measure.*

Scale is restored in the second, humanistic history of the close-up embedded in the film. The people with their wayward movements on the platform embody a contingency that is opposed to the linear, inexorable movement of the train. The two stories/histories represent two phases in the history of the cinema and of the close-up in particular. In the early cinema, the close-up is a problem—it carries the risk of being devoured (*The Big Swallow*), of being crushed (*L'arrivée* and the plethora of train films of the era), or of the hysterical, opaque, meaningless contortions of the face in the facial expression films. But with the advent of longer, feature-length narrative films this problem, this otherness of the close-up, is contained by a humanist strategy of characterization, restoring anthropocentrism and tethering the close-up to the revelation of a subjective interiority signified by a now legible facial expression. In Dubois's rather teleological argument, *L'arrivée* is the kernel, the incarnation of film history itself. The two histoires represent two phases of the history of the use of the close-up, but in *L'arrivée* they are merged and become simultaneous. It is as though *L'arrivée* portended or prophesized the future of the cinema. This historical narrative of a close-up that is domesticated through characterization has been espoused by other scholars, notably Jan Holmberg and Jill Susan Colley, although in their accounts (and most) the two histories are successive and there is no "ur-film." Yet Dubois's second histoire is not exactly that of characterization, since, if *L'arrivée* were to be generically classified, it would solicit the category of documentary rather than narrative fiction. His trajectory (interior to the film) is from an unmanageable close-up that destroys scale to a humanistic one that emphasizes the crowd and its nonmachinic haphazard movements. While the clothing and behavior of these figures may signify class, it is not facial expression that is at issue. This is crucial because the concept of facial expression (explored more fully in chapter 3) also brings into play a relation between surface and depth. While Dubois's train, emerging from the infinite depth of the vanishing point, tests and assaults the surface of the screen, in the facial expression close-up, that surface (of the face so close that it becomes aligned with the screen itself) becomes a gateway rather than a boundary, opens onto an otherwise inaccessible interiority, a "depth," a depth that conveys meaning. In this way, the close-up of characterization no longer threatens to invade the space of the spectator but enfolds itself within the diegesis of the film as simply another layer of signification.

It is impossible to overestimate the significance of the face in the cinema. In the same period in which the close-up of the face is seen as monstrous and grotesque or castrating (around 1907–13), it begins to be perceived as a crucial element of characterization in the service of narrative. As Holmberg points out, "What eventually made the 'grotesque' enlargement of the close-up acceptable, was its abilities to show the richness in detail of the actors' faces and gestures."[39] The opposition between surface and depth was invoked in order to suggest that the close-up was the privileged vehicle to provide access to a character's "interiority." This marks a critical transition point at which the early cinema turns from theater as its primary reference (actors facing the camera, medium long shots in which there is a prescribed amount of space between the characters and the edges of the frame) to the novel. When D. W. Griffith claims (falsely) to have been the first to use the close-up and "restraint in expression," "revolutionizing Motion Picture drama and founding the modern technique of the art," he is correct in a certain sense.[40] Although not the first to use the close-up as a vehicle for expression of an interiority, his practice certainly deepened and extended its consequences as a technique.[41] And it is no accident that Eisenstein invoked a novelist, Charles Dickens, as a comparison to Griffith.[42]

Within the late eighteenth-century and nineteenth-century novel, character became the instrument (conduit, medium) for furthering a new, modern concept of the self—as individual, temporally consistent, homogeneous, and branded with a unique interiority. In *The Economy of Character: Novels, Market Culture, and the Business of Inner Meaning*, Deirdre Shauna Lynch argues that in the first part of the eighteenth century in England, characters were "faceless," insofar as their faces did not point to a complex and intricate "depth" but were instead situated within a field marked by questions of social distinction, a burgeoning print culture, and a preoccupation with surface and quantity. The face's singularity was linked to its "part in upholding a foundational sort of private property," and if a face pointed to "character," it was insofar as it "indexed a social norm, a determinate place on the moral map where every person had a proper place and where distinction was contained within limits."[43] That sense of limits was the occasion for a widespread discourse on quantity—an interrogation of the distinction between a character with too many details or traits and one with just the right amount. This was a period in which caricature—the attempt to find just the right minimum number and type of traits/features that would suffice to represent a person (usually in a hyperbolic mode)—was extremely popular. The emphasis was on surface, on character as *graphic*, a matter of lines and strokes, drawing and coloring. What was at stake was the legibility of a two-dimensional surface.[44] The second half of the eighteenth century witnessed the rise of the concept of "self-expression"—of both authors and characters. "Interiority" was a construct of social and public discourses that coincided with an acceleration of commodification: "In this psychology of consumerism, commodities provide the individual with the means of symbolizing the qualities of her distinctive inner life."[45] Commodity consumerism has less to do with the consumption of products and more to do with the creation and marketing of "self-illusory experiences" linked to advertising and its images. Consumerism has an *affective* force—it is a machine for the production of desire and its surfaces are inextricably linked to a depth. Lynch argues further that this transformation of the concept of character is conjoined with a transformation in the culture of reading that responds to the rise of mass culture. "Deep truths" can readily be situated as accessible to only a subset of readers capable of a close hermeneutic reading, and in this way, the novel can be differentiated from the massive amount of pulp fiction generated by presses in a rapidly emerging mass culture.[46] This process introduced a new stratification and a "new means of locating oneself in social space."[47] In addition, the modern concept of "literature" dictates that interpretation is never completed, that the depth of characters is infinite, that there is always a residue or supplement of meaning that, in remaining opaque to the reader, guarantees the unknowable individual uniqueness of the character. "Literariness," a product of the institutionalization of literature as a discipline in the nineteenth century, authorizes the humanist reading of character as a being who is necessarily mysterious and ineffable, not fully representable, and in that resides their humanity as well as individuality.

John Frow, as well, situates character as an "affective technology of the self" in a Foucauldian manner. He reiterates Lynch's argument about the change from the neoclassical regime of the early eighteenth century to a

Romanticism consolidating the notion of an essential core of selfhood characterized by depth and interiority and cites Charles Taylor's historicization of this process: "We have come to think that we 'have' selves as we have heads. But the very idea that we have or are 'a self,' that human agency is essentially defined as 'the self,' is a linguistic reflection of our modern understanding and the radical reflexivity it involves. Being deeply embedded in this understanding, we cannot but reach for this language; but it was not always so."[48] Frow maintains that this concept of the self is embedded in an ethical or moral discourse, a disciplinary apparatus that gives literature and the analysis of character a central place in the school curriculum. It is also an effect of a moral economy, a sphere of person-to-person relations, an "everyday knowledge" that operates through the transformation of everything (other levels of knowledge) to a human scale (hence "human scale is the distinguishing feature of the logic of everyday or practical reason").[49] Its measure is dependent upon an imaginary coherence of the body situated in a lived space, and it constitutes the obviousness of "common sense," veiling its abstractness.

Early narrative cinema is inscribed directly in the wake of this novelistic and economic understanding of character and self. Its deployment of the close-up in the management of the surface/depth dichotomy is particularly conducive to the implementation of literary notions of interiority. Early film magazines and handbooks outlining how to become a "photoplay actor" extensively investigate the concept of facial expression. Because early films lacked spoken language, these discourses are particularly attentive to the status of facial expression as a legible sign—the only one capable of conveying interiority. Lists of expressions (e.g., belligerence, aggressiveness, sorrow, melancholia, fear) are produced for the benefit of those hoping to act in motion pictures. The author of *Motion Picture Acting for Professionals and Amateurs* (1916), after claiming, "The visualized story of the film is unfolded through the pictured expressions of simulated emotions . . . It is well to bear in mind that the movie artist must depend upon the gleaming eye, the distended nostril, the furrowed brow, or the compressed lips, to emphasize his emotion," provides a list of 499 emotions and illustrates them with photographs of 191 "screen stars" (figs. 2.7, 2.8).[50] The stills, however, do not convey the temporality of facial expression, its variations and mobile manifestations whose accumulation of detail adds up to the individuality signified by a proper name (a proper name always signaling the particularity and uniqueness of a person).

As Catherine Gallagher has argued, the category of fiction emerged on the basis of the deployment of the proper name as empty form, one that

IVA SHEPARD

IN

"THE DRIFTER"

CLARA KIMBALL YOUNG

Courtesy of the Gaumont Company

Cruelty, evil, vengeance, malevolence,
venom, vampire.

Courtesy of World Film Corporation

Imbecility, dementia, mesmerism, hypnotism.

2.7 & 2.8 *Motion Picture Acting for Professionals and Amateurs* (1916).

ultimately referred to "nobody": "The character came into *fictional* existence most fully only when he or she was developed as nobody *in particular....* Thinness of detail almost always indicated specific extra-textual reference. But the more characters were loaded with circumstantial and seemingly insignificant properties, the more the readers were assured that the text was at once assuming and making up for its reference to nobody at all."[51] This emptiness of the form, its avid nonreferentiality, allowed for the readers' sympathy with and affective investment in characters whose plethora of detailed traits pointed to an interiority. This is in marked opposition to the conventions of art history, where referentiality is always at play in some way in the genre of the portrait, which might seem at first glance to be the most appropriate historical predecessor of the face in close-up. The portrait, generally attached to a proper name by its title, has been conventionally the occasion for a detective-like investigation of the identity of the referent, the search for a historical proper name that would call a halt to the signifying chain, emphasizing mimesis.[52] In the cinema, after the emergence of the star system (already in effect in 1916 as demonstrated by the handbook on acting referenced earlier), the proper name is split between that of the character and that of the star (although occasionally there is an extrafilmic proper name that comes into play—e.g., W. R. Hearst in *Citizen Kane* or a known figure referenced in a historical film). This is the conundrum of the (at least) double body of filmic character.[53] The spectator must hold in tension both knowledge of the star and knowledge of the character.

There are, of course, other limits to the comparison of the character in film to that in the novel. In the novel, free, indirect discourse is the language (as opposed to direct, quoted discourse) that gives the reader access to what the character is thinking or how the character is perceiving. Rather than being quarantined within quotation marks, the character's thought can in this way merge with the discourse of the impersonal narrator. But to effect this the medium must be language, a language with a believable access to interiority. In narrative cinema, there is no comparable free, indirect discourse (even the voice-over of a character is a quoted discourse).[54] The discourse about facial expression in the early cinema is an acknowledgment that it is the visualized body, the body of the actor that is the conduit to the unspoken, nonlinguistic interiority of a character. The visual surface, particularly that of the face in close-up, must be legible as an incarnation of depth. Yet, as in the nineteenth-century novel, there must also be an unreadable supplement allowing character to exceed its formal representation—in the early cinema, its visible signs—in order to buttress a humanist notion of individuality. This essential opacity is referenced in Balázs's notion that in the close-up of the face, "we can see that there is something there that we cannot see."[55] This is the irrecoverable "beyond" or the "depth" of the face, which mirrors and repeats the unrepresentable off-screen space of the vanishing point and the rupture of the screen in Dubois's account. It is an imaginary space that is operative but not present.

Like the nineteenth-century novel, the cinema emerges in the midst of a transformation in technologies of the self that can be linked to the increasing insistence of the circulation of commodities. Cinema's advantage, however, is that, like much advertising, it is a visual medium activating the lure of the surface and the fashioning and refashioning of the body as an index to identity. These lures are instantiated in the star system, but there is a dense mixture of star and character and of exteriority and interiority. The cinematic close-up of the face is the condition of possibility of the distinctive inner life that is one of the characteristics of the individual in modernity. And the star's assumption of successive roles incarnates the accelerated rate of obsolescence of products enhancing self-definition, whose distinguishing character in commodity capitalism is not its consistency but its ability to transform. At the same time, the cinema struggles to escape from the realm of popular low culture and attain the status of an art. Griffith is exemplary in his harnessing of subjectivity, of the concept of interiority, to elevate cinema to the status of the novel and great literature. The close-up of the face, domesticating the scalar instability of the cinema, is an indispensable tool in this endeavor.

If, as early film journals and magazines suggest, the close-up is initially viewed as a monstrous and castrating image, a perversion of scale, and if, as Dubois suggests, its threat of puncturing the screen must be détourned by a focus on humanism, the transition to narrative and characterization would certainly work to assuage those fears. The close-up of the character invites a closeness, an intimacy. But why is it historically necessary to contain or domesticate the anxiety associated with the close-up, which is initially read in terms of scale (i.e., giganticism) rather than distance (i.e., closeness or intimacy)? Why the emphatic insistence upon "life-size" bodies and "normal" scale? Where does the fear of disproportion or of a massive, overwhelming scale come from? No doubt it is overdetermined, for many critics and theorists stemming from an initial compulsion to evaluate moving pictures in relation to what was seen to be their closest rival or point of comparison—the theater, where scale was a constant and the close-up unthinkable.[56] Perhaps it can be aligned with the agoraphobia theorized by Anthony Vidler as the most telling pathology of modernity in its production of an urban space of increasing complexity and illegibility.[57] But the desire for proportion takes many different forms and has a long history whose effects have lingered in an uneven development. The obsession with proportion in the human body is common to both the ancient Greeks and, in modernity, Le Corbusier, but in strikingly different incarnations.

Vitruvius, for instance, proposed that the architecture of temples should be based on the imitation of the perfectly proportioned human body, in which all parts exist in harmony. Leonardo da Vinci's *Vitruvian Man* (also known as the *Canon of Proportions* or *Proportions of Man*) is an illustration of Vitruvius's rules of proportion—the height of a man is equal to the width of his outstretched arms, creating a square enclosing the human body; the hands and feet in this configuration touch a circle whose center is the navel; the body is divided in half at the groin and by the golden section at the navel (fig. 2.9).[58] What is at stake here is a mathematically pure ideal of proportion, incarnated by the male body, and used as the measure of a transcendental aesthetics. Architecture hence mimics the greatest work of art, the human

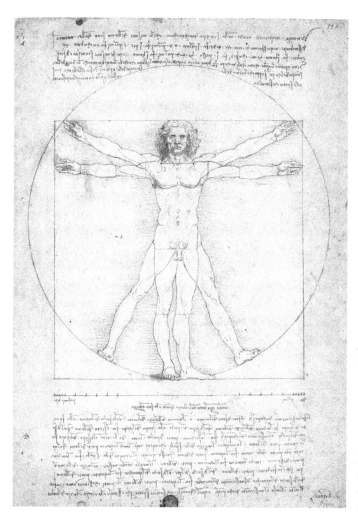

2.9 Leonardo da Vinci, *Le proporzioni del corpo umano secondo Vitruvio*, Punta metallica, penna, inchiostro marrone, tocchi d'acquerello alla testa e alle mani su carta bianco sporca, 344 × 245 mm, inv. 228; © G.A.VE Archivio fotografico—*"su concessione del Ministero dei beni e delle attività culturali e del turismo—Gallerie dell'Accademia di Venezia."*

body—but an ideal rather than a contingent or concrete body. Sergei Eisenstein's invocation of the golden section in relation to film is accompanied by a recognition of its fundamental value to the Greeks—as a method of generating a perfect unity between a whole and its parts, where each part maintains a mathematically precise relation to the whole.[59] Le Corbusier, on the other hand, although he invoked the mathematics of the golden section and the proportionality of the body, conceived of architecture first and foremost as a space designed *for* the human body, one that humans must inhabit, and therefore one whose proportions must accommodate that body.

In his treatise *The Modulor: A Harmonious Measure to the Human Scale Universally Applicable to Architecture and Mechanics* (1948), Le Corbusier embraced units of measure based on parts of the human body—elbow (cubit), finger (digit), thumb (inch), foot, pace, and so on—and disdained the move to the metric system, which was abstract and "indifferent to the stature of man."[60] These organic units were superior to the metric units because "they formed an integral part of the human body, and for that reason they were fit to serve as measures for the huts, the houses and the temples that had to be built. . . . More than that: they were infinitely rich and subtle because they formed part of the mathematics of the human body, gracious, elegant and firm, the source of that harmony which moves us."[61] Here, the body is no longer the Vitruvian ideal of an abstract mathematical purity but the generator of a mathematics of measurement that could guarantee the correct scale of the architecture that housed an empirical body. Scale moves from the realm of abstract and conceptual perfection (the fascination of mathematics) to the more clumsy or awkward, but livable, scale of the body and a form of rationalization and standardization designed to accommodate it. Each system generates its taboos in relation to a vision of corporeality that ultimately grounds an aesthetics of space. The dislocation and perversion of an architecture based on the metric system are, for Le Corbusier, a function of the fact that it loses sight of *man as measure*. In modernity, anxiety about "man as measure" is linked to the incessant rationalization of time and space, its standardization and abstraction from the realm of lived time and space.

With respect to space, this rationalization is, in effect, an assault on the body and hence an assault on the experienced anchor of the real. For knowledge of space is in close collusion with the body, its movements, and its gestures. Part of the threat of railway travel and its reduction of distance in the nineteenth century is the loss of the capacity of the body to gauge space in its relation to time and movement. Extrapolating from Gottfried Wilhelm Leibniz's analysis of space, Henri Lefebvre argues that space must, above all, be occupied—occupied not by bodies in general or corporeality itself but by a quite specific body. This body's gestures and looks mark out space, indicating direction; it is a body that demarcates, orients, and demonstrates rotation, for instance, by turning around.[62] As Lefebvre points out, for Leibniz space is "absolutely relative"—it is both abstract (accessible to a mathematical mapping) and concrete (because bodies exist in space, manifesting their material existence there). According to Lefebvre:

> There is an immediate relationship between the body and its space, between the body's deployment in space and its occupation of space. Before

producing effects in the material realm (tools and objects), before *producing itself* by drawing nourishment from that realm, and before *reproducing itself* by generating other bodies, each living body *is* space and *has* its space: it produces itself in space and also produces that space. This is a truly remarkable relationship: the body with the energies at its disposal, the living body, creates or produces its own space; conversely, the laws of space, which is to say the laws of discrimination in space, also govern the living body and the deployment of its energies.[63]

This is why space, for Lefebvre, cannot be *read* as a text. Both abstract and concrete, conceptual and material, or "the perceived, the conceived, and the lived," in his terms, it is inaccessible to a semiotic or post-structuralist interpretation whose foundational concept is a language that preexists and informs all signifying activity.[64] Instead, space is a strange conjunction of abstractness and concreteness. Although space cannot be theorized as simply *there*, a container to be filled, but must be thought as produced, it is also concrete, material, real—in the sense that it is lived, the result of a practice.

Yet, in the context of the cinema, the spectator's body is incapacitated, rendered useless, deprived of its role of demarcating space through gesture and movement. As has so often been pointed out, the spectator must become immobilized, bodiless, their senses reduced to those characterized by distance—vision and hearing. Space is not lived—at least in the sense of the ordinary or everyday experience of space in its relation to the body—but abstracted, alienated. Perhaps this is why much of film theory attempts to resuscitate this body in some form. For Pascal Bonitzer, the cutting up of space effected by montage generates a filmic world that he compares to a labyrinth—the spectator wanders through corridors of shots, confronting limits and especially the limits of vision and knowable space.[65] Famously, Walter Benjamin claimed in "The Work of Art in the Age of Mechanical Reproduction" that, in contrast to the jail-like claustrophobia of urban spaces, the film "burst this prison-world asunder by the dynamite of the tenth of a second, so that now, in the midst of its far-flung ruins and debris, we calmly and adventurously go traveling."[66] Hugo Münsterberg's theory effects a displacement of gesture and bodily movement to filmic technique: a pan mimics the turning of the head; a close-up reincarnates attention.[67] And frequently, the body's bracketing is overcome by invoking the metaphors of inhabitation—the spectator figuratively inhabits the space of the mise-en-scène.

Space in cinema is delimited by the frame, which acts both as an edge or border (against the abyss outside it) and as an apparent container (of the plenitude of objects and people within it). This twofold function can be mapped onto a distinction inspired by the one Lefebvre sees in abstract space—film is both a representation of space and a representational space (although my deployment of the terms is quite different from Lefebvre's).[68] Given its indexicality, the cinematographic image appears to transparently inscribe the things, the buildings, the beings of "real" space, which, as Lefebvre has extensively demonstrated, are already infused with ideological significance in lived space. It is as if everything in film were twice represented—as its already socially meaningful self and as the image of that social sign (as filmed). It is in this sense that the cinema is a representation *of* space—of landscape, of architecture, of fields and rooms, and of the things and beings that, tellingly, "take up" that space. Yet it is also a representational space insofar as there are fairly strict spatial determinations—aspect ratio of the frame, size of the screen, scale of the shot (close-up, medium shot, long shot), focus, and so on—that signify, in themselves, cinema and its possibilities. There is the two-dimensional space of the screen as well as the edge that separates the image from absence, from darkness. It is the space of the screen—in the darkness of the movie theater—that signifies, generating representation.

The space of narrative cinema, like that of social space, is inherently contradictory. On the one hand, that cinema posits a space that is full of meaning if not symbolism, where each location and each object carries a significance that nevertheless is careful not to assert itself as such. In Griffith's *Broken Blossoms* (1919), everything about Cheng Huan's store and home—the fans, furniture, figurines, and lamps—connotes the "Oriental." Cary Scott's home in Douglas Sirk's *All That Heaven Allows* (1955) signifies class distinctions, notions of wealth, culture, bourgeois comfort, and hierarchy. Yet the spectator is invited to accept this naturalized space that does not announce its own meaning, that is simply *there*, the place where things happen. Space itself—the space of the frame, the space of the diegesis (which can be as large as the world or even universe)—is invoked simply as vacancy, as blankness, an emptiness to be filled. Hence, space is simultaneously both full, symbolic, meaningful ("telling") and empty, neutral—as Lefebvre points out, a space "of insignificance, of semiological destitution, and of emptiness (or absence)," a container to be filled with contents.[69]

This contradiction with respect to the significance of space is accompanied by another—that of fragmentation versus unification/coherency, resolved only illusorily by a fragile activation of metonymy (a close shot, for instance, always indexing a larger space within which it is contained). Historically, film theorists have invested heavily in the coherence, legibility, and transparency of space in the classical cinema. Its very classicism consists in its having attained these goals through the production of a homogeneous space, guaranteed above all by continuity editing. But fragmentation—the discontinuity between shots—is of course the condition of the possibility of classical cinematic space and its economy. Yet the legibility or rationale of that discontinuity with respect to scale—that is, the recognizable although imprecise differences between close-up, medium shot, and long shot—invades the filmic space as a haunting reminder of difference. This is a contradiction not peculiar to film and characterizes what Lefebvre refers to as "abstract space" in general: "The fact is that abstract space contains contradictions, which the abstract form seems to resolve, but which are clearly revealed by analysis. How is this possible? How may a space be said to be at once homogeneous and divided, at once unified and fragmented? The answer lies first of all . . . in the fact that the 'logic of space,' with its apparent significance and coherence, actually conceals the violence inherent in abstraction."[70] In narrative film, the notion of a "diegesis," a virtual space that binds together the fragments that are shots, their diversity, and their inevitable exclusion of space beyond the frame, is the point of a fragile but effective coherence that denies the spatial violence of editing and framing. Its provision of an imaginary, unified space—a world, in effect, with its own spatial and temporal logic that mimes *the* world—holds at bay the violence of abstraction.[71] Bazin's frame as window on a world that extends beyond its borders, whose function of exclusion is only contingent, accidental, and does not destabilize the spectator's investment in that world, corroborates this reassuring spatial unity at the expense of a perception of the frame as cut or aggression. The frame is, in this theory, simply a necessary but benign impediment to vision.

Yet the space of the diegesis, with its depth, its foreground and background, its horizontality and verticality, is only one aspect of the space of the cinema, although it is the one most often theorized. A consideration of cinematic scale must account for a different spectatorial experience of space, one that involves a recognition that the spectator is looking at a flat surface, of a certain height and width, at a certain distance, and a diegesis whose divisions are often those of the different scales of the shot, measured not only in relation to the contents of the narrative space but also in relation to the spectator's body. In other words, cinematic scale can be measured in two ways—as the scale of the shot itself (close-up, medium shot, or long shot) or as the scale of the image projected on the screen (height and width of the screen, aspect ratio of the image).

Suggestively, shot scale, whether it is conceptualized in terms of scale (largeness versus smallness) or distance (closeness versus remoteness), is generally defined in relation to the human body as its exemplary content. David Bordwell and Kristen Thompson define a close-up as "a framing in which the scale of the object shown is relatively large; most commonly a person's head seen from the neck up, or an object of a comparable size that fills most of the screen."[72] A medium shot is "a framing in which the scale of the object shown is of moderate size; a human figure seen from the waist up would fill most of the screen."[73] Timothy Corrigan, who defines the close-up in terms of distance rather than scale, describes the close-up as "an image in which the distance between the subject and the point of view is very short, as in a 'close-up of a person's face.'"[74] The human body, as incarnated within the diegesis or in its spectatorial position, is the privileged exemplar.

Early in the history of film theory, Jean Mitry conceptualized cinematic space as a kind of box, segmented into planes determined by distance and focus in relation to a human body (the French term for shot is *plan*).[75] For Mitry, that body was the character, but insofar as the spectator is situated at the place of the camera, the focus, distance, and plane that define the shot are constituted as a reference to their body. For Mitry, then, scale becomes the primary measure of the cinema's ability to penetrate and organize space, through close-ups, medium shots, and long shots (which are, ultimately, entirely arbitrary as distinctions). From this point of view, scale becomes distinctive of the cinematic project not only in relation to the scale of the screen (the "bigger than life" quality of the movies) but internally, as the regulator of the organization of space in relation to a body—both that of the character and that of the spectator.

In da Vinci's *Vitruvian Man*, the body is framed by both a circle and a square, the purist of geometric forms, and their geometric precision is dictated by the ideal of the perfect proportionality of the human body. For Le Corbusier, the geometry of architecture must be designed above all to accommodate the human body (admittedly a standardized body), to make it comfortable and secure—at home, in a "machine for living."[76] Idealism is displaced by rationalization. The historical fixity of the frame, that is, the aspect ratio, in the cinema (particularly in comparison with painting or drawing, even photography) is accompanied by the more apparently fluid division in the scale of shots. This variation allows for a management of distance, difference, and the violation of a continuum effected by editing. There is a spatial ellipsis in a cut from long or medium shot to close-up—space is compressed much as time is compressed in a temporal ellipsis. This spatial violence that filmic abstraction entails is answered by continuity editing, which struggles to preserve the logic of a space that must be kept intact, homogeneous, and continuous. Yet it is the close-up that most frequently offers a resistance to this homogenization. The close-up always carries the threat of a certain monstrosity, a face or object filling the screen and annihilating all sense of scale. As discussed in chapter 1, the inherent despatialization of the close-up, especially of the face, is a recurrent theme in film theory, surfacing in the work of Béla Balázs, Jacques Aumont, and Gilles Deleuze, for whom the face is radically separable from the very notions of space and time.

In the early cinema, with the emergence of narrative structure, and when the rhetoric of the spatial violence of the close-up is most intense, a number of filmmakers developed a formal technique for dealing with variations of scale that reduced the threat of the close-up. The technique also works to generate a sense of depth and a lengthened duration of the shot and is, in this sense, the inheritor of the repetitive form of the chase film. In it, a character appears initially in long shot or medium long shot and then moves toward the camera, traversing in their movement the various scales of the shot until finally emerging in close-up. This occurs, for instance, in *The Curtain Pole* (AM&B, Griffith/Bitzer, 1909), *The Ingrate* (AM&B, Griffith/Bitzer, 1908) (figs. 2.10, 2.11), and, most tellingly, *Sweet and Twenty* (AM&B, Griffith/Bitzer, 1909), where a couple meeting in a love tryst wander toward the camera, pausing at the points of the long shot, medium shot, and close-up (figs. 2.12–2.14). These positions, in effect, enact the transition from long shot to medium shot or close-up while preserving the unity and homogeneity of space. Obsessively sustaining the integrity and coherence of space in the continuous long take, the perception of scale—that is, calling attention to the size of the screen, that of the image, and aspect ratio (representational space)—is transmuted into that of distance within the diegesis (represented space). Scale (the logic of large and small) is translated into distance (the logic of closer or farther). It hence suppresses the structuring ambiguity of shot size in the cinema—is it close or is it large? The early reviewers of cinematic narrative, in

2.10 & 2.11 *The Ingrate* (AM&B, Griffith/Bitzer, 1908). Courtesy of the Library of Congress.

and through their hysteria and diatribes against the close-up, saw it for what it was—a large picture.

Perspective as a system calculates distance as a relation to scale. The large is close; the small, distant. The infinitely distant would be the infinitely small—the geometric point without extension, in short, the vanishing point—the point that vanishes and can only be conceived mathematically. According to Hubert Damisch:

> The question of infinity consistently preoccupied Renaissance culture, just as it has unceasingly preoccupied geometry, *from the origin*. Finding itself inscribed, within the perspective context, in a position marked by a hole in the center of the prototype, this *original* feature (in all senses of the word) took on an emblematic value. For it is here, at this point that absented itself, so to speak, from its place, that was decided the destiny of a system that would have been unable to escape its own closure if it hadn't resorted to it [the vanishing point].[77]

In a discussion of Filippo Brunelleschi's first experiment, in which the viewer was placed behind the painting and looked out through a hole at the painting's reflection in a mirror, Damisch claims that it functioned as a self-reflexive demonstration of the very condition of perspectival representation—that the "point we today call the 'point of view' coincides, in terms of projection, with the one we call the 'vanishing point': both are situated at the intersection of the perpendicular sight line and the picture plane."[78] The place from which a perspectival representation must be viewed has an echo within the field of the painting at the vanishing point. Nevertheless, the relation between the two is asymmetrical, for the vanishing point is not an image of the point of view, which if it were represented in the painting would have to be at a virtual distance equal to that of the viewer's distance from the painting. But the vanishing point is an image of infinity and would put infinity at the back of this image of the point of view and therefore behind the viewer's head (Damisch cites Louis Marin's discussion of infinity as an "idea of what is behind one's head").[79] Obsessed by infinity, classical perspective conceived it in relation to the subject.

In perspectival representation, infinity is the unseen within and beyond the seen. It is the point where vision fails, the unrepresentable but necessary premise of representation. Within film theory, the fact that the logic of classical perspective is built into the technology of the camera lens has occasioned an understanding of the spectatorial position as a point of control and coherency, ideologically informed by a notion of the unity and mastery of subjectivity.

2.12–2.14 *Sweet and Twenty*
(AM&B, Griffith/Bitzer,
1909). Courtesy of the Library
of Congress.

Perspective is hence stabilizing. Yet Damisch takes issue with this interpretation. Although the subject gets its bearings through perspective, it is not "any the more stable" for it.[80] Instead, the allegedly dominant and masterful subject of perspective "*holds only by a thread*, however tightly stretched this might be," and Damisch compares that subject to a tightrope walker:

> The subject interpellating the painting, and interpellated by it from the point marked at its center, this subject can only get its bearings within the configuration by being reabsorbed into it, by becoming lost in it. In the sense not of a walk through it, but rather of a *transversal* of it, manifested externally by a point or hole: in ideal terms, the one through which would pass a string, perpendicular to the painting, stretched from the observer's eye to the vanishing point. So, it's not a point that perspective designates, but rather a line, one corresponding in projection to the plane marked as that of the eye, or the subject.[81]

The line is that thread from which the viewer hangs, in a fragile, because incalculable, infinity of space. Nevertheless, whether point or line, this subject is still conceived as disembodied.

The cinema would seem to perfectly instantiate Lefebvre's notion of an abstract space "that transforms the body by transporting it outside itself and into the ideal-visual realm."[82] For Lefebvre, with the advent of modernity there is an "intense, aggressive, and repressive" visualization. Reducing all sensory perception to vision, this process diminishes the subject's apprehension of a lived space—that space becomes alienated, distanced. The specta-

tor is *dispossessed* of space. For Lefebvre this is a regrettable, negative consequence of advanced capitalism, the corollary of an increasing quantification
of space that results in the elimination of the human body as measure.

The overemphasis upon vision generated the distance of the metropolitan
subject (analyzed by Georg Simmel) as opposed to the intimacy and haptic
quality of interaction in smaller, less technologically mediated, communities.[83] Although that distance is reinscribed and consistently reevaluated in
the cinema with the breakdown of shots into different scales—close-up, medium shot, long shot—it is also a distance that must be reduced or denied.
The notion of narrative cinema as a labyrinth within which the spectator is
lost but simultaneously immersed and absorbed together with all the metaphors of inhabitation seeks to redress the distance and dispossession of spectacle. This is the oxymoron of a "virtual real" space—one that is *more real*
than that of the everyday—evoking the nostalgia for a past utopic space of
closeness, intimacy, and an immediacy of sensory experience. According to
Simmel, "Spatial relations are only the condition, on the one hand, and the
symbol, on the other, of human relations."[84]

The cinema, from the outset, has played a major role in delineating the
subject's relation to space and scale. The close-up, insofar as it annihilates perspective and depth and problematizes scale, was perceived at the outset as potentially derealizing and as a quandary—hence the tirades against the close-up
in early narrative films. It is not simply the case that the ideal of human scale
was inherited from the theater, although this is a significant influence. Historically, the legibility of all shots and the organization of space in cinema

have been structured in relation to the scale of the (abstract) human body. As Bonitzer points out, when the body of a cockroach takes up the entire screen, the shot is labeled a close-up or even an extreme close-up. When the human body is entirely displayed on the screen, we call it a medium shot or medium long shot (*en plan general*). The assessment of the shot scale of the cockroach, whether or not human beings are present, is formed in relation to the human body. This is not an empirical body but an abstract or imaginary one. There is a reciprocal assurance at work here: "The impression of reality in the cinema is sustained by human stature and reciprocally."[85] The scalar distribution of shots is anthropocentric: "Hence, shots have *a priori* a content of reality at once 'objective' and subtly impregnated with subjectivity, with an implicit reference to human presence (I understand this strictly: the human stature, the imaginary body)."[86] Michel Chion maintains that the shock of the close-up is not that the small has been transformed into the large but that all elements can be represented in the same scale (the close-up) at the same time as the opposite is the case in that their sizes are understood to be incommensurable in the diegesis.[87]

The "human" of human scale is not the appeal to an essence or a natural norm but, as Frow points out, "a fantasmatic coherence projected onto a social order."[88] Conceptual bodily oppositions such as front/back, inside/outside, ingestion/regurgitation are mapped onto cinematic space despite the fact that the screen is a flat, two-dimensional space that, for instance, has no "back" or "front." I would argue that this is the most important sense in which the body comes into play in the spectator's experience of a film, rather than the appeal to the nonvisual or nonauditory senses (especially touch) made so frequently by contemporary theorists of embodiment.[89] The body at play in the formation of cinematic space is an imaginary, fantasmatic body, one whose boundaries are as psychical as they are physical (hence the resonance of figures of ingesting and devouring). While the spectator is, in a sense, disembodied, that spectator must *remember that they have a body* in order to negotiate cinematic space.

Although the human body acts as a regulator of scale in cinema, and, in Dubois's argument, humanity in close-up domesticates the force of the train threatening to breach or puncture the screen, there is always something about the close-up that is unassimilable, excessive. In its despatialization, it breaks the system of perspective; in its excessive magnitude, it destroys the hierarchy of scale. Through these deviations, it calls attention to the fundamental discontinuity of the diegesis. In this sense, it allows for per-turbation, dissonances within the structuration of a space designed to the measure of rationalization. There are by-products, barely contained and un-envisaged effects. I will take as my examples here two very different kinds of films—a classical Hollywood narrative of the early widescreen era and a contemporary art film that deliberately cuts up space in its relation to the body differently. Even in a filmmaker like Otto Preminger for whom the frame is a container characterized by fullness and presence, with no outside or alterity, loss and undecidability invade the shot, generating a disorien-tation of space, a momentary illegibility. In what is often referred to as Preminger's limit text, *Bunny Lake Is Missing* (1965), whose narrative cir-cles around an overcloseness, an excessive intimacy in the quasi-incestuous relationship between brother and sister, there is a scene in a doll hospital in which a regular, readable, and orderly space gives way to one of uncertainty, even opacity. The protagonist, Ann Lake, enters the building and climbs the stairs to speak with the old man who fixes excessively "loved" dolls. He tells her she will have to look for her daughter's doll herself, and when she descends the stairs (now dark and barely recognizable as the stairs she ascended), the space becomes uncanny, disorienting (fig. 2.15). Neon lights from the street intermittently illuminate and then darken the room, but it is the character's movement with respect to the camera that seems to warp the space and diminish its readability. The camera moves to follow her trajectory, but at points she approaches the camera so closely that the image becomes quasi-abstract (figs. 2.16, 2.17).

Within the widescreen field, the immense shadowy close-up of Ann Lake suggests a dangerous overcloseness to the camera, hence the viewer, making it difficult to interpret the spatial field. It is an excessive proximity that pro-duces at least a transitory illegibility and disorientation, witnessed by the broken dolls, fragmented simulacra of discarded human bodies. Not only does Ann's head block out space, but there is no compensation in the form of the easily legible expressivity of a face. Wong Kar-wai's *In the Mood for Love* (2000), on the other hand, produces not so much a spatial disorien-tation as an acknowledgment of the violence of abstraction, of a frame that severs. What is most striking about the deployment of scale in this film is again an excessive and sustained proximity to bodies, but in this case, the film activates the close-up differently in relation to the body, frequently undermining the expectation that the face is the privileged content of the

2.15–2.17 *Bunny Lake Is Missing* (Otto Preminger, 1965).

close-up (figs. 2.18–2.20). The possibility of expressivity and of legibility is shifted from the face to other parts of the body, resituating affect.

These instances of spatial destabilization are both the leakages and the critiques of a system that produces homogeneity through fragmentation, a logic of scale mapped as distance, and the virtual charting of a potentially navigable space. One could say that the space of the mainstream cinema simultaneously stabilizes—producing an illusory orientation of the spectator in their relation to an incomprehensible space (that of modernity, of urban space, of the ungraspability of totality in Fredric Jameson's terms)[90]—and also destabilizes, placing a different inflection on Lefebvre's notion that ab-

stract space "transforms the body by transporting it outside itself." These moments of destabilization are what Manfredo Tafuri has called the "irremediable dissonances that escape the plan of advanced capital."[91] Studies of the spaces of perspective, of modernity, and of cinema are infused with the figures of a body beside itself, or a body fragilely suspended in its relation to space. Siegfried Giedion, in his study of the organization of space, line, and architecture in modernity, characterizes the modern subject as "a tightrope dancer who, by small adjustments, keeps a continuous balance between his being and empty space," echoing Damisch's subject of perspective as tightrope walker.[92] Le Corbusier's concept of ineffable space displaces extreme affect—the cry, the terror—onto the space of architecture, transforming it into a body that is "touched, wounded, dominated, or caressed." ("The release of aesthetic

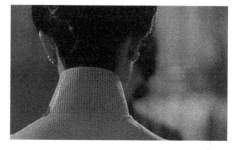

2.18–2.20 *In the Mood for Love* (Wong Kar-wai, 2000).

emotion is a special function of space.")[93] For Sergei Eisenstein, pathos in film also produces extreme affect, even ecstasy, in its etymological sense—*ex stasis*, out of a state, forcing the viewer to "be beside himself."[94]

The disembodiment associated with a cinematic space that is said to absorb or immerse the spectator is hence double-edged. It has been both disdained and embraced enthusiastically. But to the extent that the cinema is inevitably about scale in relation to a body—spectacular, monumental scale in its theatrical incarnation, shifting scales in its decoupage—that body is never lost, never truly eliminated. The cinema arises in a historical moment when space's representability has been warped by the forces of modernity—condensed by new technologies of transportation and communication (the railroad, the telegraph, the telephone), disarticulated in urban environments that are more difficultly navigable, inundated by commodities, displaced by a surfeit of representations (advertising, photography). The close-up, historically derided and applauded, carrier of spatial anomaly, imperiling the oppositions of surface versus depth and closeness versus distance, addresses a subject whose sense of location has become fragile, precarious. But the reconstructed spaces of the cinema that negotiate the hazards of the close-up offer this subject—as spectator—the simulacrum of a location and the possibility of sure navigation.

Chapter 3

At Face Value

The eye, the look, the cheeks, the mouth, the forehead, whether considered in a state of entire rest, or during their innumerable varieties of motion,—in fine, whatever is understood by physiognomy—are the most expressive, the most convincing picture of interior sensation, desires, passions, will, and of all those properties which so much exalt moral above animal life.... Physiognomy is the science or knowledge of the correspondence between the external and internal man, the visible superficies and the invisible contents.
—JOHANN CASPAR LAVATER, *Physiognomy*

Face, facade, about-face, saving face, face off, at face value, poker face, face-to-face, two-faced, faceless, putting on a face, in your face, face up to it, deface (pointing to what is perhaps the most sacrilegious act—that of removing a face). The sheer number of terms that include the concept of face signal and underline its semiotic significance and, perhaps more pertinently, its plasticity. The historical meanings of face listed in the *Oxford English Dictionary* include not only "countenance, visage" but "part of a thing which is presented, side of an object, surface, looks, aspect, aspect (of the stars), thing presented to view, appearance, form, sight, front of a building," and so on. And like the word "fact," it is linked to the Latin *facere*, to do.[1]

Inheritor of the nineteenth-century panorama's giganticism, the cinema has nevertheless made central to its strategies of magnification a thematics entirely foreign to that of the panorama and its predilection for sweeping landscapes and historical events—the thematics of the human face. While the close-up has also been used extensively to document the relevant detail and the suspense of off-screen space, it is most frequently associated with a revelation of intense human signification, with a rendering legible of the face as the signifier of the soul. As we have seen in chapter 2, the close-up of the face became inextricably linked to a problematic of characterization and the accompanying dyad interiority/exteriority. The face often names a relation between a surface and a depth, an interiority and an exteriority—it is a "window to the soul." In the later years of the first decade of the cinema, films began to focus on character as the moral, individualizing, and expressive focus of narrative, exemplified in the close-up of the face. The legibility of the face was an anchor for the intelligibility of narrative; this is one reason why so many early theorists singled out the close-up as the epitome of a medium specificity distinguishing cinema from theater. In this respect, the face connoted closeness and intimacy in comparison to an unrelenting theatrical distance. But, in addition, the close-up of the face was appropriated by the utopian discourse of a universal language searching for global meaning, negating difference. In its alleged transparency, facial expression was legible by anyone, everywhere. Paradoxically, the face is thus imbricated with both the most local of spatial algorithms (interiority/exteriority) and the most global (the concept of the universal).

The concept of facial expressivity pervades the articles and advertisements of early film journals such as *Moving Picture World*, *Motography*, *Motion Picture Magazine*, and *Motion Picture News*. Its deployment is generally aligned with both the close-up (often referred to as "close view" or "large view" beginning in 1908, as a "bust" in earlier discourses) and the absence of speech.[2] Absent language, meaning concentrates itself in the face (brought closer by the specifically cinematic technique of the close-up) and gestures of the body. But it is the face that receives the most emphasis in these discourses, signaling a fascination that would later be taken up by early film theorists such as Jean Epstein and Béla Balázs. A writer in *Motion Picture News* in 1914 states:

> Where the spoken word is eliminated, as it must be in the screen-drama, much of the meaning of the action is lost unless the audience can discern every expression of emotion upon the faces of the actors. In this picture [*The Pride of Jennico*], every facial expression is registered as if in a mirror. . . . The faces of both [the main actor and actress] are exquisitely mobile and sensitive to every changing emotion; they are "speaking faces"; every feature seems to be a tongue that carries a clear message to those who are watching the unfolding of the drama.[3]

A reader of *Motion Picture Magazine* (1914) writes in to praise the face of Clara Young: she has "an ideal face for photoplay. It is well modeled, the perfect oval, but with delicate features that are sufficiently covered with flesh not to appear sharp on the screen. Her eyes are wonderfully expressive and can alone 'speak their lines,' without the aid of gestures or facial play. Her face is particularly adapted to registering emotion. It never distorts nor grows grotesque when subject to the heavy play of anger or other passions; and it is particularly appealing when registering delicate shades of fancy, such as wistfulness, fond memories," and so on.[4] While there is no sharp distinction of sexual difference in the general discussion of facial expression in these discourses, it is clear that the faces of women are more expressive than those of men at the same time as they must maintain the balance and proportion crucial to the concept of feminine beauty. Their mobility is constrained.

The analogy between the face and language was not born with the cinema. Physiognomy, the art/pseudoscience of interpreting faces, has a long history extending from Aristotle and Giambattista Della Porta to Johann Caspar Lavater and others in the late eighteenth century to Charles Darwin and Charles Bell in the nineteenth century through the rising popularity it enjoyed in the early and mid-twentieth century with the emergence of its particularly intense association with racist discourses in the pre-Nazi and Nazi eras.[5] In almost all cases, the features of the face, their muscular contractions, and the shape of the skull are read as signs that are "spoken by" or "written on" the face. Lavater refers to the possibility of "reading the ever-present, ever-open book of the human countenance."[6] He claims that the more violent passions call out for more apparent signs and frequently compares the face to a language in need of deciphering. Lavater even uses the term "semiotics" (*Semiotik*), although he borrows it from medical semiotics and its theory of the symptom. The difficulty that emerges for physiognomy with the analogy of language is traceable to a tension within Enlightenment epistemology between its rationalist impulse favoring the arbitrary sign (in calculus, for instance) and its simultaneous embrace of the "natural sign." Language proper, it was recognized, can only be arbitrary, given the multiplicity of languages. But "natural language," epitomized by facial expression, is allegedly nonarbitrary, directly and indexically linked to the passions within. It is nature writing itself. This claim is tied to the theological concept of a Creator who has provided nature with a language easily readable by men. Nature signifies only itself. But, as David E. Wellbery claims, the natural sign is not in direct opposition to the arbitrary sign—for Enlightenment thinkers, *"the system of natural signs is the telos of all our culturally instituted systems of arbitrary signs.* The point where the two types of signs coincide, where natural and arbitrary signs become indistinguishable, is the mind of God."[7] Although developments in the nineteenth century led physiognomics to cling even more strongly to the status of a secular science, a physiognomist such as G.-B. Duchenne de Boulogne, who developed instruments allowing electricity to activate particular facial expressions by shocking the muscles, also invoked a Creator who mobilized muscles "when he wished the characteristic signs of the emotions, even the most fleeting, to be written briefly on man's face. Once this language of facial expression was created, it sufficed for him to give all human beings the instinctive faculty of always expressing their sentiments by contracting the same muscles. This rendered the language universal and immutable."[8] The idea of a universal language, although usually linked with the concept of the natural, begins to displace natural language with the intensification of colonialist projects in the nineteenth century. Facial expression, according to Duchenne, was rule-governed (he labeled these rules the "*orthography* of facial expression," extending the language analogy), but he purported to simply unveil, through careful observation and description, these rules universally ordained by nature.[9]

Discourses concerning the facial expressions of actors and their readability proliferated in the pages of early film journals and acting manuals, and they were, whether explicitly or not, haunted by the concepts of the physiognomists. They often share the physiognomists' unrelenting pursuit of a taxonomy of emotions correlated with facial expressions. Perhaps the most telling and extended discussion of facial expression in these journals is contained in a series of articles by Eugene V. Brewster titled "Expression of the Emotions" and appearing in most of the July through December 1914 issues of *Motion Picture Magazine*. Brewster at times seems to be addressing actors, exhorting them to be more sensitive to the nuanced attributes of facial expression, and at other times addressing audience members to persuade them that reading facial emotion is a skill they must develop in order to fully appreciate the photoplay. This dual address is complicated by a persistent recourse to notions of the naturalness of expression, its accessibility, its involuntary nature, and its universality. Legibility and its possibility or impossibility are constant concerns and converge with a persistent tension between the universal and the particular. Brewster mentions Darwin (*The Expression of the Emotions in Man and Animals*) explicitly and uses ideas and images drawn from works of physiognomy, physiology, phrenology, and general philosophy (Lavater,

Charles Bell [author of *Essays on the Anatomy of Expression in Painting*], Francis Warner, Herbert Spencer, Edmund Burke).[10] In fact, Brewster's work on facial expression is a vexed relay between common knowledge or common sense and a contemporary scientistic discourse.[11] This makes it a particularly interesting site for the examination of ideological understandings of the face and its significance.

The extent to which Brewster's disquisition is haunted by contradictions is exemplified in the first few pages of the second article. His argument moves rapidly through the following stages: (1) The extent and intensity of facial expression are a function of class. The most refined, aristocratic persons have learned how to control their expressions in preservation of their dignity. (2) In a progression from the lowest form of animal life to the highest class of mankind, the capacity for a wide range of fine-tuned emotions and the ability to express them increases—"An uncivilized man has fewer emotions than a civilized one has, and his face is correspondingly less expressive."[12] (3) A "savage," like a dog or a child, expresses primitive emotions (rage, fear, joy) "more decisively" than a civilized man.[13] (4) Dogs, children, and savages are closer to the "natural," while a civilized man has learned to be deceptive and hypocritical.[14] (5) Deception is natural, since we find it in the lower animals (e.g., opossums, birds, snakes)—collapsing the opposition between the natural and the civilized.[15] (6) Hence, there are two relations to the expression of emotion: deceptive and involuntary. Brewster is concerned only with the latter.[16] (7) The face nevertheless "is likely to give us away" if we try to be deceptive (hence blurring the opposition between the voluntary and the involuntary).[17] (8) Expression is like a language; children have to learn it.[18] (9) There is tremendous variety in the individual expression of emotions.[19] (10) But "we all express emotions practically the same."[20] (11) There is a scale of differences in individuals' ability to read and decipher emotions, but nevertheless our diverse readings are based on "a certain common instinct or knowledge."[21] In later articles, Brewster continues to stress the wide disparity in the expression and legibility of emotions, emphasizing particularity and individuality, but then also states, "It has now come to pass that we have practically a universal language of facial expression which nearly everybody understands," and "facial expression has become a language that all understand."[22] When discussing the concept of a language in this context, Brewster stresses the arbitrariness of its signs and claims that this is true of emotional expression as well (his example is the kiss, unknown in certain cultures, but he fails to note that this is a gesture and not an expression).[23] Then, later, he claims, "The far greater number of

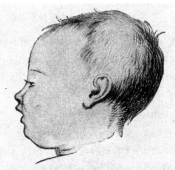

THIS CHILD IS JUST LEARNING TO EXPRESS ITS THOUGHTS BY MEANS OF ITS FACIAL MUSCLES

things and cannot help it. I wonder how many of my readers know just why that child's face is affected in that way. Again, how is it that when we see a child crying we know instantly the state of that child's feelings? And how is it that we can read the human countenance so readily and recognize a large variety of emotions and feelings merely by the expression?

There are various ways of expressing our feelings, and even the lower animals have different ways of showing them. Strike a dog with a cane, at the same time assuming a threatening attitude, and the animal will express fear in several different ways. It will probably put its tail between its legs, hold its head downward,

sadness and anger, would occur to you at once, but after that you would pause. As far as I know, nobody has ever yet attempted to make a list of such emotions and feelings, and such a list would doubtless be subject to criticism, because some would declare that certain emotions cannot be depicted by the face alone. For example, doubt and dread. Let the best actor or artist in the world try to show these two emotions, and how many of us could tell them apart? Let us make a list of some of the principal emotions and sensations, with a view of naming only those which can be depicted by the face:

Abhorrence	Derision	Longing
Admiration	Despair	Lust
Adoration	Devotion	Madness
Affection	Diffidence	Magnanimity
Alarm	Disappoint-	Malevolence
Anger	ment	Maliciousness
Anguish	Discomfiture	Meditation
Antagonism	Disdain	Meekness
Anxiety	Disgust	Melancholy
Appreciation	Dismay	Mercy
Apprehension	Distress	Misery
Arrogance	Distrust	Mockery
Artlessness	Doubt	Nobleness
Astonishment	Dread	Obedience
Avarice	Duplicity	Obstinacy
Avengement	Eagerness	Pain
Aversion	Ecstasy	Passiveness
Benevolence	Egotism	Penitence
Benignity	Enmity	Piety
Bestiality	Entreaty	Pity
Bravado	Exasperation	Pitilessness
Bravery	Fascination	Pleasure
Candor	Fear	Praise
Caprice	Ferocity	Prejudice
Captiousness	Fickleness	Prudence
Caution	Firmness	Quarrelsome-
Cheerfulness	Fury	ness

3.1 Brewster's list of some "principal emotions and expressions," from the first article in the series "Expression of the Emotions," *Motion Picture Magazine*, July 1914, 108–9.

the movements of expression, and all of the more important ones, are innate or inherited."[24] The tension throughout is between the particular and the general, the innate and the acquired, the involuntary and the voluntary, and the local and the universal—oppositions that are all imbricated with each other and that haunted classical physiognomy as well.

Brewster never questions the idea that facial expression is the sign of an interiority—feelings, emotions, anxieties. He readily accepts scientific sources that claim "the face is an index of the mind" and that the expression of emotions is due to excessive nerve force seeking an outlet.[25] Beginning the series with an extensive list of emotions, he stresses the diversification and complexity of the emotions and the scale of his task (fig. 3.1).[26] In the course

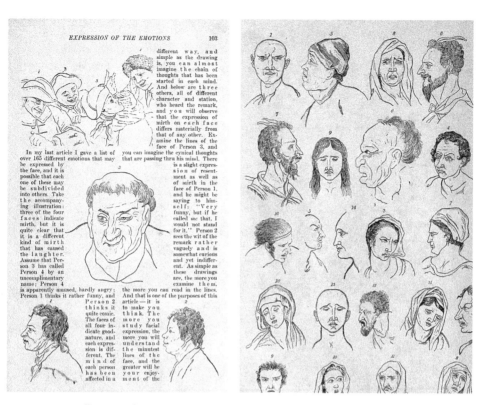

In my last article I gave a list of over 165 different emotions that may be expressed by the face, and it is possible that each one of these may be subdivided into others. Take the accompanying illustration: three of the four faces indicate mirth, but it is quite clear that it is a different kind of mirth that has caused the laughter. Assume that Person 3 has called Person 4 by an uncomplimentary name; Person 4 is apparently amused, hardly angry; Person 1 thinks it rather funny, and

different way, and simple as the drawing is, you can almost imagine the chain of thoughts that has been started in each mind. And below are three others, all of different character and station, who heard the remark, and you will observe that the expression of mirth on each face differs materially from that of any other. Examine the lines of the face of Person 3, and you can imagine the cynical thoughts that are passing thru his mind. There

is a slight expression of resentment as well as of mirth in the face of Person 1, and he might be saying to himself: "Very funny, but if he called me that, I would not stand for it." Person 2 sees the wit of the remark rather vaguely and is somewhat curious and yet indifferent. As simple as these drawings are, the more you examine them,

the more you can read in the lines. And that is one of the purposes of this article — it is to make you think. The more you study facial expression, the more you will understand the minutest lines of the face, and the greater will be your enjoyment of the

Person 2 thinks it quite comic. The faces of all four indicate good-nature, and each expression is different. The mind of each person has been affected in a

3.2 & 3.3 Illustrations for "Expression of the Emotions," drawings taken primarily from the physiognomic texts of Charles Bell, Johann Caspar Lavater, and others.

of the series, he uses two types of illustrations: drawings taken primarily from the physiognomic texts of Bell, Lavater, and others (figs. 3.2, 3.3), and still photographs of film actors and actresses, often arranged in a collage (fig. 3.4). Brewster uses the drawings to demonstrate the variability in interpretations of a single facial expression (and his are often at odds with those of the writers of the physiognomic treatises). Yet, interestingly, the still photographs of actors and actresses are almost always accompanied by a title that pinpoints the emotion displayed, as though photography and by extension cinematography were transparent and unambiguous registrations of emotion (figs. 3.5, 3.6).[27]

Brewster borrows a great deal from the treatises of physiognomy from the eighteenth century to the early years of the twentieth. His tracing of the evolution of the emotions—from the child to the adult and from the savage (often equated with the animal) to the civilized man—parallels that of the physiognomists. Although he argues that the more civilized a person is, the more capable they are of having a range of refined emotions, civilization

NORMA TALMADGE, OF THE VITAGRAPH PLAYERS, SHOWING HER
REMARKABLY EXPRESSIVE FACE UNDER DIFFERENT EMOTIONS

and suspicion. But cover the hand so that only the face is visible, and you will recognize contempt, hatred, anger or cruelty. Can you imagine John Bunny or Alice Joyce posing so as to resemble the emotions in this picture? If not, why not? That is a phase of the subject which we shall soon explore. And we shall learn why we all express emotions practically the same. And why tears come to the eyes when we are in deep sorrow. And why we frown and scowl when we are displeased.

(*To be continued*)

3.4 Illustration for "Expression of the Emotions," still photographs of Norma Talmadge arranged in a collage.

also brings with it deception, which proves to be a problem for Brewster. For in deception, the surface is a ruse; it fails to perform its task of representing a depth, hence the necessity for appealing to the superior force of the involuntary, breaking through the surface to thwart any attempt at deception. In the cinema, although Brewster does not discuss this, deception can function only if it fails, that is, if it represents deception itself for the spectator. This is one of the quandaries of subjecting an involuntary expression to what must be a voluntary art. The semiotic force at work must move from an exteriority to an interiority because, wordless, the cinema deals only with surfaces. The concept of expression is crucial here. The term "express" is derived from the Latin *expressāre* (*ex* for "out" and *pressāre* "to press"). The English term is the representation of the Latin *exprimĕre*, whose chief meanings, according to the OED, are "1. to press out; 2. to form (an image) by pressure, to represent in sculpture or painting; 3. to represent or set forth in words or actions."[28] Facial expression is an inevitable image formed by pressure, and Brewster's aim is to subject it to a sure legibility.

Physiognomy defined itself as the study of facial features or expressions as indicative of character, race, or ethnicity. Richard T. Gray maintains that it is aligned with "one of the most persistent fantasies held by the human intellect—the notion of developing a kind of penetrating interior vision that would infallibly reveal the psychological constitution of any human being at which it is directed."[29] At its inception as an empirical scientific enterprise (associated primarily with Lavater), physiognomy worked to distinguish itself from occult prophetic practices of reading faces by invoking the rational ideals of the Enlightenment. Johann Caspar Lavater's manuscript of 1775–78 was titled *Physiognomic Fragments for the Promotion of Human Understanding and Human Love* and claimed that "whether they are or are not sensible of it, all men are daily influenced by physiognomy; that ... every man, consciously or inconsciously [*sic*], understands something of physiognomy; nay, that there is not a living being which does not, at least after its manner, draw some inferences from the external to the internal; which does not judge concerning that which is not, by that which is apparent to the senses."[30] In line with the Enlightenment, physiognomy asserted the universality of the legibility of facial expression. It was a natural language in which the signs referred directly and immediately to their referent. According to Lavater, "Everything about the human body, small and large, is significant, ... nature possesses a tenthousandfold language in which it speaks to us simultaneously, ... it principally speaks in a very comprehensible, very unequivocal manner, and ... it is not nature's fault, but our own, if we fail to understand it or if we understand it incorrectly."[31] Hence, Lavater

3.5 & 3.6 Illustrations for "Expression of the Emotions," still photographs of film actors and actresses, accompanied by a title that pinpoints the emotion displayed.

presages the hermeneutic quandary that Brewster faces—all human beings have an instinctive knowledge of physiognomy, but their deficiencies in reading faces necessitate an empirical and positivistic science that can train them to do what they allegedly know instinctively. His only solution to this problem is posing the necessity of the physiognomist's genius in intuiting the meaning of a face as a precondition for breaking it down into signs that can be read by others. He is constantly juggling the desire to found an empirical, positivistic science with his profound belief in his own transempirical and uncodifiable but sure instinct. There is another way of ameliorating this conundrum—the construction of a history in which an originary ability to read faces is degraded over time by the trajectory of civilization and modernity (I will return to this later). While Lavater is also aware of the problem that haunts Brewster—that of deception or dissimulation—he confronts it by attacking the superficiality and alienation of his contemporary culture. What must be recognized is that the body in itself is only a meaningless means, a surface that effaces itself in the service of referring to a soul (the theological implications are clear).

The status of facial expression as a sign is quite complicated in Lavater's discourse. Above all, it cannot be symbolic (i.e., governed by an arbitrary code). Nevertheless, it must constitute a set of signs that are legible and teachable. In Peircean terms, for Lavater, facial expression is constituted by the signs that are closest to their referents: indexical and iconic signs. For the indexical signs, an interior passion or emotion results in the contraction of specific muscles that then produce a particular external expression (this is the precedent for Duchenne, who used electricity to produce the contractions and their allied expressions). In the case of iconic signs, the facial expressions *resemble* their referents. For instance, a large forehead points to great intelligence, a physiognomic alliance that not only helped to rationalize racism but also generated the concepts of highbrow and lowbrow culture. These signs could more readily be seen as transparent and hence natural—the eminently readable language of a Supreme Being.

The concept of a natural language poses a problem here and could almost be seen as an oxymoron. Although Lavater recognized that language—and indeed some aspects of facial expression—had to be characterized as arbitrary, the Enlightenment viewed the arbitrariness of artificially constructed languages (especially the mathematical calculus that was seen as the key to understanding) as constituting simply a detour from the sign's goal of returning to the thing itself.[32] This could be embraced as the affirmation of the primary importance of language as natural (and ultimately ordained by God). This project mandated the negation of the body, its desensualization, since the body was

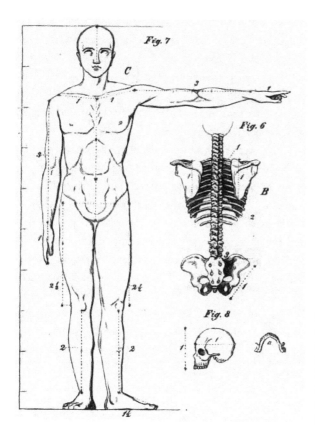

3.7 Carl Gustav Carus's unit of measurement, the "module," defined as one-third of the length of the human backbone. From *Symbolik der menschlichen Gestalt: Ein Handbuch zur Menschenkenntniss* (F. A. Brockhaus, 1857), 59.

now only a conduit for the transsensual essence of a person. This stance is very much in line with Christian theology. On the other hand, the desire of God is for a perfectly proportioned face and body. Lavater designed an instrument for cranial measurement (which was, for him, a scalar measure of intellectual capacity) and claimed, "The use of this [machine] will allow us to generate, over time, a universally comprehensible and practical proportional table for all the capacities of the human soul."[33] Carl Gustav Carus, a German physiologist and painter writing in the mid-nineteenth century, embraced the idea that the human being must be harmoniously and aesthetically proportioned. He isolated a unit of measurement derived from the human body itself—the "module," defined as one-third of the length of the human backbone—and claimed that the module was "a genuine and organic primordial measure" and hence universal (fig. 3.7).[34] Proportion was the natural plan, and any deviations from this were monstrous. Lavater wrote, "Take two, three, or four shades [silhouettes] of men remarkable for understanding; join the features so artificially that no defect shall appear, as far as relates to the act of joining; that is, take the forehead of one, add the nose of a second, the mouth of a third, the chin of a fourth, and the result of this combination of the signs of wisdom shall be folly. Folly is perhaps nothing more than the emendation of some heterogeneous addition."[35] Heterogeneity produced only aberration, abnormality.

The notion of a natural language was intimately aligned with the concept of a universal language, a desire born from the encounter with difference in the colonial enterprise. As Tani Barlow has pointed out, "It is only in the presence of difference that the claim of universality became truly compelling; only when the difference is inadvertently and irreversibly present does the exploration of and explanation for sameness become compulsory."[36] The description of the face in cinema as a universal language participates in this problematic—hence, the overdetermined tendency to invoke the primitive and racial difference in these discussions. The intimacy between these concepts is emblematized by Leibniz's use of the word "world" to demonstrate at great length that it is ultimately natural, an onomatopoeia. As Gray points out, "On the example of the word *Welt* (world), Leibniz tries to show that the articulated sounds of these letters have an originary mimetic connection to what the word itself means. He advances the hypothesis that the Old German word *Werelt* alludes to the rotation of the earth and that the root of this word can be found in the letter 'W.' He goes on to surmise that the pronunciation of this letter produces a motion that mimetically imitates the motion of the earth."[37] Hence what appears as arbitrary can be traced back to an originary natural, mimetic relationship that has simply been lost in the vagaries of language.

At the moment when the world emerges as a globe and colonialism forces a confrontation with unfamiliar differences, physiognomy presents itself as a hermeneutic system that will allay fear of the unknown. If surface differences, particularly of the face, have meaning in relation to intelligence, character, and soul, they are predictably aligned with racial differences, most frequently resulting in a hierarchy in which the European white male occupies the highest position. In 1849, Carus produced a map of the world that represented the distribution of what he termed the four human races.[38] He did not use the contemporary categories of race (Caucasian, Mongoloid, Negroid, etc.) but invented his own that only appeared to have a relation to the position of the sun and a geographic logic: "daylight peoples" (*Tagvölker*) were Europeans;

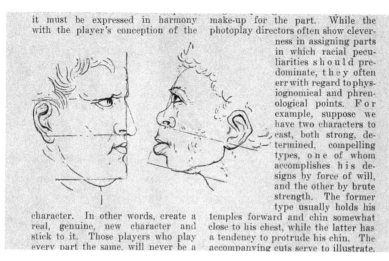

it must be expressed in harmony with the player's conception of the

character. In other words, create a real, genuine, new character and stick to it. Those players who play every part the same, will never be a

make-up for the part. While the photoplay directors often show cleverness in assigning parts in which racial peculiarities s h o u l d predominate, t h e y often err with regard to physiognomical and phrenological points. F o r example, suppose we have two characters to cast, both strong, determined, compelling types, o n e of whom accomplishes h i s designs by force of will, and the other by brute strength. The former type usually holds his temples forward and chin somewhat close to his chest, while the latter has a tendency to protrude his chin. The accompanying cuts serve to illustrate.

3.8 Eugene V. Brewster, racial profiles, "Expression of the Emotions," *Motion Picture Magazine*, September 1914, 102.

"nocturnal peoples" (*Nachtvölker*) were the Africans (the map makes it clear that Carus also includes Australians in this category); "Eastern twilight peoples" (*östliche Dämmerungsvölker*) was used for Asians; and "Western twilight peoples" (*westliche Dämmerungsvölker*) for the native peoples of North and South America.[39] The solar logic is only a ruse, and ultimately it is skin color that proves to be the decisive physiognomic sign—the "physically and intellectually inferior Negroes" are "nocturnal," while the enlightened Europeans are "daylight" peoples.[40] But Carus was primarily interested in cranioscopic measurements that would produce "objective" measurements of character and intellect.[41] These differences were linked by other physiognomists and phrenologists to the angle of incline of the skull. The *linea facialis* (facial angle) was invented by Petrus Camper, a Dutch physician, physiologist, and anthropologist, who saw it as providing the sharp dividing line between human and animal and the more gradual but marked differences between Caucasian, Asian, and African faces.[42] Physiognomic differences, the inscription of a natural, universal language, are articulated with an increasingly global consciousness.

Traces of this physiognomic impulse are more than visible in Brewster's discussion of facial expression and its legibility in film. Although he attempts to divorce this illustration from its racial implications, they return surreptitiously in his description of the significance of types in the photoplay (fig. 3.8):

While the photoplay directors often show cleverness in assigning parts where racial peculiarities should predominate, they often err with regard to physiognomic and phrenological points. For example, suppose we have two characters to cast, both strong, determined, compelling types, one of whom accomplishes his designs by force of will, and the other by brute strength. The former type usually holds his temples forward and chin somewhat close to his chest, while the latter has a tendency to protrude his chin. The accompanying cuts serve to illustrate, altho originally designed to show racial differences . . . there are certain mouldings of the facial bones and muscles and certain expressions of the countenance that everybody recognizes as denoting certain tendencies.[43]

"Force of will" is associated with the European face, while "brute strength" is allied with the African face. Relating an exteriority to an interiority, the physiognomic discourse is compelled to read surface differences as immediately meaningful, accessible to anyone. This movement from outside to inside, paradigmatic of characterization in literature and the cinema, aligned itself with a similar tropology in both psychiatry and colonialism. For Joseph Conrad, the expansionist project of colonialism involved a movement in which the horrors of traveling outward from European civilization into the heart of Africa were reflected in the interiority of the British mind. As Jennifer Green-Lewis points out, with respect to Conrad's *Heart of Darkness*, "Conradian mythologies of uncharted terrain revisited an old cliché in their studies of the human psyche, while the trope of outward-inward travel drew liberally from colonial metaphors readily at hand."[44]

The strong tendency to view the cinema itself as a universal language from the earliest years was intimately linked to and dependent upon the physiognomic claim to the immediacy and transparency of the face and skull and the advocacy of a natural, indexical language. Miriam Hansen has demonstrated compellingly and extensively that the pursuit of a universal language in film was incarnated in the transition from "primitive" cinema to the classical system of transparency. That system mandated the construction of a coherent and easily negotiable diegetic space that worked to annihilate the space and time of the spectator's physical presence in the theater. Discourses on the cinema as a transparent universal language, such as those of Frank Woods writing in the *New York Dramatic Mirror* in 1910–12, buttressed the claims of American cinema to be democratic, global, accessible to all. And, as Hansen points out, those discourses were ridden with ideological imperatives: "The universal-language metaphor had harbored totalitarian and imperialist tendencies to begin with, even in its more egalitarian and utopian instances. After the war, when the metaphor was altogether absorbed in apologetic discourse, any possible ambiguity or tension disappeared, and the progress of civilization became synonymous with the worldwide hegemony of the American film industry. . . . In the bid to control the domestic market, the superiority of American over foreign products and styles was asserted in terms of a subsumption of the particular by the universal."[45] This project required the extraction of class and ethnic specificity from an audience previously defined by its social and economic milieu and its substitution by the category of an allegedly neutral spectator that was in actuality representative of the middle class. But the recourse to the universal language theme was propped not only upon the development of a classical system that negated its own status as a language but also, perhaps even more stridently, upon the insistence that the cinematic sign was unmediated; its indexicality guaranteed that it was only a means of presenting a face that was always already legible, a "natural" sign. As Brewster points out, this transparency was crucial for the global understandability and hence exportability of the American film. Economic imperatives were interwoven with a discourse that strove to be humanist in its emphasis upon the face and the efficacy of its communication.

This refrain is taken up later by Béla Balázs, who had a much greater grasp of the techniques of cinema than Brewster but was also committed to physiognomy and the universal language theory. He claimed in *Der Sichtbare Mensch* (*The Visible Man*, 1924), "One of the preconditions of the international popularity of any film is the universal comprehensibility of facial expression and gesture. . . . The laws of the film market permit only universally comprehensible facial expressions and gestures, every nuance of which is understood by princess and working girl alike from San Francisco to Smyrna. We now already have a situation in which the film speaks the only universal, common world language understood by all."[46] Ethnic differences and specificities add only a kind of "local color," and film works teleologically toward the goal of creating "an international human type" and "an international universal humanity."[47] This argument rests on a history of origins that is elaborated in *Der Sichtbare Mensch*. In it, man originally expressed himself with his entire body; the mouth and lips were not isolated as special instruments of signification but generated only the inarticulate cry on a level with the manifestations of other corporeal organs. This is the Rousseauian ur-language of presence dissected by Jacques Derrida.[48] With the advent of speech and the word, however, the head and face became isolated and intensified as the primary sources of expression: "For the poor remnants of bodily expression that remained to us the little surface of the face sufficed, sticking up like a clumsy semaphore of the soul and signaling as best it could."[49] Printing exacerbated the problem by detaching the word from the body altogether and heightening the cultural capital of written language: "The discovery of printing gradually rendered illegible the faces of men."[50] For Balázs this is a form of disembodiment that eviscerates the soul and destroys the possibility of conveying inner emotions and experiences that transcend conventional language. With the advent of printing, people had, through lack of practice, lost access to what was actually a "universal comprehensibility of facial expression and gesture."[51] Echoing a Rousseauian theory of language, Balázs situated expression and gesture as a form of ur-language and in this way collaborated in the widespread description of film as a universal language. There was an immediacy in the readability of the face; indeed, in Balázs's theory it is not possible for the face to lie; only spoken or written language can harbor the lie. But, ironically, once this universal language, which did not have to be learned, was lost, it had to be relearned (the "re" existing in some kind of limbo since the language was originally natural, transparent and therefore not "learned" in the first place).[52] This is a narrative of loss and nostalgia, a narrative that is common to theories of a universal language. For Griffith and other proponents analyzed by Hansen, Babel is the catastrophic event of fragmentation of an originary transparent and unified language, an event that made men inaccessible to each other. This narrative yearning for a lost time is shared by physiognomy in its desire to rationalize a widespread inability to read faces despite the alleged transparency of facial expression as a natural language.

Evolutionary mythologies are rampant in physiognomy, and Balázs was no doubt aware of them. In the interwar period, Heinz Werner's *Introduction to Developmental Psychology* (1926) argued that intuitive or instinctual understanding was the originary mode of human comprehension. The "physiognomic gaze" was the "truly primordial manner of perception as such," and contemporary civilized people have lost that mode of seeing due to an emphasis upon hyperrationalization at the expense of the intuitive.[53] Similarly, Hans F. K. Günther, the notorious theorist of racism who buttressed Nazi philosophy, believed that contemporary Europeans (especially Germans) had lost the innate ability to read faces in racial terms due to the epistemological stress on calculation and the translation of all phenomena into numerical expression.[54] These works participate in a pervasive and conservative critique of modernity and technology and a cultural pessimism perhaps exemplified by Oswald Spengler's *The Decline of the West* (1918, 1922). In 1919, Rudolf Kassner, another well-known German physiognomist, published *Zahl und Gesicht* (*Number and Face*), with an introduction titled "Outline of a Universal Physiognomy." "Number" names a relation to finite, static objects and points to an epistemology sustained by the logic of identity. "Face" is its opposite and antagonist in the sense that a human face is mobile and infinitely variable, invoking an intuitive, antirationalist, even mystical approach. Kassner does not relinquish the idea that there is a relationship between the external and the internal, but it is not one of identity, as posited in Lavater's static physiognomics. The face, in this sense, goes beyond and negates the logic of identity and measurability and resides in the realm of the prerational and intuitive. According to Claudia Schmölders, Kassner "suspected that the face was the final human configuration before the human body disappeared in quantitative thought."[55] The mobility of the face is contrasted with the fixity of the mask, and, increasingly, it is the mask that is associated with modernity.

Nevertheless, Balázs cannot embrace this antimodernity, antitechnology perspective because, for him, it is the cinema, another machine of mechanical reproduction, that promises to return the face to man. The cinema has a didactic function; it will teach audiences to retrieve a lost innate skill—that of reading faces. The task of the cinema was no less than that of incarnating a machine capable of reviving the ability to read human faces—hence, the absolute centrality of the close-up and, also, of the silent cinema in Balázs's theory. However, reading and legibility are metaphoric here, since Balázs continually insists upon the immediacy of the process: "What appears on the face and in facial expression is a spiritual experience which is rendered immediately visible without the intermediary of words."[56] Hence, he must continually negotiate the tension between the cinema as a special medium with its own techniques (ones that Balázs knows quite well) and the cinema that instantiates effacement itself by destroying mediation.[57] Because the close-up generates a nearness, an intimate proximity to its object, it incarnates, ironically, this lack of mediation. In his early work, the close-up is Balázs's privileged shot, and his analysis of its powers of "despatialization" and inhabitation of another time reveals the imprint of Henri Bergson on his thinking and would later influence the work of Jacques Aumont and Gilles Deleuze. "The facial expression on a face is complete and understandable in itself and therefore we need not think of it as existing in space and time. . . . Facing an isolated face takes us out of space, our consciousness of space is cut out and we find ourselves in another dimension: that of physiognomy."[58] This dimension, together with its history of dependency upon evolutionary scenarios, leads Balázs to at least temporarily embrace an explicit racism reminiscent of Francis Galton's eugenics—in *The Visible Man*, he states, "The cinematograph is a machine that in its own way will create a living, concrete internationalism: *the unique, shared psyche of the white man.* We can go further. By suggesting a uniform ideal of beauty as the universal goal of selective breeding, the film will help to produce a uniform type of the white race."[59] Just as Lavater's *Physiognomic Fragments* were "for the promotion of human understanding and love," Balázs links his privileging of the white race to an allegedly humanistic internationalism.

Balázs's alliance with the physiognomists is inscribed in his scientism, in his assertion that cinema can be an aid to anthropology and psychology in its elaboration of group physiognomies, even to the extent of calling for "a comparative science of gesture and mimicry, with research into these in order to find the common fundamental forms of expressive movement."[60] Another tendency in Balázs leads to what Gertrude Koch has identified as the anthropomorphic extension of the face to things and an embrace of the aesthetics of expressiveness.[61] Landscapes, objects, decor—all can become faces that potentially return the gaze of the spectator, due to the "living physiognomy that all things possess."[62] Although Balázs's analysis of the face seems to isolate and favor the cinema as enabling its legibility over its intersubjectivity (the close-up over the shot/reverse shot), there is a sense in which the entire film becomes a face engaging with the spectator. This proceeds from an analysis of character point of view and an early grasp of the spectator's identification with the camera: "I have no standpoint of my own. I travel with the crowd, I fly up, I dive down, I join in the ride. And if a character in a film looks another in the eyes, he gazes down from the screen into my eyes. For the camera has my eyes and identifies them with the eyes of figures within the action; they see with my gaze."[63] But that face and those eyes can be extracted from their incarnation in a character. In an incredible passage Balázs speculates on the effect of a removal of all content, of any specific image from the film: "If you could superimpose, distort, insert without using any particular image, if you could let these techniques have a dry run, as it were, then this 'technique as such' [*'Technik an sich'*] would represent the spirit [*Geist*]."[64] Through this impossible formalist reduction, the cinema does not represent or present the face—it *becomes* a face (that, in turn, represents the spirit). The cinema as face *faces* the spectator, and the intensity of an intersubjective dream is unveiled.

The fact that the physiognomists lavishly illustrated their texts gave Brewster an extensive supply of examples for his argument in *Motion Picture*

Magazine—examples that added a veneer of scientific respectability to his discourse on a popular form of entertainment. Yet, as pointed out earlier, there is a certain incommensurability in his use of the drawings and the stills drawn from films—the captions constrain the meaning of the photographs while the drawings illustrate the diversity of interpretative possibilities. The physiognomists' deployment of illustration pointed to the reverse tendency, even before the advent of photography. Gray traces a history in the use of technologies of reproduction by the physiognomists, who preferred dealing with *representations* of faces rather than real faces. Lavater bemoaned the unreliability, contingency, and mobility of real faces, their inaccessibility to scientific observation. Because he aspired to correct and objective empiricism, the greatest difficulty in dealing with real faces was their unmeasurability—hence the recourse to artistic representations (which made his work extremely popular), made possible by an advance in printing technology, the copper etching.[65] But even more telling is the crucial place he accorded to the silhouette, developed in the middle of the eighteenth century (fig. 3.9). Lavater's physiognomics downplayed, even rejected, the aspects of facial expression that were dynamic and changeable (hence associated with the passions) and instead emphasized the hard lines and stable features of the face and head.[66] The silhouette's evacuation of detail and foregrounding of the profile was fully in line with Lavater's goal (fig. 3.10). Its accuracy was a function of its mechanical and hence proportional fidelity and did not depend upon the fallibility of the engraver's hand: "Shades [silhouettes] collect the distracted attention, confine it to an outline, and thus render the observation more simple, easy, and precise. . . . Physiognomy has no greater, more incontrovertible certainty of the truth of its object than that imparted by shade [silhouette]."[67] This is an extraordinary amount of allegiance to a representation that reduces the face to a black shadow and extracts all detail, but Lavater was aware of the silhouette's shortcomings and dismissed them as subordinate to the exact mimesis he foregrounded as its most striking characteristic:

> The silhouette of a human being or of a human face is the faintest and emptiest but—if the light has been cast on a clean surface and was sufficiently parallel to it—also the truest and most faithful image of a human being that one can give. The weakest because it is almost nothing positive; it is only negative, only a half-faced borderline. The most faithful because it is an unmediated expression of nature, like none that anyone—not even the most talented draftsman—can draw freehand from nature.[68]

3.9 Eighteenth-century instrument for tracing silhouettes.

Tellingly, Gray views the silhouette as used by Lavater in relation to a pre-photographic machine that incarnated Renaissance rules of perspective: "The silhouette is the physiognomic equivalent of the [camera] 'lucida,' the semi-transparent canvas with a rectilinear grid that was introduced into painting to allow the perfect perspectival graphing of a distant object onto the canvas."[69] Both perspective and the "physiognotrace" (as it was called) bypass human interpretation in instituting a mechanical system for the mapping of bodies in

3.10 Plate XXVI, Johann Caspar Lavater's *Essays on Physiognomy*.

space (although one models depth, the other flatness). They are both efforts to produce verisimilitude and, perhaps even more important, to construct the identity of individuals as both subject and object. Hugh Welch Diamond, an early British psychiatrist and photographer who took pictures of the insane, also saw a connection between the work of physiognomy and that of perspective as incarnated in the camera. In an 1858 issue of the *Journal of the Photographic Society*, of which he was the editor, Diamond refers to the intellectual breadth of photography and to "the physiognomist who recollects that quaint work on human faces written by a certain Neapolitan gentleman named Giovanni B. della Porta, who (strange coincidence), three centuries ago, invented the camera."[70] Diamond is clearly implying that the convergence of photography and its built-in Renaissance perspective with physiognomy and its focus upon faces as readable signs is *not* a coincidence. Rather, it buttresses his own attempt to make photography a respected instrument of psychiatric medicine.

Physiognomy promised a mode of knowing the other, whether as racial/national other or as the unfamiliar and strange other of the expanded space of the metropolis. Its popularity in the eighteenth century and beyond is demonstrated by its adoption as a kind of parlor game for the bourgeoisie. Indeed, the amateur practice of physiognomy was so widespread and Lavater's influence so extreme that, according to the *Encyclopedia Britannica* (1853–60 edition), "in many places, where the study of human character from the face became an epidemic, the people went masked through the streets."[71] In mapping interiority as the signified of exteriority, physiognomy provided a language of facial expression and gesture whose ease was guaranteed by its transparency, hence its affinity with technologies associated with photography, which was also understood as a universal language. But the "parlor game" of physiognomy also had a darker side. One of the difficulties of negotiating (and policing) the new urban spaces of anonymity lay in the necessity of differentiating between law-abiding citizens and criminals. Physiognomy, phrenology, and anthropometry were activated in this forensic process as strong measures of identity. As Carsten Zelle points out in relation to the literary topos of the horrors of having a "heart of glass," easily seen through, the metaphor reveals "a turn from the desire for transparent interpersonal communication to the terrorism of total surveillance," a turn also visible in the trajectory of mapping character and identity from physiognomy to forensic science.[72] In France in the late nineteenth century, Alphonse Bertillon (inventor of the "mug shot" still used by police) had a marked predilection for the profile for reasons very similar to those of Lavater. It registered the durable traits of the criminal and undermined the practice of disguise, facial alteration, and deception.[73]

In the second half of the nineteenth century, the police increasingly resorted to photography to register and identify criminals, creating an archive of mug shots (the "rogues' gallery," visited by victims who were expected to recognize their attackers). This was frequently perceived by the criminals themselves as an untenable form of surveillance and an invasion of privacy and was the occasion for resistance in the form of grimaces and contorted facial expressions, thwarting recognizability (fig. 3.11). As Jennifer Green-Lewis points out, the courts responded by declaring that "one's appearance is not a private concern but in effect belongs to the public domain. . . . Courts held that the face was public property."[74] In addition, the development of instantaneous photography (as opposed to the long duration of immobility required by the daguerreotype) made the practice of photographing resistant criminals easier. As Alan Sekula has shown, the Bertillon system of identification of criminals relied on indexical signs (photography) and anthropometric measurements that individualized the recidivist and inscribed a statistical methodology. Francis Galton, on the other hand, used composite photography as a symbolic sign to isolate and define certain "types": the criminal, the insane, the Jewish boy, and so on. Composite photography rested on the assumption that the superimposition of photographs of individual examples of criminals, for instance, would yield the image of the ideal or typical criminal.[75] The process of superimposition would eliminate all individual idiosyncratic differences and reveal those features that were essential to the type. The tension between the Bertillon method and the Galton method was an echo of the

3.11 "An Unwilling Subject—Photographing a Prisoner for the Rogue's Gallery at Police Headquarters," from Helen Campbell, *Darkness and Daylight, or, Lights and Shadows of New York Life. A Woman's Story of Gospel, Temperance, Mission, and Rescue Work* . . . (Hartford, CT: A. D. Worthington and Co., 1892), 692.

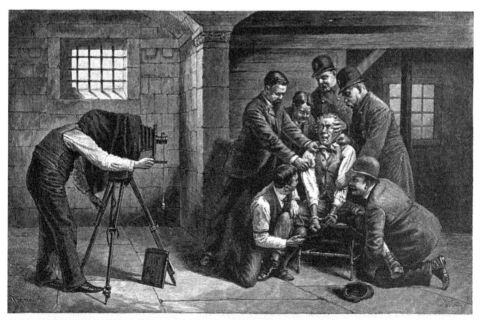

AN UNWILLING SUBJECT.— PHOTOGRAPHING A PRISONER FOR THE ROGUE'S GALLERY AT POLICE HEADQUARTERS.

recurring struggle within physiognomy between the concepts of individual and type. Although Lavater was cognizant of the myriad differences in individuals, the positing of a universal physiognomic language assumed a reading of the typical tendencies of facial configurations. Physiognomy emerged as a potential solution to the disappearance of a world in which social position was strictly circumscribed by class and gender and readability was aligned with social roles, property relations, and clothing rather than faces. But with the arrival of modernity, the uneasy category of the individual emerged as a dominant feature of the civil subject, although it was resisted by physiognomists invoking the discourse of cultural pessimism, for whom the individual was a degenerate category—unpredictable, paradoxical, and ungovernable. On the other hand, that other entity produced by modernity—the masses who haunt the city—was also unacceptable in this antimetropolitan current because the masses were "faceless," lacking distinction, uncontrollable. As Gray points out with respect to Rudolf Kassner, "The type, as Kassner's ideal, stands somewhere between the masses, those with neither individual nor typical features, and the individual, who is pure paradox and hence resists all categorization. . . . Kassner's physiognomic theory emerges, in other words, out of fear of the nameless, classless indistinction of modern cosmopolitan human beings."[76]

In the realm of the cinema, the anxious friction between individual and type emerges simultaneously with the physiognomic urge to decipher emotions and manifests itself most vividly in the star system. The star is, on the one hand, the epitome of the individual—distinctive, unique, and, as the name suggests, shining. Recognizability as an individual who appears in different roles across many films but remains the same (the double body of the star) is an important component of stardom, and the audience's knowledge of the star's proper name is crucial. The belief that anyone can rise out of the masses to become a star compensates for metropolitan anonymity. On the other hand, the star is a type—an economic category, a representational mode, one who always carries stylistic connotations of glamour (and the term "typecasting" is indicative of this status). As Edgar Morin points out, the star combines "the exceptional and the ordinary, the real and the everyday."[77] "Stardom" is manufactured and sustained by the plethora of movie magazines that arose in the 1910s. Many early film magazines saturate their opening pages with portraits of stars, producing a kind of primer for audiences.[78] One acting manual for aspirants to stardom even utilizes Galton's method of composite photography to produce the portrait of the ideal female face for the screen. Figure 3.12, which serves as the frontis-

A FILM PHANTASY

COPYRIGHT 1916 PRODUCERS SERVICE COMPANY

3.12 "A Film Phantasy," composite frontispiece for *Motion Picture Acting for Professionals and Amateurs* (1916).

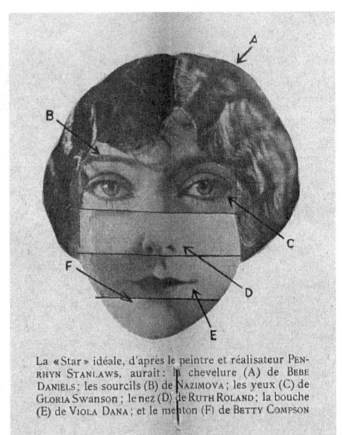

La «Star» idéale, d'après le peintre et réalisateur Pen-
rhyn Stanlaws, aurait: la chevelure (A) de Bebe
Daniels; les sourcils (B) de Nazimova; les yeux (C) de
Gloria Swanson; le nez (D) de Ruth Roland; la bouche
(E) de Viola Dana; et le menton (F) de Betty Compson

3.13 "'Star' idéale," in
Pierre Henry, "Beautés
photogéniques,"
Cinéa-Ciné, no. 17
(July 15, 1924).

piece for this manual, attempts to answer the question, "What type is most effective in the movies?" It was made by "printing through 24 photographic negative plates, one of each of the screen stars named, and the sum total is the 'First Lady of the Screen.'"[79] An article in *Cinéa-Ciné* uses the process of montage to generate the physiognomic "'Star' idéale" by combining the features of different actresses (the hair, eyes, nose, mouth, etc.) (fig. 3.13).[80] Stars exemplify the dialectic of the face in modernity: they move serially through different fictional characters who can be read in terms of their interiority while simultaneously signifying the face as pure surface, eroticized screen of glamour. If the face is a universal language, easily readable, it is also, in modernity, a cosmetic mask that does not conceal a depth. The physiognomists of the twentieth century were cognizant of this. Rudolf Kassner wrote in his 1932 book on physiognomy: "Apart from the thespian and the movie actor, who still has a face today? . . . The actor alone gained from the decadence and decline of most institutions and could thrive. Among the types, he is the one quickest and easiest to develop. He makes his appearance almost automatically, once all the other types are missing or lacking (physiognomically speaking)."[81] Ernst Jünger described the mask as a technological extension of the face, required of workers as protection in the factory and for motorists or in sports at high velocity, of soldiers in the form of gas masks, and in women's use of makeup (figs. 3.14, 3.15). He utilized photography to map this transformation. Masking procedures infiltrate everyday life; Jünger claimed, "What first strikes one in purely physiognomic terms is the masklike stiffness of the face" and referred to "this masklike appearance, which in men creates a metallic impression and in the case of women has a cosmetic effect."[82] For Jünger, photography provides a "second consciousness" for the subject who now is able to see themselves as an object.[83]

The representational technologies of physiognomy extend from the engraving to the silhouette to photography, but rarely is film used by this allegedly scientific discourse. Lavater claimed that man revealed himself only in stillness and solitude, and movement undermined the effectivity of the physiognomic gaze. As Gray points out, even into the Nazi era, the physiognomists rarely used film (as though mobility thwarted cognition). The immobile face, with fixed features allowing measurement and comparison, was the ideal. Brewster and Balázs, however, offer evidence that the cinema as representational apparatus was not irreconcilable with the dreams of physiognomy. Balázs's insistence upon the despatialization and detemporalization of the close-up of the face was his assurance that film not only was consistent with the realm of physiognomy but embodied it. Brewster's obsession with the legibility of the face, its unmediated revelation of emotion, also participated in the discourse of a universal language embraced by the physiognomists. Yet there is another well-known adherent of the silent cinema whose theory, at least in one respect, could be said to perform a resistance to physiognomy. Unlike Balázs, Jean Epstein does not analyze the cinematic face in the context of a typology or physiognomy, although he might seem to outdo Balázs's microphysiognomy in his attention to the minutest of twitches and movements on the human face. In Epstein, there is an almost erotic infatuation with the face, a concentration on detail, contingency, and movement: "The orography of the face vacillates. Seismic shocks begin. Capillary wrinkles try to split the fault. . . . A muscle bridles. The lip is laced with tics like a theater curtain."[84] Here, the mixed metaphors situate the face as comparable

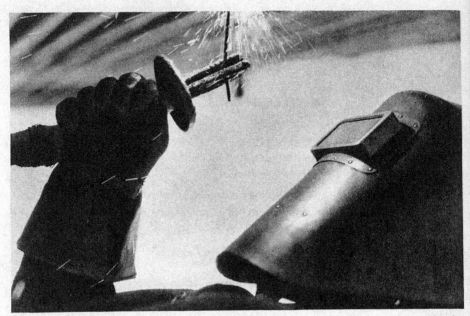

Elektriker

Die Arbeitswelt bringt mannigfaltige Gelegenheiten hervor, bei denen der Mensch in der Maske erscheint

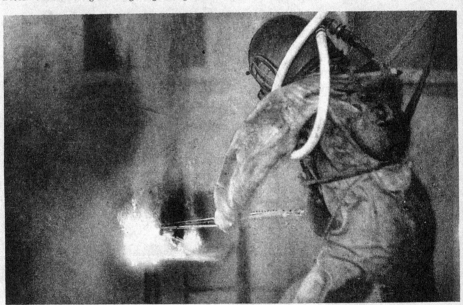

Taucher beim Schneiden von Panzerplatten unter Wasser

Im Reiche der Kosmetik

Das Klischee . . .

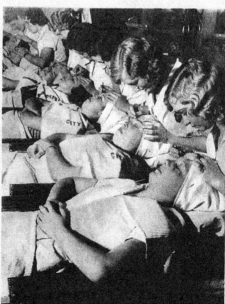

und seine Abzüge

3.14 & 3.15 Edmund Schultz and Ernst Jünger, *Die veränderte Welt: Eine Bilderfibel unserer Zeit* (Breslau: W. G. Korn, 1933), 46, 55.

to objects—there is no interiority, simply a surface that inscribes an affect that does not exist elsewhere. The face actively resists typology. Spontaneity and contingency mark the face with an unpredictability that becomes eroticized. Affect is not psychological depth but intensity, and the flow of such extreme intensities mesmerizes the spectator. Expression is therefore not, as it is for Balázs, the trace of an interiority, and the human is subsumed by movement.

Epstein's theory, like Balázs's, is wide-ranging and can by no means be reduced to the concept by which he has been pigeonholed in much of film studies—photogénie. Nevertheless, it is a crucial concept, particularly in his thinking about the filmed face. That thinking and writing are informed by an erotic infatuation, a concentration on detail, contingency, and movement. Photogénie is famously elusive and undefinable but is described by Epstein as "any aspect of things, beings or souls whose moral character is enhanced by filmic reproduction."[85] In addition, "only mobile aspects of the world, of things and souls, may see their moral value increased by filmic reproduction."[86] Cinematic movement—including slow motion and time-lapse cinematography—deviated from our everyday perception of movement. Trond Lundemo demonstrates compellingly that the vision of cinema ("the intelligence of a machine") is beyond that of the human in Epstein's discourse and that there is "an irreducible distance between the human psychological apparatus and the technology of cinema."[87] Cinema warps time (defeating the thermodynamic law of irreversibility) and at the same time gives us an access to a truer time and a time of possibility. In the close-up, this is the time of a scanning of and absorption in the face. And the close-up works to annihilate distance and overcome any separation between the "I" and the image: "Pain is within reach. If I stretch out my arm I touch you, and that is intimacy. I can count the eyelashes of this suffering. I would be able to taste the tears. Never before has a face turned to mine in that way. Ever closer it presses against me, and I follow it face to face. It's not even true that there is air between us; I consume it. It is in me like a sacrament. Maximum visual acuity."[88] The face refuses typology, and Epstein cites Edgar Allan Poe's critique of phrenology as the exclusion of the paradoxically perverse.[89] The relation to the image is not, for Epstein, as it is for Balázs, a figurative form of (nonlinguistic) reading. It is an affective bond that cannot be taught, and it is unclear to whom it is available. Photogénie is momentary, caught in glimpses, and seems to be accessible only to a refined sensibility, one attuned to cinematic specificity, and one that refuses the imperative of narrative intelligibility.

Epstein may appear to have completely escaped the ideological hold of physiognomy and found another way to theorize the face and its imaging. He does not deploy the nostalgic narrative of a loss of an originary language of facial expression, nor does his adulation of the face in close-up seem bound to the notion of identity. Nevertheless, it is not accidental that both he and Balázs single out Sessue Hayakawa as an emblematic and semantically saturated instance of the powers of the close-up, locating his appeal in a restraint that is shorthand for an inscrutable Asianness, where the slightest movement carries a barely legible meaning. But, in addition, Epstein like Balázs invests in a form of nostalgic animism, locating a projection onto the world of human characteristics as an enviable primitivism that, in his argument, surpasses the human as a form of absolute otherness:

> Moreover cinema is a language, and like all languages it is animistic, it attributes, in other words, a semblance of life to the objects it defines. The more primitive a language, the more marked this animistic tendency. . . . The almost godlike importance assumed in close-ups by parts of the human body, or by the most frigid elements in nature, has often been noted. . . . Those lives it [the cinema] creates, by summoning objects out of the shadows of indifference into the light of dramatic concern, have little in common with human life. These lives are like the life in charms and amulets, the ominous, tabooed objects of certain primitive religions.[90]

In Epstein's discourse, a modern, technologically sophisticated form of mechanical representation looks backward to the enchantment of a primitive time. Although the lure of the primitive was typical of modernisms of the 1920s, that discourse located the primitive in the realm of the *non*technological. Here, it is cinematic technology that is haunted and possessed by a primitive and animistic past. Cinema is bound up from the very start with a profound otherness.

Much later, as discussed in chapter 1, Deleuze and Guattari resuscitate this rubric with a different inflection—the face "is White Man himself, with his broad white cheeks and the black hole of his eyes."[91] But the face only attains this status within Western assemblages of power. According to Deleuze and Guattari, the societies that do not depend upon a strongly and romantically inflected concept of the face are (predictably enough) primitive societies, ones that are "collective, polyvocal, and corporeal" as opposed to signifying and subjective.[92] These "primitive" societies operate not through the face but through the body, bringing into play heterogeneous forms and substances. The face is a specifically Western, white invention.[93]

For Lavater, Duchenne, Darwin, and Galton, the face was a site for the display of emotions and identity. It was a sign, a figure that called for decipherment, reading—not the medium of intersubjectivity, of the face-to-face encounter as it would be later for writers such as Erving Goffman and Emmanuel Levinas.[94] Despite Balázs's situation of the cinema as a face facing the spectator, he can do so only by invoking an extreme scenario, reducing the cinema to its sheer technical apparatus, devoid of content. This paradoxical moment in Balázs cannot be sustained because, in his pursuit of a universal language, he must claim cinematic transparency, deny the force of mediation. To evoke the cinema as intersubjectivity, Epstein must, similarly paradoxically, dehumanize it, make it radically and excessively other to "human sensibility," transform it into the animistic "intelligence of the machine," a move that subtends his positioning of photogénie as somewhat mystical, undefinable—a "you either get it or you don't" phenomenon.

It is not accidental, then, that a privileging of the face (or the advocacy of a universal language that often accompanies it) is coincident with a claim of transparency, a denial of mediation. Face-to-face contact as immediacy, presence, and transparency represents the lost utopia, the fantasy of pure community before the "Babel-like" fall into the accelerated mediation of new technologies of representation and communication. To imagine the cinema itself as a face, as both Balázs and Epstein do at symptomatic moments in their writing, is to reclaim the presence of face-to-face communication as well as to return to the spectator a face in the midst of the ascendancy of a *mass* culture. This aspect of their arguments is, however and for the most part, concealed beneath the discourse of legibility or the accessibility of affect.

In a different historical context, and from a different field and perspective, the sociologist Erving Goffman analyzed face-to-face contact, defined as presence, as always already saturated with mediation—social, cultural, ritual. In an essay entitled "On Face-Work" (already an indication of the relation of the face to labor rather than transparency), Goffman defines face as completely abstracted from the body: "The term *face* may be defined as the positive social value a person effectively claims for himself by the line others assume he has taken during a particular contact. Face is an image of self delineated in terms of approved social attributes."[95] For Goffman, engagement in conversation is a risk that has to be negotiated, entailing a constant possibility of embarrassment, loss of face, and humiliation. Communication is not the issue. Instead, face-to-face contact is guided by a series of social rules that safeguard the preservation of face for all participants. Nevertheless, the language of universality reemerges here in intriguing ways: "Throughout this paper it has been implied that underneath their differences in culture, people everywhere are the same. If persons have a universal human nature, they themselves are not to be looked to for an explanation of it."[96] Instead, Goffman claims that it is a general principle of all societies to "mobilize their members as self-regulating participants in social encounters."[97] This leads to an apparently extreme and antihumanistic claim, almost Foucauldian in its import: "Universal human nature is not a very human thing. By acquiring it, the person becomes a kind of construct, built up not from inner psychic propensities but from moral rules that are impressed upon him from without."[98] Nevertheless, the claim of universality allows Goffman to assume a position outside of any sociohistorical specificity to outline the terms of intersubjectivity—it will always entail the production of subjects as "self-regulating participants in social encounters." Where does this concept of face come from? It is clearly not derived from Galton, Duchenne, or Darwin, who grounded their theories either in evolution or in a certain universalism based on human nature and/or difference. Instead, it is a rupture in understandings of the face that, while claiming to be universal, still derive from the experience of colonialism. For the concept of "saving face" that underlies and supports Goffman's analysis emerges in the encounter with East Asian cultures, specifically Chinese understandings of face. And while Goffman refers his readers to anthropological studies of the Chinese concept of "saving face," these references appear in footnotes, as simple addenda to the argument, rather than its source. As is clear from the etymology provided in the *OED*, the "first use" of the concepts of "saving face" or "losing face" in English appears in the communications of an English trading community in China in 1834.[99] The displacement of face as a bodily phenomenon mirroring the soul—demanding legibility, marking the particularity of the individual—to a question of social status and intersubjectivity is initiated in the (unacknowledged) contact with otherness.

The face emerges as a particularly acute problem in modernity, raising the specter of an illegible strangeness and otherness. In such a context, the notion of the face as a universal language, leveling all differences, becomes especially attractive. Tani Barlow deploys the term "colonial modernity" to indicate that modernity is inextricable from colonialism and the encounter of Western nations with difference.[100] She describes a kind of boomerang effect in which the condition of possibility of European Enlightenment and discourses on modernity is the colonial project, which revealed populations of "others" who could be positioned as primitive and unenlightened. Barlow claims that "what the universalizing gaze of the European Enlightenment had seen, after all, were the disparate peoples of the world . . . it is only in the presence of difference that the claim of universality became truly compelling."[101] The description of the face in cinema as a universal language is subtended by this colonial problematic of modernity as is the repeated tendency to align the cinema with notions of the primitive.

Miriam Hansen recognized this ideological problematic in Griffith's advocacy of a universal language. But *Intolerance* (1916) was a pivotal film for her because it allowed her to complicate this scenario by demonstrating how the film deploys a notion of language as hieroglyphics, mixing the iconic/indexical sign with a concept of writing (and hence countering the suppression of writing in the emerging classical cinema). Hieroglyphics, in addition to constituting another symptom of the colonialist project, embody the collision between a language that claims transparency and universality and a language that demands an active deciphering, between an elite language reserved for the powerful and a popular, accessible language. Hansen viewed Griffith's hieroglyphic tendency as a point of resistance to the complicit notion of a universal language and a revival of its more utopian aspects, as revealing the "tension, at least during the silent era, between the cinema's role as a universalizing, ideological idiom and its redemptive possibilities as an inclusive, heterogeneous and at times unpredictable horizon of experience."[102] For Hansen, it was not the face that held together the contradictions of modernity but a cinematic syntax that promoted a certain type of legibility in its confrontation with the contingencies and heterogeneity of a cinematic public sphere.

This is a compelling analysis, but it fails to address the persistence and tenacity of the trope of the face and its vexed condensation of particularity and universality, evidenced today in the pursuit of facial recognition technologies, Facebook and other social networks, the fascination with plastic surgery, the development of software to identify faces in digital photography platforms such as iPhoto as well as in surveillance, and the continuing insistence of the star system. The face is a highly cathected site, fragilely embracing a series of contradictions—universality/particularity, individuality/anti-individuality, rationality/irrationality, and legibility/illegibility. These tensions emerged with a vengeance in early film theory, helping to shape discourse about the cinema. Rather than resorting to the concept of a language, whether universal or hieroglyphic, it might be useful to understand the face and its deployment by activating Barlow's concept of a "historical catachresis." Barlow borrows the concept from Jacques Derrida and Gayatri Spivak but inflects it by adding the word "historical."[103] A catachresis is the misuse of a word as in "the use of the wrong word for the context" or "the use of a forced figure of speech, esp. one that involves or seems to involve strong paradox (as *blind* mouths)."[104] Spivak and Barlow analyze catachresis as a term that has no adequate referent, but whose historicity makes it legible as the form of a specific social experience. For Barlow, the concept of "woman" in Chinese has no adequate referent, yet empirical women nevertheless situate themselves in relation to it. Catachreses have an "occulted quality; they are repositories of past meaning."[105] An aspect of the specific social experience residing within the concept of the face in film theory is certainly the colonial encounter with otherness and its repercussions for identity, making the face a harbor of a scientistic physiognomy as well as its converse of illegibility and mysticism. But the more subterranean and persistent social experience (which is, nevertheless, *not* separable from colonialism), evidenced in symptomatic moments in Balázs and Epstein, is the accelerating mediation of technology and its consequences for intersubjectivity, the way in which screens, beginning with cinema, increasingly interrupt and yet mime face-to-face contact. This condition is construed as a loss, on a par with (and allied to) that of Babel and its universal language—a loss of the fantasized immediacy, transparency, and presence of face-to-face communication. The cinema both returns us to the face and takes it away.

It is only in the later years of the silent cinema that the face is sutured to revelation of character in the service of narrative. Before this consolidation, one of the earliest genres is that of the facial expression film, a single close-up of a contorting face, and that face is almost always a female face or the face of a female impersonator (a mask of a mask, as it were). *Facial Expressions* (Edison, 1902), in which a woman crosses her eyes, scrunches up her face, stretches her mouth, and so on, is perhaps the purest example (fig. 3.16). Here there is a complete absence of motivation and a pure play with the plasticity of the face. In *Anna Held* (AM&B, 1902), the woman, with wild, histrionic acting, talks, sings, gesticulates, swinging a martini glass in a performance of sheer hyperbole (fig. 3.17). Gilbert Saroni, a well-known female impersonator, enacts the malleability of the female face in *Goo Goo Eyes* (Edison, 1903), transferring his vaudeville persona to the screen (fig. 3.18). He plays a similar role in *The Old Maid in the Drawing Room* (Edison, 1901); the Edison catalog asserted, "Her facial expressions are extremely humorous and when the picture was first shown in New York City, the audience was convulsed with laughter."[106] *Sweets for the Sweet* (AM&B, 1903) is motivated by a gift of candy that is simply a pretext for a display of expressions, and *The Rose* (AM&B, 1903) is structured in a similar way (fig. 3.19). While some of these films focus on the mobility, changeability, and performativity of a peripatetic

3.16 *Facial Expressions* (Edison, 1902). Courtesy of the Library of Congress.

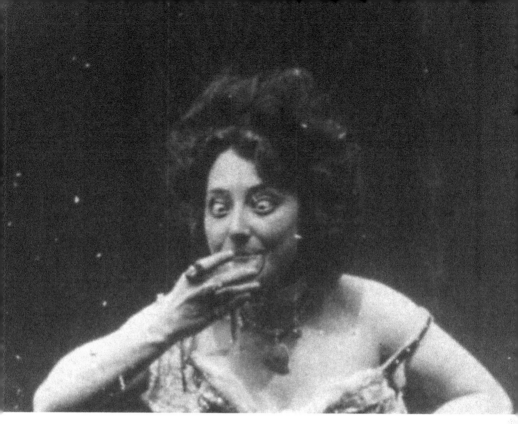

3.17 *Anna Held* (AM&B, 1902). Courtesy of the Library of Congress.

female face, others (*Facial Expressions, Goo Goo Eyes*) foreground the opacity of expression, its refusal to index an interiority. In line with Tom Gunning's "cinema of attractions," these faces directly face the spectator, refusing the profile of physiognomy. They resist physiognomic knowledge in their display of the rich contingency, multiplicity, and mobility of the cinematic image. The female face that is situated as more expressive becomes excessively, hysterically expressive and, in doing so, becomes a kind of noise in the system. The much commented upon *Photographing a Female Crook* (AM&B, 1904) displays this trajectory quite explicitly. The woman resists the identification practices of the Bertillon system as the camera reenacts that process of framing the face by moving closer and closer to its subject (fig. 3.20). Although this short film is similar to the photographic scenarios discussed earlier in which male criminals also attempt to resist the unwanted surveillance of the camera, the additional element here of the film camera gradually moving closer situates the woman as trapped in the double pincers of moving and still camera, so that her illegible facial movements/expressions are paradoxically

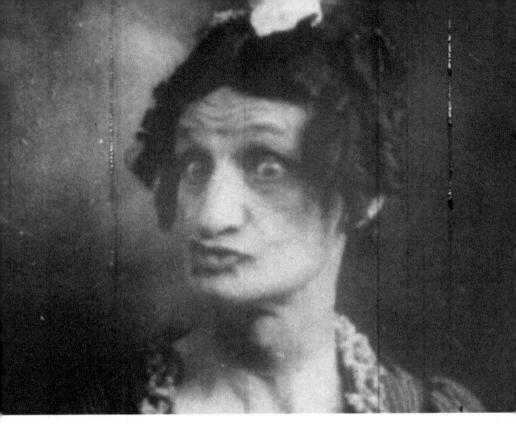

3.18 *Goo Goo Eyes* (Edison, 1903). Courtesy of the Library of Congress.

fixed by the encroachment of an apparatus representing movement itself. To assume the face as a mask rather than a transparent window is for Lavater the greatest threat to physiognomy, and in explaining the reasons for eliminating the actual face as his object of study in favor of artistic representations, it is symptomatic that he replaces the generic "he," at least momentarily, with a "she":

> But my observations must be exact; they must be repeated and tested often. How can that be possible if I have to make these observations on the sly? Isn't it presumptuous to analyze faces? And if a humble person notices that she is being observed, won't she turn away and hide her face? Indeed, it is here that I encountered one of the greatest obstacles to my studies; anyone who notices that he or she is being observed either puts up resistance or dissimulates. How can I get around this problem? Perhaps in the following way.

I retire into solitude; I place before me a medallion or a piece of antique sculpture, the sketches of a Raphael, the apostles as depicted by Van Dyck, the portraits of Houbraken. These I can observe at will.[107]

To produce usable knowledge, Lavater must turn away from the human face, which especially in the case of the woman, is prone to dissimulation and resistance.

These short films situate the woman as the site of a privileged performance of faciality. Disfiguring the face, they disallow access to an interiority.[108] To turn one's back on the camera would seem to be the greatest revolt against physiognomy. However, even at an early stage, films move to assimilate that gesture by articulating it with a meditation on the signifying powers of the

3.19 *The Rose* (AM&B, 1903). Courtesy of the Library of Congress.

3.20 *Photographing a Female Crook* (AM&B, 1904). Courtesy of the Library of Congress.

cinema itself. *One Way of Taking a Girl's Picture* (AM&B, 1904) is a demonstration of the technique of the close-up, a rationalization for the camera moving closer to its subject (figs. 3.21–3.23). *In My Lady's Boudoir* (AM&B, 1903) exploits the classical affiliation of female vanity with the mirror, requiring a detour through the image in the mirror to the woman who primps and makes herself up so that turning away from the camera is of no avail (figs. 3.24, 3.25). Given the woman's position and various poses, that mirror image is intermittently hidden, but the film's aspiration is to make all dimensions accessible, to demonstrate that the camera's vision is ubiquitous, extending even to the "other side" of its object.

The trope of feminine beauty, demanding harmony and proportion, is often at odds with the dictate that women are more emotive, with access to a greater range of facial expressions than men. But at the same time, women are more transparent precisely because they cannot control those emotions; the emotions are involuntary and burst through the facial/dermal membrane, aligning them with irrationality. Georg Simmel saw the human face as a battleground between irrationality (the uncontrolled inscription of emotions that could not be codified and was aligned with individuality) and the rational (embodied in the symmetry of the face; the twoness of the eyes, the cheeks, the ears; and the mirror structure of the two sides of the face[109]—this is why, in Simmel's view, dissymmetry is monstrous). Rationality in its generalizability was incommensurate with individuality, which always connotes a oneness, a singularity, a particularity. The latter site of the battleground articulates the face with singularity, contingency, and a certain unknowability—the very guarantees of an individuality increasingly desirable in a modern era of mass media and global networks. The former articulates it with generalizability and ultimately a universal comprehensibility. Physiognomy, for the most part, operates to reduce singularity and individuality and submit them to reason and a universal law (the notions of a natural or universal language). This struggle is played out in the contradictions of Brewster's 1914 essays attempting to deal with facial expression in the cinema. Brewster is intensely aware of the attractiveness of a singular, unspecifiable individuality and at the same time is drawn to physiognomy's apparent guarantee of a scientific ground.

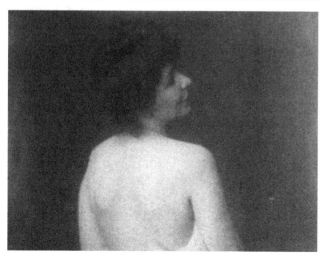

3.21–3.23 *One Way of Taking a Girl's Picture* (AM&B, 1904). Courtesy of the Library of Congress.

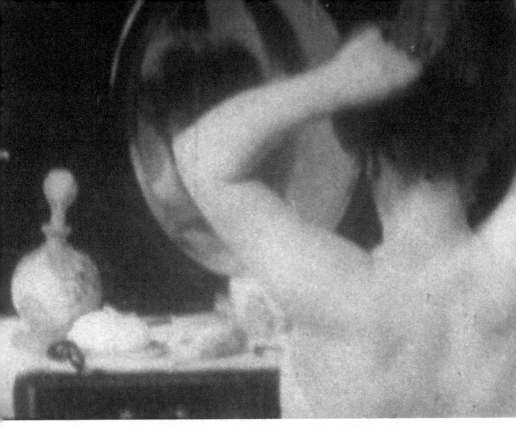

3.24 & 3.25 *In My Lady's Boudoir* (AM&B, 1903). Courtesy of the Library of Congress.

But are the concepts of the individual and the universal irreconcilable?[110] Neither are ahistorical concepts, but they achieve a quite specific inflection in modernity, whose institutions provide a normative structure of identity and individuality, a concept of what it means to be a "person," a "self." Claims to universality are always particular claims, arising in a specific sociohistorical and ideological milieu. The residue of physiognomy's particularity is, among other effects, racism. But in order to claim universality—a natural language of expression with global reach for example—particularity must be displaced *elsewhere*. The individual, with their limited ability to resist laws, regularities, conventions, and defined normalities, provides that other place increasingly in modernity, with its need to provide an escape hatch from the growing hegemony of commodity capitalism and the media networks that instantiate it. With mediation the norm, the purported immediacy of the face serves as an alternative. Its effacement of the concept of medium and promise of immediate access to signification elsewhere redoubles and certifies that of the cinema itself.

Yet, as Walter Benjamin maintained, the early years of a new technology of representation often provide the utopian promise of a postauratic aura. The daguerreotype, for example, was an inscription of a temporal duration and richness lost in the age of the instantaneous snapshot.[111] In the earliest years of the cinema, and particularly in the facial expression genre with its embrace of the grimace and nonsense, one can get a glimpse, with respect to the face and all its historical fetishizations, of more intensive scenarios of blockage, the generation of a face not as promising a hidden but legible interiority but as pure surface of transformation in time, as a proclamation that this—this face, this mutability—is all there is to be seen. There is no behind or inside. One would be tempted to call this *defacement*. As Michael Taussig has pointed out, the term "defacement" conjoins the face and sacrilege in a secular society, suggesting that the face has become sacred and that the

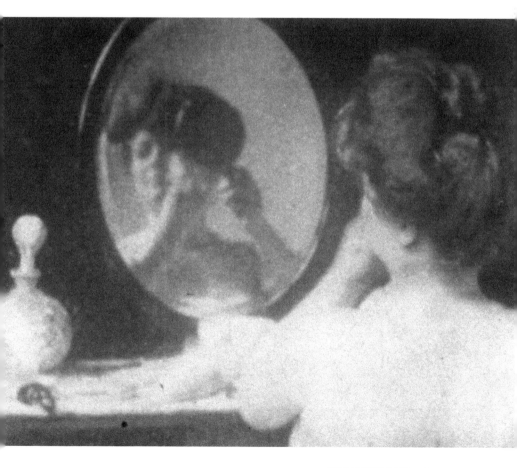

greatest transgression is that of removing or destroying a face.[112] In his view, the face participates culturally in a dialectical dance of window and mask, transparency of an interiority whose legibility is universal and impenetrable surface (the mark of a resistant singularity, i.e., individuality)—an unavoidable oscillation.[113] Attempts in the early years of the cinema to come to terms with the face as cinematic participate, ineluctably, in this tango of modernity.

PART II
SCALE/
SCREEN

Chapter 4

Screens, Female Faces, and Modernities

Prelude: Technologies of the Erotic
and the Faces of Women

Much of my interest in the cinematic close-up has been motivated by two kinds of fascination: the first with the way the close-up is used in particular films, its relation to space/scale, its relation to the face—historically situated in Western culture as a strong signifier of expressivity (and therefore of the division between inside and outside—"the face as the expression of the soul"); the second with the way in which the close-up has been used in film theory from the outset as a privileged figure of cinematic specificity (not accessible to the art that has most frequently been used as a point of comparison—theater) and as a unit of cinematic language (one of the few that is isolable). Close-ups of the faces of women act as a kind of hinge between these two concerns. They seem to occasion hyperbolic discourses that conjoin a meditation on the surplus meanings of that face with proclamations of its intimate alliance with the cinema as a machine, its filmic specificity. For Henri Langlois, for instance, Louise Brooks is "the modern actress par excellence because, like the statues of antiquity, she is outside of time. . . . She is the intelligence of the cinematographic process, she is the most perfect incarnation of photogénie" (fig. 4.1).[1] And for Roland Barthes, "Garbo belongs to that moment in cinema when capturing the human face still plunged audiences into the deepest ecstasy, when one literally lost oneself in a human image as one would in a philtre,

4.1 Louise Brooks, publicity photograph.

when the face represented a kind of absolute state of the flesh, which could be neither reached nor renounced" (fig. 4.2).[2] As the equivalent of a Platonic idea, Garbo marked a historical transition from "awe to charm." While Garbo's face is a white mask with eyes like "wounds" that are nevertheless not expressive, Audrey Hepburn's face is mobile, animated—"constituted by an infinite complexity of morphological functions." Although Barthes claims to be merely documenting a historical passage from Garbo as Idea to Hepburn

4.2 Greta Garbo, publicity photograph.

as Event, it is clear that he prefers the face of Garbo, whose function goes beyond that of expressing emotions and occasions a generalized, even transcendent, rapture. Hepburn's face, on the other hand, is earthbound, mundane, conventional. In these philosophical discourses/love letters, it seems there can be only one face—for Langlois, "There is no Garbo! There is no Dietrich! There is only Louise Brooks!"[3] The cinematic female face paradoxically combines individuality or singularity with the generalizability of a theorem.

陶樂斯德里奧最近她把頭髮截短了，而且，更把她燙捲起平，一切裝飾都變換過，如是她成為一個極摩登的姑娘，圖為她在新片 Dance Of Desire. 中化裝及其表情。

4.3 Dolores del Río in *Ling Long Women's Magazine*, no. 129 (1934).

Apparently forgotten in this awed reverence is the extent of the anxiety about magnitude and monstrous scale in the early years of the cinema discussed in chapter 2. Close-ups violated the demand for naturalistic "life-size" images and were the occasion for anxious and hostile diatribes in the press. On the one hand, close-ups were perceived as monstrous or grotesque due to their sheer size—an affront to the harmony and classical proportion associated with the human body. On the other hand, they threatened the norm of the mimetic body through an untenable and frightening fragmentation. Although there is no distinction between male and female faces in this discourse, a specifically cinematic device—the close-up—was aligned with castration, a psychic threat to masculinity. Latent in the defensive adoration of Barthes and Langlois are the traces of this trauma.

It would be highly inaccurate, of course, to suggest that only women have close-ups. But the attraction of a Rudolph Valentino or a John Wayne is more likely to be associated with the entire body. The racial otherness of Sessue Hayakawa allows him to be an exception, and both Jean Epstein and Béla Balázs are eloquent in their description of the nuances and slight tics of his facial expressions in close-up. Yet it is women's faces that are pervasive in movie and fan magazines that span cultures. Both Western and Chinese stars are the supports of the iconography of the female face in *Ling Long Women's Magazine*, published in Shanghai from 1931 to 1937 (figs. 4.3, 4.4).[4] Close-ups of men (and some of women) generally react, express, produce meaning. But the specificity of the woman's face in close-up is that it can be there simply to solicit looking—deprived of any semantic dimension. The force of Laura Mulvey's essay on visual pleasure lay in her analysis of the woman's position in the apparatus of looking constituted by cinema. As I argued many years ago, veils over a woman's face in the Hollywood cinema (exemplified by Josef von Sternberg's images of Marlene Dietrich) indicate that the depth behind the surface is only another surface.[5] An alignment with the two-dimensional image, the surface of the screen, the surface in itself, appears to come more readily to the iconography of women, who are often there simply to be envisaged—both visualized and transformed into a face.

我們的電影皇后胡蝶女士

4.4 Hu Die in *Ling Long Women's Magazine*, no. 129 (1934).

However, this face resists another discourse about the face in close-up—that which makes it the basis of the theme of the cinema as a universal language as analyzed in chapter 3. For the face as pure surface blocks its legibility, and legibility is a requirement for this theme. Born of the colonialist enterprise, which forced a recognition of difference and hence a desire for sameness, the idea of a universal language was often explicitly racist. Béla Balázs's claim that the cinema was a universal language is buttressed by a reference to "universally comprehensible facial expressions and gestures, every nuance of which is understood by princess and working girl alike from San Francisco to Smyrna."[6] He asserted that the cinema would produce and disseminate *"the unique, shared psyche of the white man"* and "a uniform type of the white race."[7] The faces of women as surface, as disallowing depth, produce noise within this system, for their faces are *seen*, not *read*—they cannot be universally legible. Interestingly, Balázs uses women who represent different classes—the princess and the working girl—to buttress his argument of universal comprehension. And the shift to race as the decisive difference is aligned with an idealized concept of desexualized, raced beauty ("a uniform type of the white race"). But he does not discuss what it is that the princess and the working girl are watching or how they might be portrayed on the screen. All of these differences—sexual, class, and racial—are in play in the search for a universal language. But women (usually white women) constitute a quite precise problem, a blockage. For while women's faces are allegedly more expressive, the abstract concept of beauty, the positioning of women in relation to looking, requires a certain immobility and hence a lack of expression, aligning the woman's face with a *screen* upon which anything can be projected.

In this prelude to a discussion of the close-up and women's faces, modernity and urban spaces, and the relation of all of these to the concept of the screen, I would like to examine two cinematic examples, from different eras and across cultures, that explicitly delineate the woman's face as having a particularly intimate relation with filmic technology—with the image, the screen, and the classical configuration of spectatorship. The first is a technological phenomenon—the tendency to use women's faces as a measure and anchor for variations in tone and color across film stocks. This is a cultural technique that has recently been "rediscovered" by artists and deployed in conflicting ways. The second is an Iranian film by Abbas Kiarostami, *Shirin*, made in 2008, that offers an intensive study of the faces of women as screens and as facing the screen. These two examples destabilize the hegemonic discourses of beauty, individuality, and universality that have been historically associated with the face.

Within the interstices of film movement in the classical era resided what is perhaps one of the most telling instances of situating the female face as screen, as technological support of the process of imaging. The leader of a 16mm or 35mm film (blank film at the beginning and end designed to protect the film during storage and threading in the projector and known as "SMPTE Universal Leader") is usually unseen by the audience unless a projectionist makes an error in threading. But sometimes spectators do catch glimpses of this concealed section, which, in addition to protection, has a twofold technical function. On the one hand, it contains a numerical countdown (8-7-6-5, etc.), with a bleep sounding at the moment of the number 2's appearance to guarantee that sound is synchronized with image. Its other technical role has to do with color timing, the process of ensuring that color balance and tonal density remain consistent across shots taken at different times or locations or perhaps with different film stock. This is done by juxtaposing a posing woman, often in close-up, with a color bar (figs. 4.5, 4.6). These images are embedded within the leader and often consist of only three or four frames so that, at twenty-four frames per second, they are barely glimpsable. They exist only as the signal of a technological function. Women's faces were used, allegedly, given their "smooth skin" and the fact that "women's skin was thought to offer a particularly nuanced tonal gauge."[8] In the Hollywood context, this skin was always white, and the technical management of color was fully aligned with the dominance of white flesh. As Richard Dyer has demonstrated with respect to lighting technology (but also color technologies), "The photographic media and, *a fortiori*, movie lighting assume, privilege and construct whiteness . . . so much so that photographing non-white people is typically construed as a problem."[9]

In the Hollywood industry, these women were referred to as "China Girls" or "China Dolls," although there is great uncertainty about the origin of this nomenclature. They appeared in every country that had a major film industry (Sweden, Germany, France, China, India, Japan), but in their U.S. incarnations they were always white. China Doll is a common name for a doll made of porcelain, a material whose clarity, whiteness, resonance, and translucence would have seemed compatible with the requirements of producing subtle color balance. Yet the term "China Doll" is also a Western stereotype referring to the racist belief that Asian women are docile, submissive, the simple carriers of meaning—the *screen* for its display.

The posing of the women brings to bear all the weighty codification of classical cinema's representation of women in relation to beauty, attractiveness, and "star qualities." The China Girls enable the incorporation of the female stereotype/icon/image into the technical apparatus to guarantee its verisimilitudinous functioning ("believable" color, matched to skin tone). The term "stereotype" traces its history to yet another technology of reproduction—printing. Originally, a stereotype was a duplicate impression in metal of an original typographical form, used in the actual printing of a text instead of the original. It thus connoted secondariness, nondifferentiation, and invariability—meanings that were displaced onto its current colloquial usage as signifying a predictable, stable, overused, and unnuanced "type." The effectivity of mechanical reproducibility is to a large extent what is at stake in the phenomenon of the China Girl. The standardization of the female face and its use as a technical measure reveal a great deal about the historical situation of that visage as ground of representation.[10]

In recent years, artists have revived and reinterrogated the China Girl in a practice that reactivates found footage. An exhibition of photographs by Julie Buck and Karin Segal, titled *Girls on Film*, consists of seventy images of China Girls, salvaged from old film leaders and subjected to a process of enlargement, editing, and digital rehabilitation, removing scratches and countering the fading of the film over time.[11] What emerge are glamorous Hollywood-style portraits, rescuing the women from their historical oblivion and returning to them the status of star. Much of the critical commentary on the exhibition as well as Buck and Segal's own discourse locates the pathos of these images in the fact that these women (office and lab assistants, secretaries, as well as some aspiring actresses) never attained the celebrity status they mimed so desperately within this concealed realm of the cinema. The artists mourn the fact that the identities of these women will never be known and harbor a desire that one of them will recognize herself in the exhibition and come forward. What we witness in the China Girl phenomenon is the hollowed-out form of the star system, its evisceration—the impossible oxymoron of the anonymous star. In these hidden "screen tests," the figure of the star is drained of its most essential traits—recognition and recognizability—and the female face becomes sheer surface. Michelle Silva's short film *China Girls* (2006), on the other hand, does not perform any digital manipulation on the images, preserving the scratches, flaws, and fading that are the marks of the work of time on celluloid and contribute to the historicization of these faces (figs. 4.7, 4.8). *China Girls* is a montage of countdowns and glimpses of China Girls, retaining the bleep at the appearance of the number 2, as well as the sounds of technicians' voices, the scratching of film against the projector's sound head, and frequency signals. The China Girls here are "left in their natural habitat of countdowns and endtones."[12] The film does not collaborate or negotiate with the star system's problematic of recognition and glamorous identity but, instead, reveals the intricate entangling of a fundamental female anonymity and crisis of recognition with the substrate of classical cinematic representation.

Also situating women in relation to the screen in a quite different but equally provocative context, Abbas Kiarostami's *Shirin* (2008) has been labeled a minimalist or conceptual film. It consists simply of looks—women's looks in close-up at what we are led to imagine is a movie screen. The evidence is the soundtrack of a film that we never see. We are confronted only with the women's faces, sometimes neutral, unreadable, sometimes following an action with their eyes or reacting to a particularly violent moment, in a theater whose audience is composed primarily of women, with a few men in shadow in the background. At least that is what the film seems to be. However, it was shot by Kiarostami in his living room, and the women are responding to his off-screen directions. They are shot in close-up, foregrounding one at a time, professional actresses (including one European, Juliette Binoche) pretending to be spectators (fig. 4.9). But there is no film. Indeed, Kiarostami did not decide what the imagined/suggested film would be (he had only a general idea of a melodrama) until after the women's "reactions" were filmed.[13] The reactions precede their source. The film allegedly screened is adapted from a well-known Persian tragic romance by Nizami Ganjavi, *Khosrow and Shirin*. The soundtrack we hear was constructed with dialogue, horses' hooves clattering, rain, footsteps, and other sound effects and a music track. *Khosrow and Shirin* is the story of a love triangle and unresolved love.

Shirin invites us to watch the women watching. Usually, a movie theater is a place where one can be confident of not being seen, of being able to see surreptitiously without being seen oneself. There is something obscene about such an exposure. *Shirin* documents, or, more accurately, presents a fiction of, modes of viewing a film (Kiarostami has said that he no longer knows how to define the difference between documentary and fiction).[14] The lighting suggests the flickering of a film, and the melodramatic music implies an intense engagement with that film. Unlike a radio drama, *Shirin* insinuates that there is something there to be seen, that the women are looking not toward a camera but toward a screen—a screen that is, ironically, off-screen.

4.5 & 4.6 China Girls from film leaders.

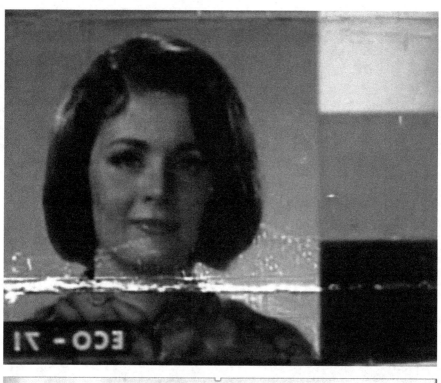

4.7 & 4.8 *China Girls* (Michelle Silva, 2006, 16mm, 3 min.).

4.9 *Shirin* (Abbas Kiarostami, 2008).

There are precedents of films that take reception as their subject matter, briefly in Godard's *Vivre sa vie* (1962) where Anna Karina, in close-up, cries during a screening of Carl Theodor Dreyer's *The Passion of Joan of Arc* (1928) and in a more extended fashion in Tsai Ming-Liang's *Goodbye, Dragon Inn* (2003), set in a dilapidated movie theater, on the verge of destruction, the attendance sparse on the final night, and the "narrative" a chronicle of missed sexual encounters. But in *Vivre sa vie*, the film is not absent—we see close-ups of Joan/Falconetti in Dreyer's film—and in *Goodbye, Dragon Inn*, we do not experience the real time of being a spectator, watching the film within the film. Instead, we are shown the activities and interactions that occupy the margins of the screen, its outside. The spectators seem to want to have nothing to do with watching the film—instead, they interact with each other through gazes or propped feet or seating choices; they wander the hallways outside the auditorium or frequent the toilets.

The women in *Shirin* look not directly at Kiarostami's camera but slightly above it, hence perpetuating the film's fictional status. They sometimes close their eyes or seem expressionless, but at intense moments they shed tears, and these moments are clearly edited to coincide with traumatic events in the narrative (e.g., when Shirin is left alone after her lover marries another for political reasons, or when Shirin kills herself at the end of the film). From that point of view, the film presents their faces as legible. But they are also, often, inscrutable, opaque. In addition, the critical response to the film often includes a commentary on the sheer beauty of the faces. (David Bordwell writes on his blog, "All are stunningly beautiful, whether young or old."[15] Kiarostami himself, when asked why he chose women rather than men to focus on, answers, "Because women are more beautiful, complicated and sensational. A combination of these three qualities makes them perfect candidates for movies and for being looked at.")[16] If the film were simply an extended investigation of the readability of faces, of how expressions are signified, or even of the infinite malleability of the face, men's faces could have been used. But it is crucial that the women are not simply looking—they are looked at. And in this sense, they signify differently, fitting well within the heritage of Barthes's and Langlois's relations to the faces of women.

In *Shirin*, the women are pretending to produce reactions to a film that is absent. In that sense as well, the film puts on display and subjects to doubt the readability of the face. That readability is manufactured through montage, in an elaborately extended Kuleshov effect in which the only "reverse shot" is a soundtrack. In this way, *Shirin* exposes the universal language trope—

the idea of the cinematic close-up as transparent and easily readable—as a carefully constructed yet fragile edifice. The face reveals only a masquerade.

The film also plays with (as do other Kiarostami films) the centrality of the shot/reverse shot construction in classical narrative cinema. If the shot/reverse shot is fundamental to the suturing effect of cinema, *Shirin* is its radical unraveling, exposing a gaping wound. We, the spectators, become the reverse shot that is never shown. Or we occupy the site of the film that is never shown. Bordwell writes that Kiarostami "has given us the first fiction film I know about the reception of a movie, or at least a heightened idea of a movie. What we see, in all these concerned, fascinated faces and hands that flutter to the face, is what we spectators look like—from the point of view of a film."[17] The fact that the story of Khosrow and Shirin was chosen in effect as an afterthought would seem to indicate that this narrative, the content of the unshown film, is irrelevant. But there is a moment toward the end of the film when Shirin, immediately after Khosrow dies, seems to directly address the audience within the film, beseeching, "And here we are. Me, Khosrow, and you, my grieving sisters. You look at his dead body and you cry. You listen to my story and you cry. Through these tears, I see your eyes. Are you shedding these tears for me, Shirin? Or for the Shirin that hides in each one of you?" Since the image is hidden, it is not possible to tell whether Shirin is addressing an internal, diegetic audience (there is wailing on the soundtrack) or whether, from the depths of a missing reverse shot, the 113 women we have seen in close-up for eighty-five minutes are being directly addressed. Or whether we are being directly addressed. The film leaves this undecidable.

The significance of films like *Shirin* and Michelle Silva's *China Girls* is that they expose the way in which women's faces are not simply a kind of privileged content of the cinema but instead are bound up in, implicated in the technology and techniques of the cinema and its apparatuses—the screen, the celluloid, the camera, the spectator. While the tropes of beauty and expressivity clearly precede the birth of the cinema, the cinema subjects them to operations of its own, inextricable from the very mode of its functioning. As the preeminent art form of the twentieth century, the cinema rehearses, in different contexts, the tension of the historical alignment of the face with, on the one hand, individuality, particularity, singularity and, on the other, a universal readability. The female face in the cinema does not seem to fit comfortably within either pole of the opposition. Although the viewer of Shirin enters the theater knowing that this is an Iranian film with its own specific cultural context, that the women wearing the *roosari* are fulfilling a particular religious convention, and that the narrative of this Persian love story "told" by the film the women watch is also historically distinctive and part of a specific cultural heritage, it is highly significant that Kiarostami situates this drama in a placeless space. We have no sense of spatial orientation; there is no establishing shot that shows the relation of the women to each other or the type of movie theater they are inhabiting (or where the theater is). This is the epitome of Marc Augé's non-place—the type of place exemplified by airports, malls, train stations, cinemas, and so forth; the type of place that one travels through and that is completely generic and recognizable no matter where it is located geographically; the type of place that undoes the concept of an anthropological place.[18] The soundtrack's narrative, *Khosrow and Shirin*, is transformed into a universal love story, accessible to all. Even the roosari, which all of the women wear, seems simply to act as a frame for the face, a cultural specificity that is annulled in an aesthetic gesture of isolating and insisting upon the face as outside of space and time—the face we are all asked to assume in the movie theater.

Recognition and the Face as Screen/Screened

Physiology and phrenology were historical responses to both urban and global confrontations with the Other. The multitudes of strangers and racial others posed problems of recognition and recognizability, both strongly linked to the legibility of the face. The face would seem to be the very locus of recognition and its potential failure. What is at stake in this problematic is a positivity, a characteristic that specifies, an identity that unifies and makes coherent and legible a person. And because gender has been for so long the buttress of all that is "natural," "universal," and the source of "stable values," it unavoidably drags along with it the premise of immediate recognition ("It's a boy" or "It's a girl" being the first and most formative moment of interpellation of identity). In this respect, it is the concepts of recognition and recognizability as social and cultural processes grounding a sexual politics that demand analysis. The concept of recognition bears within it the potential of a structuring contradiction—while the preface "re" denotes a repetition of a past event of knowing, in usage, the term is frequently employed to specify an immediate or instantaneous understanding. The *OED*'s etymology of the term traces it to the Latin *cognoscere*, to know, and the prefix *re*, "with the general sense of 'back' or 'again'"—hence, to know again.[19] "To recognize" a person, word, or place means that one has previously experienced or known that entity, and hence a comparison is being made between two moments of time, a past and a present, and a continuity between them is posited ("to recall knowledge of: make out as or perceive to be something previously known").[20] Yet recognition also bears the meanings "to perceive clearly: be fully aware of," "to acknowledge formally," and "to admit the fact or existence of"—all of which sanction the negation of the past, of the "re."[21] Recognition of someone in a meeting authorizes that person to speak, acts as a form of pointing, acknowledges an existence and a right, in the present tense.

Hence, the concept of recognition bears within it both a present entitlement or acknowledgment and a temporal doubling, a haunting of present knowledge by the past. The past instance of knowledge stamps and guarantees the present as authentic ("I recognize you"), while the present performative utterance, sanctioning speech, also acts as a form of guarantee or authorization. The dualism is particularly poignant in the case of recognizing a person. For to forget an other is often read as an insult, a de-authorization, a consignment to nonexistence, as well as evidence of a treacherous breach between past and present. And it is the face that combines both recognition's reference to history and a sense of pure presence, a face that in mainstream cinema is insistently sexually specified, gendered. To analyze the work of recognition and recognizability is to probe, warily, the very bases of the category of gender.

The cinema provides a rich and productive arena for the study of processes of recognition, particularly in relation to the human face and its deployment in close-ups and scenes with a certain affective epiphany. The star system itself, with its massive machinery promoting repetition and recognition, hinges on the simultaneous uniqueness and generality of the individual face and its continuity over a multiplicity of roles. This is generally recognized as true for the mainstream cinema of the twentieth century, but what of the avant-garde, a cinema that is usually situated outside of the star system (with the exception, perhaps, of Andy Warhol)? For it is the avant-garde that feminist film theory has embraced as a radical alternative precisely because it troubles representation and, in the process, disrupts any immediacy of recognition.[22] An obsession with the female face as screen, as support of representation but also as support of the conundrum of recognition, recognizability, and otherness, conjoins the concerns of the avant-garde with the concerns of mass culture. Both attempt to come to terms with the problem of mediation and loss—the loss precisely that of an alleged immediacy and knowability seemingly guaranteed by face-to-face communication. What is interesting to me in this respect is the extent to which it is the white female face that acts as the figure of this anxiety about legibility, both in the avant-garde and in classical cinema—two cinemas that historically have been pitted against each other.

The tendency to polarize the avant-garde and mass culture intermittently throughout the twentieth century has had a negative impact on our understanding of the intricate relations and complicities between the two. This situation has been recognized and addressed by a number of theorists, including Andreas Huyssen and Jonathan Crary, among others.[23] Here, however, I would like to focus on a particular aspect of this relationship that figures critical intersections between technologies, faces, subjectivities, and knowledges—one that is, of course, inflected by understandings of sexual difference, and one whose reading is also informed by the current interest in archaeologies of technologies (especially of mechanical and electronic reproduction). The technology here is the seemingly basic and simple one of the screen, one that we tend to take for granted as having the minor role of substrate and support of a representation.[24] Here, I would like to isolate a certain phenomenon—a tendency exhibited in two widely different types of films—to situate the "modern" female face as a screen, doubling and representing the function of the cinematic screen as support, carrier of the image.

The screen is the largely unthought ground of imagistic representation in both mass culture and the avant-garde (excluding various early experiments with split-screen, widescreen, and multiple screen processes, and at least until the advent of the notion of "expanded cinema" in the 1960s and 1970s).[25] In the realm of mass culture, the "Screen" was for a very long time simply a synonym for the Cinema. The *OED* cites a 1915 reference in a film magazine to "screen fever."[26] But the term precedes the emergence of cinema and, as the *OED* outlines, was initially used to denote a form of concealment or protection: the first definition given is "a contrivance for warding off the heat of a fire or a draught of air" (examples range from 1393 to 1899).[27] In the seventeenth and eighteenth centuries, small handheld screens, often with decoration, were produced to shield ladies' faces from the fire in a home fireplace. These screens were also like fans, according to Erkki Huhtamo, and acted as "objects of fashion, aesthetic pleasure, and erotic play. Veiling one's face behind a hand-screen incited desire and curiosity, like a mask; hiding and revealing were indistinguishable aspects of this 'screen play.'"[28] The protection extended to other potentially dangerous or uncomfortable threats, including the gaze.[29] The semantic transformation from barrier/defense to ground or support of images seems to have been consolidated with the projection of images in magic lanterns and phantasmagoria. The *OED* cites a reference from 1810: "To make Transparent Screens for the Exhibition of the Phantasmagoria." The term "screen" came to denote a surface or support for the exhibition of images. The etymological trajectory of the word traces a movement from a technology designed to protect a woman's face (from fire or the male gaze) to a technology designed to intercept a beam of light in order to make images visible on a mass scale, enabling an industry that would thrive on the exhibition of the female face.

There is an insistent and recurrent scene in Hollywood narrative cinema that plays out certain permutations of screening, identity, knowledge, and the female face. In it, a male character, constantly on the lookout for a lost object of desire, sees from behind a woman with the same hairdo as that of his lost love and with great anticipation approaches her only to find, when she turns her face toward him, that she is not the one he sought.[30] The intensity of the desire is often marked by a frenetic chase or a tracking shot moving steadily toward the woman. Often this happens in an urban setting, on the street, in the midst of crowds of nameless and unknown passersby, invoking the uniquely modern cliché of the "faceless crowd." According to Joe Milutis, "The city's relation to the face, the major trope of which is 'the faceless crowd,' is productive of one of the great cliches of the movies."[31] In the midst of overwhelming anonymity, of the faceless crowd, only one face will do, and it is one that is tauntingly suggested but absent. This scene resonates with a crisis of knowledge and knowability and can be found in films as varied as *The Fabulous Baker Boys* (1989), *Funny Face* (1957), *My Fair Lady* (1964), and *Vertigo* (1958). It marks a trauma of recognition, desire, and loss circulating around the face as screen (for the projection of a memory) and screened. But it is a trauma that is not unique to the Hollywood narrative cinema, although it may be here that it finds the terms of its most explicit enunciation as psychological trauma, embedded within the narrative. The avant-garde has also historically struggled with issues of recognition, the vacillation of knowability and unknowability, visibility and invisibility, and the screen as support of the image. And much of this interrogation has, tellingly, circulated around the trope of the female face as screen.

The historical avant-garde produced a host of experiments with light and projection, including the films of Hans Richter and Viking Eggeling, Man Ray, and Fernand Léger, as well as Marcel Duchamp's *Anemic Cinema* (1926). Not infrequently, these experiments deployed the female face or body in a privileged manner as screen, as support of the play of light and image. Man Ray's *Le retour à la raison* (1923) cuts from a suspended geometric mobile spinning and producing a play of shadows on the wall behind to the torso of a woman, itself the receptacle of or screen for the performance of light and shadow (figs. 4.10–4.12). The cut here marks a significant conjunction, a bleeding of meaning between object and subject, representation and screen, projection and surface. The first shots trace the turn of the mobile, its shadow separate from itself, doubling its movement on the wall behind. Different shots of the turning mobile and its shadow are superimposed. After the cut, the trope of the turn is taken up and reiterated by the naked torso of a woman at a window, her body acting as a screen to support the swirling play of light and shadow. No face, no limbs—just the merger of an eroticized and simultaneous fascination with breasts and with forms. The recognizability of the female body as female is not lost—to the contrary, that body is both support and supplement of representation. *Le retour à la raison* as a whole is a film obsessed with form and with the action of light and the impressionability of surfaces (many of the shots are rayograms, Man Ray's version of the photogram). Heidegger, for whom the dialectic between concealing and revealing is fundamental and whose work is permeated by metaphors of visuality, discusses the concept of the "shadow" in "The Age of the World Picture": "Everyday opinion sees in the shadow only the lack of light, if not light's complete denial. In truth, however, the shadow is a manifest, though impenetrable, testimony to the concealed emitting of light. In keeping with this concept of shadow, we experience the incalculable as that which, withdrawn from representation, is nevertheless manifest in whatever is, pointing to Being, which remains concealed."[32] For Heidegger, technology in the age when the world becomes picture is aligned with quantification, measurability, calculability, with the production, in modernity, of the object and objectivity over and against the subject of certainty and knowledge (of, in effect, the subject/object split). The avant-garde purports to interrogate cinema— as the technology of light and shadow and of movement's representation. It interrogates as well "everyday opinion," which "sees in the shadow only the lack of light, if not light's complete denial." The shadows in *Le retour* mark the body of the woman, producing it as aesthetic artifact. The shadow of the mobile in this film is separate from its object, clearly the object's projection on the wall/screen behind it. The shadows on the body of the woman, on the other hand, merge screen and object, producing that body as aesthetic surface. While it would be hazardous to "apply" Heidegger's categories of light and shadow directly to this film (or any film), it is also possible, indeed necessary, to note that *Le retour à la raison* struggles with the concept of the object

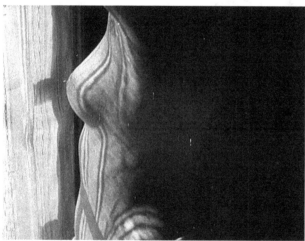

4.10–4.12 *Le retour à la raison* (Man Ray, 1923).

and its representability, struggles with mimesis and its relation to a dialectic of light and shadow, and, in the course of doing so, produces the female body as screen—screen as both access and defense (defense against capitulation to a vision of the whole). The trope of the "turn" is crucial here as well, resonating with the turn in the recurrent Hollywood scene of misrecognition discussed earlier. For the turn makes visible that which was concealed—the "other side"—an other side that does not materially exist in the two-dimensional realm of cinema but is continually evoked, imagined, assumed. Just as light reveals what was previously not accessible to vision, the turn is a constant reiteration of otherness and the limits of knowability, a denial of the sufficiency of the surface/screen. Knowledge resides *somewhere else*—behind, on the other side—or *inside*, within the depths signaled by the face.

In Man Ray's *Emak Bakia* (Basque for "leave me alone," 1926), it is the face of the woman that becomes the surface of display. Undulating lights and forms, incapable of retaining fixed or legible shapes, precede and overlay the face of the first woman, which is itself, with its prominent makeup, explicitly a painted surface (figs. 4.13, 4.14). The fleeting reflections generated by a revolving cube are projected onto the face of the second woman, who, like the first, stares directly at the camera (figs. 4.15, 4.16). The flower that introduces the image of the third woman becomes a shape projected onto a face that unhesitatingly and directly confronts the camera. All these shots foreground the act of opening one's eyes, while the plastic, mannequin-like quality of the fourth female figure is produced by doubling the representation of the eyes, using the eyelid itself as the carrier of the image (figs. 4.17, 4.18). The essential artificiality is flattened even further when her face becomes the screen for another image of her own face, upside down, now assuming the undulations and malleability of the original lights and forms.

A similar treatment of the female face emerges a bit later in the realm of mass culture—albeit in the work of a filmmaker, Busby Berkeley, who was strongly influenced by surrealism. In *Gold Diggers of 1935*, the well-known sequence "Lullaby of Broadway" opens with a woman's face, surrounded by blackness, gaining in scale as her head grows from a pinpoint on the screen to an extreme close-up (figs. 4.19, 4.20). As the woman's head rotates and she places a cigarette (a strongly marked signifier of modernity) between her lips, her face and any recognizable features are evacuated from the image and replaced by a highly stylized representation of an urban setting, which the camera gradually penetrates (figs. 4.21, 4.22). This gesture brackets a disturbing scene involving a woman's fall to her death at the height of the social frenzy

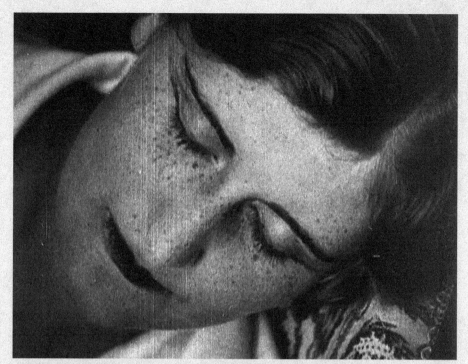

4.13 & 4.14 *Emak Bakia* (Man Ray, 1926).

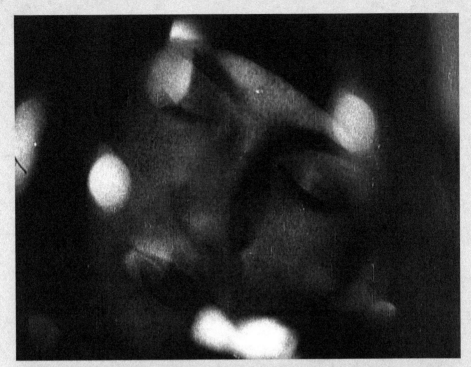

4.15 & 4.16 *Emak Bakia* (Man Ray, 1926).

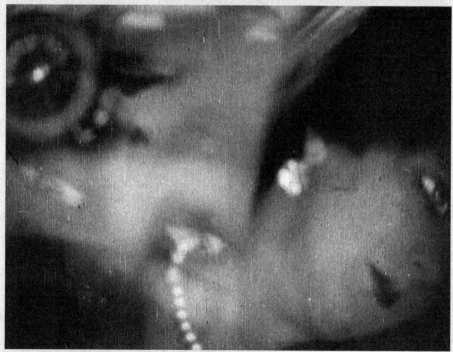

4.17 & 4.18 *Emak Bakia* (Man Ray, 1926).

4.19 & 4.20 *Gold Diggers of 1935* (Busby Berkeley, 1935).

4.21 & 4.22 *Gold Diggers of 1935* (Busby Berkeley, 1935).

of a party. Closure is attained by returning to the representation of the city, which is gradually relinquished as it dissolves into the same, now recognizable face of the woman, who turns and ultimately disappears again into the depths of the image as a point enveloped by blackness, the vanishing point of a nonperspectival image. It is not accidental that this, again, is the face of a woman, clearly specified as "modern," whose representation merges with that of a city—becomes, in effect, the screen for a city defined by a claustrophobia, a starkness, and a convoluted navigability. The special trope of cinematic modernity, the faceless crowd, is enacted through the loss of faciality and its supplementation by an urban space never quite knowable in its entirety, filled with unidentifiable strangers. By mapping the city onto the form of the female face, Berkeley intensifies the tropes of unknowability and unrecognizability. The city and the woman are both difficult to navigate, never quite specifiable, confounding the recognition traditionally aligned with the face.

For the historical avant-garde, emerging during the early years of film with an unbridled optimism about its possibilities, it was the very conditions of cinema—light, projection, movement, screen—that were at stake. But the excessively formal nature of these concerns seemed to require for its support a particular conceptualization of the female face, by definition, the *white*, Western female face. It was the face of the "modern woman," open, almost geometric in its clarity, serving to double the capacities of the screen, while signaling a certain historical specificity. For the woman's close affiliation with fashion aligns her with the perpetual production and redefinition of the new, with modernity itself. And as each new "modern" era redefines itself as new, the modern Western woman reemerges as the incarnation of the fashionable moment, whatever it might happen to be (bangs, straight hair, curly hair, short or long hair, thin eyebrows, thick eyebrows, etc.). To see the woman is to recognize most effectively and instantaneously the historical moment. In the 1960s and 1970s, this woman materializes most prominently in the avant-garde in the work of Andy Warhol and Jean-Luc Godard.

The fascination of the historical avant-garde—of László Moholy-Nagy, of Fernand Léger, of Man Ray and Marcel Duchamp—with light, reflection, and projection can be seen as an engagement with the intensive thinking of location and bodies in relation to location at the moment of the emergence of a cinematographic modernity. In the 1960s and 1970s, the filmic avant-garde, in a return to what it viewed as the ur-cinema, or the cinema before its rigidification by Hollywood classicism, and in a move deeply influenced by the historical avant-garde, resuscitated an obsession with projection and with light as

4.23 & 4.24 *Chelsea Girls*
(Andy Warhol, 1966).

medium. Andy Warhol's fixed camera stare was reminiscent of the Lumières, and he persistently explored the vicissitudes of different modes and manners of projecting his films. *Chelsea Girls* (1966) makes use of two projectors and of complex lighting schemes, coupled with the insistence upon a scriptless scenario of pure improvisation on the part of the actors. It is made up of twelve scenarios (single shots) of thirty minutes each, two projected simultaneously at all times. The specific configuration of each individual screening of this film is unique given the inevitably different rates of changing reels on the part of the projectionists.[33] The final scenario on the left, beginning with Nico crying, is an extended play with light, projection, and the face as screen.

In the beginning of this scene, Nico plays with a tape measure and a light meter, the tools of focus and lighting whose conventions are violently assaulted by the mode of filming. The coincidence of extreme affect—marked by Nico's tears in excruciatingly close close-up—and an extended and unrepentant camera stare dissolves into the reduction of face and body to a surface, a screen intercepting and displaying the movements of colored lights, textures, and patterns (in the mode of the strobe lighting so characteristic of the 1960s). The combination of excessively fast zooms in and out with the projected lights and patterns obscuring the face flattens screen space to the point where the face itself becomes the screen, blank space of reception and reflection of light (figs. 4.23, 4.24). Much as in Freud's scenario in "A Case of Paranoia Running Counter to the Psychoanalytic Theory of the Disease," the contortions of the body become the signs or symptoms of the work of an imaging system or technology, an apparatus of mechanical reproduction.[34] The fragmentation of the projected patterns combined with the extremity of the close-up troubles recognition and knowledge in their relation to the human face.

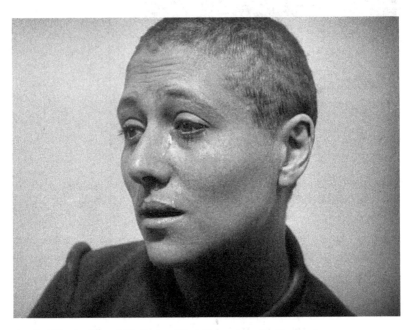

4.25 Carl Theodor Dreyer's *The Passion of Joan of Arc*, screened in *Vivre sa vie* (Jean-Luc Godard, 1962).

Jean-Luc Godard, as well, yokes together the female face and a problematics of the screen and knowability. When Nana (Anna Karina) in *Vivre sa vie* (1962) goes to the cinema, her face in close-up echoes the screen on which Dreyer's *The Passion of Joan of Arc* (1928) is playing (figs. 4.25, 4.26). A commentary on/critique of the notions of mimesis and identification (of Karina with Falconetti), the scene nevertheless resonates with the obsessive attention to faces and facing throughout the film, incarnated in the persistent return to scenes that invoke and adamantly avoid the structure of the shot/reverse shot. Yet it is the credit sequence that most explicitly situates Karina's face as both object of investigation and screen, bearer of writing and bearer of light and shadow (fig. 4.27). It is difficult to imagine Godard (or even Warhol, despite his fondness for the transgression of conventional gender identities) assigning the male face a similar function.

In Godard and Jean-Pierre Gorin's *Letter to Jane* (1972), Jane Fonda's face becomes the screen for the projection of an entire history of Hollywood facial expressions that convey, according to Godard and Gorin, only how much they know. The film consists of an extended semiotic and ideological analy-

4.26 *Vivre sa vie* (Jean-Luc Godard, 1962).

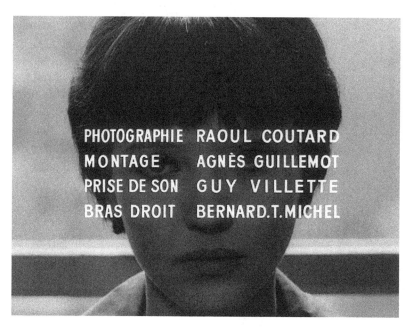

PHOTOGRAPHIE RAOUL COUTARD
MONTAGE AGNÈS GUILLEMOT
PRISE DE SON GUY VILLETTE
BRAS DROIT BERNARD.T.MICHEL

4.27 *Vivre sa vie* (Jean-Luc Godard, 1962).

4.28 *Letter to Jane* (Jean-Luc Godard and Jean-Pierre Gorin, 1972).

sis of a photograph of Jane Fonda listening to the North Vietnamese during a visit to Hanoi in 1972 (fig. 4.28). In their commentary, Godard and Gorin analyze the focus, framing, and "acting" in the photograph, and the object of their criticism, despite the fact of their awareness of a potentially problematic sexual politics, slides between the photograph itself and Jane Fonda as a "militant actress." Fonda's face, here, is isolated and acts as the screen for this masculine deconstruction, and her expression, they claim, reflects a history of similar expressions in Hollywood cinema and in politics—examples include Marlon Brando, Henry Fonda (fig. 4.29), Claudia Cardinale, and Richard Nixon. It is a "knowing expression that only says how much it knows." While Jane Fonda's face is an "expression of an expression" and a "function reflecting a function," the face of the North Vietnamese man in the background is a "function reflecting reality."[35] Godard and Gorin claim that the choice of Fonda's face (i.e., a female face) is contingent—she appeared both in their film *Tout va bien* and in the photo published in *L'Express.* Yet Fonda's presence in the photograph is, in the words of their commentary, that of a "star disguised and veiled by the absence of Max Factor." The strategy of using her face as privileged screen (screen as both ground of representation and act of concealment—of American imperialism, of New Deal humanism) also reflects the filmic history of Godard's use of the female face (as in, for instance, *Vivre sa vie*). Why, in the context of an otherwise self-conscious and politically engaged filmmaking practice, does the woman's face take on such a familiar function, simultaneously revealing in its exemplariness and concealing in its ideological work?

4.29 *Letter to Jane* (Jean-Luc Godard and Jean-Pierre Gorin, 1972).

What does it mean that these very different avant-garde practices in two historical periods—the 1920s and 1930s and the 1960s and 1970s—should persistently situate the woman's face as screen? For Huhtamo, the screen is a "liminal zone between the material and the immaterial, the real and the virtual."[36] The screen, in this sense, provides an alchemic transformation of the real into fantasy; it is a ground, a blankness upon which seemingly anything can be projected, eliciting psychoanalytic analyses. For Bertram Lewin, the support of a dream, the ground upon which its content resides, is a representation of the maternal breast, which acts as a "dream screen": "When one falls asleep, the breast is taken into one's perceptual world: it flattens out or approaches flatness, and when one wakes up it disappears, reversing the events of its entrance. A dream appears to be projected on this flattened breast— the dream screen."[37] Lewin himself has compared the dream screen to a movie screen.[38] Such a comparison yokes film viewing to a form of regression, complementing analyses by Jean-Louis Baudry and Christian Metz that also liken spectatorship to a dreaming that constitutes a psychical regression to a moment in time when perception and representation were fused. For the nursing baby, the breast is the world, and orality is paramount. There is no distinction between baby and breast—instead, this state is characterized by engulfment, immersion, a lack of the boundaries later constituted in the mirror phase. For Lewin, the dream screen represents the desire to sleep, while the contents of the dream, orchestrated by the ego and its censorship, condensation, and displacement, are attempts to awaken the sleeper. But the baby at the breast has no ego, and its sleep is pure, dreamless: "The blank dream screen is the copy of primary infantile sleep."[39] In the cinema, the narrative or action or characters tend to divert the spectator's attention from the screen as support, and a blank screen is extremely rare. But the desire to "go to the movies" is, in a sense, a desire for the screen (the "big" screen now, as opposed to the smaller screens of television and the computer, notepad, or mobile phone). This is simultaneously an anxious desire to be engulfed, to experience a nondifferentiated space—hence all the metaphors of devouring and engulfment in critical discourse on film explored in chapter 2. René Spitz, unlike Lewin, claims that the first visual percept is not the breast but the human face, specifically, the mother's face. But in the period before visual differentiation, the breast and the face merge: "The real point of juncture is to be found in the observation that the infant, while nursing at the breast, is at the same time staring at the mother's face; thus breast and face are experienced as one and indivisible."[40] For Spitz, the oral cavity is privileged as the site of the fulfillment of need, but it is also the place where the inner (the stimulations within the body, which are the only sensations of the infant at birth) and the outer (the nipple taken within the mouth) coincide: "It is here that all perception will begin; in this role the oral cavity fulfills the function of a bridge from internal reception to external reception. . . . In its nondifferentiation this world is the matrix of both introjection and projection."[41] It is significant that Spitz situates this phenomenon in relation to giganticism, noting that the "infant's face is one third the size of the adult's face," and "one begins to realize how gigantic the adult appears to the infant."[42] In this context, he cites *Gulliver's Travels*, mentioned by both Freud and Lewin, and the essential distortion of size and space experienced by the infant.

In this scenario, the dream screen of the breast is conflated with the mother's face, which might seem to offer an explanation for the tendency in both avant-garde film and mass culture to situate the woman's face as screen. But it is important to remember that the historical emergence of psychoanalysis coincides with the emergence of the cinema and its proliferation of screens. The screen is a technology of projection (a process shared with the psyche) and a ground for the mise-en-scène of desire. The scenario of the child at the mother's breast is a crucial one in psychoanalysis, and Freud associates it with the emergence of sexuality.[43] When he theorizes the birth of the drive, located between biological need and psychical desire, he refers to the way in which the child's habit of sucking its thumb is a repetition of yet a deviation from sucking at the maternal breast. The pleasure of thumb-sucking no longer has anything to do with fulfilling the original (biological) need of hunger; instead, there is an *anaclisis* in which the drive is propped upon the need but differentiated from it. Pleasure is now a function of the stimulation of the lips as an erotic zone. The original object—the milk—has been lost. Similarly, desire for the screen is desire for a technology that simulates the pleasure of breast, the face, and the blissful state of nondifferentiation of the infant (or the Imaginary in Lacanian terms). The screen here emerges as a historically specific technological prosthesis, a surface for projection (and introjection). As Bernard Stiegler points out, *"Psychoanalytic categories are formalised within a processual historicity, a historicity within which forces take shape capable of formalising such categories."*[44] In the avant-gardes of these two eras, the face at issue is a female face that, in its turn, is the face of modernity and contributes to the very conceptualization of modernity (and not just in the West, as we will presently see). These films document a crisis of legibility, recognition, and knowledge around the face, a crisis that is linked to the proliferation of technologies of representation.

In the twentieth century, hysteria, as the emblematic pathology of the nineteenth century, gives way to prosopagnosia, sometimes referred to as "face blindness." Prosopagnosia is a pathological condition characterized by an impairment in the ability to recognize faces. Although cases of these symptoms were described in the nineteenth century by Hughlings Jackson and

Jean-Martin Charcot, the condition was first named by Joachim Bodamer, a German neurologist, who in 1947 derived the term from the classical Greek *prosopon*, or "face," and *agnosia*, meaning "non-knowledge." Prosopagnosia is not sexually differentiated in the medical literature, although it is extremely relevant that the facial recognition test produced by the Prosopagnosia Research Center (Harvard and University College London) uses only the faces of women as the testing ground for the level of the pathological condition.[45]

Anxieties about the face and the potential diminishing of its power address a destabilization not only of representation but also of intersubjectivity. In the work of Emmanuel Levinas, the face is theorized as the very instantiation of the ethical relation and of intersubjectivity. The face is the marker of absolute otherness, infinite and irreducible alterity. It exceeds any possible means of appropriation—including the attempted containments of vision, knowledge, and theory, which Levinas associates with an economy of the same. But what can this mean in relation to the close-up of the face in film? Levinas's interest in the face is ineluctably linked to the extent to which the face "breaks through the form that nevertheless delimits it."[46] It does this through the reversibility of the gaze—I not only look at it, try to contain it as an image, but it looks back, it speaks to me and exceeds whatever image I might have of it. According to Levinas, the presentation of the other to the same, which is the definition of the face, is "without the intermediary of any image or sign."[47] His analysis of the face is a philosophical treatment of the originary importance of the face-to-face encounter, of its operation as the ground of sociality and of ethics. In the cinema, there is no such face-to-face encounter—the face in close-up, by definition, cannot respond to me, cannot present itself to me as an obligation or responsibility. It does not inhabit the same time or space as myself. What are the ethics of the technological reproduction of the face? And why morality, why ethics? Is it coincidental that the philosophical and theoretical obsession with the face emerges in an era of intensified mediation of that face? In an era often seen as characterized by the loss or diminishment of that face-to-face encounter, that direct and unmediated conversation in which the face breaks through form? In an era of the interface?

In Hollywood narrative film, the male character in search of the lost object of desire is subjected over and over again to the trauma of misrecognition, to the literal and metaphoric *turn* whereby the woman he confronts is not the one he knows, wants, or expects. Avant-garde film provides a mirror image of this conundrum, its articulation in the vocabulary of formalism or aesthetics. But here, in place of a missed or aborted recognition, we have the dismantling or putting into crisis of recognizability as such, the imaging of the woman as screen and the screen as site of illegibility—the collapsing together of the fascinating illegibility of the woman and that of the screen. The anxieties surrounding the diminishing power of the face as anchor of representation in a highly mediated society are exhibited differently in narrative cinema and the avant-garde. But we have to question whether, ultimately, the sexual politics of this avant-garde and of mass culture are not dangerously tangential. Whether the female face becomes in both the sign or symptom of the failure of recognition and intersubjectivity. Whether a curiously modern fear of prosopagnosia infiltrates both domains, reducing their difference— producing an affinity that any discussion of politics and aesthetics, any politics of reading, must confront.

The Female Face, the Cityscape, and Modernity in a Transcultural Context

Bertram Lewin, in the course of deciphering the implications of the dream screen, turns to the pathologies of space and scale—agoraphobia, claustrophobia, and street phobia, in which the "fear of being eaten up" (which, in the case of the Wolf Man, Freud associates with the pregenital anxiety of the oral period) is "indicated tacitly by the manifest façade."[48] In these phobias, according to Lewin, there was

> a definite, even though subordinate, latent fear of being swallowed up, or in some cases a wish to be. Hence, the breast should somehow be represented in the façade, for the breast is the first projected "eating up" organ which the baby knows, when it envelops him and puts him to sleep. I found the breast representative in the façades. The claustrum, according to the patient's oral history, was either an asylum, that is, a sheltering mother and breast; or a place of terror, that is, a devouring mother and breast. The typical agoraphobe feared that he would dissolve and become one with the wide space, which therefore represented the devouring breast, like a hostile dream screen. In the street phobias, breast and street also formed an unconscious equation. Thus the manifest façade of these topophobias was indeed like the manifest content of dreams, and in it the element analogous to the breast or dream screen could be demonstrated.[49]

The term "facade," whose etymology links it to "face," means both "the principal front of a building, that faces on to a street or open space," and "a deceptive outward appearance."[50] Freud himself uses the term primarily in this second sense, in relation to the manifest content of the dream or the phobia that acts only as a deceptive appearance and must be pierced by analysis. But he also claims that the facade in itself sometimes has significance, being subject to no or very little distortion or censorship.[51] This seems to be the way in which Lewin deploys it to explain these phobias, although for him the dream screen is not so much a manifest content but a ground for that content.

The pathologies of space—agoraphobia, claustrophobia, and phobia of the street (the last of which is sometimes referred to as agyrophobia or dromophobia)—are pathologies of modernity that respond to urbanization, increased traffic, and the general expansion of public space. The terms were first used toward the end of the nineteenth century—agoraphobia, for instance, was first described and named in 1871 by the Austrian psychiatrist Carl Otto Westphal. Anthony Vidler refers to these topophobias as the social/psychical manifestation of a generalized fear of the metropolis: "Juxtaposed in a spatial complicity that joined the fear of distance to the horror of proximity, agoraphobia and claustrophobia captured the imagination of those who attempted to characterize the special kind of anxiety engendered by the modern metropolis: on the one hand, the fear of open space, exacerbated by the scale of the squares and boulevards of the late nineteenth-century city; on the other the fear of being closed in, heightened by the increasing anxiety of private life in mass society."[52] The attempt to analyze the phobias of space is exemplified in the work of Georg Simmel ("The Metropolis and Mental Life," "The Stranger") and Siegfried Kracauer ("The Hotel Lobby").[53] This anxiety of space is fused to the face of the "modern" woman, similarly feared as unknowable and unrecognizable, hence the collapsing of female face and city in *Gold Diggers of 1935*.

In periods of rapid and destabilizing modernization, the female figure in a host of different national cinemas seems to condense all the anxieties and fears accompanying the threatened loss of traditional codes of behavior and ethical frameworks (the concept of tradition itself being a retrospective invention of modernity). It is not surprising that these anxieties would be situated in relation to sexuality, and particularly female sexuality, which, seemingly freed from traditional constraints and mores, becomes the locus of unpredictability and illegibility. And it is the "city woman," above all, who emerges as threat and instability in a number of different cultures.[54] Shanghai cinema of the 1920s and 1930s has drawn a great deal of critical attention in recent years as the site of a representational collision between East and West negotiated through the category of "modernity." The term "modernity" seems to encapsulate in a single word all the conundrums of the relations between local and global, particular and universal, and individual and general. For, insofar as modernity is indissolubly linked with a cosmopolitan urban lifestyle and forms of technological standardization as well as a mass media of commodification, it evinces a culturally unifying or homogenizing tendency that, nevertheless, emerges in unique ways in specific geographic locations. What is modernity? Is it a global phenomenon that resists geographic or cultural borders, or should we speak of multiple, plural, or alternative modernities?

For Fredric Jameson, who defines modernity as intimately and irrevocably linked with commodity capitalism, it must be thought—if it is to be thought at all—as singular. In *A Singular Modernity*, he parodies the idea of "alternate" or "alternative" modernities:

> Everyone knows the formula by now: this means that there can be a modernity for everybody which is different from the standard or hegemonic Anglo-Saxon model. Whatever you dislike about the latter, including the subaltern position it leaves you in, can be effaced by the reassuring and "cultural" notion that you can fashion your own modernity differently, so that there can be a Latin American kind, or an Indian kind or an African kind, and so forth. . . . But this is to overlook the other fundamental meaning of modernity which is that of a worldwide capitalism itself. The standardization projected by capitalist globalization in this third or late stage of the system casts considerable doubt on all these pious hopes for cultural variety in a future world colonized by a universal market order.[55]

The "singularity" of the concept of modernity is linked, for Jameson, not only to its economic base but also to the successful "colonization and commercialization of the Unconscious" constituted by mass culture and the culture industry.[56] In the context of the cinema, the process of globalization was manifested much earlier than the third stage invoked by Jameson, in the aggressive attempts of the Hollywood studios to dominate world markets with their product from the very earliest years. Because the cinema is inextricable from its technological substrate, it carries with it not only the themes and figures of a Western concept of modernity but also a way of looking, a mode of perception, hence its inevitable reception in semicolonial Shanghai, in some sectors, as yet another form of Western intrusion or imperialism. Although I believe that it must be modified to allow for the recognition of different receptions and configurations of the "modern," Jameson's monolithic concept of a singular modernity has the advantage of reminding us of the sheer force of an iconography and a technology that, from its inception, aspired to be global. There is a sense in which the cinema could be said to incarnate the very concept of modernity in at least two ways. First, it does so through its appearance (deceptive though this may be) as the absolutely new (with no representational tradition to ground it or to break away from).[57] Second, it does so through its constitutive process of uprooting and circulating images and sounds far from any localized geographic origin, a process fully consistent with that of commodification. But the cinema was also perceived, worldwide, as an embodiment of the modern in its embrace of speed, mobility, spectacle, and sheer kinetic energy.

In contrast to Jameson, Miriam Hansen, with her notion of "vernacular modernism," has pluralized the possible modes of entry into modernity.[58] The concept works to displace what had been a property of high art—an aesthetic modernism associated with literature, painting, sculpture, and so on—and relocate it in relation to a popular venue, a mass culture with no pretensions to high art: the cinema. In effect, it works both to salvage the potential of an aesthetics for cinema (over and against its positioning as "merely" popular culture) and as a means of situating the cinema in relation to a modernism with which it had previously seemed out of sync in its adoption of a classical aesthetic (theoretically sanctioned by the notion of a "classical Hollywood narrative" governed by classical values of unity, coherency, and balance). The term "vernacular" has the advantage, according to Hansen, of invoking both ordinary, everyday (i.e., nonliterary) usage and a sign system, a language, a discourse. Vernacular modernism names the specific way in which a particular culture activates a "sensory-reflexive horizon for the experience of modernization and modernity."[59] Interestingly, the two cinemas Hansen has singled out as examples of vernacular modernism are those of Hollywood and Shanghai. To situate Hollywood cinema as, ironically, a global vernacular modernism, Hansen must argue that its particular mode of accommodating a variety of ethnic and racial differences in a largely immigrant and diasporic population resulted in its broad legibility and its worldwide viability as a form having a special affinity with modernity. But while Hollywood cinema, due to its economic and representational hegemony, can be labeled a global vernacular modernism, Shanghai cinema is perceived by Hansen as a quite particular activation of Hollywood (and European) forms and techniques, a specific and telling hybridization of modern cinematic conventions and traditional Chinese aesthetic modes.

Yet the films that Hansen singles out for analysis—Shanghai cinema of the 1920s and 1930s, and particularly the left-wing films of the 1930s—activate certain tropes of female sexuality that are recognizable from both Hollywood and European (Russian, Scandinavian, French, and German especially) silent and early sound cinemas. As Hansen points out, in all of these diverse cinemas,

> the contradictions of modernity are enacted through the figure of the woman, very often, literally, across the body of the woman who tries to live them but more often than not fails, who has to become a corpse by the end of the film. . . . Women function as metonymies, if not allegories of urban modernity, figuring the city in its allure, instability, anonymity, and illegibility, which is often suggested through juxtapositions of women's faces and bodies with the lights of Shanghai, abstracted into hieroglyphics. In more narrative terms, female protagonists serve as the focus of social injustice and oppression; rape, thwarted romantic love, rejection, sacrifice, prostitution function as metaphors of a civilization in crisis.[60]

The woman has a privileged rhetorical and iconographic relation to modernity. Yet it might be argued more forcefully, as Tani E. Barlow has done, that the Enlightenment discourses of modernity in China have produced the very thinkability of a particular concept of "woman."

In these discourses, "woman" becomes the neologism *nüxing* (combining "the characters for 'female' and 'sex' in a novel way").[61] This incarnation of "woman" was that of a sexual, erotic being, defined in terms of sexual difference (*nanxing* [male sex]/*nüxing* [female sex]) and the heterosexual imperative of reproduction, theorized in terms of a social Darwinism allied with a eugenic discourse. "Women's liberation" here advocates women's choice of a marriage partner as a progressive evolutionary move, ensuring the bettering of the species.[62] *Nüxing* displaced the older *funü*—woman defined in terms of citizenship, the family, and nationalism (and later appropriated by the Chinese Communist Party to describe normative womanhood).

Nüxing is, for Barlow, a historical catachresis, stabilizing diverse elements—a myriad of sociological, political, aesthetic, and ideological imperatives. Because a catachresis has no authentic referent, it allows Barlow to circumvent the debilitating, dead-end debates over women's agency, since that "agency" is produced (and lived) differently in specific historical periods and hinges on the particular historical catachresis in play. The appearance of *nüxing* in the early twentieth century underlines the centrality of both "woman" and feminist theory to discourses of modernity and modernization, which are, from the outset, international.[63] According to Barlow, "Women in Chinese feminism, no matter which analytic subject we examine—funüjie [women's world], funü, or nüxing—is constitutionally, in a naïvely literal sense, always already an internationalized subject."[64]

Barlow's concept of "colonial modernity" (i.e., modernity as inextricable from colonialism and the encounter of Western nations with difference) enables an approach to the question/conundrum of singular or multiple modernities that offers an alternative to Jameson and Hansen.[65] It also complicates the questions of influence and dissemination considerably. She describes a kind of boomerang effect in which the condition of possibility of European Enlightenment and discourses on modernity is the colonial project, which revealed populations of "others" who could be positioned as primitive and unenlightened. Ideas about what constituted "Chineseness" played an important role in this intellectual undertaking. Subsequently, China confronted that same modernity, founded on the encounter with otherness, as other and desirable. In response to Lila Abu-Lughod's contention that feminism was disseminated from Europe to other parts of the globe, Barlow writes:

> What the universalizing gaze of the European Enlightenment had seen, after all, were the disparate peoples of the world. The dissemination of feminism returned the attention of metropolitan and colonial intellectuals to the same sites that had instigated the gaze of Enlightenment in the first instance. The logics of origin are not my primary concern; here, it is enough to propose that globally feminisms are constitutionally spectral. Generically they have arisen as gendered logics in relation to geopolitical others, which is to say that European enlightened feminism is inconceivable in the absence of colonialism, just as Chinese enlightened thought takes shape only in relation to the Great Powers and their various urbanities.[66]

By appending "colonial" to "modernity," Barlow is able not only to emphasize that Enlightenment is always fractured but also to demonstrate why the question of derivation ("Is Chinese modernity derivative of Western modernity?") is the wrong one to pose and can only result in an intellectual aporia. Yet it is significant that the concept of "colonial modernity" is singular rather than plural. The modernity of the flapper in the United States is just as colonial as the modernity of Shanghai in the 1920s and 1930s. And this is why one can trace certain recurrent themes, structures, and aesthetic strategies across a large number of national cinematic incarnations of modernity.

Shanghai cinema of the 1920s and 1930s is fascinated with the iconography of the "new woman," who is able to negotiate the space of a changing urban terrain. The trope that recurs, here and elsewhere, is that of the contaminating and corrupting transition from country to city. *Daybreak* (Sun Yu, 1933) begins with an old man watching and commenting upon the steady and relentless stream of rural people heading for the boats to the city. The crowd includes a couple, Ling Ling (Li Lili) and Zhang (Gao Zhanfei), who go to the city to work in a factory but end up separated through the machinations of their employers, Ling Ling becoming a prostitute and Zhang working at sea. Ling Ling's transformation into a prostitute is mediated by a return to the initial scene of the film where the old man again laments the exodus to the city followed by a montage of shots of city lights and high life. Earlier, after Ling Ling is raped by the factory owner's son, her flashback generates an idyllic scene of past love in a country setting. In *Twin Sisters* (1933, directed by Zheng Zhengqiu, with Hu Die playing both sisters), one sister is taken by her father to the city, where his greed motivates him to barter his daughter as a concubine to an important general. She becomes bitter and unfeeling. The other sister remains in the country only to face impoverishment and hunger for herself and her family, and finally she is forced to act as a wet nurse for her own sister, neither recognizing the other. In *New Woman* (Cai Chusheng, 1935), Wei Ming's flight to the city after her husband abandons her leads her to nearly fall into prostitution as well.

All of these examples are subtended by a very strict binary opposition between city and country, modernity and tradition. This is a codification very familiar within Hollywood and European cinemas as well—for instance in F. W. Murnau's highly allegorical *Sunrise* (1927), where the vamp from the city who visits the countryside only to lure away the good woman's husband is referred to only as "the city woman," a designation that is sufficient to evoke a myriad of evils associated with the urban. Her contamination is a function of the fact that she brings an alien hypersexuality and modernity into the countryside. And in Germany's Weimar cinema, the city is consistently aligned with a wayward sexuality, femininity gone astray, incarnated in the prostitute, the "streetwalker." But in Shanghai cinema, the difference is signaled by the additional stipulation that modernity emerges in tandem with Westernization, and that the city is always the cosmopolitan, semicolonial Shanghai, open as a trading port to persistent contact with the outside world. And yet the source of contamination does not seem to be Westernization itself but instead a distortion of sexuality in its relation to knowledge, a breakdown in categorization, a persistent commodification—all intimately linked with the figure of the woman.

In Western literature and art of the late nineteenth century and early twentieth century, the increased fascination with the figure of the prostitute, as the epitome of the female flaneur, was emblematic of the new woman's relation to urban space. The conjunction of the woman and the city suggests the potential of an intolerable and dangerous sexuality, one that is out of bounds precisely as a result of the woman's revised relation to space, her new ability to "wander" (and hence to "err"). This was perceived as a peculiarly modern phenomenon. The "painted woman" became the very figure of a modernity associated with illusion, deception, artificiality. It was becoming more and more difficult to distinguish between the well-attired prostitute and the bourgeois lady, since both were now found, unaccompanied, in the streets. The free and unanchored circulation of sexuality and money epitomized the modernity associated with the increased traffic of urban space. Walter Benjamin referred to the prostitute as an aspect of the allegory of the modern. Most significantly, the prostitute ostentatiously exhibited the commodification of the human body, the point where the body and exchange value coincided, where capitalism's ruse was exposed. It was in this sense that she represented what T. J. Clark refers to as "the danger or the price of modernity."[67] The prostitute is so resolutely linked with modernity because she demonstrates the new status of the body as exchangeable and profitable image. In the cinemas of Shanghai, Hollywood, and Europe, this commodification is also exhibited in the investment in the star system.

The narratives of prostitution do not necessarily entail a straightforward condemnation, and more often than not, in Shanghai films of the 1930s—as well as in Hollywood and European films of the period (e.g., *Blonde Venus* and *Diary of a Lost Girl*)—the figure of the prostitute is sympathetic, positioned as a victim of larger economic and social forces beyond her control. As many writers have pointed out, in Shanghai in the early years of the twentieth century, the prostitute came to displace the courtesan, who in contrast to the "streetwalker" was bound to a specific space (and who was sometimes literally constrained through foot-binding) but was also associated with a highly literary and artistic milieu, often exhibiting her own aesthetic abilities and graces.[68] Even though courtesans began to appropriate the techniques of mechanical reproduction and mass culture by circulating photographs of themselves, as Laikwan Pang has demonstrated extensively in her study of early visual culture in Shanghai (becoming, in a sense, the medium of their own demise), their domain was steadily usurped by the singsong girls, dance hostesses, and prostitutes of the new urban scene.[69] Perhaps the culminating blow was the advent of the star system and the production of a cinematic sexuality, characterized by reproducibility and mobility. While the courtesan was characterized by stasis and uniqueness, both prostitute and movie star were incarnations of a new urban mobility.

Yet I would argue that the narratives of prostitution and the quandaries of the new woman themselves, as moving as they are, cannot be considered apart from the iconography, the filmic form, that supports the intense affect associated with their representation. Through a focus on the close-up of the female face in Shanghai cinema of the 1930s and 1940s, we can trace some of the vicissitudes in a transcultural obsession with the woman as the very figure of a problematic modernity. As outlined earlier, the affect of the close-up is often linked with the representation of the face as the privileged signifier of individuality, truth, beauty, and interiority, as well as the most basic support of intersubjectivity. However, this theory and practice emerge in a Western context, as to some extent the legacy of a tradition of portraiture that strives to capture the truth of the individual, the essence of the person. Although Chinese art history contains its own, very different, history of portraiture, linked to status, privilege, and social relations, it has often been noted that the Chinese conceptualization of subjectivity and the "I" is quite different from that of the West. As Richard Vinograd points out, in *Boundaries of the Self: Chinese Portraits, 1600–1900*, "It is important to note the relatively greater emphasis on the value of individualism and the autonomous self in Western cultures in comparison to the Chinese, where family affiliations as the source of identity and the performance of social roles as the fulfillment of the self are relatively valorized."[70] In Barlow's analysis of the different terms for "woman," Vinograd's description would be inextricably linked with a particular historical period preceding the late Qing era and the early twentieth century—that which deployed the term *funü*. Nüxing, the sexual, erotic woman, the Chinese new woman, emerged within an epistemological/ideological problematic that strove to actively produce the concept of person, of individual, in relation to the division between man and woman, heteronormativity in the service of national survival, and a eugenic discourse. The cinema as a technical apparatus facilitated this objective—emerging in the West, it brought with it the traces of Western art history, including Renaissance perspective as a guarantee of verisimilitude and the technique of the facial close-up, with its promise of an access to interiority and the guarantee of individuality. The face of the woman—and the circulability of that face— has been central to modernity, to capitalism, to its mass culture and its processes of commodification. That face can carry a multiplicity of sometimes contradictory significations—modernity, timelessness, clarity, illegibility, objecthood, excessive subjectivity—but its ubiquity and semiotic centrality in modernity are linked specifically to the vicissitudes of female sexuality, its lure and threat.

The emergence of the language of universalism in theories of the human face and its readability (Darwin, Balázs) and in discourses on the silent cinema (the cinema as a universal language, a potential Esperanto) was simultaneous with the compulsion to universalize in discourses of the Enlightenment and humanism.[71] Feminism, enabled by Enlightenment thinking, was complicit in this. Thinking about feminism and the concept of "woman" inevitably entailed a recourse to the notion of the universal. To foreground "woman" as a category in the international discourse of feminist modernism was to perceive a unity and an identity that crossed all cultures, nations, races, and classes (woman as universal subject). It also aligned feminisms with the more general discourses of Enlightenment and humanism, as well as their centering of agency (and, in the case of China, with a discourse on personality, personal standing—*ren'ge* that concerned itself primarily with the deficiencies of women).[72] According to Barlow, "It is only in the presence of difference that the claim of universality became truly compelling; only when the difference is inadvertently and irreversibly present does the exploration of and explanation for sameness become compulsory."[73] The cinematic paradigm of the human face in close-up works as the assurance of a universal legibility; it stabilizes the concepts of personality, interiority, and hence individuality. The fact that the cinematic woman often confounds legibility, is represented as mysterious, unpredictable, and indecipherable, only reconfirms in a circuitous way the facial guarantee. For that very illegibility and unpredictability is legible as an attribute of her ontology—women are like that. In China, it is sexuality that defines *nüxing*, and her sexuality is random, erratic, unpredictable (especially to the extent that she does not fulfill her eugenic duty of choosing the best—or any—man).

In Shanghai films of the 1930s, the female face is both transparent and opaque, the site of the emergence of multiple contradictions and of an uneasy cultural hybridity. In many of the left-wing films with a programmatic social agenda, the female face in close-up is often the canvas that condenses and displays all the class suffering and angst of an oppressive society. It is,

4.30 & 4.31 *Twin Sisters* (Zheng Zhengqiu, 1933).

in effect, *more expressive* than that of the man, the crucial textual index of a merger of melodrama and socialist realism. According to Amy Dooling, "Leftist cinema in the 1930s appropriated the sexualized female body—often embodied by the figure of the prostitute—as a key battleground for contending (male) ideologies at the time."[74] In *Twin Sisters*, the country twin, Da Bao, forced to work as a wet nurse in her rich sister's house, is in despair over the fact that she has no money to pay for her sick husband's medical needs. As she bends over the baby's crib, she is torn by the desire to steal his expensive necklace, and her face registers this agony born of economic inequity (figs. 4.30, 4.31). The extreme closeness of the first close-up and the sheer duration of the shots registering her indecisiveness, her imagination of her pleading husband, and the trajectory of her emotions constitute her face as the primary signifying ground of the scene, the mise-en-scène of social injustice. In *Street Angel* (Yuan Muzhi, 1937), the elder of two exploited sisters, Xiao Yun, forced to become a prostitute and fatally injured by her pimp, lies dying in close-up, her face the text of her subjection. Ruan Lingyu, playing the unnamed character in *The Goddess* (Wu Yonggang, 1934), must practice prostitution in order to support her young son; as she holds him after a night's work, the sorrow of her enforced labor seems etched on her face (fig. 4.32). In the previously mentioned scene from *Daybreak*, after Ling Ling is raped, a series of close-ups link her to a fetish object of the film—a necklace made of water lilies—and this series introduces the flashback to a utopian country scene where she crafts the necklace. And in the final scenes of *New Woman*, Ruan Lingyu's face undergoes a number of transformations, from despair at her daughter's death and the ruin of her career as a writer to determination for revenge to a renewed will to live in the fa-

4.32 *The Goddess* (Wu Yonggang, 1934).

mous close-ups in which the characters for
"I want to live!" emerge as graphics from
her mouth, growing larger and larger on the
screen as she looks directly at the camera/
spectator (fig. 4.33).

4.33 *New Woman* (Cai Chusheng, 1935).

All of these scenes activating the close-up
are instances of an excessive or exaggerated
interiority. In Balázs's words, when confronted with the close-up of a face, "we
can see that there is something there that
we cannot see."[75] The visible is necessary but insufficient. In these examples,
there is something that could almost be called a hystericization of the image,
in the attempt to capture an invisible depth, or perhaps a social hermeneu-
tics that is somehow not accessible to vision, but there nevertheless. Yet this
intensive and excessive signification of interiority is accompanied by an insistence upon a pure exteriority as well. The woman's face is not simply there
as the vessel of affect but as sheer surface—a surface that in its refusal of any
"beyond," any depth, connotes only a beautiful illegibility. And this exterior-
ization is the locus of the conjunction of modernity, the woman, and the city.
It is not accidental that films such as *Crossroads* (Shen Xiling, 1937), *Street
Angel, New Woman*, and *Queen of Sports* (Sun Yu, 1934)—all films exhibiting
a fascination with the new woman—should begin with shots or pans of the
city, slow tilts upward caressing the sides of powerful and dominating modern skyscrapers. The image of the woman is often superimposed over city
lights, conflating the two in a seemingly assured invocation of modernity
itself. In *The Goddess*, city lights are consistently brought into play as Ruan
Lingyu alters her position from that of mother to prostitute or vice versa.
When her self-appointed pimp gazes out the window at the lights of the city,
her image is superimposed over those lights. The architecture of the modern
city is indissociable from the narrativization of female sexuality.

This trope, linking the modern woman and the cityscape, is characterized
by its transcultural tenacity. Why is the female face consistently associated
with the territory and architecture of a modern urban space? The city of modernity, so persistently theorized and represented in the writings of Balzac,
Poe, Simmel, Kracauer, and Benjamin, is linked with alluring and simultaneously threatening ideas of a heightened stimulation, of the crowd, of mass
culture, of anonymity and illegibility. One is suddenly surrounded by the
faces of strangers and a deformation of traditional social and community

networks (hence the discursive association of the rise of phrenology and the strangeness or unknowability of the urban other). Prostitution involves both a false contact, a fake intimacy, easily accessible and easily disownable, and the ability to map and navigate a seemingly unmanageable landscape of anonymity. Because she is lost, because she is incapable of navigating the city, the woman in *Daybreak* is sold into prostitution. Ironically, after she becomes a prostitute, she is able to find her way home again, but only to confront very limited options.

The female face, in both its representational dimensions in Shanghai cinema, can be activated as a form of assurance or stabilization of the epistemological uncertainties and dislocations of modernity. As the transparent signifier of the pathos of class suffering, her visage guarantees a legibility of the emotions, a cognitive and affective orientation. As pure illuminated surface, in collaboration with the cityscape, she carries a potential threat of illegibility, but one that is absorbed in another discursive realm affiliated with the cinema, one that also usurps the connotations of luminance—the star system. Shanghai's movie star system was in many ways similar to Hollywood's, sustained by a network of avid fans and fan magazines, extreme affect, gossip, special movie sections in newspapers, and, most of all, a proliferation and intensification of the circulation of images of faces, a kind of training in recognition. One of the most important Chinese production companies was named "Mingxing" or "Star" Film Company. Because Shanghai's movie scene, so integral a part of its modernity (or the "Shanghai Modern," as Leo Ou-Fan Lee has dubbed it), was dominated in its early years by Hollywood and European films, photos of Western stars are interspersed with those of Chinese stars. These images, for the most part, take the form of glamorous still photographs (as Laura Mulvey has noted, the star is "the glamorous impersonat[ing] the ordinary").[76] As mentioned earlier, *Ling Long Women's Magazine*, published in Shanghai from 1931 to 1937, included a movie section and frequently contained alluring photographs of both Western and Chinese stars (see figs. 4.3, 4.4).[77]

Much has been written about the peculiar phenomenon of the star, particularly the way in which the star in a film constitutes a "double body"—the body of the character in the narrative and the recognizable body of the star, with her own look, expressions, gestures, and mannerisms.[78] In the discourses surrounding the star, the opposition between public and private often collapses, so that the daily life, the routines, the activities of a star are subject to the same surveillant gaze as that of the film camera. There is strong work, a concerted effort, to produce a recognizable, identifiable person. In Shanghai, the merger of public and private, the blurring of the realms of film narrative and life narrative, has at times seemed even more intense. The story of Ruan Lingyu (the protagonist of *The Goddess*, *New Woman*, and other films), a story that has been continually written and rewritten, instantiates this most starkly. The film *New Woman* was based on the life story of Ai Xia, a young actress who had committed suicide in 1934 shortly after the appearance of a film she had both written and acted in—*A Modern Woman* (*Xiandai yi nüxing*). The tragedy was seemingly repeated when Ruan also took her life after the release of *New Woman*. Her suicide was an enormous public event occasioning countless debates over the reason for its occurrence, its relation to the hounding of the tabloid press, and its social implications for the position of women. Huge crowds attended her funeral. Michael Chang, in a nuanced analysis of movie actresses and public discourse in 1920s and 1930s Shanghai, sees the problematic of the suicide and its reception as symptomatic of a collapse of the opposition between public and private, in effect, a demand that the female star not *act*, but *be*.[79] He sees this application of a reflection theory of acting as gender-specific— the standards of "true character" (*bense*, literally "original color") and "good girl" were attached to the woman.[80] Men were allowed to make a distinction between their biographical selves and their roles.[81] The female star (*nü mingxing*), in contrast, was "understood as a naively reflective role through which some interiorized 'self' and authentic fact of 'woman' ought to be at once identified and then re-presented both on and off screen."[82]

What interests me most in this analysis is the emphasis upon a unitary and coherent "self" of both the screen and life, indivisible and fully identifiable and recognizable. In the midst of the modern city, with its anonymity and facelessness, the female star emerges as the promise of a kind of hyperindividuality that rises above the crowd, hence the insatiable desire to *know* the star that fuels fan magazines and tabloids. And because it is a *re*-cognition that is at stake, the repetitive nature of mechanical reproduction allows, ironically, a constant reassertion of individuality, uniqueness, originariness of the self. The star is hence a form of compensation for urban illegibility, anonymity, and their attendant anxieties. And the luminosity of her close-up, its aesthetic intelligibility, counters the felt loss of depth in human relations, the technologically mandated lack of face-to-face contact (the utopian nature of which is itself produced retrospectively by modernity).

In Shanghai cinema, the face of the woman oscillates between the guarantee of a knowledge of interiority, of affect, of readability (even if what is read is the pathos of class suffering) and the surface-like illegibility and deceptiveness of the city itself, epitomized by her usually enforced role as prostitute, as "painted woman." Yet, even though the illegibility and deception are contained by the star system's insistence upon a unity and transparency of the "self," there are textual leakages, moments where the contradictions subtending such a system emerge in the films, generated by the pressure of their formal work. I will briefly delineate four of these instances across the different films. In *New Woman*, the photograph of Wei Ming circulates and often functions as the instigator of events. That photograph convinces the publisher that her book is marketable because she is a beautiful woman. It is later stolen by the school trustee who harasses Wei Ming and is torn into pieces by him when she rejects him. The pieces are found by the trustee's wife, who reconstructs the photo to identify her friend, only to suspect she has an intimate relationship with her husband. As Wei Ming lies dying in her hospital bed, she is shown another photo of herself in the tabloids that spurs her will to live. After she dies, the playboy trustee throws a newspaper with her image out the window of his car and it is trampled on by hordes of marching workers. Not only are the contradictions between a revolutionary collectivity and the individualism of the new woman brought to the fore at the end of the film, but the trajectory of the photographs delineates the way in which the concept of the new woman is produced by a social/technical apparatus enabling the circulation of images.

Earlier in the film, Wei Ming is also situated as the spectator of her own image, but this time it is a film, for which a car window becomes the screen. As she rides with the trustee, Wei Ming turns in desolation to the window, and the passing scenes of the city are transformed into the memory of the event at which she first met the dastardly trustee. The "memory" is indeed a

4.34 *New Woman* (Cai Chusheng, 1935).

film, with cuts and intertitles, and the image of Wei Ming within the mise-en-scène of that film, smiling and open, contrasts with Wei Ming as spectator, scowling with anger (fig. 4.34). This splitting of subjectivity, contained by the assignment of the subjectivities to two different temporalities, past and present, is accompanied by a merging of conceptual frameworks that is more destabilizing. The urban geography, the fascinating lights of the city, occupy the same space as that of Wei Ming's represented interiority, grasped as memory. The trope associated with the new woman's surface existence, her often illegible or deceptive exteriority—the lights of the city—is confused with the stamp of her authenticity, the face as transparent access to interiority, to the genuine. The two tropological logics coexist uneasily in the same space.

In *The Goddess*, in a scene made famous by Stanley Kwan's *Center Stage* (1991), the status of the new woman as mimesis, as the representation of a representation, is demarcated. Fleeing from the police who are rounding up prostitutes, Ruan Lingyu opens a door and enters a room only to meet the man who will later exploit her. In Kwan's *Center Stage*, a quasi documentary of the life of Ruan Lingyu, Maggie Cheung, also a major star, reenacts this scene, and her repetition is interlaced with a shot of Ruan's ur-performance. In an elegant analysis of these two scenes, Jason McGrath has delineated how Cheung's performance retrospectively illuminates the status of Ruan's acting as performative realism, as the labor of constructing the image of the new woman, as a didactic lesson to the spectator teaching her how to be the new woman. And, of course, Ruan's original performance is by no means originary itself, but the putting into play of a host of images and gestures drawn from Hollywood and European cinema. It could be said that the close-up of Ruan in *The Goddess*, in which her facial expression mutates from fear to a knowing smirk, marks the moment when Ruan Lingyu becomes Marlene Dietrich, walking languidly across the room and sitting on the table to smoke in a position that best reveals her legs. Dietrich's performance is already an imitation of the classical cabaret girl, and Dietrich as movie star is herself a transcultural phenomenon, displaced from German Weimar cinema to Hollywood. The ramifications of this scene are reminiscent of Roland Barthes's analysis of beauty—only recognizable as a copy of a copy of a copy in an infinite regression of hollow guarantees.[83] Furthermore, Dietrich's image of mysteriousness and allure is generated through the arguably Orientalist mise-en-scène of Josef von Sternberg and reinforced by her association with Shanghai (in *Shanghai Express* [1932], in which she plays a prostitute), exemplifying the concept of colonial modernity. The most famous line of this film—"It took more than one man to change my name to Shanghai Lily"—is a condensation of the tropes of prostitution, promiscuity, excessive sexuality, and Shanghai as a hypermodern setting.

A final moment of disturbance in the representation of the faciality of the new woman can be located in a scene in *Daybreak*, a film that fairly rapidly toward the end generates a political discourse in favor of a revolutionary nationalism. This is again a scene where the actress mimes Marlene Dietrich, this time in relation to a quite specific film, *Dishonored* (Josef von Sternberg, 1931). At the end of *Dishonored*, Dietrich, waiting to be executed for spying, coolly applies lipstick. In *Daybreak*, Ling Ling, the country girl, has accepted her role as prostitute and consciously manipulates her sexuality. But she is a "good prostitute," or a prostitute with a "heart of gold," and she encourages her returned lover to join the revolutionary struggle. She is caught, aiding his escape, arrested, and placed before a firing squad. When she is sentenced to execution, she applies makeup and prepares for her final role. After a sympathetic young captain allows her to don country clothes for the execution, she primps and preens for the event. Ling Ling's facial expression throughout this scene is virtually illegible. Miriam Hansen argues that the aspects of this scene that resist a "male/modernist projection and stereotyping" are linked to performance and masquerade on the part of Ling Ling, who manipulates the stereotype of the "painted lady," making it her own.[84] Hansen argues, "The meanings of a film are not only determined by directorial intention and an underlying social, masculinist discourse, but are significantly shaped by other voices, such as the mode of performance and the degree of agency, however precarious, that accrues to female actors in the star system."[85] Because there were so few women screenwriters and directors in Shanghai cinema, it is tempting to attribute signifying agency to the female star, who is seen to actively resist certain sedimented understandings of femininity. But to do so is to forget that the star system itself is a representational nexus, a discourse that actively works to construct and maintain a vision of hyperindividuality, personhood, and agency. Li Lili, playing Ling Ling, at the end of *Daybreak*, does not herself undermine the ideological codification of a modern femininity, of the woman who stands in for all the anxieties of urban modernity. The disturbance of this scene is, however, linked to a certain evacuation of intelligibility in relation to the character of Ling Ling. Her perpetual smile displaces any other facial expression that might indicate comprehension (fig. 4.35). And even the smile as an invitation to commence shooting is meaningless, since the smile never disappears. The representation of Ling Ling in this scene condenses and confuses all the varied female types of Shanghai cinema—the country girl (who ironically seduces the young captain to take on a stance of resistance), the painted

4.35 *Daybreak* (Sun Yu, 1933).

prostitute (concerned only with her own image), the mime of the Western femme fatale (the reference to Dietrich in *Dishonored*). The scene collects and displays competing representations of femininity, irreconcilable contradictions, some of them (i.e., individuality vs. collectivity) a function of the sudden injection of a strong nationalist political discourse. It is a witness to the collapse of a fragile tropological structure.

Shanghai cinema of the 1930s is particularly intriguing because it exists at the nexus of, and as a point of the accumulation of, representations of the woman that aspire to be global, to cross cultures effortlessly. It could be argued that the scalar aspirations of modernity are themselves propped up by images of the woman situated as universally understandable, without national grounding, and hence appropriate for the intensified circulation and distribution that characterize capitalism. Is the "new woman" of Shanghai cinema Chinese or other? Or both—a potentially alluring and threatening hybrid? What the Shanghai star and these moments of representational disturbance demonstrate most clearly, perhaps, is that there is no "new woman"—she is a coming into being of a vision of modernity, an amalgamation of irreconcilable tropes that both perform ideological work and reveal its limits.

The Politics of Agoraphobia

The new woman, the "modern" woman, is not agoraphobic. Her problem is instead that she ventures out into the streets, even becomes a "streetwalker," transforming herself into a commodity. Yet she cannot be understood outside the problematic of an agoraphobia that plays out all the permutations of a vexed relation to space in modernity. Agoraphobia is coincident with paranoia about new, unfamiliar, and often unnavigable spaces. But it can also be analyzed in relation to a sexual politics in crisis. Agoraphobes crave the security of an enclosed space, a confined and domestic space in which their immobility can be contrasted with the frantic circulation of the marketplace. Agoraphobia is literally "fear of the public square (agora)." At the beginning of the twentieth century it is associated with domesticity and threatened by its opposite—the image of the woman transgressing the borders of the home and infiltrating the public domain through work or consumerism. The space of the domestic (and of the agoraphobe) is a space where the integrity and stability of the self—as well as its immobility, its unchangeability—can be preserved. According to Gillian Brown, capitalism in the Victorian era *requires* this concept of the person, and agoraphobia provided it with "a paradigmatic selfhood associated with female experience—or more specifically, summarized and reproduced the tradition of selfhood established by domestic ideology. . . . the agoraphobic model of self-integrity instantiates the market destiny of domesticity. The informing principle of domestic sanctuary, agoraphobia epitomizes the structure of individuality in a market economy."[86] While the market is characterized by an incessant mobility, circulation, and hence mutability, the agoraphobe clings to immobility, the stationary certainty of an enclosed space and its protection of the self. Subjectivity is formulated in spatial terms. However, capitalism operates through an insistent reliance on a fragile balancing of continuous circulation with the stability and assured identity of the individual subject. The borders of agoraphobia are always shifting. The domestic arena becomes a space of consumption (and the woman the emblematic consumer), and stores and the marketplace take on the trappings of home. In this sense, the new woman incarnates what Brown describes as "the chaos and unfamiliarity of not only a woman but a market unmoored from the modulations of immobility."[87]

Both Shanghai cinema of the 1930s and Western cinema of the same time period perform this dialectical tension incarnated in agoraphobia as a social symptom. Although most of these films do not deal directly with the domestic space of the home, preferring the labyrinth of the city, the domestic space/marketplace opposition is recast as the opposition between the idyllic, lost countryside and the complex and confounding chaos of urban life. In the city, the woman is out of place, and the fact that she can never return to the country catapults her story into tragedy. Capitalist agoraphobia's dialectic of mobility/immobility is written across her face in the two modes of her close-up—overly mobile, her features exhibit the anguish of her individual plight, the "theatrics of interiority" Brown associates with the logic of domesticity in a capitalist economy.[88] Opaque and immobile, operating only as a beautiful/glamorous surface, she ironically inhabits the role of the commodity, itself incessantly mobile and in circulation within the global marketplace. The economy of the image in modernity is most emphatically an economy of scale.

Chapter 5

The Location of the Image

Projection, Perspective, and Scale

From the Flip-Book to the Cinema

Cinematic images are projected; cinematic images are also stored. And the material nature of their existence is in each case quite different, incompatible. The question "Where is the image?" seems to be, in the first case, an issue of visibility and legibility and, in the second, one of geography, of the location of the archive. The problem of the archive today is indissociable from pressing questions about the concept of a medium and materiality in what has been described as our "postmedium" era. The mass media of the twentieth century posed a challenge to the idea of the archive precisely because of their violation of the principle of scarcity. Processes of archivization were accelerated and intensified in the nineteenth century, producing historical changes in the very terms of the archive and archivability.

What is it that is archived? Historically, it has always been an object—a text, a painting, a print, an artifact, a tool—something tangible, something consistent with the idea of storage in a location (a library, a museum, a file cabinet, an archive). The archive is a protection against time and its inevitable entropy and corruption, but with the introduction of film as an archival process, the task becomes that of preserving time, of preserving an experience of temporality. It is this experience that seems to be somehow outside the scope of the traditional archive or, perhaps more accurately, to be threatened by a certain encroaching dematerialization. Technologies of mechanical and electronic reproduction, from photography through digital media, appear to move asymptotically toward immateriality, generating images through light and electricity. The answer to the question "Where is the film?" is less assured than that concerning the physical location of a painting. Is it the celluloid strip, the projected image, the viewer's apprehension of the illusion of motion? Digital media emerge as the apparent end point of an accelerating dematerialization, so much so that it is difficult not to see the very term "digital media" as an oxymoron. Is the digital really a medium, or even a collection of media? Isn't its specificity, rather, the annihilation of the concept of a medium? Its information or representations seem to exist nowhere, and the cultural dream of the digital is a dream of immateriality, without degradation or loss. The digital archive is either everywhere or nowhere.

Controversies over the "death of cinema" in the face of digitization are often characterized by a lament over the anticipated and feared disappearance of celluloid, of the material base of the medium and its guarantee of the indexical grounding of the image. But this anxiety goes beyond the loss of indexical representation and extends to the loss of film as a material object, of reels of celluloid, sitting in cans, on shelves, in archives, accumulating the marks of time and history in their slow decomposition. This scenario invariably raises the vexed question of the ontology of the cinema—what precisely is it, or was it?—to raise the specter of André Bazin.

The dematerialization perceived to be proper to the digital is in fact preceded by the dematerialization proper, indeed necessary, for the cinema. A reel of celluloid in a can is not legible as a movie—there must be a machine, preferably, if one is interested in the "original" or "authentic" experience, a projector. From this point of view, it is not celluloid but light that defines the cinematic experience. The image must, above all, be projected. And the projecting of an image, on a large scale, to a mass audience, marks a particularly crucial historical juncture in modernity. For projection complicates the question of the location of the image. The screen intercepts a beam of light, but the perception of the moving image takes place somewhere in between the projector and screen, and the temporary, ephemeral nature of that image is reaffirmed by its continual movement and change. In addition, the projection of the moving image in the cinema, unlike the representation of movement in the optical toys that preceded it, allows for a monumental scale more reminiscent of the nineteenth-century panorama, one paving the way for the spectacle that would dominate the twentieth. An advertisement of the American Biograph Company in 1900 proclaimed: "Our Films Are Seven

Times the Size of Others, We Show Twice as Many Pictures Per Second, and Our Pictures on the Canvas Are LARGER, BRIGHTER, STEADIER and More INTERESTING Than Others."[1]

The intensification of the obsession to represent time and movement in the nineteenth century is witnessed by the proliferation of optical toys of all sorts—the phenakistoscope, the praxinoscope, the zoetrope, the kineograph or flip-book, and a host of other miniature machines and gadgets exploiting the illusions produced by the intermittent display of images. Long marginalized as simple prefigurations or anticipations of the cinema, these optical toys have assumed a prominent position within the last decade in the disciplines of film history, the history of science, history of technology, and art history. Why this renewed interest in optical toys (or philosophical toys, as they are also called) at this particular historical moment? Why the irrepressible debates about teleology and technological progress, and why this insistence upon an attention to the losers or failures of history?

What emerges in the historiography of this period is a discourse contesting the linear narrative of an era existing only to anticipate cinema, of artifacts definable only as "precinema" or "protocinema"—a discourse of uneven development, overdetermination, staggered levels.[2] It is a history resistant to the logic of origins and "first times," acknowledging simultaneously the earlier embodiment of what later emerges as "new" and the persistence of the allegedly outmoded. In many ways, its historical logic seems to echo that of psychoanalysis, which in its turn resists traditional historiography. According to Michel de Certeau, there are two different "strategies of time" involved here. For psychoanalysis, the past and the present are fully imbricated, locked in a struggle in which "forgetting" is no longer a simple accident but a defensive weapon aimed against the past. In Certeau's words, the past "resurfaces, it troubles, it turns the present's feeling of being 'at home' into an illusion."[3] Traditional historiography, on the other hand, solidifies its notions about knowledge, power, and "objectivity" by effecting a "clean break" between the past and the present. The past is spatially isolated; it exists in museums and archives, which neutralize and sanitize its psychical impact. The forms of relation between past and present posited in psychoanalysis are those of imbrication, repetition, substitution; in historiography, they are succession, correlation, disjunction.[4] Certeau is convinced that it is precisely these differences, together with psychoanalysis's insistence upon the vital interconnections between past and present, that make possible a "renewal" of historiography.

Hence, the phrase "from the flip-book to the cinema" used as the title of this section does not name a linear or teleological progression whereby the flip-book merely paves the way for the cinema and then disappears, exhausted by its own inadequacy. Nor does it suggest that the cinema emerges as the historical victor, as more technologically or aesthetically mature than the optical toys of the nineteenth century. Indeed, it could be said that the cinema, immaterial product of a beam of light, is haunted by the flip-book, by the miniature, touchable, manipulable, opaque image. Relations of imbrication, repetition, and substitution between the two media signal an unresolved and ideologically inflected series of tensions between materiality and abstraction, the tactile and the visible, closeness and distance, the miniature and the larger-than-life, partiality and transcendence. More relevant here than narratives of the steady advance of science would be the anecdotes that strike us as historically perverse or "regressive": the scenario of Max Skladanowsky, forced to give up his Bioskop projections when denied a license, cutting up strips of film into frames and reassembling them into a flip-book, or of Étienne-Jules Marey laboriously cutting out the images from a strip of film, overlapping them, and rephotographing them to mimic single-plate chronophotography. These were two widely different events with different determinants but nevertheless both evoking the specter of return, of detour, of a historical stuttering.

But to return to my earlier question: Why this revival of the historical fascination with optical toys? Why now? For Walter Benjamin, in a well-known and often cited section of "Theses on the Philosophy of History," history inevitably conjures an irreducible imbrication of the present and the past:

> The true picture of the past flits by. The past can be seized only as an image which flashes up at the instant when it can be recognized and is never seen again. . . . For every image of the past that is not recognized by the present as one of its own concerns threatens to disappear irretrievably. . . . To articulate the past historically does not mean to recognize it "the way it really was" (Ranke). It means to seize hold of a memory as it flashes up at a moment of danger.[5]

If this is the instant when the past as image can be recognized, and recognized as one of its own concerns, it is undoubtedly because we are yet again witnessing the emergence of a new technology of representation—the digital—that strikes us as having a somewhat alarming power and expansiveness, a potential to revolutionize modes of perception and even intellection. Digital media raise issues that demand a renewed vigilance to what we know or would like to know about the emergence of new technologies of representation.

For the digital seems to move beyond previous media by incorporating them all (even the loop characteristic of optical toys, as Lev Manovich has pointed out) and by proffering the vision (or nightmare) of a medium without materiality, of pure abstraction incarnated as a series of zeroes and ones, sheer presence and absence, the code.[6] Even light, that most diaphanous of materialities, is transformed into numerical form in the digital camera. In English, a telling symptom of this imperative of abstraction in the digital is its linguistic repression of touch. The first definition of "digital" listed in the *Oxford English Dictionary* is "of or pertaining to a finger, or to the fingers or digits." The transition from the digit to the digital is effected, first, by defining the most pertinent characteristic of the finger as its discreteness, its differentiation from the other fingers, and, second, by emphasizing the way in which the fingers lend themselves to counting, enumeration.[7] Yet what is elided here is the finger's preeminent status as the organ of touch, of contact, of sensation, of connection with the concrete. It could be said that the unconscious of the digital, that most abstract of logics/forms of representation, is touch.[8]

At first glance, it might seem that the history of technologies for the representation of movement traces the trajectory of a transition from optical toy to cinema, from manipulability to projection, from touch to sight, from materiality to abstraction. And certainly, there can be no doubt that the cinema has displaced the optical toy as the primary embodiment of a fascination with the illusion of movement. Nevertheless, we have only to point out the well-documented insertion of cinematic exhibition practices within a strongly established magic lantern culture (much older than the nineteenth-century rage for optical toys) to establish the complexity and convoluted nature of any such trajectory. Yet I would still argue that there is a crucial although incomplete displacement of touch by sight, materiality by abstraction, and that the residue of this incompletion is a certain ideologically inflected nostalgia. To that end, I will trace the instability of these oppositions that seem to haunt the search for a technology capable of adequately representing movement and time and producing both as the possession/experience of a viewer.

The flip-book itself, in terms of patents at any rate, was a relative latecomer in the parade of gadgets and inventions. In 1868, John Barnes Linnett patented the kineograph, or "movement writer" (the name no doubt inspired by the fact that movement was written, inscribed, contained within the pages of a book), although it is generally agreed that flip-books were widely used earlier in the nineteenth century and possibly even in the eighteenth. Also called a thumb book, it contained pages that held successive phases of a movement that, when held by the thumb and flipped, produced an uncannily smooth illusion of motion. The images were initially drawn, and until the advent of instantaneous photography, figures had to pose in position for each separately taken photograph. The popularity of the flip-book is exemplary testimony to the attractions of miniaturizing movement's representation and to the pleasures of tactility. The book could be held, owned, possessed. In this microcosm of movement, the viewer could oblige its figures to repeat, over and over again, the most convoluted actions. In its transportability, the flip-book is reminiscent of the thaumatrope, which exploited the theory of the afterimage but was incapable of depicting movement. The flip-book demanded a certain closeness between viewer and image, embodying the urge Benjamin associated with modernity—the urge "to get hold of an object at very close range by way of its likeness, its reproduction."[9] Unlike projection techniques (of the magic lantern, for instance), it produced an apparent immediacy and intimacy in the relation between the viewer, the apparatus, and the image. Unlike a regular book, a novel for instance, for which the reader must unfold its pages in a time that bears no relation to the time of the narrative, the speed of the flip-book viewer's thumb in releasing the pages is crucially connected to the effectiveness of the illusion of movement obtained. Nevertheless, what Susan Stewart has written about the miniature printed book has a certain relevance for the flip-book as well: "The social space of the miniature book might be seen as the social space, in miniature, of all books: the book as talisman to the body and emblem of the self; the book as microcosm and macrocosm; the book as commodity and knowledge, fact and fiction."[10] Herman Casler's mutoscope (patented in 1894), somewhat more sophisticated but based on the same principle as the flip-book, mimicked the physical configuration of Edison's kinetoscope. Yet it retained both the significance of tactility in the hand cranking necessary to mobilize the image and the insistence upon the solitary viewer of the smaller flip-book.

Earlier apparatuses designed to produce an illusion of movement, although less exemplarily tactile than the flip-book, were distinguished by their manipulability, the miniature scale of the illusion, their invitation to play, and their orientation toward either the single viewer or very small groups of viewers in a domestic rather than public setting. Joseph Plateau's phenakistoscope (1832) and anorthoscope (1836), Michael Faraday's wheel (1831), Simon von Stampfer's stroboscopic discs (1832), William Horner's Daedalum or zoetrope

(1834), and Charles-Émile Reynaud's praxinoscope (1877) all required the co-ordination of hand and eye, the spinning of a wheel or the sliding of a series of images through the apparatus, the changing of slides, strips of images, or wheels.[11] Unprojected and generally opaque, the image of movement could more readily be seen as both an ocular and a tactile possession. The reduced form of seriality of the loop constituted a type of miniaturization of time and movement, its repetition a guarantee of its materiality.

As discussed in chapter 1, Susan Stewart has connected the phenomenon of miniaturization with the domesticity and interiority associated with the bourgeois subject, exemplified, perhaps, by the dollhouse. The miniature can be truly appreciated only within the context of the home, and the status of optical toys as scientific experiment was very quickly displaced by their status as commodities designed to fill some of the leisure time of an increasingly powerful urban middle class. Within the bourgeois parlor, the optical toy provided a microcosm inside a microcosm, a miniature world of movement and action controlled by the bourgeois subject who was thereby reassured of their individuality and inviolable interiority. Conforming to the space and time of the individual subject, "the miniature, linked to nostalgic versions of childhood and history, presents a diminutive, and thereby manipulable, version of experience, a version which is domesticated and protected from contamination."[12] Scale is registered traditionally in reference to the body, and the smaller-than-life representation of motion confirms the stature of the subject, their transcendent view upon the world of things and actions. Tom Thumb, in Charlotte Yonge's children's book *The History of Sir Thomas Thumb* (1856), evokes a sense of corporeal wonder in two senses—named after a diminutive part of the body, he also nestles within the hand: "He was no larger than the green top of the twayblade blossom, and though perfect in all his limbs, it was not possible to feel that a thing so light and soft rested on the hand."[13] The domesticity of the miniature, its ensconcement within the regime of play and entertainment, does not, however, completely isolate it from the scientific. The miniature exists nowhere in nature but emerges as a cultural phenomenon, the product of a technology, part of whose fascination lies in the wonder of the diminutive, the very effort of seeing beyond the limits of the scale of everyday life. It is thus allied with the vision of the microscope: "That the world of things can open itself to reveal a secret life—indeed, to reveal a set of actions and hence a narrativity and history outside the given field of perception—is a constant daydream that the miniature presents. This is the daydream of the microscope: the daydream of life inside life, of significance multiplied infinitely *within* significance."[14] The daydream of life within life is also the logic of the toy, particularly the mechanical toy. The vision of children is a vision on a different scale—close to the earth, to things.

According to the *Oxford English Dictionary*, the leading sense of the word "toy," established only fairly recently, in the late eighteenth century and early nineteenth century, is "a material object for children or others to play with (often an imitation of some familiar object); a plaything; also, something contrived for amusement rather than for practical use (esp. in phrase *a mere toy*)."[15] But the most salient meaning in relation to its usage in the term "optical toy" has to do with the intimate relation between the toy and animation. The child's toy is brought to life in play; it is a witness to the fantastic transformation from the inanimate to the animate. The optical toy is antiphantasmagoric in this respect—it does not hide the work of its operation but instead flaunts it. A full appreciation of the illusion of movement provided by this toy is dependent upon a recognition of the stasis that is its foundation. The viewer must recognize the fundamental fixity of the image, its depiction of arrested life, before the movement can lay claim to the totality of its fascination. A hesitation in the transition from still to moving image underscores the wondrous nature of its effects, its alliance with the toy that takes on life.

Hence, unlike the various attempts to align the illusion of movement with projection—the magic lantern shows both earlier and later and the cinema (usually seen as the telos of the optical toy)—the optical toy depended upon miniaturization, the materiality and opaqueness of an image that was quite tangible, and the proximity of the single viewer (simultaneously the operator of the device) to the image. However, as Jonathan Crary has argued, there is undoubtedly an abstraction at work here.[16] While the pages of the flip-book or the strips of images in the praxinoscope were quite tangible, indeed, demanded to be held, the image of movement itself was nowhere but in the perception of the viewer—immaterial, abstract, and thus open to practices of manipulation and deception. The toys could not work without this fundamental dependence upon an evanescent, intangible image. The tangibility of the apparatus and the materiality of the images operated as a form of resistance to this abstraction, assuring the viewer that the image of movement could be produced at will, through the labor of the body, and could, indeed, be owned as a commodity, situated within the most domesticated of places, among other material objects that displayed the social ascendancy of the middle class. Often these toys were elaborately handcrafted and elegantly designed, becoming themselves—outside of any function—the prized objects.

This insistence upon materiality also characterized the epistemological discourse on these toys, the "philosophical" or scientific aspect of the "philosophical toy." The items were sold as educational toys whose aim was to instruct the populace about the functioning of the eye, the work of vision. Plateau's phenakistoscope, often situated as the originating moment of the obsession with such apparatuses, was designed to illustrate the observations of Peter Mark Roget and Michael Faraday about optical illusions in viewing spokes of a turning wheel through vertical apertures. Plateau not only elaborated the principles of the effect but invented the phenakistiscope to demonstrate it. In 1830, he wrote, "If several objects, progressively different in form and position, are presented to the eye for very short intervals and sufficiently close together, the impressions they make upon the retina will join together without being confused, and one will believe one is seeing a single object gradually changing form and position."[17] The retina was conceptualized as a slate or screen that retains, if only briefly, imprints or impressions. According to A. R. Luria, "The psychology of the nineteenth century regarded perception as a passive imprint made by external stimuli on the retina, and later in the visual cortex."[18] A strong enough stimulus or force will *impress itself* upon the retina, causing actual physical changes often described in terms reminiscent of engraving, printing, or other processes of mechanical reproduction. Hermann von Helmholtz, for whom the eye was analogous to a camera obscura, claimed, "On the surface of this membrane [the retina] a real optical image is projected of the external objects in view, which is inverted and very much reduced in size."[19] He buttressed this explanation by citing the "fact" that, when removing an eye from a corpse and pointing it toward the light, a small inverted image can be seen sharply defined on the retina. Helmholtz's invention of the ophthalmoscope in 1850 and his discussions of the image formed on the dead retina appear to have prepared the ground for a massive investment in the late nineteenth century in the idea that the retina acts like a photographic plate and retains the last image before death.[20] Even within this fictional realm, however, it is only at the moment of death that the image is stabilized for any length of time—in general, we are dealing with fleeting impressions of short duration. Nevertheless, in nineteenth-century theories of vision, there is always a material inscription, and the lingering, the delay of that trace is stipulated as the basis of the illusion of movement in the optical toy.

The toys "worked," but the theory of persistence of vision has been largely discredited within the realm of cognitive psychology and replaced by theories of the phi phenomenon, masking, and critical flicker fusion.[21] The assumptions underlying the theory of persistence of vision—retinal retention, the physiological duration of images—have been rejected in favor of an insistence upon the question of critical thresholds beyond which the human eye is incapable of perceiving difference.[22] The theory of persistence of vision may be "wrong," but the question remains: Why was it so firmly ensconced, and what function did it serve in the nineteenth century? The answer has at least partially to do with a denial of the accelerating abstraction linked to capitalism, with a clinging to the idea of the materiality of the image, its touchability, its concreteness. The theory that purportedly explained the effect of the optical toy—persistence of vision, in locating the image on the retina of a dead eye—insisted that the image is *not nowhere* (to the contrary, it is indeed *embodied*).

It is not possible to claim that the optical toy and projection constitute separate successive historical stages or even that they have nothing to do with each other. The magic lantern was produced as a toy in the second half of the nineteenth century, and the lantern's prior exhibition of projection to a large audience preceded the emergence of the optical toy craze of the early part of that century. The Kinora, the miniature mutoscope developed for home use by the Lumières in 1896, was extremely popular well into the era of the cinema (approximately 1912). Plateau's phenakistoscope inspired a number of attempts to project the illusion of movement, including T. W. Naylor's "Phantasmagoria for the Exhibition of Moving Figures" (1843), Franz von Uchatius's merger of the phenakistoscope and magic lantern in 1845, Louis Jules Duboscq's Lanterne Photogénique (1853–54), Gomez Santa Maria's Dinascope (1868), and a host of others.[23] Uchatius's description of his aims clearly indicates that he understood the advantages of scale allowed by projection: he was attempting to produce "an apparatus by means of which moving images can be represented on a wall, at the size which one desires, and with a clarity which Stampfer's disc does not obtain. . . . Although a moving image has already been obtained which may be viewed by a greater number of people at the same time, one would still wish to be able to produce this image on the wall at the desired size and thus to be able to show it in a large auditorium."[24]

The ability to hold the instrument of represented movement in one's hand lends the image a closeness, a contingency, a possessability that differs markedly from the experience of projection. The transition is from a viewer who looks down at an image and plays with it to a stably positioned spectator who looks up, at a distanced, seemingly immaterial image. Optical toys and projection seem to entertain every conceivable historical relation: precession, succession, and simultaneity. Projection both precedes (in the magic lantern) and succeeds (in the cinema) the optical toy; in addition, the two simultaneously share the middle years of the nineteenth century in an ongoing struggle between domestic and public space. It is clearly a dialectical relation of negation and incorporation, inversion and opposition. Nevertheless, projection achieved and maintained a hegemony in the production of the illusion of movement for much of the twentieth century.

The various technical developments associated with the intermittent projection of motion—finding an effective shutter speed, automation, agreement upon a fixed aspect ratio—stabilized, regularized, and standardized the image at the expense of its dematerialization. The image is carried, transported, on a luminous beam, and for the sedentary viewer in this configuration, nothing is tangible. As Dominique Païni points out:

> Projection arises from a little-known history belonging to the fields of physics, of geometry, of optics, of psychology, of pictorial representation, of show business (*spectacle*). In its shortest definition, the most ordinary dictionary relays the equivocal character of the word: the action of projecting images on a screen and the representation of a volume on a flat surface. Spectacle and geometry, fields of activity far from each other, are mixed in the same word. With the slide or the film, it is nonetheless a matter of a comparable result: a volume transferred to a surface, illusion and geometric codification, mirage and science.[25]

According to Païni and from an art historical perspective, the image can be achieved in two ways: through its attachment to a material support (he is thinking here of painting, frescoes, and the like, but one could also add optical toys) and through the interception of a beam of light by a surface (the screen) that is totally foreign to the image. In the first case, the image is made visible through direct or ambient light; in the second, the image is "dependent on the light that traverses the transparent veil of its support. . . . In this 'other' history, light no longer encounters an image, nor bathes it, nor illuminates it. Light penetrates it at first, then transports it, duplicates it in dematerializing it, sometimes temporalizing and sublimating it . . . since the projection of an image mixes in a single composite the image and the light necessary for its exhibition, it associates *representing* and *exhibiting*. Vision equals light and light is identified with the sense of sight."[26] Projection of the illusion of motion collapses representation and exhibition and calls up the notion of spectacle. It magnifies the image whose scale is no longer dominated by the scale of a body but by that of an architecture, of the abstract authority of spectacle and a collective, public life. The abstraction and dematerialization associated with projection as an operation are perhaps most provocatively confronted in a 1973 film by Anthony McCall, *Line Describing a Cone*. Imageless, the film deals only with the projected beam of light, beginning as a thin, laser-like beam and gradually developing over thirty minutes into the full shape of a cone. In the words of one critic, "It demystifies the leap from celluloid to projected image by showing what exists, semi-tangibly, in between."[27] Rather than treating projected light as a mere carrier of the image, the film transforms that beam into an object, so much so that the viewer experiences an irresistible compulsion to reach out and touch it, a gesture leading only to disappointment. The viewer, who is not restricted to a single point of view but encouraged to move around, through and under the beam, must turn their back on the screen and ultimately face the projector itself.[28]

Line Describing a Cone directly confronts the abstraction and dematerialization associated with projection. The classical narrative film of Hollywood, on the other hand, denies these processes through the production of the image as a world—concrete, material, absorbing. The spectator of this cinema, unlike the viewer of the optical toy, is kept in the dark, as it were, in relation to knowledge of the origin of the image. This spectator must turn their back on the apparatus in order to perceive the illusion of movement, generating an epistemological uncertainty as to the status of the image: Is it material or immaterial? Close or distant? Concrete or abstract?

With cinema and the accomplished projection of the illusion of movement came an increase not only in abstraction but also in scale. Now untouchable, at a distance, the image became gigantic, larger than life. The viewer, who could dominate, manipulate the optical toy, controlling the speed and timing of its production/generation of movement, became dominated, overwhelmed, and dispossessed in relation to an image that seemed to be liberated from the obligation of dimension. While the miniature appears completely intelligible and knowable, the gigantic, as Stewart has argued, exceeds the viewer's grasp and incarnates the limited possibility of partial knowledge. The growth of capitalism and a consumer economy precisely situates the subject as epistemologically inadequate, as incapable of ever actually mapping or understanding the totality of social forces that determine the subject's position. As Guy Debord argues in *The Society of the Spectacle*, the giganticism of the spectacle is particularly in synchrony with the effects of capitalist production: "The *success* of this production [of the workers], that is, the abundance it generates, is experienced by its producers only as an *abundance of dispossession*. All time, all space, becomes *foreign* to them as their own alienated productions accumulate. The spectacle is a map of this new world—a map drawn to the scale of the territory itself."[29] In cinematic projection, the distance of the image is a measure of this dispossession, its intangibility a sign of the increasing abstraction of a consumer economy.

Nevertheless, there is also a sense in which the cinema has worked ceaselessly to repudiate this abstraction and to generate its own forms of possession of the image. The dream of the tangible, of the haptic (of the optical toy in effect) is incorporated within the cinema through the production of effects of proximity. These effects are most visible, perhaps, in the technique of the close-up, a figure that has been absolutely central to the development of a film language as well as the theory of that language. The close-up works to actualize, to make present, that which it contains—to bring the image within reach. It seems to address the question posed by Maurice Blanchot—"What happens when what you see, even though from a distance, seems to touch you with a grasping contact, when the matter of seeing is a sort of touch, when seeing is a *contact* at a distance?"[30] While on the one hand, the close-up works to magnify, to exaggerate the scale of the image, its giganticism, it also, by necessity, deals with the detail, the miniature. Its logic is that of the microscope—to expand vision by moving ever closer and revealing worlds within worlds. In the close-up, miniaturization and magnification complement one another. The miniature is absorbed within, indeed becomes, the gigantic, the larger-than-life of the cinema, exemplifying the dialectic of distance and proximity so crucial to modernity.[31]

The cinema does not overcome or defeat the optical toy through some kind of fatality associated with a teleological history of advance or technological progression. To the contrary, it exhibits a form of active nostalgia for or semiotic envy of the materiality, the tangibility of that toy's image. In the wake of an increasing abstraction and its attendant destabilization, the cinema's compensation lies in its production for the spectator of an illusory possession of time and movement in a congealed form—that of the temporal condensation of narrative and the spatial expansion of the close-up.

With the ever more elaborate abstraction and dematerialization of the digital, the optical toy has assumed an increasing significance. One might even argue that the optical toy has reemerged in the mobile phone with its touchscreen technology. Here, the viewer can not only hold the machine that generates movement but also control the scale of the image with two fingers. However, it also seems that the historical optical toy has become more important in its own right—not only in the history of science and technology and in a new archaeology of media, but also within the domain of the museum. In the last few years, the number of special exhibits devoted to the optical toy and its role in a history of visual culture has increased substantially. The optical toy—often elaborately and elegantly decorated—has become the centerpiece of a certain nostalgia. Its promise that the representation of movement need not be accompanied by the loss of materiality and tangibility is incarnated in its embrace of a painterly ideal. The running, jumping, and mutating figures of the phenakistoscope, the zoetrope, or the praxinoscope are often meticulously drawn or beautifully painted, works of art in their own right. Although the optical toy's historical emergence coincided with that of photography, it clung to a painterly aesthetic, emphasizing—against the evanescence of projection— the image's attachment to a material support. This aesthetic of the optical toy makes it highly amenable to incorporation within the museum. What might be called the museumification of the optical toy, its emergence as an objet d'art, celebrates the memory of that viewer who, for a brief moment of historical time, seemed to hold movement in their hands.

Projection and the Avant-Garde

Writing in 1925, László Moholy-Nagy foregrounded light as the medium of photography and film. Light was not so much dematerializing as it was a new material, no longer that which simply facilitated access to other, seemingly more material objects. His experiments with photograms made light both agent and mold of the representation, and in his short film *Ein Lichtspiel Schwarz-Weiss-Grau* (1930), recognition of the material object or its parts is completely subordinated to the tracing and recording of the play of projected and reflected light and shadow (fig. 5.1).[32] At the opening of the film, the sheerness and transparency of film as a strip of frames is exhibited as an overture to the tracking of the projected image suffused with light. More radically, perhaps, in his theoretical writings, Moholy-Nagy envisaged a utopian future that would "attach the greatest importance to kinetic, projected composition, probably even with interpenetrating beams and masses of light floating freely in the room without a direct plane of projection; the instruments will continually be improved so that it will be able to embrace far larger fields of tension."[33] Moholy-Nagy also imagined a projection plane divided into different obliquely positioned planes and a projection screen in the shape of a sphere (or a segment of a sphere), instead of the traditional flat rectangular screen. In this construct, more than one film could be projected simultaneously, and, most intriguingly, these films would not be projected onto a fixed location of the screen; instead, the process of projection itself would be mobile, freed from the rigidity of convention.[34] As mentioned in the previous chapter, the historical avant-garde produced numerous other experiments with light and projection, including the films of Richter and Eggeling, Man Ray, and Fernand Léger, as well as Marcel Duchamp's *Anemic Cinema* (1926).

This was the historical moment—the 1920s—of a frenzied optimism about the potential of cinema to produce a radically new vision. And it is crucial that part of this celebratory discourse and experimentation involved the disengagement of projection and of light as a particularly malleable medium,

5.1 *Ein Lichtspiel Schwarz-Weiss-Grau* (László Moholy-Nagy, 1930).

independent of that which was projected and that which was illuminated. While the projection of an image on a large scale, in theaters, to a mass audience, marked a transition from the production of an illusion of movement as toy, as tangible and possessable commodity, to the spectacular forms of image production and dissemination characterizing the twentieth century, that process of projection was also perceived by the avant-garde as a distinctly new aesthetic language, capable of dodging, in its dematerialization, the discourse of commodification. Later, one could also trace a persistent fascination with the projection beam in films as diverse as Orson Welles's *Citizen Kane* (1941), Max Ophuls's *Caught* (1949), and Isaac Julien's *Looking for Langston* (1988)—in each case, the projection beam as cone of light (made manifest by the swirling of dust or smoke) signifying Cinema itself.

Yet the very concept of projection requires some theoretical and historical unraveling. "To project" once signified "to work an alchemical transformation by casting the philosopher's stone over base metal in the hope of turning an inferior amalgam into pure gold."[35] Projection effects a change at the material level but through a cause that partakes of immateriality, invisibility, inscrutability. Projection also indicates the action of throwing, ejecting, propelling away from oneself. To project is literally to throw forward (the distance between projector and screen is called a "throw" by film projectionists). In geometry, the term fixes a certain conceptualization of space and vision in relation to points and lines. A straight line or "ray" connects each point of a figure to an intercepting surface or plane—the resulting image is a projection of the original. Sight is imagined as straight line, arrow, ray, linear directionality (invoking, as Païni points out, "the letter of Albertian theory—sight as light beam").[36] A basic assumption here is the transformation, the alchemic transmogrification as it were, of three-dimensional space into two-dimensional space, a mapping or reduction of sensory, tactile space into purely visual space. The affinity of this way of thinking with perspectival constructions of the real is apparent. Projection also names quite specifically the representation on a flat surface of a sphere or a section of a sphere (pre-eminently, the globe), hence its strong connection with mapping.

Yet the mathematical and scientific claims of the concept of projection coexist with the less mappable, less calculable notion of projection as an attribute of subjectivity (its invocation within the discourses of behaviorism, general psychology, psychoanalysis). This inflection has had crucial reverberations within aesthetic theory as well, when the spectator/viewer is conceptualized as a point of origin in relation to an image. An entry in the supplement to Diderot and D'Alembert's *Encyclopedia* heralds a continuing discussion of the necessary limits of illusion in art—the illusion cannot and must not be complete.[37] As such, it would risk the loss of a pleasure associated with the moment of recognition of the object's fabrication. Lack is built into the concept of aesthetic illusion—not only as the impossibility of the aesthetic object's attempted substitution for the real but as a necessary prerequisite for a specifically aesthetic fascination and enjoyment, based in part on the notion of projection.

In E. H. Gombrich's view, there must be some sort of gap, absence, or lack to enable the most important spectatorial activity, which he labels "projection." Far from being "taken in" by the illusion, the viewer actively participates in the construction of an impression of the real and is led by experience and expectation to "project." In the essay "Conditions of Illusion," he claims, "When we say that the blots and brushstrokes of the impressionist landscapes 'suddenly come to life,' we mean we have been led to project a landscape into these dabs of pigment."[38] Gombrich outlines two conditions that must be met in order to support the illusion: (1) the viewer must be assured that they can close the gap or incompletion that is a necessary consequence of the limits of the medium; (2) the viewer "must be given a 'screen,' an empty or ill-defined area onto which he can project the expected image."[39] The screen is exploited by those artists who know how to produce "expressive absence" and are educated as to the "power of indeterminate forms." Yet, beyond the skill of the artist, it is the very structure of the apparatus of painting, of the ritualized forms of viewing, that generates the screen, receiver of the viewer's projections: "The distance from the canvas weakens the beholder's power of discrimination and creates a blur which mobilizes his projective faculty. The indistinct parts of the canvas become a screen."[40] Far from an insistence upon mimesis or verisimilitude, this is a demand for blankness, illegibility, and absence as the support of illusion. It is noteworthy that Gombrich has recourse to a cinematic vocabulary—projection, screen—in order to specify the conditions of illusion in pictorial art. Both Roland Barthes and Christian Metz have emphasized the projective powers of cinema, particularly in comparison with photography (in photography, according to Barthes, "this has been" overpowers "here I am").[41] Not only light in its transience and quasi immateriality, but something of the self is thrown out at the screen. (This was the basis, in the 1970s, for apparatus theory's insistence that the spectator be included as a component of cinema.)

Nevertheless, it is within psychoanalysis, arising, as is often noted, at the same historical moment as the cinema, that projection receives its most sophisticated theorization, and one that ultimately returns to the project of a mapping of subjectivity in relation to space. Projection is instrumental in the establishment of the opposition between internal and external, subject and object. In Freudian theory, the infant expels and projects into the external world what it finds in itself of the unpleasurable, and incorporates or retains what is pleasurable (projection and introjection both being conceived on the model of the oral drives). In this way, the child constructs for itself—even before it attains the status of subjecthood—the territories and spaces, both internal and external, that will constitute its world. Hence, the paranoid activation of projection is only an intensification and perversion (in the sense of a "turning away from" rather than a pathology) of what Freud describes as a normal, nonpathogenic mechanism, fundamental to the establishment of an opposition between ego and external world and hence crucial to any epistemology that posits a subject and an object of knowledge. In "Negation," Freud points to the originary nature of the nondifferentiation between subject and object: "The antithesis between subjective and objective does not exist from the first. It only comes into being from the fact that thinking possesses the capacity to bring before the mind once more something that has once been perceived, by reproducing it as a presentation without the external object having still to be there."[42] It is the assumption of representation, based on absence, that is the condition of possibility of subjectivity. And theoretical systems, according to Freud (even, and perhaps especially, his own), are produced through a mechanism not unlike that of paranoid projection.

In a telling discussion of female paranoia, what is at stake for Freud is the projection not of a desire or drive but of an aspect of the body itself, whose position in space thus becomes confused, dislocated. In the only case of female paranoia Freud treats, described in "A Case of Paranoia Running Counter to the Psychoanalytical Theory of the Disease," the woman's delusion concerns being photographed. This case involves a young woman who, during lovemaking with a male friend, hears a noise—a knock or tick— which she interprets as the sound of a camera, photographing her in order to compromise her. In his analysis, Freud doubts the very existence of the noise: "I do not believe that the clock ever ticked or that any noise was to be heard at all. The woman's situation justified a sensation of throbbing in the clitoris. This was what she subsequently projected as a perception of an external object."[43] Female paranoia thus finds its psychoanalytic explanation in the projection of a bodily sensation from inside to outside, in a relocation in external reality.

Whether projection involves the displacement of bodily sensation, the loss of the measure of one's physical pleasure, or simply the destabilization of a fragile boundary separating subject and object, in psychoanalysis it is a concept that names a disorientation, a mapping gone awry (but, it should be said, a fundamental disorientation, a grounding alienation). And it is not accidental that this intensive theorization of a spatiopsychical instability should coincide with the emergence of technological projection on a massive scale, with the growing dominance of the cinema as both a mode of addressing disorientation and a mode of orienting the subject to new spaces. As Jean Laplanche and J. B. Pontalis point out in *The Language of Psychoanalysis*, one of the senses of projection is "comparable to the cinematographic one: the subject sends out into the external world an image of something that exists in him in an unconscious way. Projection is defined here as a mode of *refusal to recognise* (*méconnaissance*) which has as its counterpart the subject's ability to recognise in others precisely what he refuses to acknowledge in himself."[44]

In the works of the historical avant-garde, the cinematic play of light is disorienting because it dematerializes location, undoes solidity, and destabilizes the spectator's assurance of position. In the 1960s and 1970s, another avant-garde also pursued an obsession with projection and with light as a medium. This obsession is present in the work of figures such as Andy Warhol, Anthony McCall, Peter Kubelka, Paul Sharits, Michael Snow, and many others. Filmmakers such as Tony Conrad, with *The Flicker* (1965), and Peter Kubelka, with *Arnulf Rainer* (1960), took this logic of interrogating projection and foregrounding light as medium to an extreme by emptying the image of all content. The "flicker film," with its carefully sequenced alternations of white and black frames, produced a stroboscopic effect. Representation, if it could be called this, extended beyond the screen to invade the space of the theater or screening room itself. Space was effectively sculpted by the light generated by projection (and sculpture is, ironically, usually thought to be one of the arts most densely laden with matter, with materiality). Nevertheless, the flicker film still anticipated an immobile, indeed transfixed spectator—the spectator of theatrical space. It is with work like that of Anthony McCall that projection exceeds the confines of the screen and becomes the aesthetic event itself. *Line Describing a Cone* (1973) was discussed earlier in this chapter, but an even more radical example of McCall's production of aesthetic objects that he calls "film" but that do not rely on the materials we normally associate with the medium (such as the flat screen and projected image missing in *Line Describing a Cone*) is an installation piece of

1975 entitled *Long Film for Ambient Light*. Lacking camera, film, projector, and screen, the piece dealt only with space, light, and duration. As Jonathan Walley described it, "The work consisted of an empty Manhattan loft, its windows covered with diffusion paper, lit in the evening by a single bare lightbulb hanging from the ceiling. It lasted for twenty-four hours, during which time spectators could come and go as they pleased, moving about the space at will."[45] Walley, resuscitating a term coined by Ken Jacobs, refers to McCall's work and similar works by Paul Sharits and others as "paracinema." Strongly influenced by Conceptual art, these works are "radically dematerialized," according to Walley, and find an affinity with Conceptual art's challenge to both art as commodification and the notion of modernist art as reflecting incessantly upon medium specificity (instead, they reveal how the concept of a medium is constantly historically changing). What is at stake here is an "idea of cinema" that is based on subtracting the very matter or elements that we usually associate with the medium.

Because much of this work is in the form of installations or performances, it effectively displaces the concept of cinema from theatrical exhibition and resituates it in the museum. Païni claims these works are critical of mediatic power, a position that would seem to be confirmed by McCall's description of *Line Describing a Cone* as anti-illusionary:

> It deals with the projected light beam itself, rather than treating the light beam as a mere carrier of coded information, which is decoded when it strikes a flat surface.... *Line Describing a Cone* deals with one of the irreducible conditions of film: projected light. It deals with this phenomenon directly, independently of any other considerations. It is the first film to exist in real, three-dimensional space. This film exists only in the present: the moment of projection. It refers to nothing beyond this real time. It contains no illusion. It is a primary experience, not secondary: i.e., the space is real, not referential; the time is real, not referential.[46]

But if the power of conventional/classical cinema already is seen to lie less in any illusionary power than in its move toward dematerialization (and away from the tangibility of the optical toy), in its projection of an image viewable by mass audiences as public spectacle—all of which hinges on the notion that an image can be carried on a beam of light—if this is the case, why is an exacerbation of this process of dematerialization viewed as a contestation? I think the answer lies in a return to the history of the effects of projection and scale, together with the fate of the body and location in modernity.

Within the conventional cinema, projection enables the "bigger than life" scale of the image, a scale that can seem overwhelming—and certainly was in the earliest years of the cinema. But scale as a problem is also internalized as the relation of the body of the spectator to the articulations of the image as close-up, medium shot, and long shot. When Le Corbusier sought, in the early years of the twentieth century, to outline the need for a new visual measure, he pointed to music as a model. The scale in music breaks up the continuum of sound and allows for recording and archival procedures. For his visual measure, he fastened upon the human body as a reference point, citing the age-old tradition of correlating units of measure to parts of the human body—elbow (cubit), finger (digit), thumb (inch), foot, pace, and so on. Architecture designs a space that a human body must inhabit; for Le Corbusier, this demands a resistance to the pure abstraction of the metric scale.[47] Film provides an abstract space populated by virtual bodies and invites a form of figurative inhabitation by the spectator. The rules of continuity editing dictate that this space must appear navigable and inhabitable, its directions securely orienting a spectator. Continuity editing, from this perspective, would represent a form of domestication (or reembodiment) of scale from within. As outlined in chapter 2, in the early years of the cinema there was a strong resistance to the close-up for its violation of human scale—gigantic scale was both fascinating and disturbing. All of this suggests that the cinema (and its theorization) has struggled with a fundamental disorientation, its complex attempts to orient subjects to spaces responding to a form of dislocation specific to the advent of modernity and its abstraction of time, space, and vision. The concepts of absorption and inhabitation, the fascination with being incorporated or enveloped by an image, are symptoms of an uncertainty and anxiety about the individual's relation to an increasingly incomprehensible social network, a deficiency that Fredric Jameson has eloquently described as the problem of cognitive mapping, an inability to deal with the "growing contradiction between lived experience and structure."[48]

The larger-than-life spectacle of the cinema takes up where the panorama of the nineteenth century left off and inherits its uncertain spatial location of an image. According to Jonathan Crary, in the panorama, "audience members occasionally tossed coins at the image as a way of determining how far away it was."[49] Like the panorama, but even more intensively, the cinema generates a confusion about the location of the image, abstracting location itself. The virtuality of the image indicates not a question about its substance or materiality but an undecidability as to where it is. We might see the desire to lose oneself in an image as an outgrowth of the destabilization of scale (as proportionate representation), mapping, and dimension that accompanies modernization and its technologies of dedistancing and overstimulation. The projection of images accelerates these tendencies.

The works of an expanded cinema or a "paracinema" are, in a sense, antiprojection (even McCall's *Line Describing a Cone*) to the extent that projection implies as one of its effects the mapping of a three-dimensional space onto a two-dimensional plane.[50] For these works demand that the three-dimensional space of reception be activated, that the spectator/viewer become unfixed, mobile, cognizant of that space. This is a return to three-dimensional space not as a form of realism but as a resuscitation of the body as a measure of scale. Here, the invocation of sculpture is absolutely crucial. As McCall points out, when you watch a film or video, "you enter the elsewhere of the moving image, and you leave your physical body behind, which remains rooted to the spot. To study sculpture—or to explore architectural space—you must walk, measuring what you see with your eyes and your physical body."[51]

The viewer of *Line Describing a Cone*, on the other hand, reaches out to touch the light, the projection beam, but encounters only space. The works of paracinema or expanded cinema are a counterweight to the delocalization of the image associated with projection. They deal directly with the loss of location of the image so that, even while it could be said that these works are radically *not* about the image, they are about a spatial disorientation caused by the projection of the image. If dematerialization is the project of this "cinema," to what effect? These works, in exacerbating dematerialization but insisting on location, seek to engage with the complex reorganization of body, scale, and image that characterizes modernity and is perhaps best exemplified by the cinema. Like Le Corbusier, they work to reengage the body of the viewer as measure (of scale, distance, and materiality). And in this sense, they generate a rethinking of the location of the image, and the location of location.

Projection, Mapping, and Perspective

To project an image in the cinema is to produce a two-dimensional representation of a three-dimensional world (the second, "geometric," definition of Païni). A volume is projected onto a surface. In this sense, projection is a technique with an intimate historical connection to cartography as well as the development of Renaissance perspective. A map is generated through the projection of a sphere (the globe) onto a flat plane. However, this devel-

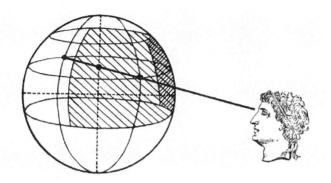

5.2 Ptolemy's third method of mapping, from Samuel Y. Edgerton, *The Renaissance Rediscovery of Linear Perspective* (New York: Basic Books, 1975). Thanks to Samuel Edgerton for permission to reprint this image.

opment in cartography—the use of projection—did not appear in Europe until after 1400, when Ptolemy's *Geographia* first reemerged and generated widespread interest in Florence. Medieval maps were portolan charts that were produced based on seamen's accounts of the geography of coastlines and wind directions. They did not accurately represent position or location but were used to ascertain the directions to various ports and harbors. Although written in AD 140, Ptolemy's *Geographia* had no impact on mapping practices until the Renaissance's resuscitation of a fascination with classical texts. It did not so much expand knowledge of geography as provide a rigorous system for mapping the surface of the world based on a theory of space as unified and mathematically precise. The ancient world conceptualized the earth as a sphere divided by meridians between the poles (longitudes) and parallels encircling it (latitudes).[52] The difficulty lay in generating a flat representation of these curved lines. According to Samuel Y. Edgerton, Ptolemy's *Geographia* "now showed how to project the coordinates of any geographic location in the world, and how to compensate for the distortion of the spherical surface when stretched out on a two-dimensional plane."[53]

Edgerton has argued that the rediscovery of Ptolemy's *Geographia* in the early fifteenth century in Florence is indissociable from the Renaissance rediscovery of perspective by such figures as Filippo Brunelleschi and Leon Battista Alberti. Ptolemy's third method of mapping situates the viewer in relation to the globe in a precise position in order to produce a two-dimensional map (fig. 5.2). It also locates Syrene (Σ, the center of the

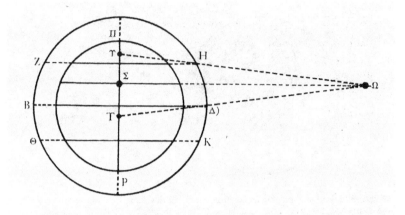

5.3 Ptolemy's third method of mapping, from Samuel Y. Edgerton, *The Renaissance Rediscovery of Linear Perspective* (New York: Basic Books, 1975). Thanks to Samuel Edgerton for permission to reprint this image.

oikumene [the known world in ancient times]) as the central point in a perspectival construction organized for the viewer.[54] Edgerton claims that this point is for all intents and purposes the same as Alberti's "centric point" as described in *De pictura* and hence equivalent to the vanishing point, resting on the horizon (the meridian linking the North and South Poles [Π and P in fig. 5.3]). The viewer's position (Ω) is on a line linked to this central point, and hence the latitude through Syrene would be the only one appearing to the viewer as a straight line while all other latitudes would appear as ellipses, turned concavely toward this line. According to Edgerton, "What he [Ptolemy] is talking about here is nothing less than the *horizon line* principle—a principle which was not to be scientifically applied to a pictorial situation until Brunelleschi's mirror experiment."[55] The points Υ and T mark the edges of the known world, resulting in Ptolemy's map of the world (fig. 5.4).

The great advantage of Ptolemy's mapping procedure was the grid system of latitude and longitude, which "reduced the traditional heterogeneity of the world's surface to complete geometrical uniformity . . . and thereby gave powerful impetus to the Renaissance rationalization of the world."[56] This grid system is echoed by Alberti's *velo* (veil), a gridded instrument for the production of accurate form and perspective (fig. 5.5), described by Alberti in *On Painting* in this way: "It is like this: a veil loosely woven of fine thread, dyed whatever color you please, divided up by thicker threads into as many parallel square sections as you like, and stretched on a frame. I set this up

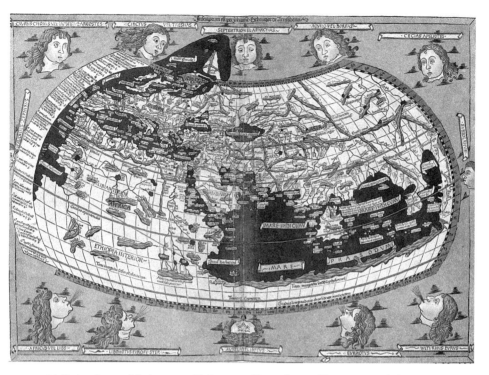

5.4 Ptolemy's map of the known world. A 1482 world map illustrated by Donnus Nicholas Germanus, constructed using Ptolemy's system.

between the eye and the object to be represented, so that the visual pyramid passes through the loose weave of the veil."[57] The space of the map is most similar to that of perspective in its homogeneity and rationality. Position and location constitute the central values of the map that, because it is the result of the projection of a sphere onto a plane surface, necessarily entails inaccuracies in other qualities (shape, area, distance, direction). A flat map is most reliable in the areas (points or lines) where it is tangential to the globe but becomes increasingly inaccurate as it strays from those points or lines (which, in a map of any practical value, it must do). This is particularly the case with scale. As David Greenhood points out, "There is no flat, large-region map in which the scale is true and is the same constant scale, measuring in all directions from any and every point. This is possible only on a globe."[58] The most widely used and hence familiar map is the Mercator cylindrical projection, developed by the Flemish geographer and cartographer Gerardus Mercator in 1569. Although its primary purpose was nautical, it has been widely disseminated in educational atlases and maps, and its shapes and areas have had,

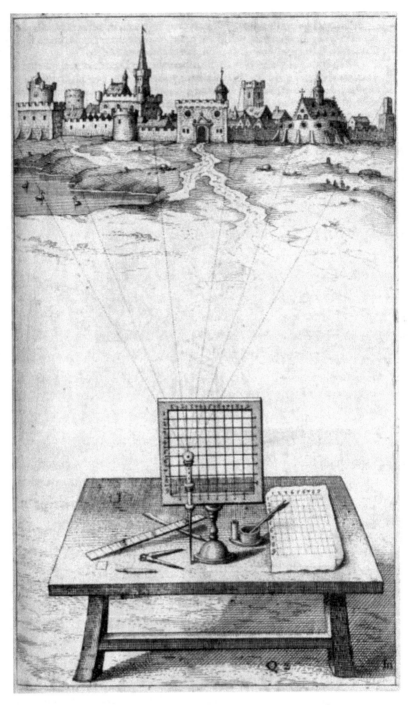

5.5 Alberti's *velo*. From Robert Fludd (1574–1637), *Utriusque cosmic maioris scilicet et minoris metaphysica* (Oppenhemii: Ære Johan-Theodori de Bry, typis Hieronymi Galleri, 1617–21).

perhaps, the greatest influence on the popular recognizability of the scale of continents. However, because it is a cylindrical map, its accuracy is greatest at the equator and diminishes toward the poles as its scale increases toward infinity. On the Mercator map, Africa appears to be the same size as Europe when it is actually three times as large; the area of Alaska on the map is equal to that of Brazil, although Brazil has five times the area of Alaska; Greenland seems to be larger than Africa, although Africa's area is fourteen times greater than Greenland's.[59] Generated during the age of European exploration and colonialism, the Mercator map has often been criticized for its Eurocentrism and for diminishing the size of countries and continents in the global South. Cartographers frequently acknowledge the political implications of procedures of mapping in the face of accusations of cartographic imperialism.[60]

The inevitable flaws and falsifications of maps are widely recognized, while the illusionism involved in perspectival representation striving for "realism" in its depiction of space is disavowed. As Erwin Panofsky points out, the picture in Renaissance perspective is transformed into Alberti's window, and the "material surface upon which the individual figures or objects are drawn or painted or carved is thus negated, and instead reinterpreted as a mere 'picture plane.' Upon this picture plane is projected the spatial continuum which is seen through it and which is understood to contain all the various individual objects."[61] Although both mapping and perspective generate an abstraction of space, the constructed nature of that space is foregrounded in mapping and undermined in aesthetic perspective through the figure of the transparent window and the illusion of three-dimensionality. Despite the fact that they are both undergirded by a geometric optics, there are a number of crucial differences between mapping and perspective. A map does not produce the illusion of a "beyond" lurking behind its surface. Nor does it necessarily imply a continuous and activated space beyond its frame that is only contingently "cut off" from the space of the representation. Svetlana Alpers, in distinguishing between a southern, Italian use of perspective and the northern, Dutch style of description and observation of the seventeenth century, claims that there is no stable point of view for the subject in Dutch painting—rather, the painting is viewed, like a cartographic projection, "from nowhere."[62] While any claims to scientificity might be argued as situating the map's viewer as "nowhere," positionless, a map is nevertheless a geometric construction that presupposes a location for the eye of the viewer, and its scale purports to be proportional to the "real" space of that viewer.[63] Most important, both the map and perspective engender a homogeneous space in which all points are defined in terms of position, location. Panofsky, in the beginning of his book, quotes Ernst Cassirer (from whom he borrows the concept of "symbolic form") at length:

The ultimate basis of the homogeneity of geometric space is that all its elements, the "points" which are joined in it, are mere determinants of position, possessing no independent content of their own outside of this relation, this position which they occupy in relation to each other. Their reality is exhausted in their reciprocal relation: it is a purely functional and not a substantial reality. . . . Hence homogeneous space is never given space, but space produced by construction. . . . [In the space of immediate perception] there is no strict homogeneity of position and direction; each place has its own mode and its own value. Visual space and tactical space [*Tastraum*] are both anisotropic and unhomogeneous in contrast to the metric space of Euclidean geometry: "the main directions of organization—before-behind, above-below, right-left—are dissimilar in both physiological spaces."[64]

The space of both perspective and mapping is a systematic space, a measurable space. In both cases, the spatial representation is about location, positioning, "knowing where one is." The grids of latitude and longitude in mapping and the network of orthogonals and transversals in perspective situate both places and viewers in a stable and knowable site.

Alberti's discussion of perspective is inextricably linked with his analysis of proportion and scale. Largeness and smallness are for him purely comparative qualities, but the ultimate arbiter of scale is the human body, which, whether gigantic (as with Hercules) or diminutive, retains "correct" proportionality ("a very small man is proportional to a very large one; for there was the same proportion of span to stride, and of foot to the remaining parts of the body in Evander as there was in Hercules, whom Gellius conjectures was taller and bigger than other men").[65] And proportion in the visual pyramid of perspective is a reflection of that corporeal proportion. The horizon, according to Alberti, should be placed no higher than the height of a man standing at the lower border of the painting's frame, echoing, internalizing, and confirming the point of view of the spectator.

In the cinema, nearness and farness are ineluctably linked with the scale of the shot—close-up, medium shot, *plan américain*, long shot—insofar as size becomes the signifier of distance (close-ups are not simply huge or monstrous [though they are that as well]—they are close, intimate). Yet this correspondence between size and distance in representation is not an invention of the cinema but instead a function of Renaissance perspective, which precisely and mathematically calculates and maps this diminution and enlargement of things proportionally, on a two-dimensional surface in relation to a place that is both there and not there—the vanishing point. Scale, perspective, proportion, and the body are ineluctably bound together in classical representation. In the history of film theory, the fascination with perspective as a system for the ordering of space and subjectivity seems to have occupied a very brief but striking moment, involving figures writing in the 1970s such as Jean-Louis Baudry, Jean-Louis Comolli, Christian Metz, and Stephen Heath, among others. The French concept of a *dispositif* or cinematic apparatus (as it was translated in English) loomed large in these debates, and because quattrocento perspective presented itself as the most regulated or rule-like visual system and the most fully aligned with the idea of a machine or an apparatus (of which it had various incarnations: the camera obscura, camera lucida, etc.), it held a prominent place in what is often referred to as 1970s film theory. The work of Jean Pèlerin Viator, Leon Battista Alberti, and contemporary theorists such as Pierre Francastel and Marcelin Pleynet was cited to buttress arguments about the ideological implications of the single-point perspective that was "built into" the camera lens. The insistence of perspective in the cinematic image appeared to corroborate the regularity and rationality of a highly legible space and its seemingly endless, indeed infinite, coherence. But since the 1970s, perspective has more or less disappeared as a focus, the reasons for which have something to do with the incommensurability of an accelerating micro-historicist tendency in film studies with the sheer breadth and lack of specificity of perspective as a historical phenomenon that spans not decades but centuries. As Hubert Damisch was to argue insistently, however, "There is a great danger of treating perspective as just one object among others, if not as a simple product or effect, whereas it interests us here primarily as something that is *productive* of effects, insofar as its capacity, its power to inform extends well beyond the limits of the era in which it was born. Without any doubt, our period is much more massively 'informed' by the perspective paradigm, thanks to photography, film, and now video, than was the fifteenth century."[66] Damisch's book (tellingly entitled *The Origin of Perspective*) engages throughout with an intense struggle over precisely what history is, how it can be thought.

For the film theorists of the 1970s, perspective was understood primarily in relation to the positioning of a subject-spectator, one who was centered and empowered by the system (all of the subsequent arguments about passivity vs. activity [i.e., agency] were entirely misdirected). The primary references were not, actually, those of art history but of current theories of ideology, psychoanalysis, and subject positioning, particularly those of Louis Althusser and Jacques Lacan. Perspective was not perceived as of another, antiquated era but as persisting in or revived by photographic technologies. Consistent with the delineation of the cinema as an apparatus that includes the spectator, these film theorists were above all concerned to investigate the relation between perspective and the production of subjectivity as a position. Baudry viewed *perspectiva artificialis* as a revolutionary new mode of representation: "This system, recentering or at least displacing the center (which settles itself in the eye), will ensure the setting up of the 'subject' as the active center and origin of meaning."[67] In cinema, perspective contributes to the positioning of the spectator as disembodied and as the origin of a transcendent vision. For Metz, the vanishing point "inscribes an empty emplacement for the spectator-subject, an all-powerful position which is that of God himself, or more broadly of some ultimate signified."[68] Comolli, who is invested in explicating the ideological implications of a technique that had been situated (by Jean-Patrick Lebel and others) as scientifically neutral—"founded in a real body of knowledge"—situates the cinema and photography as inheritors of a Renaissance code that structured a lasting humanism and prepared the way for bourgeois ideology.[69] More sensitive to the way in which movement (of the camera, of figures in the field) is capable of disrupting perspective, Stephen Heath describes Renaissance perspective as a powerful, even utopian, ideal (of the complicity of eye and knowledge, of the power of optics and geometry) that is not always strictly implemented in the history of painting. In the cinema, movement produces the possibility of interfering with that ideal "with which nonetheless it is immediately involved, historically, industrially, ideologically."[70] Although there are significant differences between these figures, all strive to situate perspective's ideological work in relation to the constitution of a subject who is above all, in place, positioned stably as a point of vision, possessing mastery of both vision and knowledge. The homogeneous and unified space generated by perspective corroborates this notion of subjectivity. This approach tends to privilege the monocular status of perspective, its relation to theories of the rectilinear propagation of light rays, its situating of the eye as the center of a visible space that can be explicated mathematically. Yet there are many other aspects of the perspective system that have been dealt with extensively in art history—the vanishing point and its relation to the conceptualization of infinity, the projection involved in mapping a three-dimensional object onto a two-dimensional surface, scale and recession, the construction of a space that contests the limits of the frame while requiring it, the relation of perspective to point of view. The theorists of the 1970s were more likely to cite the sociologist Pierre Francastel and Marxist Louis Althusser than art historians (although Marcelin Pleynet, editor of *Tel Quel*, was a significant exception). Perhaps the most glaring art historical omission in 1970s film theory is Erwin Panofsky, whose extraordinary essay, *Perspective as Symbolic Form*, written in 1925, was not, it should be noted, translated into English until 1991, but whose work on Albrecht Dürer and his relation to perspective was written in English in 1943, while Panofsky was at Princeton.

A number of art historians have aggressively criticized film theorists' analysis of perspective, including Damisch, but perhaps most famously Jonathan Crary, who claims that perspective in the era of the camera obscura constitutes an entirely different paradigm than that governing the construction and circulation of images in modernity, for which the stereoscope offers itself as the exemplary technology. The production of depth in stereoscopic imagery is a function of its activation of binocular vision, generating an entirely different kind of space than that of quattrocento perspective. However, because Crary focuses primarily upon modernity's discipline of a body haunted by failure, prone to visual illusions, and the consequent severance of the image from its referent enabling the accelerating circulation and exchange of images, he is only peripherally interested in the qualities of the space of the binocular image. Nevertheless, his description of the visual experience of the stereoscope is one of the most eloquent and compelling sections of the book. The figures are "cut-outs," hovering, suspended, unanchored by a space that could provide a viable ground. The exploitation of the effects of the stereoscope requires the placement of objects in different planes—foreground and middle ground in particular—and the production of a discontinuous, disaggregated space. To suggest that the figures appear as "cut-outs" is to claim that they are, paradoxically, flattened, two-dimensional, and that they are disengaged from the space in which they reside. The sense of depth here hinges upon the separability of different planes of the image. In contrast to monocular perspective, this space is not unified, homogeneous, and coherent but simply occupies the areas where there are no figures or objects. This is why the stereoscope strikes Crary as decidedly uncanny, *un*real. The cut-out bodies have no "other side" (unlike the "behind" and "beyond" whose imagination is enabled and encouraged by the space of monocular perspective). If they were to turn, they would reveal only an emptiness, a void (perhaps this is why 3D cinema

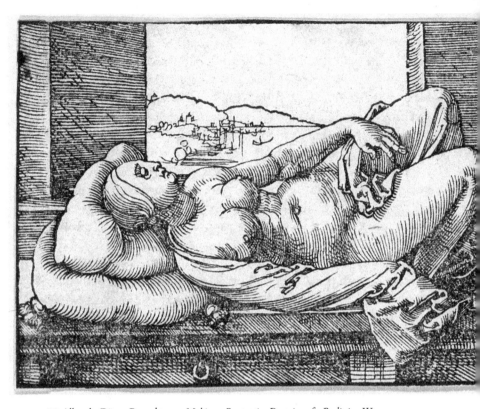

5.6 Albrecht Dürer, *Draughtsman Making a Perspective Drawing of a Reclining Woman*, woodcut (ca. 1600).

favors the *z* axis, movement toward and away from the camera). Henri Lefebvre has stressed the significance of the "turn" in the body's production of a space that simultaneously produces it. While, as Crary argues, the body of the stereoscope observer is more fully involved in the repetitive movements of changing cards and working the apparatus, the bodies in the field of vision are surreal and paradoxically flat, without volume.[71]

Such a body is in sharp contrast to that represented, somewhat perplexingly, in an image presented repeatedly as exemplary of the system (and the lure) of perspective. I am thinking of Dürer's woodcut *Draughtsman Making a Perspective Drawing of a Reclining Woman* (ca. 1600) (fig. 5.6). There is nothing particularly perspectival about the woodcut itself (other than the angles of the windows, table, and screen—a minimal depth is suggested here), but it represents the process of perspective by situating a nude female body as the object of a drawing generated by an apparatus similar to Alberti's *velo*—a

grid of lines to segment the body, a stiletto eyepiece to keep the artist's eye in place, and another grid for the proportional transfer of these segments. The female body is voluminous, its curves and fleshiness emphasized. In a chapter entitled "The Proportions Which a Perfectly Formed Man's Body Should Possess" in a fifteenth-century Italian handbook on painting, Cennino Cennini writes: "Take note that, before going any farther, I will give you the exact proportions of a man. Those of a woman I will disregard, for she does not have any set proportion. . . . I will not tell you about the irrational animals, because you will never discover any system of proportion in them."[72] Women were perceived as unmeasurable, uncontainable within any rational boundaries. Refuting linearity and rationality, the female body would, indeed, seem an unlikely subject for the demonstration of perspective (a difficulty compounded by an unlikely angle on a reclining figure, whose foreshortening must be pronounced). One is accustomed to see in illustrations of perspective

5.7 *Città ideale-Urbino*, tempera on panel, anonymous (ca. 1470).

a subject matter that echoes and repeats, even accents, the linear geometry that subtends the perspectival system (e.g., the Urbino, Baltimore, and Berlin panels of the Ideal City analyzed extensively by Damisch or, in film, the insistent perspective of the opening titles of Otto Preminger's *The Cardinal* [1963]) (figs. 5.7, 5.8). Here there is an almost excessive or hyperbolic insistence upon linearity and the geometry of the vanishing point. However, the woodcut conjoins two of Dürer's most pressing concerns—the theoretical basis of perspective and the mathematical calculation of the proportions of the human body. Problems of scale and proportion are, of course, intimately linked to questions of perspective. This is not the only instance in which Dürer attempted to contain the body by a grid. In his studies of the proportions of the human body (influenced by Vitruvius), various parts—here the face and the foot—were encased within a network of straight lines (figs. 5.9, 5.10). It is telling that both of these examples involve a *turn*—from the profile of the face to a frontal view; from a side view of the foot to a view of the centering of its heel. Panofsky, in his study of Dürer, argues that a concern with perspective is intimately linked to an obsession with bodily proportion: "Perspective, one might say, is a mathematical method of organizing space so as to meet the requirements of both 'correctness' and 'harmony,' and is thus fundamentally akin to a discipline which sought to achieve precisely the same thing with respect to the human and animal body: the theory of proportions."[73] Dürer's emphasis on bodily proportion echoes that of Alberti described earlier. But the female body is resistant.

Feminist art historians and cultural theorists have, understandably and correctly, criticized Dürer's woodcut for its subjection of the body of the woman to the controlling and masterful gaze of the artist and his mathe-

5.8 *The Cardinal* (Otto Preminger, 1963).

matical apparatus. Svetlana Alpers, for instance, claims that "Dürer's wood-cut tellingly reveals it [the active confidence in human powers] in the rela-tionship of the male artist to the female observed who offers her naked body to him to draw. The attitude toward women in this art—toward the central image of the female nude in particular—is part and parcel of a command-ing attitude taken toward the possession of the world."[74] "Possession of the world" is in collusion with mapping, perspective, and proprietorship of the woman's body. And Lynda Nead, analyzing the woodcut, writes, "Geometry and perspective impose a controlling order on the female body. . . . In con-trast to the curves and undulating lines of the female section, the male com-partment is scattered with sharp, vertical forms; the draughtsman himself is up and is alert and absorbed. Woman offers herself to the controlling disci-pline of illusionistic art. With her bent legs closest to the screen, the image recalls not simply the life class but also the gynaecological examination."[75] It is undoubtedly not accidental that Dürer conjoined the question of the nude and the question of perspective in writing of his admiration for the Italians: "I highly praise the Italians with regard to their nudes and, above all, to perspective."[76] Barbara Freedman speculates about what would hap-pen if we adopted the woman's perspective: the woman "lies comfortably relaxed; the artist sits upright, rigidly constrained by his fixed position."[77]

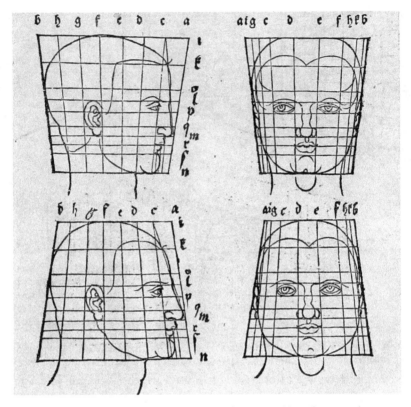

5.9 Albrecht Dürer, *Four Books on Human Proportion* (Hierinn sind begriffen vier Bücher von menschlicher Proportion) (Nürnberg: Hieronymus Formschneyder, 1528), p. 174.

In a sense, speculation is not necessary. Dürer also subjected a male figure to the same apparatus (in the service of portraiture this time) in *A Draughtsman Taking Details for a Portrait* (fig. 5.11). This is a very different picture, in which the upright, dignified sitter mirrors the upright, dignified artist. Reflecting each other ad infinitum, they are the confirmation and corroboration of reason itself.

I find it more interesting to speculate about what Dürer's draftsman saw and drew, which is not so easily imaginable. Feet toward the apparatus? The body reclining in a position that would seem more difficult to configure? What role does the female body play in a system that, as so many thinkers have noted, makes possible the very conceptualization of infinity? As Damisch has pointed out, Renaissance culture was obsessed with the question of infinity, hence its embrace of the vanishing point, "this point that ab-

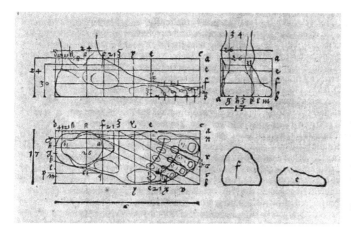

5.10 Albrecht Dürer, *Four Books on Human Proportion* (Hierinn sind begriffen vier Bücher von menschlicher Proportion) (Nürnberg: Hieronymus Formschneyder, 1528), p. 65.

sented itself, so to speak, from its place."[78] Panofsky states that in perspectival representation, "The picture has become a mere 'slice' of reality, to the extent and in the sense that *imagined* space [one thinks here of the diegesis in film] now reaches out in all directions beyond *represented* space, that precisely the finiteness of the picture makes perceptible the infiniteness and continuity of the space."[79] The frame, masquerading as a limit, instead points to limitlessness. For Brian Rotman, perspectival space is a "projected, coordinated space; a space in which every position is signifiable in relation to the horizon and centric ray as axes and the vanishing point as origin of coordinates. (Indeed, the mathematical space appropriate to perspectival images is that of projective geometry which, in order to study the effect upon plane figures of changing the position of the point of projection, postulates a point of infinity as its origin.)"[80] The vanishing point is both infinity and origin. Hence, one of the principal effects, if not determinants, of perspectival space can be seen as the emergence of the concept of infinity. For Panofsky, perspective, hinging upon the idea of a point of view, marks a desecularization, a transition from a theocracy to an anthropocracy. It is a desecularization that generates a concept of infinity opposed to the closed sphere of the heavens and earth posited by early Christian theology.

But what does Dürer's draftsman draw in this space constructed as infinite? The history of art provides us with a number of possible responses, including the photograph *The Urban Nude* (Lucien Clergue, 1981) (fig. 5.12), with its strict geometric lines and articulation of the female body with architecture. Yet perhaps the most fascinating (and telling) is Gustave Courbet's

5.11 *A Draughtsman Taking Details for a Portrait, Using a Perspective Apparatus for Drawing onto Glass*, from *Course in the Art of Drawing* by Albrecht Dürer, published Nuremberg 1525. Private collection, the Stapleton Collection/Bridgeman Images.

L'origine du monde (*Origin of the World* [1866]) (fig. 5.13), in which the less linear and more awkward positioning of the body closely mimes the position of Dürer's model. In a sense, this image could be said to represent or figure Dürer's draftsman's vision (not in the sense of biographically ascertainable influence but in the sense of a desire that haunts perspectival representation and repeats itself in various forms). For the lines of force connecting the interior spectator/artist of Dürer's woodcut to the body of the woman are directed toward the female genitals, centering the female sexual organ. In Courbet's *L'origine du monde*, it is the gaze of the spectator of the painting itself whose attention is drawn to the centering of the female genitals as *origin*. Although, given the absence of straight lines, it would be fairly difficult to

5.12 *The Urban Nude* (Lucien Clergue, 1981) © 2020 Lucien Clergue/Artists Rights Society (ARS), New York/SAIF, Paris.

locate the vanishing point of *L'origine du monde*, it is nevertheless clear that it is not literally coincident with the female sexual organ. Still, that organ could be described as the centering point of the organization of space and gaze in the painting. It is a vanishing point in that it is both interior and exterior to the painting—if this is, indeed, the *origin* of the world, it is not the visible genitals but the womb they conceal behind them, the Freudian site of the uncanny. It is a figurative vanishing point, working at the same time to fix a view and to suggest infinity. It is the source of the obscene (in the etymological sense of "off-stage"), since it generates the imagination of a space that exceeds the boundaries of the frame. According to Rotman, "Many early Renaissance painters, as if to emphasize the essential otherness and exteriority of this location, placed the vanishing point inside a hole: a framed opening, such as a door, a window, a mirror, or even another painting, within the visual scene. This had the effect of doubling the pull exerted by the vanishing point on the spectator, and at the same time, by invoking the potentially unlimited iteration of a frame within a frame, of pushing the vanishing point out to an infinite, unreal, numinous distance."[81] In art historical discourse, Courbet's *L'origine du monde* is frequently compared to his paintings of caves (e.g., *The*

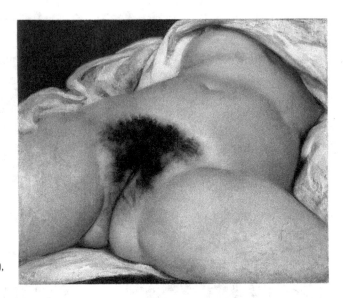

5.13 *L'origine du monde*
(Gustave Courbet, 1866),
Paris, Musée d'Orsay.

Source of the Loue, ca. 1865), bringing the female body in line with a landscape, one that suggests a hidden interiority, inaccessible to vision.

Dürer's image, honing in on the fetishized site of a generative absence, of the source of human reproduction, is a woodcut, following in the wake of the printing press as one of the earliest modes of mechanical reproduction, presaging the endangerment of the entire concept of the original. Courbet's *Origine* is a unique painting (one that for many years was lost, as Linda Nochlin points out in an amusing treatment of the repetitive search for the original in art history).[82] Yet both the painting's title and its content are clearly references to human reproduction. *L'origine du monde* can be so (i.e., the origin of the world) only if the world is conflated with the subject (for this is really the origin of the subject, the birth of the individual). In other words, for the painting to be adequate to its title, the point of view of the subject must be equal to the world. In a sense, this is precisely what perspective does. It generates a point of view, that of the observer (equivalent to the linguistic shifter) beholding the painting, which simulates that of the painter painting the painting, both occupying a site mirroring that of the vanishing point. At the same time, it generates a space that is homogeneous, coherent, and extensive—one that is infinitely expansive, that is, a world. Perspective produces subject and object simultaneously. For Panofsky, it is "a translation of psychophysiological space into mathematical

5.14 Marcel Duchamp, *Étant Donnés: 1. La Chute d'Eau, 2. Le Gaz d'Éclairage* (Given: 1. The Waterfall, 2. The Illuminating Gas) (1946–66) © Association Marcel Duchamp/ADAGP, Paris/Artists Rights Society (ARS), New York 2020.

space; in other words, an objectification of the subjective."[83] Perspective involves both stable and mathematically exact rules, but it is contingent upon the concept of an individual who adopts a subjective point of view.[84] In this sense, just as the Dürer woodcut is a representation of perspective as system, *Origine* can also be seen as a meditation on perspective as a paradigm of knowledge, revolving around the ultimate unknown of the female body.

Marcel Duchamp's last work, *Étant donnés* (full title: *Étant Donnés: 1. La Chute d'Eau, 2. Le Gaz d'Éclairage* [Given: 1. The waterfall, 2. The illuminating gas]), created in secrecy between 1946 and 1966, is a further extension of this problematic (fig. 5.14). Positioning its viewer explicitly as a voyeur, the tableau is blocked by a huge wooden door with two side-by-side peepholes. Only one person can see the work at a time, and, looking through the holes, one sees a strangely bucolic scene: a crumbling stone wall, trees and a waterfall in the background, and, in the foreground, a nude woman reclining in the manner of Courbet's nude in *L'origine du monde*, holding a small gas lamp aloft in her left hand. The genitals here seem to be off-center and malformed. Jean-François Lyotard analyzes this work explicitly in relation to perspective and its imperatives. According to Lyotard, this is not a figurative but a literal localizing of the female genitals as vanishing point: "The vanishing point of the 'cube' (in the perspectivist sense) of *Given* would be given by the vulva. A slightly plunging perspective, the voyeur's eye being placed higher up (at a height of 1.536 meters) than the table that supports the nude. . . . This immutable distance nails the eyes to their viewing point and the woman to her optimum point of exhibition (vanishing point). The voyeur is a viewer without dimension, reduced to his point."[85] In this sense, the room that is the centerpiece of the installation mimics the camera obscura and the system of perspectival representation. For Lyotard, the work implements a mechanism that is allied with the cinema, despite the fact that Duchamp attempted to tear it away from the filmic and relegate it to the realm of the photographic—he refers to "the fate reserved here for the voyeur: he sees suddenly, in the snapshot of the opening of the diaphragm. Because of this he sees no more than is seen by a sensitive film, he is impressed, like the film. *Augenblick*, point in time, no time at all."[86] Contained in the work, as the support of the tableau of the naked woman, is an invisible checkered floor. This is the perspectival grid that, in Lyotard's view, must remain hidden in this "laying out" of the female body as the exemplary instance of the vanishing point and all it implies about infinity. But it is the crucial support of this discourse and its hidden geometry. This is an extension of Dürer's problematic, but does it imply a change?

For the film theorists of the 1970s, perspective was above all a stabilizing system, constituting a subject-spectator whose major attributes were mastery, unity, and control. But this involved privileging disembodiment, monocular vision, and a rationalizable vision. What is lost here is the founding exorbitance of the concept of infinity, of that which escapes vision. It is an exorbitance that in the history of art has been conflated with the female body. For Damisch, "vanishing point" is "a phrase that nicely characterizes the opposition between a fixed point and its being pushed into infinity."[87] Damisch takes issue with film theory's assumption that perspective is a stabilizing system. Although the subject gets its bearings through perspective, it is not "any the more stable" for it.[88] Instead, the allegedly dominant and masterful subject of perspective "*holds only by a thread*, however tightly stretched this might be," and Damisch compares that subject to a tightrope walker.[89]

5.15 *Bunny Lake Is Missing* (Otto Preminger, 1965).

Stephen Heath claims that perspective in the cinema is markedly different from perspective in painting primarily due to movement and the constant need to restabilize shifting perspectives. This is certainly true, but there is another aspect of cinema that destabilizes perspective, particularly in its relation to the human body. Perspective cannot tolerate extremes. Film theorists have often noted that it is the "normal" lens (50mm) that puts into play most precisely the perspective system. Wide-angle lenses exaggerate and telephoto lenses diminish the effects of perspective. In terms of faces and bodies, the closer the object to the camera, the greater the distension of proportions and the corresponding loss of a relation between the body and space. This is, perhaps, because the body becomes space, the only space available to the spectator. In classical cinema, this has often been exploited as exceptional—as moments of intense psychologization such as close-ups from Preminger's *Bunny Lake Is Missing* (1965; fig. 5.15) and his *Whirlpool* (1950; fig. 5.16). But in the realm of the avant-garde, Willard Maas and Marie Menken's extraordinary *Geography of the Body* (1943) makes that distortion central (figs. 5.17, 5.18).[90] Here, the body is characterized by sexual indifferentiation, indeed, unrecognizability at moments. An ear can easily be misread as a vagina. Perspective works only to problematize an already illegible space. Maas and Menken used dime-store magnifying lenses to film extreme close-ups of various parts of each other's bodies, accompanied on the soundtrack by a surrealist poem

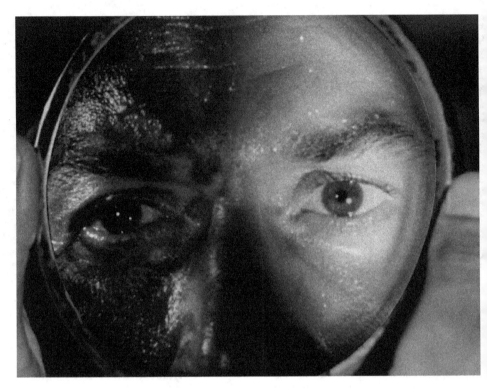

5.16 *Whirlpool* (Otto Preminger, 1950).

written and recited by George Barker. The soundtrack and the filming of the body transform it into a terrain, a space for the exercise of a colonialist gaze. Yet the excessive closeness and magnification simply guarantee that what ought to be the most knowable of spaces—one's own body—becomes the site of the unrecognizable. In this film, the metaphor of the body as a landscape is hystericized. Space is no longer mappable, negotiable in the ease of a familiar paradigm, and it is the body that acts as the foil. *Geography of the Body* demonstrates that although perspective may be built into the lens of the camera, this does not limit filmmaking to a reconfiguration of the presuppositions of the classical perspective system, a system that, as we have seen, is not so easily hypostasized. Perspective is, in its own right, a highly complex system, coordinating subject and object, surface and depth, finitude and infinity, male and female—a system from which we cannot claim to have fully escaped.

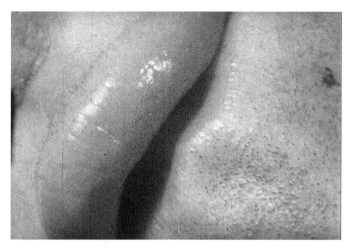

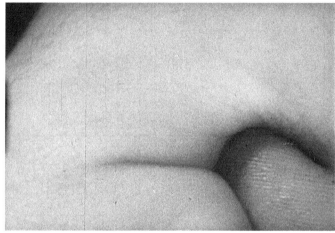

5.17 & 5.18 *Geography of the Body* (Willard Maas and Marie Menken, 1943).

Vertical Perspective/Disorientation

Maps and perspective have in common a mandate to provide a sense of orientation for the subject/viewer, to allow that subject to know where they are in relation to an ordered space. Although perspective is generally associated with the production of "realism," this is not necessarily its primary effect, since animation will often make use of perspective to develop its space—often a space of fantasy. The criticisms of perspectival "realism" tend to distinguish it from *vision* and are familiar—perspective is a form of monocular vision versus the binocular vision of everyday life; perspective involves the projection of three-dimensional objects on a flat plane versus the curved surface of the retina. Panofsky also distinguishes *perspectival* space from what he refers to as *psychophysiological* space (the space of everyday life). Psychophysiological space does not know the concept of infinity. Instead, it is always a bounded space, circumscribed by the limits of the eye. In addition, it is not homogeneous; each place has its own mode and its own value. Front, back, above, below, left, and right are different from each other and linked to the position of the body. According to Panofsky, the intended purpose of perspective is "to realize in the representation of space precisely that homogeneity and boundlessness foreign to the direct experience of that space . . . it negates the differences between front and back, between right and left, between bodies and intervening space ('empty' space), so that the sum of all the parts of space and all its contents are absorbed into a single 'quantum continuum.'"[91] Perspectival space abstracts from psychophysiological space in order to facilitate orientation, location, and navigation. And the very notion of infinity is harnessed in the figure of the vanishing point that organizes the system.

But there is another kind of perspective, or perhaps a paraperspective, that is associated with the accelerating proliferation of maps in media of all sorts, as well as the pervasiveness of the aerial view. Drones, surveillance cameras, military aerial photography, and the zooming and floating vision facilitated by Google Earth disconcert and disrupt the spatial regime of linear perspective. Hito Steyerl places what she calls "vertical perspective" (the view from above) in relation to a general condition of destabilization and displacement in contemporary life—free fall.[92] This condition is linked to a general sense of political, moral, and metaphysical groundlessness, the inability to find a stable foundation for thought or observation. Spatially, this is manifested in the loss of the horizon. In perspectival systems, the horizon orients and locates the subject both as measure (in Alberti's rules for perspective, as mentioned previously, the horizon can be situated no higher than the height of a human body standing on the lower frame line) and as the stable mirror/echo of the vanishing point located upon it. In navigation, the horizon orients, directs, and forms the basis for the determination of geographic position. In aerial images, in contrast, the horizon is annihilated or, at the very least, destabilized, shifting. The viewer is similarly deprived of a stable position and could more accurately be described as suspended, hovering, or perhaps "hanging," perpetually on the brink. According to Steyerl, "With the loss of horizon also comes the departure of a stable paradigm of orientation, which has situated concepts of subject and object, of time and space, throughout modernity. In falling, the lines of the horizon shatter, twirl around, and su-

5.19 "The Blue Marble," view of the earth as seen by the Apollo 17 crew traveling toward the moon (1972).

perimpose."[93] Of course, as Steyerl herself points out, the horizon, even in linear perspective and the navigation based upon it, is a fiction, a denial of the curvature of the earth. It offers an illusory stability and a secure position of vision, commanding a homogeneous space.

The quintessential aerial image is that of the earth as a globe, floating in a black void. This image breaks from that of the earlier globe of colonialism and its homogeneity (see chapter 1). As Laura Kurgan points out, the ur-image here is the 1972 view of the earth as seen by the Apollo 17 crew traveling to the moon (fig. 5.19). Known as "The Blue Marble," this representation has been remade in different versions ("The Blue Marble 2002," "The Blue Marble: The Next Generation, 2005," "The Blue Marble: The Next Generation 2012) and was even used as the default screen of the iPhone.[94] Kurgan demonstrates that there is a marked shift from the 1972 NASA image to the 2005 and 2012 versions. Whereas the 1972 image is a homogeneous view— "handcrafted witness to earthly totality," the later images are composite images, generated by a patchwork of satellite data, an assemblage of different perspectives.[95] Despite their virtuality, they carry with them great authority and a claim to truth. Kurgan claims that "their basis in remotely sensed data helps us understand what has become of truth in the era of the digital data stream: it is intimately related to resolution, to measurability, to the construction of a reliable algorithm for translating between representation and reality. The fact that they are virtual images does not make them any less true, but it should make us pause and consider what we mean today by truth."[96] Satellite imaging marks a crucial turn away from perspectival imaging and its construction of space. The Global Positioning System (GPS) is foremost in a series of events that "amount to a cataclysmic shift in our ability to navigate, inhabit, and define the spatial realms."[97] Like Steyerl, Kurgan believes that this shift can be described in terms of a loss of center and orientation.

Originally, GPS was a technology of the military and dependent upon data received from twenty-four satellites orbiting the earth (the U.S. Air Force currently maintains thirty-one satellites). Gradually, it became available to the public and for commercial uses with "selective availability"; eventually, by 2000, the full system was available freely. It is now deployed to guide missile systems at the same time it can be used by mobile phones to access directions and locations. Its specific capability is that of precise positioning, what Kurgan labels "the technology of looking close up at a distance": "Every view from a satellite is an experiment with the technology of looking close up at a distance, remotely examining and representing something as small as fifty centimeters of the ground from a height of four hundred miles in the sky."[98] The GPS might be seen as offering a stable orientation through its ability to pinpoint locations with impressive accuracy. However, as Peter Galison has demonstrated, GPS is based on the assumptions of Einstein's relativity— there is no stable spatial and temporal location; all is in flux. The calculation of location and distance in this system is based on temporal differentiation. The receiver's distance from the satellite is calculated as a function of the temporal difference between the satellite's emission of a signal and the receiver's reception of that signal. Because the satellite's clocks, traveling at a speed of 12,500 miles per hour, were slow compared with the earth, and gravitational forces led to the clocks running fast, there was a constant discrepancy, and relativistic time, according to Galison, had to be built "deep into the machine."[99] In addition, "So accurate had the system become that even 'fixed' parts of the earth's landmass revealed themselves to be in motion, an unending shuffle of continents drifting over the surface of the planet on backs of tectonic plates."[100] This vision of shifting, instability, and decentering of land masses is a far cry from the controversy concerning the scale of continents on Mercator maps, although it is undoubtedly no less ideological. Kurgan refers to this system as "a visual regime that is inherently decentering, that disorients under the banner of orientation."[101]

What are the effects of this accelerating dominance of vertical perspective and the "view from above"? Google Earth gives one the sense that any location anywhere in the world can be made visible. Although GPS seems to offer us the knowledge of exactly where we are and where we are going, this seemingly secure orientation is undergirded by another, more fundamental form of disorientation. Although the satellite image appears as transparently legible, as Kurgan points out, "In the end, it seems, embedded in the very structure of the techno-scientific, militarized, 'objective' image is something more disorienting, an 'emptiness and abstraction' that resists sovereign control and opens itself to other sorts of interpretation."[102] As Kurgan rightly claims, these interpretations are always political. The image is a heterogeneous collection of data that must be actively read. Seeing is largely disabled as a mode of knowing—there is no longer even the illusion that "seeing is believing" because the image is a concatenation of multiple perspectives and a mathematics that is quite different from that of the geometry that supports/configures linear perspective.

Linear perspective and the vertical view are different visual and epistemological forms of managing spatial location and orientation. Perspectival representation is an investment in the stability and immobility of position in relation to a space understood as ordered, geometric, and homogeneous. Within this system, however, disorientation is not absent but persists as a threat that must be mastered through suppression or repression. In our contemporary era of digital, militarized, and surveillant vision—the "view from above" and its concomitant erasure of the horizon—disorientation is constitutive, structuring even though it is not embraced by experience. Disorientation is not so much a menace to be repressed or foreclosed as it is an instrument to be deployed in the service of a pursuit of precise localization and hence possession of a space understood as global. Each system is organized around a mode of address to its interpellated subject, which is also a solicitation, an appeal, an alliance with a historically specific form of commodification. Perspective as a representational system underlies the visual technologies of modernity of the twentieth century—photography and cinema, the *mass* media. The conceptualization of the mass or the masses is based on a presumption of homogeneity, if not a preexistent homogeneity, one that can be molded, produced, propped upon the annihilation of difference (usually racial, ethnic, sexual). The irony of linear perspective has always been that it generates a notion of objectivity at the same time that it produces a point of view, an affirmation of subjectivity. But that subjectivity is exhausted by its recognition/understanding/conceptualization as a position, one that can indeed be occupied by anyone, the deindividualized individual.[103] Today, the idea of the homogeneous mass is shattered by demographic targeting and, beyond that, by finer and finer specifications of the desires of the subject based on a history (of buying, of browsing, of associating, liking, and disliking), assuming a multiplicity of perspectives and a heterogeneity of desire. This pinpointing, the isolation and identification of consumer longing and aspiration, echoes and redoubles the ambition of pinpointing and localization of any place on earth, the conquering of space through its reduction to smaller and smaller bits. The slippages of a perspectival era—Cubism, Preminger's use of an extreme wide-angle lens for grotesque effects, *Geography of the Body* and its disconcerting of location—were just that: slippages, exceptions in relation to a norm. Now, the norm itself is a form of disorientation, decentering, loss of the support/guarantee of a horizon. The subject, zooming through space on Google Earth or floating in the air surveying the earth, may momentarily lose their bearing but can be reassured that the very technologies of disorientation allow a distinct and intensified localization and an access to all the space of the globe. It is increasingly difficult to be "off the grid."

Chapter 6

The Concept of Immersion

Mediated Space, Media Space, and the
Location of the Subject

One of the most remarkable achievements of classical Hollywood narrative was undoubtedly its construction of a plausible space that the spectator could understand as inhabitable, navigable, homogeneous, and continuous. This was a full space, within which events could take place—any events, a plethora of stories. But despite this cinema's extensive deployment of off-screen space and the suggestion of infinite depths, the inescapable limit was the fact of the screen, a clearly localizable screen housed in a theater that incarnated the destiny of the moviegoer. Roland Barthes attempted to come to grips with the pleasures of cinema by proposing an oscillation between two spaces— that provided by the film and that associated with all the marginalia of the theatrical setting: "letting oneself be fascinated *twice over*, by the image and by its surroundings—as if I had two bodies at the same time: a narcissistic body which gazes, lost, into the engulfing mirror, and a perverse body, ready to fetishize not the image but precisely what exceeds it: the texture of the sound, the hall, the darkness, the obscure mass of the other bodies, the rays of light, entering the theater, leaving the hall."[1] But what he does not acknowledge explicitly is that one cannot inhabit both spaces at the same time. To the extent that one is "engulfed" in the film's diegesis, one cannot be aware of the space of the theater, no matter how ornamental or alluring. And to the extent that one is attentive to and delights in the supplemental detail of the theatrical setting, one blinds oneself to/loses sight of the diegesis. Barthes would like to make this a dialectical movement but, instead, it is an either/or.

Today, one experiences a whiff of nostalgia reading Barthes's description of his relation and nonrelation to the screen in the movie theater, at the idea of a designated *place* for the viewing of moving images that might constitute in itself a distraction. In contrast, screen culture now has become strikingly heterogeneous and pervasive. Screen sizes now range from the miniature touchscreen of the iPhone and iPad to the immense scale of IMAX. Images are mobile and transportable, savable and recyclable, called up at will and often ephemeral. They can be viewed virtually anywhere. And to that extent, where they are viewed becomes less and less significant, even in the case of IMAX, which although it requires a specialized theater, projection, and screen, heavily weights Barthes's first form of fascination with the image—that of engulfment. In IMAX, the bloated image exceeds the screen, swells, distends, and infiltrates the space of the spectator. If Hollywood's promise was that of taking the viewer to another place by denying their own location in the theater, IMAX holds out the allure of annihilating that location, hence the pervasive and persistent discourse of "immersion." The concept of immersion suggests a transport of the subject into the image but also a bleeding of the image beyond the screen into the auditorium so that the very question of place or location becomes nebulous. References to immersion are ubiquitous in advertising for IMAX, 3D, digital surround sound, and virtual reality. The concept is symptomatic of larger questions concerning subjectivity, spatiality, and mediation. I will focus here on two technologies that have been consistently and emphatically allied with the discourse of immersion: IMAX and digital surround sound systems.

Monstrous Screens, IMAX, and the Sublime

Contemporary urban landscapes are often populated with gigantic screens, emphasizing the monumentality of the image. Projected onto buildings, or screens on buildings, these images call out to a mobile spectator, an occasional spectator, a spectator who is often distracted by the countless other stimuli of the modern city. The most densely populated metropolises—New York, Hong Kong, Tokyo, Shanghai—seem to exhibit most strikingly this culture of colossal screens (fig. 6.1). In most cases, but not all, the images bear the transparent messages of a rampant commodification. A seemingly

6.1 Urban screens, photograph by author.

more subtle example would be the transformation of a corporation's office building into a prestigious aesthetic object, flaunting the nebulous concepts of "taste" and "value." On December 4, 2004, Chanel opened its largest boutique on the elite Chuo-dori Avenue of the Ginza district of Tokyo (designed by American architect Peter Marino). During the day, the structure seems to be an ordinary office building with transparent windows allowing workers to see outside, but at night, the two-hundred-foot-tall, ten-story façade becomes an enormous screen, a high-tech version of Chanel's signature tweed (fig. 6.2). According to C. C. Sullivan in *Architectural Lighting Magazine*, this is achieved by "a mix of solar-control glazings and optical materials in a three-layer wall system with integrated white LEDs. Electrochromic glass—which changes in opacity depending on a current applied through the material—became a means to achieve the many competing functions of the illuminated walls. During the day, the glass turns transparent; at night it changes to translucent, making the building surfaces essentially a large backlit screen." Abstract patterns, figural images, and messages, all in a tasteful black and white, glide across the surface of the building. In the same article,

6.2 Chanel facade, Tokyo, photograph by author.

Matthew Tanteri, a collaborating architect, claims, "The important thing it had to achieve was becoming media, rather than a fixed graphic. So while the façade also acts as lighting for the building, it's a communication tool with imagery, logos, and branding."[2] Becoming media. While architecture has always been a medium, this exhortation situates the screen as the quintessential support of media, a screen that increasingly permeates both domestic and public space.

From January 16 through February 12, 2007, New York's Museum of Modern Art (MoMA) projected Doug Aitken's *Sleepwalkers* on five large screens on the sides of the museum (fig. 6.3). The work was advertised as a "Large-Scale Cinematic Installation to Be Projected onto the Facades of the Museum of Modern Art" and a "Major Public Artwork." Aitken himself spoke of turning the museum inside out. The exhibit was (necessarily) free, and MoMA provided a set of instructions on how to view it that prescribed a specific tra-

6.3 Doug Aitken, *Sleepwalkers* (2007).

jectory and certain limitations (no portable seating; no food, beverages, pets, or cigarettes in the Sculpture Garden). What strikes me about this installation is its uncanny formal resemblance to the massive screens of commodification discussed earlier. The overwhelming size of the images seems to situate them unconsciously within the framework of a genre whose conventions are already known and overly familiar. The installation attempts to occupy a site that is already crowded, that already dictates its own urban and architectural logic. What determines—or overdetermines—this representational proximity, this affinity between the realm of aesthetics and the forms of commodification, particularly in relation to scale? I will return to this question later.

As demonstrated in chapter 2, the cinema was also understood at the time of its emergence in terms of scale—it was "bigger than life." The twentieth century will undoubtedly be seen as the era of the *cinematic* screen, a restricted and localized screen (situated primarily within a theatrical space). And outside of a few isolated experiments such as Abel Gance's use of three-screen sections (Polyvision) in *Napoléon* in 1927 as well as widescreen experiments of the 1950s, this cinema was also characterized by a surprisingly stable screen and frame size through most of that century (the dominant frame ratio initially being that used by Thomas Edison for the kinetoscope in

1889 and later standardized for the entire industry—first at 1.33:1 in the silent era, then at 1.375:1 in 1932, remaining in place until the widescreen formats such as Cinerama in the early 1950s). But in recent years, the screen—particularly in relation to its size—has been increasingly widely diversified, subject to both miniaturization and magnification, and in many cases uprooted from a stable location. The small size of the mobile phone is associated primarily with ideologies of individual agency and ownership as well as transportability, while the gigantic screens of the urban environment and IMAX become public spectacle.

With IMAX, size is the central and defining characteristic, so much so that the films themselves must entail subjects of a certain grandeur and ungraspability, self-reflexively conjuring up narratives of magnitude. IMAX seems to have fulfilled the early cinematic aspirations associated with the phrase "bigger than life." The emergent history of IMAX was dominated by nature and exploration films, seemingly transcending the comparatively minute human scale of characters and plots. Examples include documentaries such as *Legends of the Sky* (1971), *Man Belongs to Earth* (originally shown at Expo '74 in Spokane), *Living Planet* (1979), and *The Eruption of Mount St. Helens!* (1980). The IMAX website describes *Man Belongs to Earth* in this way: "A fascinating exploration of the fragility of earth's resources, this film was the standout sensation at Spokane's Expo '74. From the dazzling opening shots of the Grand Canyon to a dramatic oil-rig fire at the end, the huge images are a provocative illustration of the U.S. Pavilion's motto: 'The Earth Does Not Belong to Man; Man Belongs to the Earth.'"[3] The era of expos was that of a growing familiarity with images of the earth produced through aerial views, as well as views from space. As mentioned in chapter 5, the Apollo 17 crew, traveling to the moon, generated the widely disseminated "Blue Marble" photograph in 1972; even earlier, after Stewart Brand insisted upon NASA's release of a satellite image of the entire earth, he published the image on the cover of the first edition of the *Whole Earth Catalogue* (1968). The earliest IMAX films were significantly shorter than traditional feature-length films, ranging from seventeen minutes to half an hour, at least partially determining the avoidance of fiction and the classical narrative, whose norms at that point in cinematic history required a certain duration. IMAX emerged from and found a home in world fairs and expositions as a performance of the capabilities of image technologies—the films were less about subjects than about the very fact of the technology. Migrating to specialized venues associated with museums and science centers, the films were presented as an educational experience, often touristic (and imperialistic).[4] Since the early 2000s, Digital Media Remastering

6.4 Cinerama
advertisement.

(DMR) has been used to generate IMAX feature fiction films, and many films have since incorporated sections shot with IMAX cameras and film stock, enabling a wider range of content for the form. Feature films shot entirely in IMAX are rare (*Penguins* [2019] was the first) but are beginning to emerge.

The advertising rhetoric for IMAX reiterates and refashions that for widescreen in the 1950s and focuses on the concept of "immersion." The IMAX website claims that IMAX is "The World's Most Immersive Movie Experience." "You," that is, the spectator, are not observing the space revealed on the screen—you are inside of it. For John Belton, the "illusion of limitless horizontal vision" in Cinerama and CinemaScope intensified the spectator's sense of immersion or absorption in the space of the film (much of the advertising for these processes emphasized the spatial relocation of the spectator from their seat to the world provided by the cinema [fig. 6.4]).[5] IMAX ads

also insist that the spaces of film and spectator are confused and entangled. Objects or persons in the film reach out of the screen into the space of the audience, or the spectator is sucked into the world of the film, erasing all borders between representational space and the space of the viewer (figs. 6.5, 6.6). At times, this is presented as an effect of IMAX alone; at others, 3D processes buttress the IMAX effect. In this scenario, there is no "off-screen space." All of the world has become media, and as a consequence, there is no mediation.

The paradox of IMAX is that its development and expansion in theaters coincided with the accelerating minimization of screen size—on computers, laptops, and notepads and culminating in handheld mobile devices such as the iPhone. Films are now viewable on the smallest of screens as well as the largest. Although David Lynch, in defense of the large screen, has categorically insisted (using various expletives) that if you view a film on an iPhone, you simply haven't seen the film, the mobility of images is a pervasive cultural phenomenon that must be confronted.[6] Perhaps it is not so much a question of whether it is the "same image," but how technologies with such extreme differences of scale can inhabit the same media network. What is the work of "scale" in contemporary media, and how does it configure or reconfigure space, location, and subjectivity?

6.5 & 6.6 IMAX 3D
advertisements.

At first glance, the iPhone, unlike IMAX, would not seem to provide an immersive experience. Immersion connotes a transport of the subject into the image, and the iPhone appears to give its user an unprecedented control over the screen. But if immersion, with its alliance with water, fluids, liquidity, indexes an absorption in a substance that is overwhelming and all-encompassing, there is a sense in which the user of the iPhone could be described as immersed. In fact, this has been the social anxiety concerning iPhones—young people, absorbed in their iPhones, are lost to the world. They no longer have face-to-face conversations; they are no longer where they are. They have fled the real. This fear of the danger of iPhones is reminiscent of historical diatribes against the movies for their irresistible influence on young and malleable minds, particularly in relation to images of sex and violence. In the case of the iPhone, what is feared is a form of temporal and spatial immersion, absenting oneself from a specific time and location. The geography of the iPhone is that of "elsewhere," the elsewhere of a seemingly unmappable, uncognizable network.

Yet immersion is a very vague, imprecise analytical concept, and we should be suspicious of its easy transfer between advertising and journalistic discourses and critical theoretical discourses on the media. While a number of scholars have noted that the concept of immersion is deployed in advertising for widescreen formats and IMAX, there also seems to be an infiltration of its symbolic penumbra, a contagion of its dream within their own critical language. Haidee Wasson describes the experience of IMAX in these terms: "With IMAX you find yourself moving into and out of great heights and depths, traveling downward to the bottom of the sea or upward to the stars," or "IMAX engulfs its spectators, stretching the limits of human vision through its expansive screen and immersive aesthetic."[7] For Charles Acland, "IMAX films soar. Especially through the simulation of motion, they encourage a momentary joy in being placed in a space shuttle, on a scuba dive, or on the wing of a fighter jet."[8] Immersion is used to describe the experience not only of IMAX but of new technologies such as virtual imaging. It is the lure, the desire, the alleged fascination of the industry itself. But what does it mean to be immersed? And why is it the focus of a contemporary desire? Obviously figural (although it is often seen as literal), the tropology denies the physical location of the spectator. I propose to read the concept of immersion as symptomatic, as a claim that points to a work of spatial restructuring in a screen-saturated social economy.

IMAX is about excess—one of its movie theater intros deploys the traditional movie countdown from 10 to 1 (which gradually enlarges the numbers until they become gigantic) and inserts the words "See more, hear more, feel more," ending with the IMAX slogan, "Think Big." As of this writing, the largest IMAX screen is in Sydney, Australia, and is approximately eight stories high. IMAX screens can be ten times the size of a traditional cinema screen. The clarity and resolution of the image is made possible by a frame size that dwarfs that of conventional 70mm film (three times larger). With the perforations placed horizontally rather than vertically, the film must run through the projector at extremely elevated speeds. The very high resolution of the image allows spectators to be positioned closer to the screen. In a typical IMAX theater, the seats are set at a significantly steeper angle and all rows are located within one screen height, whereas in a conventional movie theater, rows can be within eight to twelve screen heights. As Allan Stegeman points out in an article claiming that IMAX and other large-screen formats can compete effectively with high-definition television, "An Imax image occupies 60° to 120° of the audience's lateral field of vision and 40° to 80° of the vertical field of view, and an Omnimax image occupies approximately 180° in the audience's horizontal field of vision, and 125° vertically—the large-screen format effectively destroys the viewer's awareness of the film's actual frame line."[9]

It is this desired annihilation of the frame line that I would like to focus on here. While CinemaScope claimed to compete with the spectator's peripheral vision, IMAX and other large formats attempt to exceed the eye in all dimensions so that the image appears to be uncontained. The frame in cinema is not only a technical necessity adjudicating the relation to temporality (twenty-four frames per second) and the production of an illusion of motion, but also a link between cinema and the history of Western painting, particularly in its inscription of perspective as a rule of space. The frame demarcates the space of the representation as a special place, one that obeys different dictates for legibility. Or, as Jacques Derrida has pointed out, the frame, as parergon, is neither part of the work nor outside the work but gives rise to the work.[10] The frame is the condition of possibility of representation. In the history of cinema, the frame lends to the film's composition a containment and a limit that rivaled the limit of the two-dimensional surface of the screen. Both could be contested, but the frame and the screen were themselves activated to produce the concepts of off-screen space and depth of field as domains of the imaginary.

If the frame constitutes a limit—a fully visible limit—in the experience of the spectator in conventional cinema, what does it mean to remove that limit by using technology to exceed the physiological limits of the spectator's vision? IMAX clearly has limits, but they are generally not of a visible order in the spectator's experience. It strives against limits, as seen in this ad from the IMAX corporation: "People say our screen curves down at the edges. It doesn't. That's the earth." The limit of the IMAX screen merges with that of the earth, which is to say that it has no artificial or cultural limit. What is the lure of this idea of boundlessness?

In the history of aesthetic theory, this concept has been most frequently associated with that of the sublime in its philosophical formulation. For Longinus, the sublime was a function of language, of rhetoric, and its excess was located in its association with an appeal to affect that transcended the recipient's rationality. It was therefore the "beyond" of rhetoric because it could not be taught, was subject to no rules or assured tropology—indeed, it was a kind of scandal of rhetoric, destroying the notion of techne.[11] In Edmund Burke's analysis, "sublime objects are vast in their dimensions."[12] Here, the eye is given a privileged position, standing in metonymically for the entire body ("as in this discourse we chiefly attach ourselves to the sublime, as it affects the eye").[13] For Burke, the sublime is associated with passion, awe, and terror and with a pain that proves to be pleasurable. And this abstraction of pain from pleasure is in many instances a bodily phenomenon—both terror and pain produce a tension, contraction, or "violent emotion of the nerves."[14] This is the sublime, as long as any possibility of actual danger is removed. In a section of the book entitled "Why Visual Objects of Great Dimension Are Sublime," Burke buttresses his argument with a detailed discussion of the physiology of the eye, particularly its susceptibility to a kind of violent stimulation, a forceful impression on the retina produced by the light emanating from all points of the object seen: "Though the image of one point should cause but a small tension of this membrane, another, and another, and another stroke, must in their progress cause a very great one, until it arrives at last to the highest degree; and the whole capacity of the eye, vibrating in all its parts must approach near to the nature of what causes pain, and consequently must produce an idea of the sublime."[15] Yet darkness, or the deprivation of light, is also associated with the sublime because the withdrawal from light causes the pupil to dilate and the eye to strain to see what it cannot. Here, again, tension and pain are associated with the sublime.

Hence the sublime, in one of its earliest formulations, is conceptualized as an assault on the eye. Paul Virilio has referred to IMAX as "cataract surgery," designed to rescue the cinema from the proliferation of small screens by, in effect, welding the eye to the technology.[16] From another point of view, the visual field of the IMAX film, overwhelming that of the spectator, is an assault on the eye, exceeding its capacities in a sheer demonstration of imagistic power. But why should pain and even terror produce the particular pleasure associated with the sublime? For Kant, it is a pleasure that can only be produced through a detour, and it is the detour that causes pain preparatory to the pleasure of discovering the power and extension of reason.

Pain is produced as a result of a striking consciousness of human inadequacy, finitude. Infinity, in the mathematical sense, is not sublime because it is dependent upon a notion of endless progression, each moment of which annihilates the preceding ones so that the mathematical infinite is abstracted from any true intuition of totality. Nature—the ocean, a vast mountainous landscape, a tremendous thunderstorm—may be the occasion for the sense of the sublime, according to Kant, but none of these can be designated as a "sublime object" because the sublime is an attribute of subjectivity. And it is, ultimately, a correlative of the realization of the simultaneous possibility and impossibility of a finite representation of the infinite. Apprehension falls short, and while the subject cannot comprehend the notion of the infinite (imagination is inevitably inadequate), it grasps its own sensuous and imaginative inadequacy as a failure that is nullified by reason—the ability, that is, to form a concept of infinity as totality: "The quality of the feeling of the sublime consists in being, in respect of the faculty of aesthetic judging, a feeling of displeasure at an object, which yet, at the same time, is represented as purposive—a representation which derives its possibility from the fact that the subject's very incapacity betrays the consciousness of an unlimited capacity of the same subject, and that the mind can aesthetically judge the latter only through the former."[17] It is the faculty of the subject that is unlimited, so that infinity resides not in the world—which would be threatening and incomprehensible—but instead as a power within the subject. This is entirely consistent, as I will try to demonstrate later, with the representation of the subject's relation to infinity within the system of quattrocento perspective. Hence, the sublime is produced under the pressure to hold the infinite in thought, to conceptualize it as a totality. The fact that this is possible is for Kant a validation of the superiority of reason, of its movement beyond the sensuous—it is "supersensual." This, in turn, is a validation of the human, of the ability of human reason to exceed the boundaries or limitations of its spatiotemporal localization. Infinity, in a sense, resides within the subject. But the "unlimited faculty" (i.e., reason) is based upon lack/inadequacy.

Hence, the concept of the sublime grapples with the notion of infinity and its representability, although this is not the term Kant would have used. Yet there is another way of thinking and representing infinity that is not usually articulated with the sublime. Renaissance perspective, inherited by the cinema, constitutes infinity as a point—a perpetually receding point, the vanishing point—which mirrors the position of the subject contemplating the painting. Like Kant's reason in at least one respect, it acts as an imprimatur of a mastery that takes form by going beyond, even annihilating, the subject's sensory and spatiotemporal localization, all the singularities/particularities of incarnation in a finite body limited by the reach of its senses. At least this reading of perspective is that of apparatus theory in film studies, the legacy of Jean-Louis Baudry, Jean-Louis Comolli, and others in the 1970s. And it is that of Erwin Panofsky as well. Panofsky analyzed Renaissance perspective as the symptom and instantiation of a new concept—that of infinity, embodied in the vanishing point.[18] Yet this was a representational infinity that confirmed and reassured the human subject, replacing a theocracy with an individualizing humanism.[19] In a way, it could be seen as a secularization of the sublime.

Perspective produces an illusion of depth in the image—potentially endless depth guaranteed by the vanishing point marking the "place" of infinity. It allows for the simulation of the three-dimensional on a two-dimensional surface. However, both modernity and postmodernity have been characterized as a regime of the surface, a decimation of depth. As Fredric Jameson has famously written: "A new kind of flatness or depthlessness, a new kind of superficiality in the most literal sense [is] perhaps the supreme formal feature of all the postmodernisms."[20] How, or is, the infinite thought or represented in such a context? Where is the sublime? In a provocative essay entitled "Notes on Surface: Toward a Genealogy of Flatness," David Joselit has argued that, in the case of painting, illusionistic recession has been transposed into lateral extension. He cites Clement Greenberg, who claims that the abstract expressionists utilized huge canvases to compensate for the spatial loss of illusionistic depth.[21] Indeed, this lateral extension can be seen in the movement toward larger and larger screens, culminating in IMAX, but also in the embedding of smaller screens such as the iPhone in complex and extensive networks whose scope and scale are challenges to individual comprehension. The intricacy of these networks contributes to what Jameson has labeled the problem of cognitive mapping. This suggests that infinity is no longer conceptualizable in relation to depth and recession, as in a humanist perspectival system, but instead in relation to questions of scale, extension, and uncognizable networks. For a network, in theory, has no closure. This does not herald a break with the disembodiment or delocalization of perspectival illusionism, but a shifting or displacement of the subject's relation to space, scale, and location that shares with Kant's sublime a lack in relation to knowledge and imagination. From Joselit's point of view, the increasing emphasis upon surface and flatness in aesthetic representation cannot be divorced from late capitalism's production of the self as image, as a commodity of surfaces. In other words, there is a conflation of psychological and optical flatness that generates a politics of the visualizable self and motivates the incessant work of the stereotype (whether racial, sexual, ethnic, or other).

The *Oxford English Dictionary* defines the sublime as "set or raised aloft, high up" and traces its etymology to the Latin *sublimis*, a combination of *sub* (up to) and *limen* (lintel, literally the top piece of a door). The sublime is consistently defined by philosophers in relation to concepts of largeness, height, greatness, magnitude. For Burke, visual objects of "great dimension" are sublime. Kant claims, "Sublime is the name given to what is absolutely great," and "the infinite is absolutely (not merely comparatively) great."[22] The sublime is associated with formlessness, boundlessness, and excess beyond limit. It is not surprising in this context that IMAX has been analyzed by invoking the concept of the sublime (Haidee Wasson and Alison Griffiths refer to Burke's sublime in particular), especially insofar as the terror associated with the sublime, for both Burke and Kant, must be experienced from a position of safety. The sublime is an aesthetic category, and it is inevitably chained to affect, whether awe, terror, pleasure, or fear—and most frequently a combination of these. The advertising for and the analysis of IMAX are obsessed with its involvement of the subject in a gripping experience—hence, the discourse of immersion. IMAX is described as above all a visceral experience, requiring a form of bodily participation. Unlike the disembodiment of the classical perspectival system, the body seems to be what is above all at stake in discourses on IMAX. The IMAX sublime, if there is such a thing, here deviates from Kant's, for whom the sublime was sublime only on condition that it exceed the sensuous, proclaim the irrelevance of the subject's spatiotemporal presence in favor of the infinite grasp of reason. The discourse of immersion would seem to rescue the body from its nullification by both Renaissance perspective and the Kantian sublime, making us once again present to ourselves.[23]

But I would like to argue that immersion as a category is symptomatic, and one has to ask what this body is. The body here is a bundle of senses— primarily vision, hearing, and touch. But this appeal to the body as sensory experience, as the satiation of all the claims for its pleasure, does not revive an access to spatiotemporal presence or localization. Instead, it radically de-localizes the subject once again, grasping for more to see, more to hear, more to feel in an ever-expanding elsewhere. IMAX emerged from the world fairs and expos that constituted exhibitionistic displays of the ever-expanding powers of technology (what David Nye has called the "technological sublime").[24] It is telling that one of the works of this early tendency toward magnification of the scale of the image and proliferation of screens was Charles and Ray Eames's iconic *Powers of Ten: About the Relative Size of Things in the Universe* (1977).[25] The Eames Office website claims that "in this film, Charles and Ray employed the system of exponential powers to visualize the importance of scale."[26] *Powers of Ten* was preceded by and based on Kees Boeke's book

Cosmic View (1957) and the Eames's earlier work *A Rough Sketch of a Proposed Film Dealing with the Powers of Ten and the Relative Size of Things in the Universe* (1968). The 1977 film illustrates a movement from a couple having a picnic in Chicago (tellingly centered on the man's hand) (fig. 6.8) to the edge of the universe and back to the interior of the body by exponentially increasing the "camera's" distance from the couple, reversing the trajectory, and decreasing that distance to the point of inhabiting the body itself (figs. 6.7, 6.9). The mirrored movement—first outward to outer space and then inward to the depths of the microscopic—suggests an ontological mirroring as well: the "world" of the infinitesimally small echoes the forms populating the enormity of the galaxies, making both "graspable," legible, in the same terms. This imperialist, colonizing mode of knowledge is fully compatible with the Cold War context and competitive world fair milieu within which the IBM-sponsored *Powers of Ten* emerges.[27] The constancy and placelessness of the reassuring, well-educated male voice-over (of Philip Morrison) confirms the accessibility and stability of this knowledge.

Working with an animation stand, the filmmakers used flat photographs and drawings from various sources: NASA, the Chicago Aerial Survey, time-exposure photography with telescopes, Robert Hooke's *Micrographia* (1665), scanning electron microscopes, transmission electron micrographs, bubble chamber photos, and so on.[28] Alex Funke, one of the film technicians, describes the process in the following way:

> *Powers of Ten* is essentially one continuous animation-stand truck shot. The animation was photographed in a series of ten-second moves, made in such a way that the apparent acceleration is constant. Every ten-second period begins with a big close-up of the center of a large image, and ends on a field ten times larger. At the center of each image—there were more than a hundred of them—was an inserted, ten times reduced view of the entire preceding scene, to assure continuity of detail and color. The successive moves were linked by in-camera dissolves.[29]

Funke describes changes in size in the film in relation to a "truck shot" (tracking shot, in which the distance between the camera and its object changes) rather than a zoom (in which it is the focal length of the camera lens that is altered). Nevertheless, the film is almost always described as a long zooming shot, undoubtedly at least partially due to the title of its initiating source, the book *Cosmic Zoom* (in which the term is even less applicable). However, it is crucial that the zoom is appealed to as specifying the experience of *Powers*

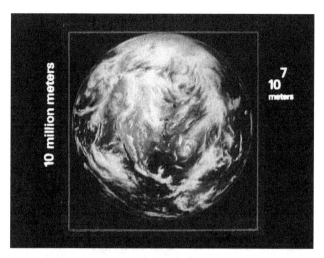

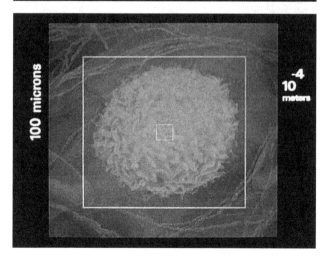

6.7–6.9 *Powers of Ten*
(Charles and Ray Eames,
1977).

of Ten. The use of the term "zoom" is symptomatic of a generalized way of seeing that is tethered to a particular epistemological position (I will return to this shortly).

The human body would seem to be central to this demonstration, primarily as a marker of scale and as the threshold of a trajectory from the gigantic to the infinitesimally small. Yet the film is instead an allegory of the nullification of the body and its location, acting only as a nostalgic citation of a time when the human body was the ground and reference for measurement, replacing it with a mechanical mathematical formula for the progressions of scale. The limits of the "camera's" trip in both directions are, of course, the limits of human knowledge—at the moment. But the film suggests that this movement is infinitely extendable, and it is not accidental that technologies of knowledge and technologies of the image are inseparable here. Human vision, with the aid of imaging technologies, is infinitely extendable, and knowledge is embedded in that vision. But I have spoken only of the represented body—the inhabitant of the picnic blanket—not of the spectatorial body. The film appears to be, and has been marketed as, a combination of a long zoom out to the outermost edges of the universe and a long zoom in to the smallest particles within the human body (ending with quarks). But, as outlined earlier, it is a manufactured zoom, suturing together heterogeneous still images derived from different sources, and the dissolves between them further blur the film's discontinuities and ruptures in the service of the illusion of a smooth, unified, progressive vision. As Zachary Horton has pointed out, *Powers of Ten* "produces a scalar continuum that enacts at the same time a total representational system (anything found within the totality of the world exists somewhere along its scalar axis) and a contiguous field that eliminates any discontinuities in the ordering of the universe."[30] The spectatorial eye is fully aligned with the technological eye—not with the vision of the represented "characters," the man and the woman—and its travels are limited only by the current state of technologies of imaging/knowledge. Yet there is a sense not only that it is disembodied or delocalized but that it is potentially everywhere, able to see and hence know everything.

Why is the idea of the zoom, despite its lack of accuracy, so central to this endeavor? Contrasting our contemporary moment to "the fixed perspective of Renaissance art" and other visual phenomena, Steven Johnson has described the zoom as the distinctive way of seeing of contemporary life. Referring to the "long zoom" of Google Earth, satellite imaging, DNA, and fractal geometry, among other phenomena, he points to the term's inclusion of the scales of the smallest and the largest, outside of the question of whether they are visible to the human eye.[31] Google Earth's movement through different scales would seem to be exemplary in this respect (although, at present, it excludes the microscopic), seemingly making the entire earth accessible to any viewer. But although the zoom is certainly part of the program's experience, it is not the smooth, homogeneous zoom of *Powers of Ten*. As Mark Dorrian points out in an essay included in the anthology *Seeing from Above: The Aerial View in Visual Culture*, Google Earth is constituted by a "panoply of geospatial data sets produced by orbiting satellites and lower-level image-capture devices, which are then digitally sutured together to form the global image. . . . With its evidently constructed patchwork, the visual rhetoric of the globe no longer enunciates the 'wholeness of the object' but rather the 'wholeness of its searchability,' for everything that retards vision tends to be drained away."[32] What *is* hidden, according to Dorrian, is the politics of resolution of Google Earth, where high resolution is reserved for areas with the greatest real estate value and the Third World becomes "lo-res." Nevertheless, while the zoom has mutated from its deployment in *Powers of Ten* (in both, the zoom is manufactured, but in the film the seams are concealed), it is still a crucial vehicle of vision and knowledge, suturing together a plethora of scales, situating the viewer in a position of illusory dominance. The OED links the original meaning of the word "zoom" to a buzzing or humming sound produced by high speed. It defines the cinematographic use of the term as "the action of increasing or decreasing magnification of an image smoothly and quickly." In the elision of sound by vision, velocity is still at issue. Unlike a tracking shot, which confronts the resistances of place and matter, a zoom easily annihilates the distance between subject and object of vision, aligning itself with a host of technologies that strive to negate distance (the railroad, the telephone, television). Both Google Earth and *Powers of Ten* promote a mastery of space and a liberation from time (Google, in particular, has affiliated itself with the notion of instantaneity). The sense of wandering through time of the tracking shot has faded in the face of the omnipresent zoom. The zoom encompasses both the miniature and the gigantic, the components of cells and the extent of the universe, and the possibility of traveling from one to the other virtually instantaneously.

I would like to bring into play here another, quite different, film, one that, along with *Powers of Ten*, is also not an IMAX film but could be said to have IMAX aspirations and at the same time struggle with earlier modes of representation. The contradictions and clashes between the two problematics are quite striking in their visibility. Like *Powers of Ten*, Terrence Malick's *Tree of Life* (2011) strives to articulate the everyday with the grandeur and sublimity of the universe. Sections of *Tree of Life* were filmed in IMAX and originally designed to be exhibited separately in IMAX theaters. But the film was released in traditional theaters and included these sections, whose only gain from IMAX filming was increased resolution but not scale. The film makes ample use of what I would call the "IMAX shot," inevitably a point-of-view shot moving forward toward the horizon, over a cliff, down a waterfall, over the ocean, and so on (fig. 6.10). This is in effect a simulation of a point-of-view shot, an impossible point-of-view shot that is thereby depsychologized. It is also one of the primary generators of the discourse of immersion. In *Tree of Life* it is combined with shots reminiscent of educational nature IMAX films but clearly deployed here to evoke the sublime. These are the "birth of the universe shots," often accompanied by moving and swelling classical or religious music—here, Zbigniew Preisner's *Requiem for My Friend* (fig. 6.11). Malick refused to use computer-generated imagery (CGI) to produce his cosmic special effects and instead achieved them by returning to techniques reminiscent of those utilized in the early years of the cinema: milk poured

6.10 The "IMAX shot," *Tree of Life* (Terrence Malick, 2011).

through funnels, various chemicals, fluorescent dyes, carbon dioxide, smoke, unidentifiable objects shot so closely that they seem gigantic and overwhelming in the tradition of the scale models discussed in this book's introduction.[33] This is a form of special effect that exploited the spectator's inability to ascertain dimension, their failure to negotiate imagistic space with respect to the scale of everyday life. The illegibility of the distance between camera and object is translated into that between spectator and image. *Tree of Life* is in many ways about scale—both temporal and spatial. Eons in the life of the universe are juxtaposed with memories of a single lifetime. Ontogeny recapitulates phylogeny but only in the sense of a flattening of time. The cosmic sequences detach themselves from the heritage of the IMAX educational film but not simply because they are not situated within an educational or scientific context (despite the fact that Malick enlisted scientific experts on imaging technologies in the generation of these sequences). Instead, there is an intertwining of recognizability and unrecognizability in the series of images. In the sense that they strive to represent the unrepresentable, they inhabit the problematic of the sublime.

But this is not the sublime of Burke or Kant, though it has affinities with them. Malick's sublime is also lodged within the family scenes, which are

6.11 Birth of the universe, *Tree of Life* (Terrence Malick, 2011).

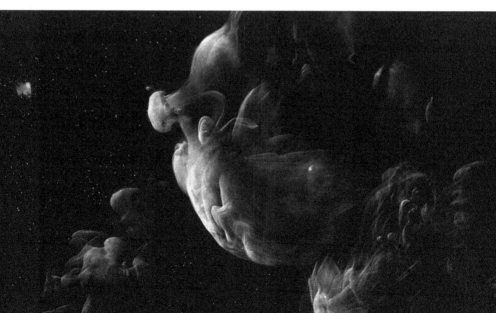

curiously decontextualized. Point of view is fractured despite the fact that retrospectively the film seems to locate itself in the memory of Jack, the character played by Sean Penn. His memories arise in a non-place—the elegant glass skyscrapers of an urban milieu where the scale of the architecture, in its turn, seems to partake of the sublime. But within the diegesis of memory, time is fractured in the service of a significant condensation often aimed toward the production of affect. Jump cuts are consistently deployed, the film's dialogue is truncated and inarticulate, and the images sometimes seem as impossible as those of the cosmic sequences. Time is not organic but fractured, as though the aspiration to the sublime of memory were riddled with contradictions. There is an Oedipus complex. But it is both a hyperbolization of the Oedipus complex and its mere citation, its shorthand. The concatenation of cosmic images, both microcosmic and macrocosmic, that punctuate the narrative are its parergon, the frame that invades the picture, for the cinematic techniques of the narrative partake of the same condensation of time and evocation of awe as those of the cosmic sequences—to make individual memory as sublime as the infinite wonder of the cosmos. As an effect of this, the narrative scenes seem dislocated, derealized, but nevertheless, or perhaps as a consequence, sublime. Yet these images, in their sublimity, are not far removed, particularly at certain points in the depiction of the mother, from those of commercial advertising, which also strives to package life into moments of condensed bliss. Movement becomes life in a form of instantaneous gesture that aims at reproducibility, distributability, and a common consensus of the good life. At these moments, the sublime appears to be in collusion with the commodity form.

Jean-François Lyotard claims that the sublime marks the point of incommensurability between thought and the world, between representation and the indeterminate. For Lyotard, Burke's primary contribution to the thinking of the sublime was his yoking of it to privation—"privation of light, terror of darkness; privation of others, terror of solitude; privation of language, terror of silence; privation of objects, terror of emptiness; privation of life, terror of death. What is terrifying is that the *It happens that* does not happen, that it stops happening."[34] This is for Lyotard what links the sublime to the avant-garde—a discourse that pursues not the question "What is happening?" but "Is it happening?" and produces itself as a pursuit of the indeterminate. The avant-garde's continual striving for innovation is designed as a denial of a finality of art that would assure us that *it* has happened and lead us to cease asking the question. Unfortunately, however, this can bring the avant-garde dangerously close to the mechanism of capitalism, which is also that of continual innovation:

There is something of the sublime in capitalist economy. It is not academic, it is not physiocratic, it admits of no nature. It is, in a sense, an economy regulated by an Idea—infinite wealth or power. It does not manage to present any example from reality to verify this Idea. In making science subordinate to itself through technologies, especially those of language, it only succeeds, on the contrary, in making reality increasingly ungraspable, subject to doubt, unsteady. . . . Hidden in the cynicism of innovation is certainly the despair that nothing further will happen. But innovating means to behave as though lots of things happened, and to make them happen. Through innovation, the will affirms its hegemony over time. It thus conforms to the metaphysics of capital, which is a technology of time. . . . The avant-gardist task remains that of undoing the presumption of the mind with respect to time. The sublime feeling is the name of this privation.[35]

Capitalism's collusion with the sublime, particularly in its insistent innovation in the realm of technology and especially technologies of imaging, does not mean that the concept of the sublime is inevitably complicit. Malick, in *Tree of Life*, is no doubt attempting to resist the capitalist logic of innovation as well as commercialism's hollowing out and abstraction of the image. The film resuscitates a heavily theological discourse, locating its thinking of infinity there, grasping for a way to deal with indeterminacy and to produce a sublime that is outside of capitalism's hegemonic hold over time. Yet the veering of its images toward those of advertising should act as a warning of the vulnerability of the logic of the sublime—especially of attempting to locate the sublime in everyday life—to the spatiotemporal coordinates of commodification. For the logic of the IMAX sublime—perhaps the technological sublime par excellence—is also harnessed to that of capitalism in another way, insofar as it operates under the umbrella of the discourse of immersion, producing an illusion that depth and ready access to the body are still with us, and concealing its radical delocalization and dislocation of a subject seemingly empowered in the face of a world defined as infinite extension.

The Trope of the Turn and the Production
of Sound Space

While both classical and contemporary film theory have productively dissected the relation between the visible and the invisible in cinema through a concentration on off-screen space as the preeminent "blind space," much less attention has been paid to that other dimension of invisibility—that which is behind, the "other side" of bodies and of things. Because the film image is two-dimensional, the activation of perspective and overlapping figures is clearly involved in the production of the effect of three-dimensionality, but this is true of a painting or a photograph as well. The cinema has an added advantage—movement, which aids in carving out the space of the diegesis. The "turn"—of both characters' bodies and the body of the camera—is a crucial trope in this respect. The "turn" in classical Hollywood films is often activated in the service of scenes of misrecognition, where it reveals a mistaken identity. For the turn makes visible that which was concealed—the "other side"—an other side that does not materially exist in the two-dimensional realm of cinema but is continually evoked, imagined, assumed. The turn is a constant reiteration of otherness and the limits of knowability, a denial of the sufficiency of the screen as surface. Knowledge resides *somewhere else*— behind, on the other side. But the turn also confirms that there *is* another side, in what could be labeled a "virtual dimension." Nevertheless, given the physical immobility of the spectator, the necessity of facing forward to see the screen, that turn must be delegated to someone or something else— character, figure, camera. Navigable space is on the side of the screen. What are the effects of this delegation to figure or camera of a bodily gesture that is critical to the subject's relation to space, of a body's fundamental capability, as Henri Lefebvre has pointed out, "of indicating direction by a gesture, of defining rotation by turning round, of demarcating and orienting space"?[36] In Lefebvre's analysis, space cannot be conceived of as an empty container, ready and able to accept any content. Space is, above all, *occupied*: "There is an immediate relationship between the body and its space, between the body's deployment in space and its occupation of space . . . each living body *is* space and *has* its space: it produces itself in space and also produces that space."[37] Yet, in the context of the cinema, the spectator's body is incapacitated, rendered useless, deprived of its role of demarcating space through gesture and movement. As has so often been pointed out, the spectator must become immobilized, bodiless, their senses reduced to those characterized by distance—vision and hearing. Space is not lived—at least in the sense of the ordinary or everyday experience of space in its relation to the body—but abstracted, alienated. The turn that helps to demarcate and define space is, in the cinema, a *represented* turn, and the space is a *represented* space. But there is another turn at issue here, one that must be prohibited. One thing the spectator must not do is turn around to look at the back of the auditorium.

The turn that demarcates and orients space must be relocated on the side of the screen.

Increasingly today we are confronted with the delocalizing effects of contemporary media networks. The subject's relation to space, the sense of "where" one is, has been corroded by the proliferation of virtual spaces and the displacement of the question "where" to that of "who" one is (e.g., the Facebook phenomenon and other social media). But delocalization has been an aspect of many if not all modern technologies of representation and communication—the telephone, the railroad, the telegraph, radio, cinema, television. Modern media have systematically worked to disengage "place" from a specific site and make it transportable, exchangeable, commodifiable. Do recent digital technologies—mobile phones, IMAX, digital surround sound—simply intensify this general tendency, or can they be seen as different, historically discontinuous? Their promise is that of the expansion of space to envelop the spectator, to surround them in the production of a vicariously lived space. This would seem to be a commodification without object—the commodification of environment.

The turn in classical cinema—of the character, of the camera—can be seen as compensatory. It works to reduce the sense of film as a two-dimensional medium and buttress the spectatorial experience of volume, of depth, of a full space. It was often markedly absent in the earliest silent cinema, where characters were positioned theatrically, facing the camera/audience (for example, in *The Bride Retires* [1902], where the bride directly faces the audience instead of her husband). With the advent of sustained narrative, this position morphed into its opposite—the taboo against looking at the camera, the insistence upon an autonomous space of the narrative, completely disengaged from the space of the viewer. Since the viewer was no longer "there," this opened up the possibility of the character's turning away from the camera, seemingly inconceivable in much early silent film. However, even the earliest films played with this frontality and its relation to the "back" space— sometimes explicitly. In *In My Lady's Boudoir* (1903), the female character's back is to the camera, but this receives compensation through the fact that her face is reflected in the mirror for the benefit of the spectator (see figs. 3.24, 3.25). Here there is a concerted attempt to grapple with the inevitable two-dimensionality of film, its flatness and material limits as a surface.

But, again, this conceptualization of front and back and the turn concerns the space of the diegesis and not that of the spectator. Both the turning character and the turning camera mark out the space of the diegesis and delineate its volume. Yet the spectator's space is defined differently. Vision is directional, and the spectator who turns around and no longer faces the film will miss a part of it, making that particular turn taboo, prohibited. Nevertheless, the space behind the spectator has not been entirely neglected. Often it has been activated by theorists in intriguing ways. Jean-Louis Baudry refers to the directionality of "reality" in the cinema: "In any case this 'reality' comes from behind the spectator's head, and if he looked at it directly he would see nothing except the moving beams from an already veiled light source."[38] The veracity/actuality of the diegesis is evacuated by the turn. Deploying Plato's allegory of the cave in which the prisoners are chained since infancy, allowed only to look ahead at the screen of shadows, Baudry cites Plato's imaginary scenario of turning around: "Suppose one of them were set free and forced suddenly to stand up, turn his head, and walk with eyes lifted to the light; all these movements would be painful, and he would be too dazzled to make out objects."[39] In Baudry's analogy, it is the turn toward the projector that breaks the illusion of the apparatus, but it also connotes a certain violence, a dazzlement of vision. Christian Metz's transcendental identification with the camera and with the pure act of perception becomes in the screening an identification with that other part of the apparatus—the projector, "an apparatus the spectator has behind him, *at the back of his head*, that is, precisely where fantasy locates the 'focus' of all vision."[40] In a discussion of the way in which Renaissance perspective, from the outset, was linked to the concept of infinity, Hubert Damisch refers to infinity as "an idea of what's behind one's head."[41] Hence, the non-place of this "behind" in the theater is not empty but instead replete with the subject's relations to illusion, the real, fantasy, and infinity, as well as answerable to a certain taboo against the gaze in support of representation. The separation between "front" and "back" spaces in relation to media has also been conceptualized as a structure of the social availability of knowledge and ignorance by Anthony Giddens. Citing the work of Erving Goffman and Edward Hall, Giddens claims that the "front" space of society constitutes an open, accessible space for the general public, a place of transparency and visibility. But the "back" space is "the locus of social information that is hidden."[42] According to Jonathan Sterne, "Giddens and John Thompson both argue that the rise of the mass media has coincided with the growth of forms of communication that entail very small front spaces (relatively little available information) in relation to relatively large back spaces (lots of unknown factors)."[43] All of the arguments of 1970s film theory about concealing the apparatus and hiding the work of the production of a film would seem to confirm this assertion. It is arguable that the "back spaces" of digital media are larger still. The spatial categories of front and back are aligned with a form of social engineering of the availability of information. The back spaces are those that are withheld, secret, deliberately opaque.

But 1970s film theory was primarily interested in cinema as a visual medium, with only occasional references to sound. Although one cannot see what is behind one's head, one can hear it. And this three-dimensionality of sound is increasingly referenced by film theorists. For instance, in a consideration of cinema and the ear, Thomas Elsaesser and Malte Hagener claim that "hearing is always a three-dimensional, spatial perception, i.e. it creates an acoustic space, because we hear in all directions," and quote Mirjam Schaub: "The main 'anthropological' task of hearing . . . [is] to stabilize our body in space, hold it up, facilitate a three-dimensional orientation and, above all, ensure an all-round security that includes even those spaces, objects and events that we cannot see, especially what goes on behind our backs. Whereas the eye searches and plunders, the ear listens in on what is plundering us. The ear is the organ of fear."[44] The ear is associated with a sense of balance and with contributing strongly to the apprehension of the body's location in space. Cinematic space is molded as much by sound as by the dialectic of on-screen and off-screen space. Sound, as the material displacement or vibration of airwaves, affects the entire body and not just the ears. Michel Chion similarly stresses the fact that hearing "is omnidirectional. We cannot see what is behind us, but we can hear all around."[45] Although all of these considerations allude to a phenomenological conceptualization of hearing and are part of what Jonathan Sterne terms the "audio-visual litany," that is, the string of characteristics that are supposed to be natural to sound and hence dehistoricized, it is significant that these specific traits are becoming more fundamental in recent years to our understanding of cinematic sound. The shift seems to be linked to the alterations in sound reproduction of the 1960s and 1970s, the era of rock concerts and high-fidelity records, which produced a more discerning listener, unable to accept the unnuanced sound reproduction of earlier years. But it is also a function of the increasing mobility of sound—it accompanies us everywhere, and in the theater, it has begun to invade the space previously erased or at least reduced by classical cinema, the space of the auditorium. But what does it do there?

One of the major debates in 1930s attempts to grapple with sound circulated around the question of sound perspective. Sound perspective refers to the spectator's sense of a sound's location in space and is determined by a number of factors, including volume, frequency, the balance with other sounds, and the amount of reverberation. It can be an effect of microphone placement or of postproduction manipulations. In conflict in the debate were the values of spatial realism (the localizability of an event, the matching of image and sound) and the intelligibility of dialogue (which would be lost at a certain distance if strict sound perspective were maintained). As Rick Altman has shown, intelligibility of dialogue generally won out (except in very special cases), undermining the perceived necessity of spatial fidelity of sound to image. What was lost were all the qualities, including reverberation, that might be used to spatialize a sound.[46] The debate was settled, according to James Lastra, by "close miking and a certain 'frontality.'"[47] As Emily Thompson has pointed out, radio and other modern deployments of sound, including soundproofing and the use of a directional flow of sound in theaters, were a crucial reference point: "This kind of sound was everywhere. In its commodified nature, in its direct and nonreverberant quality, in its emphasis on the signal and freedom from noise, and in its ability to transcend traditional constraints of time and space, the sound of the sound track was just another constituent of the modern soundscape."[48] The technical possibility of producing reverberation in the studio, independently of the space of the original recording, freed sound from "any architectural location in which a sound might be created: it was nothing but an effect, a quality that could be meted out at will and added in any quantity of any electrical signal."[49] In a sense, sound was both everywhere and nowhere. What was at stake in these debates were the limits of acceptability of the spacelessness of sound. A spaceless sound is one that can be more easily disengaged from its specific geographic, historical, and political location and subjected to circulation as a commodity.

The sound perspective debates of the 1930s have somewhat uncannily reemerged with the production of new multichannel systems, surround sound, digital sound, and the consequent proliferation of speakers throughout the auditorium. With respect to questions of sound space, there are at least two ramifications of these changes. One would be the accelerated annihilation of the sense of the specific space of the auditorium in which a film is projected. Michel Chion claims that the choice of architecture and building plans for new movie theaters has "mercilessly vanquished" reverberation—"the result is that the sound feels very present and very neutral, but suddenly one no longer has the feeling of the real dimensions of the room, no matter how big it is."[50] It is arguable that, perhaps with the exception of ostentatious picture palaces that called attention to themselves, movie theaters have always been designed to reduce a sense of their own specific spatial properties in order to "host" any number of diegetic spaces proposed by a stream of ever-changing films. In order to allow audiences to "go elsewhere," theaters must become non-spaces or "non-places," to adopt Marc Augé's term to describe airports, shopping malls, and any institutional space that is eminently recognizable in a generic sense that has nothing to do with its specific location. But for Chion, this process has intensified—theatrical sound has become so "pure" and neutral that it has reduced any distinction between cinema sound and a good home stereo system. Collective sound has been displaced by personal sound. This pursuit of spatial anonymity characterizes the space of cinematic exhibition. But the second ramification of the proliferation of multichannel systems and surround sound concerns the space produced by the film, its diegetic space. For the multiplication of potential sound sources exacerbates the issue of the localizability of sound. It appears to demand a greater precision in matching sound and space and hence, in a sense, to respatialize sound. Chion defines as the "superfield" the space produced in multichannel films by ambient sounds that surround the visual space and "can issue from loudspeakers outside the physical boundaries of the screen."[51] According to Chion, the fact that these sounds are more precisely located spatially releases contemporary narrative film from the classical obligation of providing an establishing shot (typically used to orient the spectator in relation to the use of close-ups and medium shots that fragment that space). This results in a contemporary filmic style of fast editing and more insistent use of close-ups because the "superfield provides a continuous and constant consciousness of all the space surrounding the dramatic action."[52] Modern soundtracks endow the image track with a greater recognizability. Yet echoing the sound perspective debates of the 1930s, many sound technicians have been reticent about "too much" sound realism (spatialization), about overuse of the speakers spread over the auditorium, due to the potential distraction of the spectator's attention away from the screen. If sound has traditionally been used to tell us where to look, what is visually important, its leakage into the auditorium presents a potential difficulty. Again, hearkening back to the 1930s debates, this is particularly true in the case of dialogue, which must be both intelligible and "present," intimately bound to the image of the person, whether visible or invisible, that is, just over there, on the other side of the frame, in what has traditionally been specified as the most significant form of off-screen space in narrative film. Current sound practice tends to locate dialogue in the speakers behind the screen, just as classical practice dictated.

Ambient noise—leaves rustling, train whistles in the distance, birds, rain, and so on—and music, forms of sound that can be more easily dissociable and independent of the image, are more likely to be channeled to the speakers in the auditorium.

In an experiment intended to challenge conventional uses of multichannel sound and expand its possibilities, Christos Manolas and Sandra Pauletto produced a short narrative film in 2009 with a small number of austere images and a large number of spatialized sounds, hoping to demonstrate that multichannel sound could strongly direct the spectator's reading of the geography of the narrative—extending to the internal and external states of a character. In one instance, a character's spoken dialogue emanated from a speaker behind the screen, but his thoughts were emitted from the rear speaker in the auditorium, mapping the distinction between real and imaginary onto that between front and back, as though sound spatialization required that the unreal always and literally come from behind. As long as the spectator understood that the rear voice was interior monologue, they would not be tempted to turn and look behind.

While many contemporary films restrict the use of surround speakers in conventional ways, others use digital surround systems that reject classical norms, leading Mark Kerins to suggest that Chion's concept of the "superfield" is already outdated. The superfield is continuous and autonomous in relation to the image, and its stability allows a heightened discontinuity in the image track. Kerins claims, however, that there are many recent films in which the soundtrack is discontinuous, precisely matching the image track by changing sound perspective with each newly spatialized image (the first scene in *Saving Private Ryan* is his privileged example). Kerins labels this new 360-degree space the "ultrafield." The discontinuity in classical terms of this space is so extreme that it even encourages the violation of the 180-degree rule. The 180-degree rule, in Kerins's account, assumes that the space behind the camera (and, by extension, the space behind the spectator) is irrelevant to the narrative and can be suppressed. This places the viewer "outside of the world" and "not in it."[53] By violating the 180-degree rule, these films imply that "the camera cannot capture all the action without *turning around* to shoot 'behind' the audience."[54] There are a number of issues here, perhaps first and foremost the idea that the camera might be able to "capture all the action." Since the camera is the construction of the possibility of "seeing" the "action," this assertion implies that we are witnessing a documentary event, of which we can see more or less. But because what we see—in both documentary and fiction—is a function of the camera's vison, there is no "all," a portion of which the camera can see. Granted, that "behind" is in quotation marks here; nevertheless, the language of immersion and being "in the middle of the action" recurs frequently in Kerins's discourse, which echoes that of the advertising for new film technologies—not only digital surround sound but also IMAX, 3D, and so on—as discussed earlier.

While even the classical film attempted to absorb its audience, to bring the spectator into the diegesis, this rhetoric seems to have become more insistent with each "new" technology. According to Kerins, in films using immersive sound, "the audience is literally *placed* in the dramatic space of the movie, shifting the conception of cinema from something 'to be watched from the outside'—with audience members taking in a scene *in front of them*—to something 'to be personally experienced'—with audience members literally placed *in the middle* of the diegetic environment and action."[55] The problem is that, unlike the characters, the spectators continue to face forward. The true blind space is still behind them. The taboo nature of this space is indicated very clearly by the fact that sound designers continue to be wary of overlocalizing or overspatializing sounds to the extent that the spectator is distracted and pulled away from the image/screen. This is evidenced most tellingly in what they refer to as the "exit door effect" or the "exit sign effect," in which, hypothetically, the spectator would try to localize a sound and turn away from the screen in order to identify its source. Kerins suggests that the exit door effect is no longer as pressing a concern after more than two decades of multichannel sound and the "training" or "recalibration" of audiences, but he does so in the context of a discussion about why, despite the potential of surround sound, directors continue to be extremely conservative in their use of it. Outside of a few instances, the rear speakers are generally used for ambient effects that do not call out for a specific localization.

Dolby's website introduces Dolby Atmos (short for atmosphere), a recent technical development in sound, with the promise to the moviegoing public that they will "Feel Every Dimension"—not just hear every dimension but feel its bodily impact. Dolby Atmos is based on audio objects governed by metadata rather than on channels, more precisely locating and scaling sounds and purportedly capable of working with any theater's configuration of speakers. On the Dolby website, the examples of sounds appropriate for this system are those taken, tellingly, from a sublime nature—birds, a waterfall, a thunderstorm, and so on—and the sublimity of the cinematic image corresponds to that of the sound. Sound is "seen" as its source is pinpointed in the movement from speaker to speaker in the auditorium, tracing the path of a helicopter seed. In the scene from *Life of Pi* used on the website, the directionality of the sounds of fish flutters is reversed from left-right to right-left on the cut from the tiger's point of view to Pi's, violating the classical sound editing rule of staggering sound cuts and image cuts to conceal the fact of the cut. "You," according to Dolby, are the subject of a constant movement—"you" are "propelled into the story," and "you" are "transported into a powerfully moving cinema experience"—a reiteration of the discourse of immersion characterizing the advertising of IMAX and 3D.[56] In fact, immersion now has a technical definition in relation to sound: immersive sound is "the term used to describe sound that emanates from sources beyond the horizontal plane by means of enhanced spatial properties such as additional height and overhead speakers and localized apparent sound sources within the auditorium."[57] While this definition strikes one as dry and technical, without the affective valence of the usual discussions of immersion, the article begins with the description of an immersive sound experience:

> Imagine stepping from life and being totally immersed in the story during your next cinema experience. Hearing everything as if you were actually there in the scene. Close your eyes. You're at a cafe in Paris, around you dishes are clanking and patrons are engaged in conversations. A woman is shouting from a third-floor window and birds are chirping in the trees. High overhead, a jet cruises by, and you subconsciously note that it's departing to the east. You hear the familiar footsteps of your date approaching behind you. You hear all these details exactly where they belong. This is the goal of Immersive Sound, the next big advance in cinema technology.[58]

The fact that "you" are asked to close your eyes is symptomatic of the continuing tensions between three-dimensional sound and two-dimensional image localization. To "hear all these details exactly where they belong" requires denying the visual space that does not support (or supports only figuratively) the sound space. The Dolby Atmos website situates the difference of this technology in a more powerful bass and overhead sound that "heightens the realism of your cinematic experience." Finally, your own location is made irrelevant: "no matter where you sit in the theatre," you will have access to this moving experience.[59]

Why this insistent rhetoric refining and insisting upon the immersion of the spectator in the diegesis? Why does it, beyond the promises of classical cinema, produce a contract that pledges the film will enter the space of the auditorium and envelop the spectator? Why the insistence upon "enlarging" the diegesis (the space of fantasy), as if it were not large enough already? Why deny the crucial (and necessary) incommensurability of the space of the spectator and that of the diegesis? It would be a mistake to try to understand surround sound as separate from IMAX and 3D, other attempts to expand the space of the diegesis in as many directions as possible. Surround sound and multichannel systems, by moving sound into the space of the auditorium, assist in this annihilation of the frame line.

By locating us everywhere, in an other space, the rhetoric of immersion reduces the compelling nature of location, of the body's ability, as Lefebvre points out, of demarcating and analyzing, not to mention producing, space, in a particular historical and social context. The emphasis upon disembodiment in 1970s film theory was, perhaps, always more about delocalization, about the erasure of the spectator's space in favor of another space. For the body has been increasingly in play in terms of the number of senses the cinema seeks to activate (perhaps impacting a recent trend in film theory positing a "haptic" cinema). The spectator is a body, but a body defined entirely by its senses and the heightening of those senses. Jonathan Crary has delineated a historical process producing the separability and isolation of the senses. Modern media purport to reunite them, but only at the expense of their derealization and dislocation/relocation.[60] This delocalization is, of course, not specific to cinema, which cannot be understood outside a network of new media configurations. Elsaesser and Hagener emphasize mobility—the movement from speaker to speaker in digital surround sound as a reflection of the increasing mobility of sound systems since the Sony Walkman of the 1970s.[61] And this is, assuredly, correct. But the Sony Walkman and the iPod, smartphone, and other devices not only move us but also extract us and abstract us from the space we are navigating. The space we enter with these devices is more commodifiable, less apt to make us question where we are— not necessarily only geographically but also historically, socially, politically.

Perhaps the most striking delocalization masquerading as localization is the map posted in urban space that specifies "You are here" (fig. 6.12). This is a rather large point representing "you," but it is still a point. A point that in mathematics is without extension, takes up no space. The same is true, despite its mobility, of the point that represents "you" in Google Maps as you navigate an unknown territory. This is not only surveillance—"they" know where you are—but the reduction of your spatiality, the fact that the body is

6.12 "You are here" sign, photograph by author.

itself a space, to a point. This only seems "natural" because we are accustomed to thinking of ourselves as points within a network. Social media ameliorate this by purportedly giving "you" an identity—but where are you when you post on social media?

So, why have I emphasized the "turn" and its function in both classical cinema and the cinema of today? The turn in classical cinema had a quite precise effect—that of indicating the lost dimension of the image—within the diegesis. There was no question of the spectator themselves turning, looking away from the screen. That turn invokes the possibility of another space, the missing space, behind the spectator. Surround sound, in its most current uses, hopes to make this space palpable, to conquer the otherwise and formerly taboo space of the rear of the theater, the back of the spectator—perhaps the "last" territory. But it must do so very carefully, with restraint. For the spectator, turning and looking behind is not just a refusal of the screen but an acknowledgment of the existence of an exit.

Immersion and Location: The "Unattainable Endpoint of Media History"

It is revealing to examine more closely the ways that technicians have approached the question of immersion. Just as technicians during the emergence of the classical narrative system in Hollywood spoke frequently and insistently of the "impression of reality" as a crucial consideration in film production, "immersion" has emerged as a goal in technical discourse, to be managed through precise strategies. For instance, Pierre Hugues Routhier describes four aspects ("axes") of the "immersive experience" that are activated differently by different media.[62] The first axis is seclusion, which measures the degree to which the viewer/user is isolated from their surroundings. In full seclusion, this is a complete sensory isolation from the "real," and Routhier associates it with virtual reality (VR) and simulation experiences (while film and television are aligned with low seclusion). The second axis is navigation and refers to physical mobility of the user in the media environment. There are two measures of navigability: the number of degrees of freedom (DOF) and range. In DOF, which is deployed as a technical term and used by other writers, it is the body whose directionality is measured.[63] In "real life," the human body has 6 DOF—the head can rotate up and down, left and right, and sideways (the 3 rotational DOF). The entire body can walk forward and backward, left and right, or up and down (the 3 translation DOF). Television and standard theatrical films have "0 DOF": "The experience is fixed in an object, and independent of the user's movements. This level is called passive viewing, as the level of user engagement is minimal. Changes in user gaze and posture have no effect on the experience."[64] The concept of DOF is strongly aligned with the earlier discussion of the "turn" in relation to the spectator in the auditorium with surround sound and the necessity of restraining movement. Navigation in the cinema is derealized, present only figuratively, though it remains a persistent metaphor.

Interaction is the third axis of the "immersion experience" and dictates the extent to which the user/spectator is able to alter the media environment. According to Routhier, this excludes not only classical cinema and television viewing but also what is often referred to as "interactive" narratives in these realms (this would include the allegedly "interactive" film *Bandersnatch*

(2018), part of the *Dark Mirror* series on Netflix). In these texts, one can choose a direction of the narrative, but the choices "do not change the actual content," which is already dictated for the viewer. Routhier therefore considers this form of "interactivity" as, instead, an aspect of navigation. True interaction involves both input and output and is characteristic of immersive gaming and professional simulation (medical, flight, etc.). The final axis, "modelization," refers to the question of whether the representation is indexical of the real ("Analog Capture") or virtual (artificially created). It is linked to immersion because it "has a direct impact on" navigation and interaction, which can be made available only through a certain amount of digitization.

Routhier's goal in constructing this taxonomy is to give media makers a tool to aid them in deciding which technologies should be used given their representational objectives. He makes it clear that narrative does not require, but in fact is undermined by, an increase in navigability and interactivity. An increase in seclusion, navigation, interaction, and digital modelization is appropriate for simulation experiences (with sensory gloves, suits, shoes, etc.). Gaming and professional uses of these elements reside between narrative and simulation, the two poles on the charts Routhier provides. His taxonomy is allegedly superior to existing forms of classification (augmented reality, VR, etc.) and is crucial for dealing with the current "exploding landscape of immersion."[65] Nowhere does Routhier attempt to define the experience of immersion. Instead, it is fractured by and within each of these categories—there are, for instance, partial and full forms of seclusion (from "reality"). The implication, however, is that full immersion would entail a system with the highest levels of seclusion, navigability, interactivity, and virtuality—a system that would, in effect, provide its own "world," a world that the user/spectator could inhabit. It would provide a new location for the delocalized and dislocated spectator, a location with no relation to actual place or geography. This is why it is defined as an "experience."

Many media theorists are careful to point out that total immersion is an ideal goal that will never be reached. Quoting from Janet Murray's book *Hamlet on the Holodeck* to the effect that "we" enjoy immersion in a different reality and the ability to navigate it, Britta Neitzel writes, "The total immersion that Murray aims at, which claims all our attention and our entire apparatus of perception, is a myth and must remain a myth: a mythical, unattainable endpoint of media history that emerges in visions of the total loss of reality . . . and became the subject of popular discourses in films such as *The Matrix* (Andy & Larry Wachowski, USA 1999)."[66] Neitzel claims, instead, that "the distinction between being here and being there can never be completely eliminated. Immersion is an ambivalent phenomenon that means simultaneously being here and there."[67] In her dissertation, Allison Whitney outlines five "myths" concerning IMAX. The third myth is "The IMAX viewer is absorbed into the image," and the fifth is "An IMAX movie is the closest thing to being there." However, Whitney goes on to argue that each of these myths has an element of truth and speaks to "the extent to which 3D technology extends IMAX's unique conflation of theater space and the visual space of the film."[68] Still, it is clear that the dream of IMAX, the aspiration explicit in its advertising, is the goal of total immersion.[69]

This dream is so intense that it can, as mentioned earlier, bleed into critical discourse surrounding IMAX and give sustenance to certain persistent fantasies of immersion. Tim Recuber focuses on the "reenchantment" of cinematic space through new technologies of spectatorial absorption: "Although previous art critics and historians have described art reception as immersive or absorbing (e.g., Benjamin, 1968), this notion was used metaphorically, to describe the degree to which one was emotionally or intellectually involved with a work of art. Today, this metaphor, and the ideal it represents, is replaced with an actual technological immersion in the lived space of the theater."[70] And later, he claims that "viewers are no longer simply voyeurs; they are participants in an immersive sensory environment."[71] It is true that Recuber is quite skeptical of the way in which this technology is employed for the construction of an intense sensorial spectacle (at the expense of "nuanced writing, directing and acting" and "to the detriment of lived social space").[72] Invoking the work of Lefebvre and Edward Soja, he calls for a "thirdspace" that would provide alternative and more meaningful geographies, although he does not define this space in any detail. However, in his deployment of the concept of reenchantment and acceptance of the idea of immersion, Recuber collaborates with the enthusiastic discourse of the industry and its promise to take the spectator elsewhere—what Nigel Thrift refers to as the mass production of phenomenological encounter.[73] Immersion is a seductive concept. And this leads to its often unquestioned acceptance as an aesthetic phenomenon that requires analysis. Robin Curtis claims that immersion must be understood not only as a perceptual impression but also as aligned with the aesthetic effect of empathy ("immersion and empathy are so closely related that they can be considered as synonymous").[74] Marie-Laure Ryan also treats immersion as an aesthetic phenomenon that needs to be understood, primarily through the construction of a taxonomy. Immersion in a literary text hinges upon the creation of a seemingly inhabitable space, a world. It is "an imaginative relationship to a *world projected by a text*," whether that text is a novel, a film, or a video game.[75] Ryan persistently invokes the end term of the combination of immersion, interactivity, and narrativity, working together, as "total art." But here it is not Neitzel's "unattainable endpoint of media history," but a dream and a desire that might one day be achieved, an aesthetic to be valued and celebrated. The goal of Alison Griffiths's *Shivers Down Your Spine*, a detailed and erudite analysis of cathedrals, panoramas, museums, and IMAX cinema, is to identify "resonances across these spectacular forms of entertainment that can better help us grasp the nature of immersive viewing."[76] This suggests that there is a transhistorical mode of immersive spectatorship despite the historical specificity of these different media. Immersion is defined by Griffiths as the "sensation of entering a space."[77]

For all of these writers, immersion is ineluctably linked with the notion of another space, environment, or world provided by the medium and the consequent dislocation of the spectator. Even if the argument is tempered by the idea that the spectator is always aware of their actual location in the theater— "knowing" that they are both here and there, aware of the medium as an interface—immersion is always about the provision of an elsewhere designed as a lure. The question that is not posed is, Why? Why this insistent desire to locate the spectator in another place, and why does the invocation of immersion tend to become increasingly described as literal (or total) in relation to modes of media that seek to annihilate the frame in contemporary culture? The ideas of total immersion or total art as the inevitable end point of media history are not simply wrong—or not wrong in any simple way. They speak to a symptomatic crisis of location, a despatialization, a reconceptualization of position, scale, and infinity that undergird the mechanisms of late capitalism and its incessant expansion of commodification. The film technician's concept of "the impression of reality" was also taken up by theorists of classical cinema in the 1970s, but it was subjected to an interrogation informed by linguistics, an ideological dismantling, a psychoanalytic investigation. Recent theoretical approaches have situated themselves as a rejection of the earlier "linguistic turn" of semiotics, structuralism, and poststructuralism. Embracing immersion as a viable aesthetic is consistent with a new enthusiasm for affect theory and phenomenology in media studies (especially film studies). Phenomenology and affect theory have affinities with the aspirations of new "immersive" technologies insofar as they strive to make the body, emotions, and the senses determinant in understanding, an assurance that they are going beyond (or before) language (and hence reading, interpretation). This is, as Mark Andrejevic has argued incisively in the context of the increasing importance of "datafication" and the simultaneous emergence of affect theory and "new materialism," a claim to be postinterpretive, postexplanatory, and postpsychoanalytic, "eliding the realm of the subconscious [sic], desire, and the psychoanalytic subject," ignoring failure and the "structuring deadlock."[78] It is also, inevitably, depoliticizing. At the level of the body and the senses, things tend to become universal, eliding cultural, social, and historical differences. Kristin Veel, in an analysis of the notion of cyberspace, invokes the work of George Lakoff, Mark Johnson, and Mark Turner to avoid Foucault's "imprecise" concept of "heterotopia": "They claim that all our experiences, knowledge, and thinking derive from small temporal and spatial stories that are not culturally determined but universally linked to the human body. Our consciousness conceives of everything that goes on around us as spatial stories, which are comprehended in correlation with the experience of our own body."[79] This is an attempt to narrow and simultaneously individualize knowledge. And, as with every invocation of the universal, it is a removal of the political or ideological implications of space-building in its relation to dominance and subjection, and here sidesteps the way in which space can be and has for a long time been detached from the body.

The vicissitudes of scale discussed throughout this book in relation to cinema constitute early stages of a reconfiguration and abstraction of space and its corollary dislocation of the spectator. "Immersion" would seem to be the final stage—hence the invocation of it as an ultimate end point or goal of media history. In the earliest years of the cinema, the scale of the close-up produced anxiety and horror and was often viewed as "monstrous," especially when associated with the human body. The close-up was ultimately precariously managed through its incorporation within strategies of narrativization and characterization/individualization. In the same vein, directors are often instructed to avoid close-ups in IMAX, whose size could be terrifying. The technology is seen to be more compatible with extensive landscapes that reaffirm its own grandeur. The spectator's inability to gauge scale, its fundamental immeasurability in films, was also exploited in the utilization of the scale model, and later, through CGI. With IMAX, there is a complete capitulation to the pleasures of the gigantic and the "bigger than life." "Immersion" is premised upon the loss of the spectator's actual space and the provision of an imaginary one with its own scalar logic. Scale and location are inextricably intertwined.

The breaking of the frame in cinema, the frameless aspirations of VR, invoke a sense of extension and boundlessness. Whereas infinity was once conceptualized in relation to depth in perspectival systems, by a point that was "vanishing," infinity today is linked to labyrinthine and extended networks, surfaces without depths. On the other hand, as space seems to expand endlessly in IMAX, it contracts elsewhere. Instantaneous communication through telephone, television, and computer as well as high-speed transportation on airplanes work to erase or even destroy space as extension. Space becomes a blockage to be overcome in the service of dedistancing the world—in other words, globalization. Large screens such as IMAX and "immersive" experiences would appear to compensate for the everyday compression of space, giving the spectator access to an expanded and limitless diegesis. The spectator is presented with a commodified experience of space, a space that is elsewhere disappearing. This is, of course, a space that is only illusorily livable, inhabitable. As is the space of globalization, which Peter Sloterdijk associates with the "tearing-away of meaning from lived situations."[80] Sloterdijk bemoans this decontextualization and offers an alternative:

> Once distances are seemingly only there to be overcome, once national cultures only exist to mingle with other traditions, once all the earth's surfaces only represent the immobile counterparts to their elegant collections as geographical maps and aerial photographs, and once space as such means no more than the nothingness between two electronic workplaces—then we can predict the direction which the resistance against these de-realizations will take: sooner or later, the culture of presence will have to assert its rights once more against the culture of imagination and memory.[81]

Sloterdijk lauds this "culture of presence" as the "rediscovery" of slowness and spatial extension and associates it with the "local" (but only insofar as local space is posited as heterogeneous to global space, not simply its subset). To exist is to be embedded, to be where one is, to be situated and indwelling in a space that is uncompressible. This situatedness resists the contracted world, the globalized world in which space is destroyed. One who is truly at home in an extended, uncompressed space with all its encumbrances "stops measuring and reducing; they project themselves into the habitual at a scale of one to one. Indwelling . . . can neither be reduced true to scale nor expanded beyond a certain degree."[82] Scale becomes real once again.

Sloterdijk's nostalgia for presence and embeddedness is both reactionary and impossible. His "local," as he himself admits, must be exclusive, self-preferential, selective, and protectionist. It must guard against the "others," and if it admits some others, it must produce other others at the edge of its boundaries. This is not, he claims, the "summary of a far right party manifesto," but an invocation of the "human" and "real human spheres," reminding us once again that the concept of the human, along with that of the universal, is often oppressive in its grasping for the apolitical and the undifferentiated, and here, the harmonious gated enclave.[83] This nostalgia for the life-size, a scale of one-to-one, shared by Paul Virilio, neglects the fact that these local realms of slow time and extended space are infiltrated by cell phones, laptops, televisions, and IMAX.[84] Contemporary understandings of space—the local, the global, the extraterrestrial—have been irrevocably altered in an ever-expanding media environment. One only has to consider the way in which the word "zoom" has been torn from its technical cinematic meaning and become what Steven Johnson has described as the distinctive way of seeing of contemporary life. The OED links the original meaning of the word to a buzzing or humming sound produced by high speed, and the cinematographic use, dropping the sound but retaining the velocity, is defined as "the action of increasing or decreasing magnification of an image smoothly and quickly." The "zoom" encompasses both the miniature and the gigantic, the components of cells and the extent of the universe, and the possibility of traveling from one to the other virtually instantaneously. The close-up is another cinematic term that has drifted into the world of the everyday, here to signify a concentrated view of the minute.

The historical process of disengaging scale from the human body was not initiated by the cinema, but cinema certainly aided and abetted that endeavor. The anxieties (and pleasures) surrounding gigantic scale, the "bigger than life," can be seen in the earliest films (*The Big Swallow*, *The Man with the Rubber Head*) and the perceived monstrosity of any close-up of the face. The demand for "life-size" images in the early twentieth century presages today's call for a return to a scale of one-to-one. Marshall McLuhan claimed that every new media technology could be defined by the change of scale it introduces. IMAX seeks to capitalize on this, and as Dorrian points out, in the case of Google Earth, which presents itself as the ultimate mapping technology, "what strikes one about Google is the constant insistence on the colossal, the gargantuan and the exorbitant."[85] Google's name is derived from the googol in mathematics, the almost unthinkable, enormous number of 10 to the power of 100. Google is about the colonization of knowledge, about the availability of any space whatever (although, as noted earlier, there is a politics of resolution establishing a hierarchy of places in its algorithms). And just as immersion is posited by many as total art, the end point of media history, Google strives to be the terminal point of knowledge (or at least data):

> The planet, this earth, when qualified by Google appears to transform into an informational utopia—or even, in Kevin Kelly's eschatological phrase, a new "Eden of everything"—that then exists as the final point on an expanding scale in whose lower reaches those earlier utopias of entertainment and science that were first branded as "lands" and then "worlds" find their place. The virtual globe that Google Earth presents is surely the symbolic counterpart of the corporation's mission to make everything available to you: Google gives you the world, and indeed, after the launch of Google Sky, the cosmos as well.[86]

It is not coincidental that one of the most pervasive uses of the word "scale" today, as mentioned in the introduction, is that by corporations, where "to scale" a business means to expand in a way that will generate more profits: *"'Scale' is increasingly being used as shorthand for 'scale up' ("to grow or expand in a proportional and usually profitable way") and as a noun that means 'proportional growth especially of production or profit' and/or 'a large market position.'"*[87] Scale in this scenario facilitates the transformation of everything into a commodity for everyone. The scalar logic of media (especially its striving for immersion) goes beyond things and markets phenomenological experiences. The fragility and precariousness of location, the spatial displacement and disorientation required of its spectators, open up the possibility of inhabiting an infinite number of worlds. Consumption—the possession of commodities, of views, of spaces, the marketability of the globe—compensates for this disorientation and loss of location.

The solution, however, is not to clamor for a Luddite resistance to new media technologies and a return to an unmediated, local, extended, and life-size realm. Just as the concept of photogénie in early film theory exploited the potential despatialization of the close-up in order to celebrate contingency (and hence to define "immersion" as something other than the inhabitation of another world), it is possible to activate the fissures and ruptures of mediated spaces to make delocalization and disorientation productive, generative, political—to exploit the hidden incommensurability of scales generated by technological cultures, to dismantle the homogeneity of space embodied in the zoom. Willard Maas and Marie Mencken's *Geography of the Body* (1943) parodies the travelogue form, the idea that the cinema can take us to other, more exotic places, at the same time that it uses the close-up in the service of unfamiliarity, unrecognizability rather than physiognomic identity. Not knowing where one is, being lost can be both destabilizing and ecstatic. To err/error is to make a mistake, to be wrong, but it is also etymologically traceable to the meaning of wandering or going astray. It connotes both a mistake or deviation from a norm and a resistance to maintaining a direct and teleological trajectory. Wandering, one resists the increasing, neo-colonizing mapping and datafication of space and is inevitably confronted by the unknown.

Notes

Introduction

Epigraph: Robert Smithson, "A Cinematic Atopia," in *Robert Smithson, the Collected Writings*, ed. Jack Flam (Berkeley: University of California Press, 1996), 141.

1 See Béla Balázs, *Theory of the Film: Character and Growth of a New Art*, trans. Edith Bone (New York: Dover, 1970); Jean Epstein, "*Bonjour cinéma* and Other Writings," trans. Tom Milne, *Afterimage* 10 (1981): 8–39; Gilles Deleuze, *Cinema 1: The Movement-Image*, trans. Hugh Tomlinson and Barbara Habberjam (Minneapolis: University of Minnesota Press, 1986). Also see my article "The Close-Up: Scale and Detail in the Cinema," *differences: A Journal of Feminist Cultural Studies* 14, no. 3 (Fall 2003): 89–111.

2 Sergei Eisenstein, *Au-délà des étoiles*, trans. from Russian into French by Jacques Aumont et al. (Paris: Union Général d'Editions, 1974), 229. Translations into English within the text are my own.

3 Eisenstein, *Au-déla des étoiles*, 112.

4 Noël Burch, *Life to Those Shadows* (Berkeley: University of California Press, 1990), 202. There are a number of excellent readings of this short film, including Tom Gunning, "The Impossible Body of Early Film," in *Corporeality in Early Cinema*, ed. Marina Dahlquist et al. (Bloomington: Indiana University Press, 2018), 13–24; and Akira Mizuta Lippit, *Atomic Light (Shadow Optics)* (Minneapolis: University of Minnesota Press, 2005), 71–73.

5 Serge Daney, "The Forbidden Zoom," *Framework: The Journal of Cinema and Media*, no. 32/33 (1986): 177.

6 John Belton, "The Bionic Eye: Zoom Esthetics," *Cinéaste* 11, no. 1 (Winter 1980–81): 21. This is the authentic version of Belton's essay, which had been published earlier by *Film Comment* in an altered form, adding a coauthor and substantially changing the content without consulting Belton. See John Belton and Lyle Tector, "The Bionic Eye: The Aesthetics of the Zoom," *Film Comment* 16, no. 5 (September–October 1980): 12.

7 *Oxford English Dictionary*, 2nd ed. (Oxford: Oxford University Press, 1989; online ed., 2016), s.v. "scale, n. 3," accessed August 2, 2016, https://www.oed.com.

8 *Oxford English Dictionary*, s.v. "scale, n. 2," accessed August 2, 2016, https://www.oed.com.

9 Andrew Kirby, "Popular Culture, Academic Discourse, and the Incongruities of Scale," in *Geographies of Power: Placing Scale*, ed. Andrew Herod and Melissa W. Wright (Malden, MA: Blackwell, 2002), 74.

10 Sallie Marston, Keith Woodward, and John Paul Jones III, "Scale," in *Dictionary of Human Geography*, ed. Derrek Gregory et al., 5th ed. (Malden, MA: Wiley-Blackwell, 2009), 665.

11 "What Does 'Scale the Business' Mean? How a Common Word Became a Staple of Business Jargon," Merriam-Webster, accessed July 27, 2019, https://www.merriam-webster.com/words-at-play/scale-the-business-meaning-origin.

12 See Sallie A. Marston, "The Social Construction of Scale," *Progress in Human Geography* 24, no. 2 (2000): 219–42; Sallie A. Marston and Neil Smith, "States, Scales, and Households: Limits to Scale Thinking?," *Progress in Human Geography* 25, no. 4 (2001): 615–19.

13 Marston, Woodward, and Jones, "Scale," 666.

14 Joan Kee and Emanuele Lugli, "Scale to Size: An Introduction," in *To Scale*, ed. Joan Kee and Emanuele Lugli (West Sussex: Wiley Blackwell, 2015), 10.

15 Anne Wagner, "Scale in Sculpture: The Sixties and Henry Moore: Rothenstein Lecture," in *Tate Papers*, no. 15 (Spring 2011), https://www.tate.org.uk/research/publications/tate-papers/15/scale-in-sculpture-the-sixties-and-henry-moore.

16 Emanuele Lugli, *The Making of Measure and the Promise of Sameness* (Chicago: University of Chicago Press, 2019), 214.

17 Robert Tavernor, *Smoot's Ear: The Measure of Humanity* (New Haven, CT: Yale University Press), 2007.

18 Tavernor, *Smoot's Ear*, xvi.

19 Oliver Wendell Holmes, "The Stereoscope and the Stereograph," in *Classic Essays on Photography*, ed. Alan Trachtenberg (New Haven, CT: Leete's Island Books, 1980), 81.

20 See Jan Holmberg's dissertation on the close-up, "Förtätade bilder: Filmens närbilder I historisk och teoretisk belysning" (PhD diss., Stockholms Universitet [Sweden], 2000), ProQuest Dissertations Publishing (CA36980). I am grateful to Jan Holmberg for providing me with an English translation of chapter 3, "Large and Small."

21 Jeremy Blatter, "Constructing Scale," in *Paper Worlds: Printing Knowledge in Early Modern Europe* (Cambridge, MA: Collection of Historical Scientific Instruments, Houghton Library, Harvard University, 2010), 73–74, exhibition catalog.

22 Jorge Louis Borges, "Of Exactitude in Science," in *Jorges Luis Borges: Collected Fictions*, trans. Andrew Hurley (New York: Penguin Books, 1999), 325.

23 Computer-generated imagery (CGI) may seem to have obliterated the necessity of scale models, but it still operates in relation to the production of scales and scalar systems, and scale models themselves have not disappeared.

24 See Joseph A. Ball, "Theory of Mechanical Miniatures in Cinematography," *Transactions of SMPE*, no. 18 (May 1924): 119–26; and G. F. Hutchins, "Dimen-

sional Analysis as an Aid to Miniature Cinematography," *Journal of the Society of Motion Picture Engineers* 14, no. 4 (1930): 377–83, for the early discussion of these issues, mostly revolving around the search for an algorithm that would accurately translate linear scale into frame rate. The term "miniature" was most frequently used to denote a scale model at this time. The discussion following Ball's essay is noteworthy for its focus on human scale and expectations that would undermine the audience's perception of a human as gigantic. The argument was that audiences would perceive a human walking in slow motion as more likely to denote a human being subjected to a lack of gravity, for instance, walking on the moon, than to perceive the human as gigantic. Since walking on the moon would only become a common image more than forty years later, this is a striking illustration of the persistence and embeddedness of human scale as a norm. See also Sarine Waltenspül, "The Camera as a Scaling Instrument: Focus on Cinematographic Modelling Techniques," trans. Burke Barrett, in *Too Big to Scale—On Scaling Space, Numbers, Time and Energy*, ed. Forian Dombois and Julie Harboe (Zurich: Verlag Scheidegger & Spiess AG, 2017), 33–48, for an intriguing discussion of the scaling of "size via the detour of time" (43) and the contradictory doubleness of the cinematographic scale model, which is scaled differently in both profilmic space (smaller) and screen space (larger). I am grateful to Florian Dombois for alerting me to this work and to the phenomenon of film rate manipulation. For more discussion of the scale model (miniature) and its relation to temporality, see Raymond Fielding, *The Technique of Special Effects Cinematography*, 4th ed. (London: Focal Press, 1985), 322–86.

25 Robert Smithson, "A Cinematic Utopia," in *Robert Smithson: The Collected Writings*, ed. Jack Flam (Berkeley: University of California Press, 1996), 141.

26 Cited in Marta Braun, *Picturing Time: The Work of Etienne-Jules Marey (1830–1904)* (Chicago: University of Chicago Press, 1992), 155. See esp. 155–56 for a discussion of Marey's attempts to develop a motion picture camera.

27 See Tom Gunning, "Phantasmagoria and the Manufacturing of Illusions and Wonder: Towards a Cultural Optics of the Cinematic Apparatus," in *The Cinema, a New Technology for the 20th Century*, ed. André Gaudreault, Catherine Russell, and Pierre Veronneau (Lausanne: Editions Payot Lausanne, 2004), 31–44.

28 Katharina Loew, "Magic Mirrors: The Schüfftan Process," in *Special Effects: New Histories/Theories/Contexts*, ed. Dan North, Bob Rehak, and Michael S. Duffy (London: Palgrave, 2015), 63. As Loew argues, the Schüfftan process standardized and commodified the bricoleur-like production of special effects that had previously been associated with art and handicraft in relation to singular filmic challenges that demanded varying approaches. For a discussion of the Schüfftan process, see also Fielding, *The Technique of Special Effects Cinematography*, 61–68.

29 Loew, "Magic Mirrors," 65.

30 Loew, "Magic Mirrors," 66.

31 Le Corbusier, *The Modulor: A Harmonious Measure to the Human Scale Universally Applicable to Architecture and Mechanics* (Cambridge, MA: Harvard University Press, 1954), 20.

32 Le Corbusier, *The Modulor*, 19.

33 Christopher Lukinbeal, "Scale: An Unstable Representational Analogy," *Media Fields Journal*, no. 4 (2012): 2; quoting Witold Kulu, *Measures of Men*, trans. R. Szreter (Princeton, NJ: Princeton University Press, 1986), 100.

34 The current definition of the meter is based on the speed of light—it is the distance traveled by light in a specific fraction (1/299,792,458) of a second. This illustrates a move away from the guarantee of measure incarnated in a tactile object and toward the abstraction of measurement (this trajectory is also that of the kilogram).

35 Peter Sloterdijk, *Spheres*, vol. 2, *Globes, Macrospherology*, trans. Wieland Hoban (South Pasadena, CA: Semiotext(e), 2014), 868.

36 Quoted in Peter H. Brothers, "Japan's Nuclear Nightmare: How the Bomb Became a Beast Called Godzilla," *Cineaste* 36, no. 3 (Summer 2011): 36.

37 Wikipedia, "Godzilla," accessed August 5, 2016, https://en.wikipedia.org/w /index.php?title=Godzilla_(1954_film)&oldid=731652267.

38 Kwame Owusu, "The New Godzilla Is 350 Feet Tall! Biggest Godzilla Ever!," *Movie Tribute*, February 28, 2014, https://www.movietribute.com/874/new -Godzilla-is-350-feet-tall-biggest-godzilla-ever/.

39 See Fatimah Tobing Rony, *The Third Eye: Race, Cinema, and Ethnographic Spectacle* (Durham, NC: Duke University Press, 1996).

40 Sloterdijk, *Spheres*, 2:785.

41 Sloterdijk, *Spheres*, 2:936.

42 Pascal Bonitzer, "Les dieux et les quarks," *Cahiers du cinéma*, no. 295 (December 1978): 8 (my translation).

43 Bonitzer, "Les dieux et les quarks," 8 (my translation).

44 André Bazin, "The Ontology of the Photographic Image," in *What Is Cinema?*, ed. and trans. Hugh Gray (Berkeley: University of California Press, 2005), 1:12.

45 Epstein, "*Bonjour cinéma* and Other Writings," 13.

46 See Bill Brown, "Thing Theory," *Critical Inquiry* 28, no. 1 (Autumn 2001): 1–22; Bill Brown, *A Sense of Things: The Object Matter of American Literature* (Chicago: University of Chicago Press, 2004); Jane Bennett, *Vibrant Matter: A Political Ecology of Things* (Durham, NC: Duke University Press, 2010); Karen Barad, *Meeting the Universe Halfway: Quantum Physics and the Entanglement of Matter and Meaning* (Durham, NC: Duke University Press, 2007).

47 Barad, *Meeting the Universe Halfway*, 245.

48 Barad, *Meeting the Universe Halfway*, 149.

49 Zachary K. Horton, "Mediating Scale: From the Cosmic Zoom to Trans-scalar Ecology" (PhD diss., University of California, Santa Barbara, 2015), 92.

50 Horton, "Mediating Scale," 76.

51 See Jonathan Crary, *24/7: Late Capitalism and the Ends of Sleep* (New York: Verso, 2014); Sloterdijk, *Spheres*, vol. 2; Paul Virilio, *Open Sky*, trans. Julie Rose (New York: Verso, 2008).

52 Virilio, *Open Sky*, 44.

53 Hito Steyerl, "In Free Fall: A Thought Experiment on Vertical Perspective," in *The Wretched of the Screen*, ed. Julieta Aranda, Brian Kuan Wood, and Anton Vidokle (Berlin: Sternberg Press/e-flux journal, 2013), 12–30. However, it is important to note that for Steyerl there is no return to a pretechnological era.

54 Robert Bird, "How to Keep Communism Aloft: Labor, Energy, and the Model Cosmos in Soviet Cinema," *e-flux journal*, no. 88 (February 2018): 9.

Chapter 1. The Delirium of a Minimal Unit

A primitive version of chapter 1 was published in *differences: A Journal of Feminist Cultural Studies* 14, no. 3 (Fall 2003).

1 See Donald L. Fredericksen, *The Aesthetic of Isolation in Film Theory: Hugo Münsterberg* (New York: Arno, 1977); Noël Carroll, "Film/Mind Analogies: The Case of Hugo Munsterberg," *Journal of Aesthetics and Art Criticism* 46, no. 4 (1988): 489–99. For a brief discussion of Münsterberg's pioneering of "psychotechnics," see Friedrich Kittler, *Discourse Networks 1800/1900*, trans. Michael Metteer with Chris Cullens (Stanford, CA: Stanford University Press, 1990), 225–26; Kittler, *Gramophone, Film, Typewriter*, trans. Geoffrey Winthrop-Young and Michael Wutz (Stanford, CA: Stanford University Press, 1999), 159–60; and Kittler, *Optical Media: Berlin Lectures 1999*, trans. Anthony Enns (Cambridge: Polity, 2010), 175. See also Giuliana Bruno, "Film, Aesthetics, Science: Hugo Münsterberg's Laboratory of Moving Images," *Grey Room* 36 (Summer 2009): 88–113, which argues that the technical instruments of Münsterberg's experimental laboratory at Harvard were closely connected to his theory of film, which was, for Münsterberg, a "laboratory of emotion" (100).

2 The revolver is often used as a privileged example of the close-up, here and in Christian Metz, *Film Language: A Semiotics of the Cinema*, trans. Michael Taylor (New York: Oxford University Press, 1974), 67; and Jean Epstein, "The Cinema Seen from Etna" and "On Certain Characteristics of *Photogénie*," trans. Stuart Liebman, in *Jean Epstein: Critical Essays and New Translations*, ed. Sarah Keller and Jason N. Paul (Amsterdam: Amsterdam University Press, 2012), 290, 295.

3 Hugo Münsterberg, *Hugo Münsterberg on Film: The Photoplay—A Psychological Study and Other Writings*, ed. Allan Langdale (New York: Routledge, 2002), 86.

4 Münsterberg, *Hugo Münsterberg on Film*, 86–87.

5 Münsterberg, *Hugo Münsterberg on Film*, 62.

6 Münsterberg, *Hugo Münsterberg on Film*, 117.

7 Münsterberg, *Hugo Münsterberg on Film*, 153.

8   Rudolf Arnheim, *Film as Art* (Berkeley: University of California Press, 1964), 82.

9   Louis Delluc is often cited as the first to use the term *photogénie* in relation to film. However, the word itself precedes him, and Epstein's attempt to define it, while acknowledging Delluc, goes far beyond him in its intricacy. See Louis Delluc, "Photogéne," in *Film Theory: Critical Concepts in Media and Cultural Studies*, vol. 1, ed. Philip Simpson, Andrew Utterson, and K. J. Sheperdson (New York: Routledge, 2004), 49–51.

10 Jean Epstein, *"Bonjour cinéma* and Other Writings," trans. Tom Milne, *Afterimage* 10 (1981): 20.

11 Jean Epstein, "Magnification and Other Writings," *October*, no. 3 (Spring 1977): 9.

12 Epstein, "Magnification," 13.

13 Epstein, "Magnification," 13.

14 Jean Epstein, "The Delirium of a Machine," trans. Christophe Wall-Romana, in *Jean Epstein: Critical Essays and New Translations*, ed. Sarah Keller and Jason N. Paul (Amsterdam: Amsterdam University Press, 2012), 373.

15 Epstein, "The Delirium of a Machine," 372.

16 Stephen Heath, "Screen Images, Film Memory," *Edinburgh '76 Magazine* 1 (1976): 36.

17 Gertrude Koch, "Béla Balázs: The Physiognomy of Things," trans. Miriam Hansen, *New German Critique* 40 (Winter 1987): 167–77.

18 As Maggie Hennefeld points out in her book on women and early comedy, *Specters of Slapstick and Silent Film Comediennes* (New York: Columbia University Press, 2018), a number of silent films thematize a phantasmatic detachability of limbs such as hands and legs and exploit their comic effects. Examples include *The Thieving Hand* (Blackton, 1908), *The Kitchen Maid's Dream* (Vitagraph, 1907), *The Dancing Legs* (Vitagraph, 1908), and *Scullion's Dream* (*Le rêve des marmitons*; Pathé, 1908). However, these early films do not include close-ups isolating only the hand or leg, but ensconce these body parts within the diegetic space, where they dance or work or thieve. Even Segundo de Chomón's *Le roi des dollars* (Pathé Frères, 1905), which does use a close-up of a detached pair of hands, situates them in relation to a minimalist mise-en-scène in which they perform magic tricks with coins, a glass bowl, and a man's head. This organization of space is quite different from that of the close-up of the face, which lacks this orienting space. While the films do detach the limbs from the body, they move and assume their usual functions in relation to a virtual body. For an astute discussion of the limitations of Balázs's anthropocentric yoking of the close-up to the face in the context of the film work of Jean Painlevé, see James Cahill, *Zoological Surrealism: The Nonhuman Cinema of Jean Painlevé* (Minneapolis: University of Minnesota Press, 2019), esp. 71–85.

19 Béla Balázs, *Theory of the Film: Character and Growth of a New Art*, trans. Edith Bone (New York: Dover, 1970), 61.

20 Balázs, *Theory of the Film*, 61.

21 Balázs, *Theory of the Film*, 61.

22 Gilles Deleuze, *Cinema 1: The Movement Image*, trans. Hugh Tomlinson and Barbara Habberjam (Minneapolis: University of Minnesota Press, 1986), 95–96.

23 Griffith claimed in an advertisement in the *New York Dramatic Mirror* that he was the inventor of the close-up, but there are many instances that were earlier than his films. *New York Dramatic Mirror*, December 3, 1913, 36.

24 Pascal Bonitzer, *Le champ aveugle: Essais sur le cinéma* (Paris: Gallimard, 1982), 29 (my translation).

25 Jacques Aumont, *Du visage au cinéma* (Paris: Éditions de l'Etoile/Cahiers du cinéma, 1992), 84 (my translation).

26 Epstein, "Magnification," 9.

27 Münsterberg, *Hugo Münsterberg on Film*, 90.

28 Sergei Eisenstein, *Film Form: Essays in Film Theory*, trans. and ed. Jay Leyda (San Diego: Harcourt, 1949), 243.

29 Eisenstein, *Film Form*, 238.

30 The English translation of this passage is my own, from Sergei Eisenstein, *Au-delà des étoiles*, trans. from Russian into French by Jacques Aumont et al. (Paris: Union Général d'Éditions, 1974), 229.

31 Walter Benjamin, "The Work of Art in the Age of Mechanical Reproduction," in *Illuminations*, trans. Harry Zohn, ed. Hannah Arendt (New York: Schocken Books, 1969), 223.

32 Metz, *Film Language*, 67. Why is it that the revolver recurs time and again in discourses about the close-up as a kind of privileged content, a requirement of discussion about the form? Epstein, Metz, and Balázs all isolate the close-up of a revolver as exemplary. Metz, characteristically, would like to abstract it from any symbolic connotations—it is simply the instantiation of the "here is," the index of actualization that could be applied to any close-up. But is it accidental that it is a revolver? Especially when the revolver in the history of conceptualizing the close-up has been obsessively central, repetitively invoked? The revolver has a kind of insistent materiality—heavy, reflective, evocative. Evocative of death, of course. And suspense. But precisely because it has these associations, it can be foregrounded as an indicator of something that goes beyond narrative and stereotypical renderings. The revolver seems to *mean*, even beyond any plot characteristics, perhaps because it is infused, overladen with its previous usages in cinema. It is a kind of metacinematic instance, referring the close-up back to the ability of cinema to produce suspense, to generate questions of what will happen next, but also to dwell in the moment, the instant. What is this thing? See Epstein, "*Bonjour cinéma* and Other Writings," 22; Béla Balázs, *Early Film*

Theory: Visible Man and the Spirit of Film, ed. Erica Carter, trans. Rodney Livingstone (New York: Berghahn Books, 2010), 38.

33 Balázs, *Theory of the Film*, 60.

34 Balázs, *Theory of the Film*, 60.

35 Balázs, *Theory of the Film*, 58.

36 Aumont, *Du visage au cinéma*, 85.

37 Deleuze, *Cinema 1*, 88.

38 Deleuze, *Cinema 1*, 87.

39 Deleuze, *Cinema 1*, 88.

40 "Facialization," in Brian Massumi's translation of Gilles Deleuze and Félix Guattari's *A Thousand Plateaus: Capitalism and Schizophrenia* (Minneapolis: University of Minnesota Press, 1987), strikes me as more felicitous.

41 Deleuze, *Cinema 1*, 99.

42 Aumont, *Du visage au cinéma*, 15. The grandiose or totalizing tendencies of these statements are evidenced by the return of the term "man" used in a generic sense.

43 Balázs, *Theory of the Film*, 76.

44 Balázs, *Theory of the Film*, 76.

45 Balázs, *Theory of the Film*, 44–45.

46 Balázs, *Theory of the Film*, 39.

47 Susan Stewart, *On Longing: Narratives of the Miniature, the Gigantic, the Souvenir, the Collection* (Durham, NC: Duke University Press, 1993), 127.

48 Walter Benjamin, "On Some Motifs in Baudelaire," in *Illuminations*, trans. Harry Zohn, ed. Hannah Arendt (New York: Schocken Books, 1969), 188.

49 Noa Steimatsky, in her excellent analysis in *The Face on Film* (New York: Oxford University Press, 2017), has argued that my notion of the close-up in film theory as remembered image does not adequately account for Epstein's view of photogénie (38n25). She links her argument to Epstein's emphasis on the brevity of photogénie, his desire to find it in the "ordinary" run of mainstream American cinema with its insistence on continuity editing, and his association of it with "presentness" and the cathecting of desire—all of which undermine the possibility of an *aprés coup* effect. These are all certainly claims that Epstein makes, but they do not necessarily hold up in his ecstatic descriptions of close-ups, and my reading is a symptomatic one. His prose evokes the time of an extended contemplation that contradicts the incessant unfolding of events in time that he also values in film. However, it is undeniable that Epstein is extremely sensitive to the temporality of film and its alliance with movement (photogénie is indissociable from movement for Epstein). But this sensitivity is more visible in his discussions of slow motion, time-lapse photography, and camera movement than in his discussions of the close-up and photogénie. It is true that Epstein emphasizes the brevity of photogénie—"the value of the photogenic is measured in seconds," "the photogenic is like a spark that appears in fits and

starts" ("Magnification," 9). And his descriptions of close-ups of the face tend to dwell on moments of hesitation before movement, breaking into a smile, and so on, the manifold beginnings and anticipations of facial expression. Nevertheless, because the close-up is extracted from the spatiotemporal coordinates of the narrative space, it floats in a region beyond space and time, and this is why I align Epstein's theory, along with that of many others, with a synchronic dimension, a halting of time that still includes movement but no progression. Granted, Epstein's writings about cinema are infused with contradictions, but the specific form of the contradiction about time and the close-up is particularly intriguing.

50 Laura Mulvey, "Visual Pleasure and Narrative Cinema," in *Narrative, Apparatus, Ideology: A Film Theory Reader*, ed. Philip Rosen (New York: Columbia University Press, 1986), 203.

51 Michael Chanan, *The Dream That Kicks: The Prehistory and Early Years of Cinema in Britain* (London: Routledge and Kegan Paul, 1980), 41.

52 This essay is a critical text for Naomi Schor in *Reading in Detail: Aesthetics and the Feminine* (New York: Methuen, 1987), 81–84, where she traces Barthes's relation to Hegelian aesthetics.

53 Epstein, "*Bonjour cinéma* and Other Writings," 22.

54 Bonitzer, *Le champ aveugle*, 30.

55 Roland Barthes, "The Face of Garbo," in *Mythologies*, trans. Annette Lavers (New York: Hill and Wang, 1972), 56.

56 Deleuze and Guattari, *A Thousand Plateaus*, 181, 175–76.

57 Deleuze and Guattari, *A Thousand Plateaus*, 171.

58 Aumont, *Du visage au cinéma*, 60.

59 Eisenstein, *Film Form*, 34–35.

60 Balázs, *Theory of the Film*, 55.

61 Stewart, *On Longing*, 79–80.

62 Guy Debord, *Society of the Spectacle* (Detroit: Black and Red, 1977), 29.

63 Stewart, *On Longing*, 91.

64 Stewart, *On Longing*, 70, xii.

65 Epstein, "Magnification," 13.

66 Stewart, *On Longing*, 70.

67 Robert Morris, "Notes on Sculpture," in *Minimal Art: A Critical Anthology*, ed. Gregory Battcock (New York: E. P. Dutton, 1968), 230.

68 Morris, "Notes on Sculpture," 231.

69 Morris, "Notes on Sculpture," 231.

70 Noël Burch, *Theory of Film Practice* (Princeton, NJ: Princeton University Press, 1981), 35.

Chapter 2. The Cinematic Manufacture of Scale

Epigraph: "Notes," *The Chap-Book* 5 (July 15, 1896): 239–40. Sections of chapter 2 appeared in *Realism and the Audiovisual Media*, ed. Lucia Nagib and Cecilia Antakly de Mello (Hampshire: Palgrave Macmillan, 2009); and in *NTU (National Taiwan University) Studies in Language and Literature*, no. 20 (December 2008).

1 Charles Musser, "The May Irwin Kiss: Performance and the Beginnings of Cinema," in *Visual Delights—Two: Exhibition and Reception*, ed. Vanessa Toulmin and Simon Popple (Eastleigh, UK: John Libbey, 2005), 103. See also Linda Williams, *Screening Sex* (Durham, NC: Duke University Press, 2008), 26–33, for an analysis of the ambivalent reception of Edison's *The Kiss* (1896).

2 Philippe Dubois, "Le gros plan primitive," *Revue belge du cinéma*, no. 10 (Winter 1984–85): 15 (my translation).

3 Dubois, "Le gros plan primitive," 14 (my translation).

4 Dubois, "Le gros plan primitive," 14 (my translation).

5 See Tom Gunning, "Cinema of Attractions: Early Film, Its Spectator and the Avant-Garde," in *Early Cinema: Space, Frame, Narrative*, ed. Thomas Elsaesser (London: British Film Institute, 1990), 56–63. See also Tom Gunning, "In Your Face: Physiognomy, Photography, and the Gnostic Mission of Early Film," *Modernism/Modernity* 4, no. 1 (January 1997): 1–29.

6 See also Georges Méliès, *La lanterne magique* (1903); *Water Flea and Rotifers* (Charles Urban Trading Company, Great Britain, 1903); *Le microscope de Jacques* (Pathé Frères, France, 1910); and *The Love Microbe* (Biograph, USA, 1907).

7 Jan Holmberg, "Closing In: Telescopes, Early Cinema, and the Technological Conditions of De-distancing," in *Moving Images: From Edison to the Webcam*, ed. John Fullerton and Astrid Söderbergh Widding (Sydney: John Libbey, 2000), 84.

8 For a discussion of the use of catastrophe as an arbitrary ending in early silent films, see Noël Burch, *Life to Those Shadows* (Berkeley: University of California Press, 1990), 191–93. For a discussion of female performers and catastrophe, see Maggie Hennefeld, *Specters of Slapstick and Silent Film Comediennes* (New York: Columbia University Press, 2018), esp. 31–53.

9 Burch, *Life to Those Shadows*, 89.

10 See Jill Susan Colley, "Unearthing the Close-Up: Spectatorship, Anxiety, and Abstraction in Early Cinema" (PhD diss., State University of New York at Buffalo, 1998), ProQuest Dissertations Publishing (9905254).

11 Thomas Edison quoted in Terry Ramsaye, *A Million and One Nights: A History of the Motion Picture through 1925* (New York: Simon and Schuster, 1986), 130; John Belton, *Widescreen Cinema* (Cambridge, MA: Harvard University Press, 1992), 242n76.

12 See Holmberg's dissertation on the close-up, "Förtätade bilder: Filmens närbilder I historisk och teoretisk belysning" (PhD diss., Stockholms Universitet

[Sweden], 2000), ProQuest Dissertations Publishing (CA36980). I am grateful to Jan Holmberg for providing me with an English translation of chapter 3, "Large and Small."

13 Yhcam, "Cinematography (April 20, 1912)," in *French Film Theory and Criticism: A History/Anthology, 1907–1939*, vol. 1, *1907–1929*, ed. Richard Abel (Princeton, NJ: Princeton University Press, 1988), 72.

14 H. F. Hoffman, "Cutting Off the Feet," *Moving Picture World* 12, no. 1 (April 6, 1912): 53.

15 Hoffman, "Cutting Off the Feet," 53.

16 "Too Near the Camera," *Moving Picture World* 8, no. 12 (March 25, 1911): 633–34.

17 "Too Near the Camera," 633–34. See also "The Size of the Picture," *Moving Picture World* 8, no. 10 (March 11, 1911): 527; and Jan Holmberg's analysis of side-by-side articles regarding masking and the close-up in "Large and Small."

18 Harry Furniss, "Those Awful Cinematograph Faces," *Motography*, May 3, 1913, 329.

19 Furniss, "Those Awful Cinematograph Faces," 330.

20 "The Factor of Uniformity," *Moving Picture World* 5, no. 4 (July 24, 1909): 115–16.

21 "The Factor of Uniformity," 115.

22 "The Factor of Uniformity," 116.

23 "The Factor of Uniformity," 116.

24 See, for instance, anon., "Faces," *Moving Picture World* 21, no. 1 (July 4, 1914): 56; Louis Reeves Harrison, "Eyes and Lips," *Moving Picture World* 8, no. 7 (February 18, 1911): 348–49; Frank Woods, "Spectator's" Comments," *New York Dramatic Mirror*, March 22, 1911, 28; and Thomas Bedding, "The Modern Way in Moving Picture Making," *Moving Picture World* 4, no. 13 (March 27, 1909): 360.

25 Philippe Carcassonne, "Les paradoxes du gros plan," *Cinématographe*, no. 24 (February 1977): 4.

26 Carcassonne, "Les paradoxes du gros plan," 5.

27 Ken Knabb, ed. and trans., *The Situationist International Anthology*, rev. ed. (Berkeley: Bureau of Public Secrets, 2006), 52, 67.

28 Carcassonne, "Les paradoxes du gros plan," 5.

29 Dubois, "Le gros plan primitive," 21.

30 Dubois, "Le gros plan primitive," 21.

31 Dubois, "Le gros plan primitive," 22.

32 Dubois, "Le gros plan primitive," 21.

33 Dubois, "Le gros plan primitive," 21. For Dubois, Epstein's infatuation with the close-up as an object of desire is only the flip side of this fear and involves the same drive. In both cases, the close-up is perceived as jeopardizing the boundary between the two heterogeneous spaces, as threatening to puncture the screen and merge the space of the film with that of the spectator.

34 Dubois, "Le gros plan primitive," 21.

35 Dubois, "Le gros plan primitive," 25.

36 Dubois, "Le gros plan primitive," 28.

37 Dubois, "Le gros plan primitive," 30. Dubois's use of the term *détournement* differs from that of the situationists, for whom the concept had radical, not conservative, implications.

38 Dubois, "Le gros plan primitive," 28.

39 Holmberg, "Large and Small," 12.

40 This statement appeared in an ad taken out by Griffith in the *New York Dramatic Mirror*, December 3, 1913, 36.

41 See Tom Gunning, *D. W. Griffith and the Origins of American Narrative Film: The Early Years at Biograph* (Champaign: University of Illinois Press, 1994), 32–35, for a historical overview of film theory's understanding of Griffith's use of the close-up as a critical part of a new cinematic language that no longer relied upon theatrical tradition. See also Gunning's own intervention in this debate: "Rather than a conflict between an outmoded theatricality and a discovery of the essential possibilities of film, this transformation can be more accurately understood as a transformation from a cinema of attractions to one based on narrative integration" (35).

42 Sergei Eisenstein, "Dickens, Griffith, and the Film Today," in *Film Form: Essays in Film Theory*, ed. and trans. Jay Leyda (San Diego: Harcourt, 1949), 195–255.

43 Deirdre Shauna Lynch, *The Economy of Character: Novels, Market Culture, and the Business of Inner Meaning* (Chicago: University of Chicago Press, 1998), 33.

44 Lynch, *The Economy of Character*, 38.

45 Lynch, *The Economy of Character*, 145.

46 Lynch, *The Economy of Character*, 147.

47 Lynch, *The Economy of Character*, 129.

48 Quoted in John Frow, *Character and Person* (Oxford: Oxford University Press, 2014), 63. However, Frow is careful to point out that "Taylor's notion of the self is—like Mauss's—a notion of the successive mutations of a continuously developing entity which reaches its fullest form in modernity" (95). This is an idea that both Frow and Lynch resist.

49 Frow, *Character and Person*, 120.

50 Jean Bernique, *Motion Picture Acting for Professionals and Amateurs: A Technical Treatise on Make-Up, Costumes and Expression* (Chicago: Producers Service Company, 1916), 21, 43–149. See also Frances Agnew, *Motion Picture Acting* (New York: Reliance Newspaper Syndicate, 1913), 42. Agnew advocates a form of method acting in which the actor must imagine a situation that calls forth the emotion in order to produce the correct facial expression.

51 Catherine Gallagher, *Nobody's Story: The Vanishing Acts of Women Writers in the Marketplace, 1670–1920* (Berkeley: University of California Press, 1994), 174.

52 See Georges Didi-Huberman, "The Portrait, the Individual and the Singular: Remarks on the Legacy of Aby Warburg," in *The Image of the Individual: Por-*

traits in the Renaissance, ed. Nicholas Mann and Luke Syson (London: British Museum Press, 1998), 165–88; Georges Didi-Huberman, "The Art of Not Describing: Vermeer—The Detail and the Patch," *History of the Human Sciences* 2, no. 2 (June 1, 1989): 135–69. Didi-Huberman writes, "The picture is always considered to be a ciphered text, and the cipher, like a treasure-chest, or a skeleton hidden in a cupboard, is always there waiting to be found, somehow *behind the painting*, not enclosed within the material density of the paint: it will be the solution to the enigma posed by the picture, its 'motive' or the 'admission' of its secret meaning" ("The Art of Not Describing," 137).

53 See Jean-Louis Comolli, "Historical Fiction: A Body Too Much," *Screen* 19, no. 2 (Summer 1978): 41–53.

54 I would contest Pasolini's argument that the stylized point-of-view shot is equivalent to free indirect discourse. First, his examples are all taken from modernist films (Antonioni, Godard, etc.) rather than classical narrative, but, more important, the point-of-view shot in cinema is always accompanied by a residue of the real in excess of the character, even if that shot is distorted, out of focus. A flashback is a particularly good example of this, since a flashback in classical narrative very quickly loses its subjective status and becomes a scene on a level with any other scene in the film. See Pier Paolo Pasolini, *Heretical Empiricism*, ed. Louise K. Barnett, trans. Ben Lawton and Louise K. Barnett (Bloomington: Indiana University Press, 1988), 175.

55 Béla Balázs, *Theory of the Film: Character and Growth of a New Art*, trans. Edith Bone (New York: Dover, 1970), 76.

56 See Yuri Tsivian, *Early Cinema in Russia and Its Cultural Reception* (Chicago: University of Chicago Press, 1994), 197. See also Ben Brewster and Lea Jacobs, *Theatre to Cinema: Stage Pictorialism and the Early Feature Film* (New York: Oxford University Press, 1997).

57 See Anthony Vidler, *Warped Space: Art, Architecture, and Anxiety in Modern Culture* (Cambridge, MA: MIT Press, 2000).

58 See Kimberly Elam, *Geometry of Design: Studies in Proportion and Composition* (New York: Princeton Architectural Press, 2001), 12–17.

59 Sergei Eisenstein, *Nonindifferent Nature: Film and the Structure of Things*, trans. Herbert Marshall (Cambridge: Cambridge University Press, 1987), 18–22. As John Belton has pointed out to me, "The golden section is a key term in the discourse about aspect ratio, especially during the 1929–30 widescreen era, at which time paintings were cited as models for the selection of a widescreen aspect ratio." John Belton, private communication with the author, November 2019.

60 Le Corbusier, *The Modulor: A Harmonious Measure to the Human Scale Universally Applicable to Architecture and Mechanics* (Cambridge, MA: Harvard University Press, 1954), 20.

61 Le Corbusier, *The Modulor*, 19.

62 Henri Lefebvre, *The Production of Space*, trans. Donald Nicholson-Smith (Malden, MA: Blackwell, 1991), 170.

63 Lefebvre, *The Production of Space*, 170.

64 Lefebvre, *The Production of Space*, 39.

65 Pascal Bonitzer, "Partial Vision: Film and the Labyrinth," trans. Fabrice Ziolkowski, *Wide Angle* 4, no. 4 (1981): 56–63.

66 Walter Benjamin, "The Work of Art in the Age of Mechanical Reproduction," in *Illuminations*, trans. Harry Zohn, ed. Hannah Arendt (New York: Schocken Books, 1969), 236.

67 See Hugo Münsterberg, *Hugo Münsterberg on Film: The Photoplay—A Psychological Study and Other Writings*, ed. Allan Langdale (New York: Routledge, 2002).

68 Lefebvre himself insists upon breaking the antagonistic relation of the binary opposition between "representations of space" and "representational space" by adding a third term—"spatial practice," manifested in the competence and performance of users of specific spaces; spatial practice is a particular perception of space. Representations of space, for Lefebvre, are ways of conceiving space and are associated with architects, urban planners, and the use of such notions as the golden section. It is the representational space, in this schema, that is associated with art (but also with inhabitants and users of space)—it is the arena in which the imagination seeks to "change and appropriate" socially dominated space. This is "lived" space. Hence, my use of the opposition, which remains binary in my schema of film space, is only inspired by Lefebvre, since I am dealing only with space as represented and experienced in film, a representational system. Lefebvre's notion of representational space might be useful in thinking about individual filmmakers' spatial practices, but I am more concerned here with cinema as an apparatus. See Lefebvre, *The Production of Space*, esp. 38–40, for a fuller discussion of these categories.

69 Lefebvre, *The Production of Space*, 349.

70 Lefebvre, *The Production of Space*, 306.

71 One might well ask why abstraction is a form of "violence" for Lefebvre. A clue can be found in the etymology of the word "abstract," which stems from Latin *abs* (from, away from) and *tractus* (past participle of *trahere*, to draw)—hence, to "draw away from." The term "abstract" is associated with some form of subtraction (from an entity that would otherwise be "whole"): to withdraw, remove, take away, extract. Early usage also associated it with theft—"to remove unlawfully or dishonestly; to steal, purloin" (*Oxford English Dictionary*, 3rd ed. [Oxford: Oxford University Press, 2021; online ed., 2021], s.v. "abstract," accessed March 24, 2021, https://www.oed.com).

72 David Bordwell and Kristin Thompson, *Film Art: An Introduction*, 7th ed. (New York: McGraw-Hill, 2004), 501.

73 Bordwell and Thompson, *Film Art*, 504.

74 Timothy Corrigan, *A Short Guide to Writing about Film*, 5th ed. (New York: Pearson Longman, 2004), 177.

75 Jean Mitry, *The Aesthetics and Psychology of the Cinema*, trans. Christopher King (Bloomington: Indiana University Press, 1997), 59.

76 Le Corbusier, *Towards a New Architecture*, trans. Frederick Etchells (New York: Dover, 1986), 4.

77 Hubert Damisch, *The Origin of Perspective*, trans. John Goodman (Cambridge, MA: MIT Press, 1994), 388.

78 Damisch, *The Origin of Perspective*, 120.

79 Damisch, *The Origin of Perspective*, 121n.

80 Damisch, *The Origin of Perspective*, 388.

81 Damisch, *The Origin of Perspective*, 389.

82 Lefebvre, *The Production of Space*, 309.

83 See Georg Simmel, "The Metropolis and Mental Life," in *The Sociology of Georg Simmel*, trans. and ed. Kurt H. Wolff (London: Collier-Macmillan, 1950), 409–24.

84 Georg Simmel, "The Sociology of Space," in *Simmel on Culture: Selected Writings*, ed. David Frisby and Mike Featherstone (London: Sage, 1997), 137–38.

85 Pascal Bonitzer, "Les dieux and les quarks," *Cahiers du cinéma*, no. 295 (December 1978): 8.

86 Bonitzer, "Les dieux and les quarks," 8.

87 Michel Chion, "Cours sur l'échelle" (unpublished manuscript), 16. I am grateful to Michel Chion for providing me with this manuscript.

88 Frow, *Character and Person*, 122.

89 See, for example, Vivian Sobchack, *Carnal Thoughts: Embodiment and Moving Image Culture* (Berkeley: University of California Press, 2004); Laura Marks, *The Skin of the Film: Intercultural Cinema, Embodiment, and the Senses* (Durham, NC: Duke University Press, 2000); Laura Marks, *Touch: Sensuous Theory and Multisensory Media* (Minneapolis: University of Minnesota Press, 2002); and Linda Williams, "Film Bodies: Gender, Genre, and Excess," *Film Quarterly* 44, no. 4 (1991): 2–13.

90 Fredric Jameson, "Cognitive Mapping," in *Marxism and the Interpretation of Culture*, ed. Cary Nelson and Lawrence Grossberg (Champaign: University of Illinois Press, 1988), 349.

91 Manfredo Tafuri, *Architecture and Utopia: Design and Capitalist Development*, trans. Barbara Luigi La Penta (Cambridge, MA: MIT Press, 1976), 137.

92 Quoted in Vidler, *Warped Space*, 50; originally in Siegfried Giedion, *Space, Time and Architecture: The Growth of a New Tradition* (Cambridge, MA: Harvard University Press, 1941).

93 Quoted in Vidler, *Warped Space*, 54; originally in Le Corbusier, *The New World of Space* (New York: Reynal and Hitchcock, 1948), 8.

94 Eisenstein, *Nonindifferent Nature*, 27.

Chapter 3. At Face Value

Epigraph: Johann Caspar Lavater, *Physiognomy; or, The Corresponding Analogy between the Conformation of the Features and the Ruling Passions of the Mind* (London: Cowie, Low, and Co. in the Poultry, 1826). An earlier version of a section of chapter 3 appeared in *New German Critique* 122 (Summer 2014).

1   *Oxford English Dictionary*, 3rd ed. (Oxford: Oxford University Press, 2009; online ed., 2021), s.v. "face," accessed March 24, 2021, https://www.oed.com.

2   Eileen Bowser cites William Christy Cabanne's division of shots into "knee figure," "bust figure," and "big head." In this taxonomy, the human body is used to scale images. See Bowser, *The Transformation of Cinema*, vol. 2, *1907–1915* (Berkeley: University of California Press, 1990), 283n12. See also Joyce E. Jesionowski, *Thinking in Pictures: Dramatic Structure in D. W. Griffith's Biograph Films* (Berkeley: University of California Press, 1987), 7. Bowser also points out that the term "close view" often referred to a shot in which the entire body of the actor is shown, with the head at the top of the frame and the feet touching the bottom. Before 1909–10, shots of actors generally left a third of the frame above the actor's head and showed floor or ground beneath their feet (the camera being located about twelve feet from the actor). The term "close view" in 1909–10 is comparative, referring to a shot in which the camera is nine feet from the actor. In the period 1908–12, close-ups were used to show objects, letters, and so on that could clarify the narrative but were rarely used to display a human face. Close-ups were more common before 1908, in the facial expression films and as emblematic shots at the beginning or end of a film. See Bowser, *The Transformation of Cinema*, esp. chap. 6: "Acting: The Camera's Closer View," 87–102.

3   "'The Pride of Jennico' Filmed," *Motion Picture News* 9, no. 8 (February 28, 1914): 27.

4   "Great Artist Contest," *Motion Picture Magazine* 8, no. 7 (August 1914): 164.

5   Although a well-known tract known as *Physiognomia* was frequently attributed to Aristotle, classical scholars now tend to agree that this was likely not written by Aristotle himself but by another author in the third century BCE. See, for example, Charles B. Schmitt and Dilwyn Knox, eds., *Pseudo-Aristoteles Latinus: A Guide to Latin Works Falsely Attributed to Aristotle before 1500* (London: Warburg Institute, 1985), 45–49. For other famous thinkers of physiognomy, see Giambattista Della Porta, *De humana physiognomonia libri IIII*, 1586, Public Domain Review, accessed August 23, 2019, https://publicdomainreview.org /collections/giambattista-della-portas-de-humana-physiognomonia-libri-iiii -1586/; Johann Caspar Lavater, *Essays on Physiognomy: For the Promotion of the Knowledge and the Love of Mankind*, trans. Thomas Holcroft, vols. 2 and 3 (London: C. Wittingham, 1804); Charles Darwin, *The Expression of the Emotions in Man and Animals*, ed. Joe Cain and Sharon Messenger (London:

Penguin Classics, 2009); Sir Charles Bell, *Essays on the Anatomy of Expression in Painting* (1806; Birmingham: Classics of Medicine Library, 1984). For more on physiognomy's use in the eugenics movement, see the work of Sir Francis Galton, who coined the term "eugenics," including *Hereditary Genius* (1869; New York: Appleton, 1883); *Inquiries into Human Faculty and Its Development* (1883; London: J. M. Dent, 1911); and *Natural Inheritance* (London: Macmillan, 1889). For a history of the eugenics movement in the late nineteenth century and early twentieth century, see Lyndsay Andrew Farrall, *The Origins and Growth of the English Eugenics Movement 1865–1925* (Bloomington: Indiana University Press, 1969).

6 Johann Caspar Lavater, *Physiognomy; or, The Corresponding Analogy between the Conformation of the Features and the Ruling Passions of the Mind* (London: Cowie, Low, and Co. in the Poultry, 1826), 19.

7 David E. Wellbery, *Lessing's Laocoon: Semiotics and Aesthetics in the Age of Reason* (Cambridge: Cambridge University Press, 1984), 28.

8 G.-B. Duchenne de Boulogne, *The Mechanism of Human Facial Expression*, ed. and trans. R. Andrew Cuthbertson (Cambridge: Cambridge University Press, 1990), 19.

9 Duchenne de Boulogne, *The Mechanism of Human Facial Expression*, 34.

10 Eugene V. Brewster, "Expression of the Emotions," *Motion Picture Magazine*, September 1914, 98–101. On pp. 99–100, Brewster refers to Francis Warner as Francis Walker, but the quote he uses is from Francis Warner, *Physical Expression: Its Modes and Principles* (London: Kegan, Paul, Trench and Co., 1885), 194–95. This is an interesting slip, since Francis A. Walker was an economist who argued that immigration was a cause of the degeneration and exhaustion of Anglo-Saxon stock and linked this to "race suicide." See John Higham, *Strangers in the Land: Patterns of American Nativism, 1860–1925* (New Brunswick, NJ: Rutgers University Press, 2002), 147.

11 Brewster was a lawyer, politician, and sometime film director who, with J. Stuart Blackton, was a founding editor of *Motion Picture Story Magazine*, which later became *Motion Picture Magazine*. See Kathryn H. Fuller, "*Motion Picture Story Magazine* and the Gendered Construction of the Movie Fan," in *In the Eye of the Beholder: Critical Perspectives in Popular Film and Television*, ed. Gary Richard Edgerton, Michael T. Marsden, and Jack Nachbar (Bowling Green, OH: Bowling Green State University Popular Press, 1997), 97–98.

12 Eugene V. Brewster, "Expression of the Emotions," *Motion Picture Magazine*, August 1914, 101.

13 Brewster, "Expression of the Emotions," August 1914, 101.

14 Brewster, "Expression of the Emotions" August 1914, 102.

15 Brewster, "Expression of the Emotions," August 1914, 102.

16 Brewster, "Expression of the Emotions," August 1914, 102.

17 Brewster, "Expression of the Emotions," August 1914, 107.

18 Brewster, "Expression of the Emotions," August 1914, 107.

19 Brewster, "Expression of the Emotions," August 1914, 106.

20 Brewster, "Expression of the Emotions," August 1914, 109.

21 Brewster, "Expression of the Emotions," August 1914, 106.

22 Eugene V. Brewster, "Expression of the Emotions," *Motion Picture Magazine*, October 1914, 114.

23 Brewster, "Expression of the Emotions," October 1914, 115.

24 Brewster, "Expression of the Emotions," October 1914, 118.

25 Warner, *Physical Expression*, 193.

26 Eugene V. Brewster, "Expression of the Emotions," *Motion Picture Magazine*, July 1914, 108–9.

27 Interestingly, Brewster does not use the captions in the physiognomic text illustrations that, like his film still captions, pinpoint the emotion being displayed.

28 *Oxford English Dictionary*, 2nd ed. (Oxford: Oxford University Press, 1989; online ed., 2021), s.v. "express," accessed March 24, 2021, https://www.oed.com.

29 Richard T. Gray, *About Face: German Physiognomic Thought from Lavater to Auschwitz* (Detroit: Wayne State University Press, 2004), xvii.

30 Lavater, *Essays on Physiognomy* (1804), 2:31.

31 Quoted in Gray, *About Face*, 160.

32 See Gray, *About Face*; Wellbery, *Lessing's Laocoon*.

33 Quoted in Gray, *About Face*, 111.

34 Quoted in Gray, *About Face*, 116.

35 Lavater, *Essays on Physiognomy* (1804), 3:98–99.

36 Tani E. Barlow, *The Question of Women in Chinese Feminism* (Durham, NC: Duke University Press, 2004), 363.

37 Gray, *About Face*, 19.

38 Gray, *About Face*, 125.

39 Gray, *About Face*, 124.

40 Gray, *About Face*, 125.

41 Gray, *About Face*, 131.

42 Gray, *About Face*, 229.

43 Brewster, "Expression of the Emotions," September 1914, 102.

44 Jennifer Green-Lewis, *Framing the Victorians: Photography and the Culture of Realism* (Ithaca, NY: Cornell University Press, 1996), 148.

45 Miriam Hansen, *Babel and Babylon: Spectatorship in American Silent Film* (Cambridge, MA: Harvard University Press, 1991), 78–79. For her earlier work on film and the concept of a universal language, see Miriam Hansen, "Universal Language and Democratic Culture: Myths of Origin in Early American Cinema," in *Mythos und Aufklärung in der Amerikanischen Literatur/Myth and Enlightenment in American Literature: In Honor of Hans Joaching-Lang*, ed. Dieter Meindl and Friedrich W. Horlacher (Erlangen: Universitätsbund Erlangen-Nürnberg, 1985), 321–51.

46 Béla Balázs, *Theory of the Film: Character and Growth of a New Art.*, trans. Edith Bone (New York: Dover, 1970), 44–45. Although *Theory of the Film* was published in 1945, the chapter in which this statement and the following quotes from *Theory of the Film* appear is reprinted from *Der Sichtbare Mensch* (1924). However, Balázs, like Brewster, is inconsistent in his assessments of film as a language. In "Visual Culture," he relays the story of a Siberian girl who sees a film for the first time and misreads close-ups as a cutting of the human body into pieces. This initiates a discussion of how films have taught us to see. Balázs, *Theory of the Film*, 34–35.

47 Balázs, *Theory of the Film*, 45.

48 Jacques Derrida, *Of Grammatology*, trans. Gayatri Chakravorty Spivak (Baltimore: Johns Hopkins University Press, 1997).

49 Balázs, *Theory of the Film*, 41.

50 Balázs, *Theory of the Film*, 39.

51 Balázs, *Theory of the Film*, 44–45.

52 Or, as John Belton has elegantly put it, "What makes it an ur-language is that it is apparently never learned, only re-learned once forgotten." Personal correspondence with the author.

53 Gray, *About Face*, 181.

54 Gray, *About Face*, 265–66.

55 Claudia Schmölders, *Hitler's Face: The Biography of an Image*, trans. Adrian Daub (Philadelphia: University of Pennsylvania Press, 2009), 56. Schmölders also comments on Kassner's idea that the only remaining faces of the period were those of the actor and the athlete (the Jew and the American)—"the actor alone gained from the decadence and decline of most institutions" (98).

56 Balázs, *Theory of the Film*, 40. Étienne Balibar refers to the "scattered meaning of the universal" and outlines its three modalities (real, fictional, symbolic) in "Ambiguous Universality," *differences: A Journal of Feminist Cultural Studies* 7, no. 1 (Spring 1995): 49. Balázs's notion of universality would seem to correspond to Balibar's second, fictional universality insofar as it negotiates between the concepts of the universal and the individual. For Balibar, this concept of (fictional) universality *requires* what seems to be its opposite—the free play of individuality constructed as such by state ideology.

57 The close-up, as a single shot whose temporality is crucial, is homogeneous and resists the differentiation of the cut. Sergei Eisenstein criticized Balázs in 1926 for his championing of the cameraman and the single shot, isolated from the work of montage. The continuity and homogeneity of the single shot were crucial for the claim of immediacy and a universal readability, and Eisenstein is understandably suspicious of the denial of heterogeneity generated by the phenomenological and physiognomic assumptions underlying this claim. See Sergei Eisenstein, "Béla Forgets the Scissors," in *The Film Factory: Russian and Soviet Cinema in Documents 1896–1939*, ed. Ian Christie and Richard Taylor (New York: Routledge, 1994).

58 Balázs, *Theory of the Film*, 61.

59 Béla Balázs, *Early Film Theory: Visible Man and the Spirit of Film*, ed. Erica Carter, trans. Rodney Livingstone (New York: Berghahn Books, 2010), 14.

60 Balázs, *Theory of the Film*, 81.

61 See Gertrude Koch, "Béla Balázs: The Physiognomy of Things," trans. Miriam Hansen, *New German Critique*, no. 40 (1987): 167–77.

62 Balázs, *Early Film Theory*, 46. Compare this notion of objects returning the gaze with Walter Benjamin, "On Some Motifs in Baudelaire," in *Illuminations*, trans. Harry Zohn, ed. Hannah Arendt (New York: Schocken Books, 1969), 188.

63 Balázs, *Theory of the Film*, 99.

64 Quoted in Koch, "Béla Balázs," 171. This passage is translated in Balázs, *Early Film Theory* as follows: "If we could dissolve, distort, duplicate and superimpose a particular image, if, in other words, we could let the cinematic technology run on empty, as it were, then the technology 'in itself' would depict mind in itself" (169). This statement is preceded by the claim, "Our entire psychic apparatus is revealed in these transformations."

65 Gray, *About Face*, 339.

66 Lavater's emphasis on the hard features of the face was at least partially a response to intensive criticism of his work on the part of Georg Christoph Lichtenberg and others who stressed the mobility and changeability of the passions and emotions displayed by the face and the inadequacy of Lavater's association of static features (the nose, the forehead) with specific qualities. In response, Lavater claimed that he was interested not in the emotions but in the relatively fixed aspects of character and opposed physiognomy to pathognomy (the analysis of affects). From this point of view, physiognomy provided a more favorable platform for racism and Günther's later denial of history in support of essence.

67 Johann Caspar Lavater, *Essays on Physiognomy: Designed to Promote the Knowledge and the Love of Mankind*, trans. Thomas Holcroft (London: William Tegg and Co., 1850), 189.

68 Johann Caspar Lavater, *Physiognomische Fragmente*, quoted in Christoph Siegrist, "'Letters of the Divine Alphabet'—Lavater's Concept of Physiognomy," in *The Faces of Physiognomy: Interdisciplinary Approaches to Johann Caspar Lavater*, ed. Ellis Shookman (Columbia, SC: Camden House, 1993), 33.

69 Gray, *About Face*, 342.

70 Hugh Welch Diamond, "Editorial," *Journal of the Photographic Society of London* 5, no. 70 (September 21, 1858): 21. Della Porta was known both for his work on optics and perspective and for a short work on physiognomy comparing the faces of men with those of animals. See Green-Lewis, *Framing the Victorians*, for a fuller discussion of Diamond and his relation to photography.

71 Quoted in Green-Lewis, *Framing the Victorians*, 152.

72 Carsten Zelle, "Soul Semiology: On Lavater's Physiognomic Principles," in *The Faces of Physiognomy: Interdisciplinary Approaches to Johann Caspar Lavater*, ed. Ellis Shookman (Columbia, SC: Camden House, 1993), 40.

73 The profile was only part of Bertillon's expansive system for identifying recidivists. This system included anthropometric and other data that could be easily filed and retrieved. See Alan Sekula, "The Body and the Archive," *October*, no. 39 (Winter 1986): 3–64.

74 Green-Lewis, *Framing the Victorians*, 199–200.

75 See Sekula, "The Body and the Archive."

76 Gray, *About Face*, 204–5.

77 Edgar Morin, *The Stars*, trans. Richard Howard (Minneapolis: University of Minnesota Press, 2005), 14.

78 See, for example, *Cinéa-Ciné*, no. 17 (July 15, 1924), front pages.

79 Jean Bernique, *Motion Picture Acting for Professionals and Amateurs: A Technical Treatise on Make-Up, Costumes and Expression* (Chicago: Producers Service Company, 1916), 15–16. The twenty-four actresses photographed include Lillian Gish, Mae Marsh, Fannie Ward, Anita Stewart, and others. The chapter is titled "A Film Phantasy."

80 Pierre Henry, "Beautés photogéniques," *Cinéa-Ciné*, no. 17 (July 15, 1924), 18–19.

81 Quoted in Schmölders, *Hitler's Face*, 98.

82 Quoted in Brigitte Werneburg, "Ernst Jünger and the Transformed World," trans. Christopher Phillips, *October*, no. 62 (Autumn 1992): 54, from the original German by Ernst Jünger, *Der Arbeiter* (Hamburg: Hanseatische Verlagsanstalt, 1932), 117.

83 Quoted in Werneburg, "Ernst Jünger," 52, from the original German by Ernst Jünger, *"Ober den Schmerz,"* in his *Blätter und Stein* (Hamburg: Hanseatische Verlagsanstalt, 1934), 201.

84 Jean Epstein, "Magnification and Other Writings," trans. Stuart Liebman, *October*, no. 3 (Spring 1977): 9.

85 Jean Epstein, "On Certain Characteristics of *Photogénie*," trans. Stuart Liebman, in *Jean Epstein: Critical Essays and New Translations*, ed. Sarah Keller and Jason N. Paul (Amsterdam: Amsterdam University Press, 2012), 293

86 See Jean Epstein, *"Bonjour cinéma* and Other Writings," trans. Tom Milne, *Afterimage*, no. 10 (1981): 20–21.

87 Trond Lundemo, "A Temporal Perspective: Jean Epstein's Writings on Temporality and Subjectivity," in *Jean Epstein: Critical Essays and New Translations*, ed. Sarah Keller and Jason N. Paul (Amsterdam: Amsterdam University Press, 2012), 217. Epstein's position here differs considerably from that of Balázs (for whom cinematic techniques are an incarnation of the soul or mind (*Geist*). See Balázs, *Early Film Theory*, 169.

88 Epstein, "Magnification and Other Writings," 13.

89 See Edgar Allan Poe, "The Imp of the Perverse" (1850), in *Complete Stories and Poems of Edgar Allan Poe* (Garden City, NY: Doubleday, 1966), 272; Katie Kirtland, "The Cinema of the Kaleidoscope," in *Jean Epstein: Critical Essays and*

New Translations, ed. Sarah Keller and Jason N. Paul (Amsterdam: Amsterdam University Press, 2012), 102.

90   Epstein, *"Bonjour cinema* and Other Writings," 22.

91   Gilles Deleuze and Félix Guattari, *A Thousand Plateaus: Capitalism and Schizophrenia*, trans. Brian Massumi (Minneapolis: University of Minnesota Press, 1987), 176.

92   Deleuze and Guattari, *A Thousand Plateaus*, 175.

93   Deleuze and Guattari, *A Thousand Plateaus*, 176–77, 181. Deleuze and Guattari do not advocate, however, a return to a polymorphous primitivism of the body but the effacement of the face, anonymity (188–91).

94   See Emmanuel Levinas, *Totality and Infinity: An Essay on Exteriority*, trans. Alphonso Lingis (Pittsburgh: Duquesne University Press, 1969), 14.

95   Erving Goffman, "On Face-Work: An Analysis of Ritual Elements in Social Interaction," in *Interaction Ritual: Essays on Face-to-Face Behavior* (New York: Pantheon, 1967), 5.

96   Goffman, "On Face-Work," 44.

97   Goffman, "On Face-Work," 44.

98   Goffman, "On Face-Work," 45.

99   *Oxford English Dictionary*, 3rd ed. (Oxford: Oxford University Press, 2009; online ed., 2021), s.v. "saving face," accessed March 24, 2021, https://www.oed.com.

100 Barlow, *The Question of Women*, 87–91.

101 Barlow, *The Question of Women*, 65, 363.

102 Hansen, *Babel and Babylon*, 19.

103 Barlow, *The Question of Women*, 1–2.

104 *Webster's Third New International Dictionary, Unabridged, the Collegiate Edition Online*, s.v. "catachresis," accessed September 6, 2019, https://www.merriam-webster.com/dictionary/catachresis.

105 Barlow, *The Question of Women*, 34.

106 Charles Musser, *Before the Nickelodeon: Edwin S. Porter and the Edison Manufacturing Company* (Berkeley: University of California Press, 1991), 169.

107 Quoted in Gray, *About Face*, 338.

108 For a provocative reading of these early facial expression films in the context of the physiognomic project, see Tom Gunning, "In Your Face: Physiognomy, Photography, and the Gnostic Mission of Early Film," *Modernism/Modernity* 4, no. 1 (January 1997): 1–29. He argues that the "grimace" in these films indicates noise, the lack of meaning.

109 See Georg Simmel, "The Aesthetic Significance of the Face," in *Georg Simmel: 1858–1918: A Collection of Essays*, ed. Kurt Wolff, trans. Lore Ferguson (Columbus: Ohio State University Press, 1959), 276–81.

110 See Étienne Balibar, "Ambiguous Universality," *differences: A Journal of Feminist Cultural Studies* 7, no. 1 (Spring 1995): 48–74.

111 See Walter Benjamin, "A Small History of Photography," in *One-Way Street and Other Writings*, trans. Edmund Jephcott and Kingsley Shorter (London: Verso, 1985), 245.

112 Michael Taussig, *Defacement: Public Secrecy and the Labor of the Negative* (Stanford, CA: Stanford University Press, 1999), 2–3.

113 Taussig, *Defacement*, 229.

Chapter 4. Screens, Female Faces, and Modernities

Different sections of chapter 4 were published in *Gender and Chinese Cinema*, trans. into Chinese by Li Shuling, ed. He Chengzhou and Wang Lingzhen (Nanjing: Nanjing University Press, 2012); *The Question of Gender: Joan Scott's Critical Feminism*, ed. Elizabeth Weed and Judith Butler (Bloomington: Indiana University Press, 2011); and in Italian in *La Valle dell'Eden*, no. 19 (July–December 2007).

1 Henri Langlois quoted in James Card, "The 'Intense Isolation' of Louise Brooks," *Sight and Sound* 27, no. 5 (Summer 1958): 241.

2 Roland Barthes, "The Face of Garbo," in *Mythologies*, trans. Annette Lavers (New York: Hill and Wang, 1972), 56–57.

3 Barry Paris, *Louise Brooks: A Biography* (Minneapolis: University of Minnesota Press, 2000), 440.

4 Dolores del Río in *Ling Long Women's Magazine*, no. 129 (1934): 226, accessed August 25, 2020, https://archive.org/details/linglong_1934_129/page/n34/mode/2up; Hu Die in *Ling Long Women's Magazine*, no. 129 (1934): 225, accessed August 25, 2020, https://archive.org/details/linglong_1934_129/page/n32/mode/2up.

5 See Mary Ann Doane, "Veiling Over Desire," in *Femmes Fatales* (New York: Routledge, 1991), 49.

6 Béla Balázs, *Theory of the Film: Character and Growth of a New Art*, trans. Edith Bone (New York: Dover, 1970), 44–45.

7 Béla Balázs, *Early Film Theory: Visible Man and the Spirit of Film*, ed. Erica Carter, trans. Rodney Livingstone (New York: Berghahn Books, 2011), 14.

8 "Artists Reveal and Reinterpret Captivating Imagery," *Artdaily.org*, July 16, 2005, https://artdaily.cc/news/14311/Artists-Reveal-and-Reinterpret-Captivating-Imagery#.XfAacy3My8o. I am indebted to Oliver Gaycken for bringing to my attention the relevance of the China Dolls to my work on screening the female face.

9 Richard Dyer, *White: Essays on Race and Culture* (New York: Routledge, 2013), 89.

10 When I first wrote this section on the China Girl, there was very little written about the phenomenon, although images of China Girls had been used in a

number of avant-garde films. But since that time, there has been a renewed interest in the China Girl. Genevieve Yue, in "The China Girl on the Margins of Film," *October*, no. 153 (Summer 2015): 96–116, delineates a detailed history of the technology of the China Girl and provides close analyses of some of the avant-garde films that have referenced the phenomenon (Owen Land, *Film in Which There Appear Edge Lettering, Sprocket Holes, Dirt Particles, Etc.* [1965]; Morgan Fisher, *Standard Gauge* [1984]; Barbara Hammer, *Sanctus* [1990]; as well as the projection performance by Sandra Gibson and Luis Recoder, *A Sourceful of Secrets* [2012]). The Chicago Film Society also has a website, the Leader Ladies Project, that contains an archive of submitted images of China Girls, accessed August 26, 2020, https://www.chicagofilmsociety.org/projects /leaderladies/.

11 *Girls on Film* has been exhibited at the Fogg Art Museum, Harvard University (2005); at Anthology Film Archives, New York (2005); at the Columbus College of Art and Design, Columbus, Ohio (2006); and the Center for Contemporary Art, Tel Aviv (2008). See Julie Buck's website for more details: http://www.juliebuck.com. Several images can be seen in Ken Gewertz, "A Bevy of Unknown Beauties," *Harvard University Gazette*, July 21, 2005, https://news.harvard.edu/gazette/story/2005/07/a-bevy-of-unknown -beauties/.

12 Michelle Silva, *China Girls* (2006, 16mm, 3 min.), Canyon Cinema description, accessed January 26, 2012, http://canyoncinema.com/catalog/film/?i=4116.

13 Khatereh Khodaei, "*Shirin* as Described by Kiarostami," *Offscreen.com* 13, no. 1 (January 2009), https://offscreen.com/view/shirin_kiarostami.

14 See Jonathan Rosenbaum, "Shirin as Mirror," *Cinema Guild Home Video*, accessed August 26, 2020, http://cinemaguild.com/homevideo/ess_shirin .htm; Geoff Andrew, "Abbas Kiarostami," Guardian Interviews at the BFI, *Guardian*, April 28, 2005, https://www.theguardian.com/film/2005/apr/28 /hayfilmfestival2005.guardianhayfestival.

15 David Bordwell, "The Movie Looks Back at Us," April 1, 2009, http://www .davidbordwell.net/blog/2009/04/01/the-movie-looks-back-at-us/.

16 Khodaei, "*Shirin* as Described by Kiarostami."

17 Bordwell, "The Movie Looks Back at Us."

18 See Marc Augé, *Non-places: Introduction to an Anthropology of Supermodernity*, trans. John Howe (New York: Verso, 1995).

19 *Oxford English Dictionary*, 3rd ed. (Oxford: Oxford University Press, 2009; online ed., 2018), s.v. "recognize, v. 2," accessed March 27, 2021, https://www .oed.com.

20 *Webster's Third New International Dictionary of the English Language*, unabridged (Springfield, MA: G. & C. Merriam Co., 1961), s.v. "recognize."

21 *Webster's Third New International Dictionary of the English Language*, s.v. "recognize."

22 Its interrogation of an everyday certainty, of a seemingly unquestionable banality, has drawn various feminisms, historically, to the avant-garde. The avant-garde was a crucial concern in the 1970s and early 1980s during the heyday of "theory" within feminist film studies. In "Visual Pleasure and Narrative Cinema," most famously perhaps, Laura Mulvey characterized the avant-garde as a negation of Hollywood cinema's complicity in the patriarchal ordering of sexual difference: "The first blow against the monolithic accumulation of traditional film conventions (already undertaken by radical filmmakers) is to free the look of the camera into its materiality in time and space and the look of the audience into dialectics, passionate detachment." Laura Mulvey, "Visual Pleasure and Narrative Cinema," in *Narrative, Apparatus, Ideology: A Film Theory Reader*, ed. Philip Rosen (New York: Columbia University Press, 1986), 209. Much of the feminist film practice of the 1970s and 1980s (I am thinking here of films like those of Mulvey and Wollen, Sally Potter's *Thriller* [1979], Babette Mangolte's *What Maisie Knew* [1975], and Anthony McCall, Jane Weinstock, Claire Pajaczkowska, and Andrew Tyndall's *Sigmund Freud's Dora* [1979]) embraced a project of negation, a systematic interrogation and undermining of classical codes of sexual looking and imaging. It is this negativity at the heart of an affirmation of feminism that is most intriguing. Yet it was often a negativity lodged in formal categories, susceptible to the tendency to equate aesthetic radicalism with political radicalism, collapsing politics into aesthetics.

23 Andreas Huyssen, *After the Great Divide: Modernism, Mass Culture, Postmodernism* (Bloomington: Indiana University Press, 1986); Jonathan Crary, *Techniques of the Observer: On Vision and Modernity in the Nineteenth Century* (Cambridge, MA: MIT Press, 1992).

24 For a lucid discussion of the screen as surface and its relation to texture, see Giuliana Bruno, *Surface: Matters of Aesthetics, Materiality, and Media* (Chicago: University of Chicago Press, 2014).

25 See Ariel Rogers, *Cinematic Appeals: The Experience of New Movie Technologies* (New York: Columbia University Press, 2013).

26 *Oxford English Dictionary*, https://www.oed.com.

27 *Oxford English Dictionary*, https://www.oed.com.

28 Erkki Huhtamo, "Elements of Screenology: Toward an Archaeology of the Screen," *ICONICS* 7 (2000): 35.

29 In this respect, it is very interesting to note that the term "purdah," designating the veil worn over a woman's face in certain Islamic societies, is derived from the Hindi and Urdu "parda," meaning "screen," "curtain," or "veil." It can refer to the veil over a woman's face, an architectural screen used to divide female and male spaces, or the entire system of sexual segregation practiced in many Islamic and Hindu cultures. "Purdah" does not experience the semantic slippage from screen as divide or protection to screen as the surface of projection of images that characterizes the English term; it is used primarily to indicate a form of

protection, segregation, or isolation. I am indebted to Corey Creekmur for alerting me to the multiple meanings of this term. Some examples of definitions include the following:

1. "purdah, system of seclusion of women practiced by some Muslim and Hindu peoples. The word *purdah* also refers to a curtain or screen used to keep women separate from men and strangers, used primarily in India." "Purdah," Microsoft Encarta Online Encyclopedia 2008, http://encarta.msn.com © 1997–2008 Microsoft Corporation. All Rights Reserved.

2. "purdah, An Urdu word meaning 'curtain' or 'screen' and referring to a system of sex-role differentiation marked by strong physical and social segregation. Purdah is maintained by the segregation of physical space within the household and by the use of articles of clothing such as the veil. It is largely associated with Islamic religion and culture but immensely variable in the form and degree of observance amongst Islamic peoples." *A Dictionary of Sociology*, originally published by Oxford University Press 1998, http://www.encyclopedia.com/doc /1088-purdah.html.

3. "purdah, Etymology: Hindi & Urdu *parda*, literally, screen, veil Date:1865
   1: seclusion of women from public observation among Muslims and some Hindus especially in India
   2: a state of seclusion or concealment." http://www.merriam-webster.com /dictionary/purdah.

30 I am indebted to Joe Milutis for calling my attention to this scenario. See his intriguing website devoted to the representation of the face, F2F, accessed November 14, 2006, http://www.hyperrhiz.net/issue01/f2f/.

31 Milutis, F2F.

32 Martin Heidegger, *The Question Concerning Technology and Other Essays*, trans. William Lovitt (New York: Harper and Row, 1977), 154.

33 Unfortunately, the DVD fixes the relation of right screen to left screen, erasing the original appeal to contingency in the screening situation. In addition, the DVD deviates from the strict projection instructions included whenever the 16mm film is screened. These provide for staggering the timing of the reels on the different projectors so that the final scene ends with only Nico on the left side, outlasting the other reel with the Ondine-as-Pope sketch.

34 In this analysis, Freud claims that the woman's perception of a "click" she associates with a camera photographing her in a compromising position is actually a projection of a "sensation of throbbing in the clitoris. This was what she subsequently projected as a perception of an external object." Sigmund Freud, "A Case of Paranoia Running Counter to the Psychoanalytical Theory of the Disease" (1915), in *The Standard Edition of the Complete Psychological Works of Sigmund Freud*, trans. and ed. James Strachey (London: Hogarth Press, 1953–74), 14:104.

35 It is interesting to compare Godard and Gorin's analysis here with Barthes's conceptualization of both the woodcutter's and the revolutionary's relation to language as denotative and operational in *Mythologies* (145–46). Because these two types of workers "act" language, their words are closer to the real than those of the myth or the mythologist. Barthes and Godard/Gorin share a semiotic-political fantasy of linguistic transparency. In addition, Godard and Gorin isolate Jane Fonda's face, which, unlike that of the North Vietnamese soldier, is designated by them as eminently separable from its context, the visual insistence of an eternal, ahistorical truth of pity. While the North Vietnamese soldier's face demands a concrete, material, historical context, when confronted with Jane Fonda's look, there is "no reverse shot possible."

36 Huhtamo, "Elements of Screenology," 34.

37 Bertram D. Lewin, "Sleep, the Mouth and the Dream Screen," *Psychoanalytic Quarterly*, 15, no. 4 (1949): 421.

38 See especially Bertram D. Lewin, "Reconsideration of the Dream Screen," *Psychoanalytic Quarterly* 22, no. 2 (1953): 174–99.

39 Lewin, "Sleep, the Mouth and the Dream Screen," 422.

40 René A. Spitz, "The Primal Cavity," *Psychoanalytic Study of the Child* 10, no. 1 (1955): 219.

41 Spitz, "The Primal Cavity," 220, 238.

42 Spitz, "The Primal Cavity," 217–18.

43 See Sigmund Freud, "Three Essays on the Theory of Sexuality" (1905), in *The Standard Edition of the Complete Psychological Works of Sigmund Freud*, trans. and ed. James Strachey (London: Hogarth Press, 1953–74), 7:125–243.

44 Bernard Stiegler, "Pharmacology of Desire: Drive-Based Capitalism and Libidinal Dis-economy," trans. Daniel Ross, *New Formations* 72 (2011): 161. This statement appears in the midst of a critique of Marcuse for employing a distinction between a structural (psychoanalytic) level and a historical level. For Stiegler, psychoanalytic categories are always already historical, and there is no ontology of desire.

45 In the new faces recognition test, not the famous faces recognition test, where both celebrity men and women are used. See "Understanding Prosopagnosia," accessed December 4, 2006, https://www.faceblind.org/research/.

46 Emmanuel Levinas, *Totality and Infinity: An Essay on Exteriority*, trans. Alphonso Lingis (Pittsburgh: Duquesne University Press, 1969), 198.

47 Levinas, *Totality and Infinity*, 200.

48 Lewin, "Reconsideration of the Dream Screen," 194.

49 Lewin, "Reconsideration of the Dream Screen," 194–95.

50 *Lexico.com* (Oxford: Oxford University Press, 2020), s.v. "facade," accessed April 15, 2021, https://en.oxforddictionaries.com/definition/facade.

51 See, for example, Sigmund Freud, "The Interpretation of Dreams" (1900), in *The Standard Edition of the Complete Psychological Works of Sigmund Freud*, trans. and ed. James Strachey (London: Hogarth Press, 1953–74), 5:489–90.

52 Anthony Vidler, "Psychopathologies of Modern Space: Metropolitan Fear from Agoraphobia to Estrangement," in *Rediscovering History: Culture, Politics, and the Psyche*, ed. Michael Roth (Stanford, CA: Stanford University Press, 1994), 12.

53 See Georg Simmel, "The Metropolis and Mental Life" and "The Stranger," in *The Sociology of Georg Simmel*, trans. and ed. Kurt H. Wolff (London: Collier-Macmillan, 1950), 409–24, 402–8; Siegfried Kracauer, "The Hotel Lobby," in *The Mass Ornament: Weimar Essays*, trans. and ed. Thomas Y. Levin (Cambridge, MA: Harvard University Press, 1995), 173–85.

54 For excellent analyses of modernity, the urban, and femininity in Shanghai, see Yingjin Zhang, *The City in Modern Chinese Literature and Film* (Stanford, CA: Stanford University Press, 1996), esp. chap. 7; Leo Ou-Fan Lee, *Shanghai Modern: The Flowering of a New Urban Culture in China, 1930–1945* (Cambridge, MA: Harvard University Press, 2001); and Zhang Zhen, *An Amorous History of the Silver Screen: Shanghai Cinema, 1896–1937* (Chicago: University of Chicago Press, 2005).

55 Fredric Jameson, *A Singular Modernity: Essay on the Ontology of the Present* (New York: Verso, 2002), 12–13.

56 Jameson, *A Singular Modernity*, 12.

57 In recent years, film historians such as Charles Musser and Tom Gunning have undermined this myth by revealing the important connections between earlier forms of entertainment, including vaudeville, melodrama, and carnival attractions, and the emerging cinema. See Charles Musser, *History of the American Cinema*, vol. 1, *The Emergence of Cinema: The American Screen to 1907* (Berkeley: University of California Press, 1990); Tom Gunning, "The Cinema of Attractions: Early Film, Its Spectator and the Avant-Garde," in *Early Cinema: Space, Frame, Narrative*, ed. Thomas Elsaesser (London: British Film Institute, 1990).

58 See, for instance, Miriam Bratu Hansen, "The Mass Production of the Senses: Classical Cinema as Vernacular Modernism," in *Reinventing Film Studies*, ed. Christine Gledhill and Linda Williams (London: Arnold, 2000), 332–50; Hansen, "Fallen Women, Rising Stars, New Horizons: Shanghai Silent Film as Vernacular Modernism," *Film Quarterly* 54, no. 1 (2000): 10–22.

59 Hansen, "Fallen Women," 10.

60 Hansen, "Fallen Women," 15.

61 Tani E. Barlow, *The Question of Women in Chinese Feminism* (Durham, NC: Duke University Press, 2004), 78.

62 See Barlow, *The Question of Women*, esp. chapter 3, for an extensive and detailed analysis of Chinese feminist discourses (authored by both men and women) of the early twentieth century that outline the necessity for women's parity in terms of Darwinian theory, eugenics, nationalism, and modernity.

63 As has been frequently pointed out, feminist theorizing in early twentieth-century China was dominated by men anxious about the positioning of China

as a nation, in relation to the West and in relation to what was considered modernity and progressive thought. The liberation of women was perceived as indispensable to the development of a modern, enlightened nation, hence the currency of feminism as a sign that one was "modern." See, for instance, Amy Dooling, *Women's Literary Feminism in Twentieth-Century China* (London: Palgrave Macmillan, 2005); Rey Chow, *Woman and Chinese Modernity: The Politics of Reading between West and East* (Minneapolis: University of Minnesota Press, 1991); and Barlow, *The Question of Women*.

64 Barlow, *The Question of Women*, 71.

65 Of course, it is necessary to point out that Jameson's analysis foregrounds the terrain of economics (late capitalism) as well as ideology, while Barlow focuses on a critical form of intellectual history.

66 Barlow, *The Question of Women*, 65. In a sense, this analysis of the boomerang effect of colonial modernity is similar to Hansen's emphasis on immigration (the arrival of the other) as the basis for the development of a cinematic language that claimed to be universal and globally legible. Yet the process seems to be more benign in Hansen's analysis since the Hollywood cinema works to accommodate a range of ethnic differences *in the audience* with the aim of legibility rather than transforming those differences into tropes by means of and against which the discourse (of Enlightenment) can rationalize itself.

67 T. J. Clark, *The Painting of Modern Life: Paris in the Art of Manet and His Followers* (Princeton, NJ: Princeton University Press, 1999), 103.

68 See, for instance, Andrew D. Field, "Selling Souls in Sin City: Shanghai Singing and Dancing Hostesses in Print, Film, and Politics, 1920–49," in *Cinema and Urban Culture in Shanghai, 1922–1943*, ed. Yingjin Zhang (Stanford, CA: Stanford University Press, 1999), 99–127.

69 See Laikwan Pang, *The Distorting Mirror: Visual Modernity in China* (Honolulu: University of Hawai'i Press, 2007), esp. chapter 2.

70 Richard Vinograd, *Boundaries of the Self: Chinese Portraits, 1600–1900* (New York: Cambridge University Press, 1992), 1.

71 See Miriam Bratu Hansen, *Babel and Babylon: Spectatorship in American Film* (Cambridge, MA: Harvard University Press, 1991), 76–89.

72 Barlow, *The Question of Women*, 114–24.

73 Barlow, *The Question of Women*, 363.

74 Dooling, *Women's Literary Feminism*, 24.

75 Balázs, *Theory of the Film*, 76.

76 Mulvey, "Visual Pleasure and Narrative Cinema," 202.

77 *Ling Long Women's Magazine*, no. 129 (1934), 225, 226, https://archive.org/details/linglong_1934_129/page/n32/mode/2up; https://archive.org/details/linglong_1934_129/page/n34/mode/2up.

78 See, for example, Richard deCordova, *Picture Personalities: The Emergence of the Star System in America* (Champaign: University of Illinois Press, 2001);

Christine Gledhill, ed., *Stardom: Industry of Desire* (London: Routledge, 1991); Richard Dyer and Paul McDonald, *Stars*, 2nd ed. (London: British Film Institute, 2008); and Jean-Louis Comolli, "Historical Fiction: A Body Too Much," *Screen* 19, no. 2 (Summer 1978): 41–53.

79 Michael Chang, "The Good, the Bad, and the Beautiful: Movie Actresses and Public Discourse in Shanghai, 1920s–1930s," in *Cinema and Urban Culture in Shanghai, 1922–1943*, ed. Yingjin Zhang (Stanford, CA: Stanford University Press, 1999), 156.

80 Chang, "The Good, the Bad, and the Beautiful," 129.

81 Katherine Hui-ling Chou's essay "Acting and Beyond: The Queer Stardom and Body Enactment of 'Leslie Cheung'" (accessed August 29, 2020, http://www.airitilibrary.com/Publication/alDetailPrint?DocID=20702663-200901-201005250065-201005250065-217-248) demonstrates that this confusion of role and life/personality can also emerge in relation to a male star (her example is Leslie Cheung). But it is crucial to note that this dissolution of boundaries between representation and the real was sutured to the trope of gayness, not masculinity.

82 Chang, "The Good, the Bad, and the Beautiful," 132.

83 See Roland Barthes, *S/Z*, trans. Richard Miller (New York: Hill and Wang, 1974), 33–35.

84 Hansen, "Fallen Women," 16, 18–20.

85 Hansen, "Fallen Women," 16.

86 Gillian Brown, *Domestic Individualism: Imagining Self in Nineteenth-Century America* (Berkeley: University of California Press, 1992), 137, 139.

87 Brown, *Domestic Individualism*, 145.

88 Brown, *Domestic Individualism*, 139.

Chapter 5. The Location of the Image

An earlier version of a section of chapter 5 was published in *The Art of Projection*, ed. Stan Douglas and Christopher Eamon (Stuttgart: Hatje Cantz, 2009); and in Chinese in *Chung-wai Literary Quarterly*, no. 423 (December 2008).

1 George C. Pratt, *Spellbound in Darkness: A History of the Silent Film* (Greenwich, CT: New York Graphic Society, 1973), 18.

2 However, even one of the most exemplary treatments of this period—Laurent Mannoni, *The Great Art of Light and Shadow: Archaeology of the Cinema*, trans. and ed. Richard Crangle (Exeter: University of Exeter Press, 2000)—still structures the history of optical toys and devices as a teleological movement toward cinema.

3 Michel de Certeau, *Heterologies: Discourse on the Other*, trans. Brian Massumi (Minneapolis: University of Minnesota Press, 1986), 4–5.

4 Certeau, *Heterologies*, 4.

5 Walter Benjamin, "Theses on the Philosophy of History," in *Illuminations*, trans. Harry Zohn, ed. Hannah Arendt (New York: Schocken Books, 1969), 255.

6 Lev Manovich, *The Language of New Media* (Cambridge, MA: MIT Press, 2001), 314–22.

7 For a fascinating discussion of fingers and the digital, see Aden Evens, "Concerning the Digital," *differences: A Journal of Feminist Cultural Studies* 14, no. 2 (Summer 2003): 49–77.

8 In this context, Hiroshi Ishii's Tangible Media Group at the MIT Media Lab exemplifies a unique effort to conjoin the digital and the tangible. One of its projects, "Tangible Bits," seeks to give "physical form to digital information, seamlessly coupling the dual worlds of bits and atoms." The discourse reveals a nostalgia for that which the digital seems to neglect or exclude—touch. See MIT Media Lab, Tangible Media Group, "The Vision: Tangible Bits," January 2005, http://tangible.media.mit.edu/projects.

9 Walter Benjamin, "The Work of Art in the Age of Mechanical Reproduction," in *Illuminations*, trans. Harry Zohn, ed. Hannah Arendt (New York: Schocken Books, 1969), 223.

10 Susan Stewart, *On Longing: Narratives of the Miniature, the Gigantic, the Souvenir, the Collection* (Durham, NC: Duke University Press, 1993), 41.

11 Although Plateau's anorthoscope was devised in 1828, it was not presented to the Académie des sciences in Brussels or marketed until 1836.

12 Stewart, *On Longing*, 69.

13 Charlotte M. Yonge, *The History of Sir Thomas Thumb* (Edinburgh: Thomas Constable, 1856), 21.

14 Stewart, *On Longing*, 54. Early silent films often displayed a fascination for magnification and microscopic images that revealed an unfamiliar world unseen by the naked eye. Examples include *The Love Microbe* (Wallace McCutcheon, 1907), *Cheese Mites* (1903, BFI National Archive), *Water Flea and Rotifers Pond Life* (1903, BFI National Archive), and *Le microscope de Jacques* (1910, BFI National Archive).

15 *Oxford English Dictionary*, 2nd ed. (Oxford: Oxford University Press, 1989), s.v. "toy," accessed March 27, 2021, https://www.oed.com.

16 Jonathan Crary, *Techniques of the Observer: On Vision and Modernity in the Nineteenth Century* (Cambridge, MA: MIT Press, 1992), 97–136.

17 Joseph A. F. Plateau quoted in Georges Sadoul, *Histoire générale du cinéma*, vol. 1 (Paris: Denoel, 1948), 25.

18 A. R. Luria, *The Working Brain*, trans. Basil Haigh (New York: Basic Books, 1973), 229, quoted in Michael Chanan, *The Dream That Kicks: The Prehistory and Early Years of Cinema in Britain* (London: Routledge and Kegan Paul, 1980), 57.

19 Hermann von Helmholtz, *Treatise on Physiological Optics*, trans. and ed. James P. C. Southall (Menasha, WI: Optical Society of America, 1924), 1:91.

20 See Arthur B. Evans, "Optograms and Fiction: Photo in a Dead Man's Eye," *Science Fiction Studies* 20, no. 3 (November 1993): 341–61.

21 See, for instance, Joseph Anderson and Barbara Anderson, "Motion Perception in Motion Pictures," and Bill Nichols and Susan J. Lederman, "Flicker and Motion in Film," both in *The Cinematic Apparatus*, ed. Teresa de Lauretis and Stephen Heath (London: Macmillan, 1980), 76–95, 96–105. Research into the perception of motion in cinema is ongoing and in flux. For an explanation of critical flicker fusion and apparent motion, see David Bordwell and Kristen Thompson, *Film Art: An Introduction*, 5th ed. (New York: McGraw-Hill, 1997), 4, 33.

22 Chanan, *The Dream That Kicks*, 59. As early as 1916, Hugo Münsterberg, in one of the first extended theories of film, questioned the validity of persistence of vision and, influenced by the 1912 studies of Max Wertheimer, proposed that the viewer fills in the gap between two still images and that motion is "superadded by the action of the mind." Hugo Münsterberg, *The Film: A Psychological Study* (New York: Dover, 1970), 29. For a more extensive discussion of the theory of persistence of vision and the afterimage, see Mary Ann Doane, *The Emergence of Cinematic Time: Modernity, Contingency, the Archive* (Cambridge, MA: Harvard University Press, 2002), 69–107.

23 See Mannoni, *The Great Art of Light and Shadow*, 223–47.

24 Quoted in Mannoni, *The Great Art of Light and Shadow*, 225–26.

25 Dominique Païni, "Should We Put an End to Projection?," trans. Rosalind Krauss, *October*, no. 110 (Fall 2004): 24.

26 Païni, "Should We Put an End to Projection?," 24, 27.

27 Genevieve Yue quoted in Laurent Mannoni, Werner Nekes, and Marina Warner, *Eyes, Lies and Illusions: The Art of Perception* (London: Hayward Gallery, 2004), 170.

28 Anthony McCall describes the film in these terms: "It deals with the projected light beam itself, rather than treating the light beam as a mere carrier of coded information, which is decoded when it strikes a flat surface. . . . *Line Describing a Cone* deals with one of the irreducible conditions of film: projected light. It deals with this phenomenon directly, independently of any other considerations. It is the first film to exist in real, three-dimensional space. This film exists only in the present: the moment of projection. It refers to nothing beyond this real time. It contains no illusion. It is a primary experience, not secondary: i.e., the space is real, not referential; the time is real, not referential." Mannoni, Nekes, and Warner, *Eyes, Lies and Illusions*, 170.

29 Guy Debord, *The Society of the Spectacle*, trans. Donald Nicholson-Smith (New York: Zone Books, 1995), 23.

30 Maurice Blanchot, *The Gaze of Orpheus*, ed. P. Adams Sitney, trans. Lydia Davis (Barrytown, NY: Station Hill, 1981), 75; quoted in Jan Holmberg, "Closing In:

Telescopes, Early Cinema, and the Technological Conditions of De-distancing," in *Moving Images: From Edison to the Webcam*, ed. John Fullerton and Astrid Söderbergh Widding (Sydney: John Libbey, 2000), 83.

31 See Holmberg, "Closing In," 84–85.

32 The "object" of the film is ostensibly one of Moholy-Nagy's kinetic sculptures, "Licht-Raum-Modulator," which is overwhelmed by the play of light and shadow it itself generates.

33 László Moholy-Nagy, *Painting, Photography, Film*, trans. Janet Seligman (Cambridge, MA: MIT Press, 1969), 26.

34 Moholy-Nagy, *Painting, Photography, Film*, 41.

35 Barbara Maria Stafford and Frances Terpak, *Devices of Wonder: From the World in a Box to Images on a Screen* (Los Angeles: Getty Research Institute, 2001), 82.

36 Païni, "Should We Put an End to Projection?," 27.

37 M. (Jean-François) Marmontel, 1777, "Illusion," Tome 3:560, in *Suppléments à l'Encyclopédie ou Dictionnaire raisonné des Sciences, des Arts & des Métiers par une Société de Gens de lettres*, ed. Jean-Baptiste Robinet, University of Chicago: ARTFL Encyclopédie Project (Autumn 2017 Edition), ed. Robert Morrissey and Glenn Roe, https://encyclopedie.uchicago.edu/.

38 E. H. Gombrich, "Conditions of Illusion," *Art and Illusion: A Study in the Psychology of Pictorial Representation* (Princeton, NJ: Princeton University Press, 1969), 203.

39 Gombrich, "Conditions of Illusion," 208.

40 Gombrich, "Conditions of Illusion," 222.

41 See Roland Barthes, *Camera Lucida: Reflections on Photography*, trans. Richard Howard (New York: Hill and Wang, 1981), 77. See also Christian Metz, *The Imaginary Signifier: Psychoanalysis and the Cinema*, trans. Celia Britton et al. (Bloomington: Indiana University Press, 1982), 50.

42 Sigmund Freud, "Negation" (1925), in *The Standard Edition of the Complete Psychological Works of Sigmund Freud*, trans. and ed. James Strachey (London: Hogarth Press, 1953–74), 19:237.

43 Sigmund Freud, "A Case of Paranoia Running Counter to the Psychoanalytical Theory of the Disease" (1915), in *The Standard Edition of the Complete Psychological Works of Sigmund Freud*, trans. and ed. James Strachey (London: Hogarth Press, 1953–74), 14:270.

44 Jean Laplanche and J. B. Pontalis, "Projection," in *The Language of Psychoanalysis*, trans. Donald Nicholson-Smith, intro. Daniel Lagache (New York: Norton, 1973), 354.

45 Jonathan Walley, "The Material of Film and the Idea of Cinema: Contrasting Practices in Sixties and Seventies Avant-Garde Film," *October*, no. 103 (Winter 2003): 20.

46 Anthony McCall, "*Line Describing a Cone* and Related Films," *October*, no. 103 (Winter 2003): 42.

47 Le Corbusier, *The Modulor: A Harmonious Measure to the Human Scale Universally Applicable to Architecture and Mechanics* (Cambridge, MA: Harvard University Press, 1954), 15–21.

48 Fredric Jameson, "Cognitive Mapping," in *Marxism and the Interpretation of Culture*, ed. Cary Nelson and Lawrence Grossberg (Champaign: University of Illinois Press, 1988), 349.

49 Jonathan Crary, "Géricault, the Panorama, and Sites of Reality in the Early Nineteenth Century," *Grey Room* 9 (Fall 2002): 19.

50 This is one of the standard definitions of projection. In the cinema, projection produces a relation between one two-dimensional image (the film frame) and another (the projected image). However, the celluloid support of the film frame *is* three-dimensional, no matter how attenuated (and reduced the thickness of) that three-dimensionality may be. It is that thickness—though slight—that materiality, that is lost in the projection of the image on the screen.

51 Anthony McCall et al., "Round Table: The Projected Image in Contemporary Art," *October*, no. 104 (Spring 2003): 76.

52 Samuel Y. Edgerton, *The Renaissance Rediscovery of Linear Perspective* (New York: Basic Books, 1975), 91–105.

53 Edgerton, *The Renaissance Rediscovery*, 100.

54 Syrene is modern Aswan in Egypt.

55 Edgerton, *The Renaissance Rediscovery*, 107.

56 Edgerton, *The Renaissance Rediscovery*, 113.

57 Leon Battista Alberti, *On Painting*, trans. Cecil Grayson, intro. Martin Kemp (London: Penguin, 2005), 65.

58 David Greenhood, *Mapping* (Chicago: University of Chicago Press, 2018), 118.

59 Wikipedia, "Mercator Projection," accessed July 27, 2018, https://en.wikipedia .org/wiki/Mercator_projection.

60 In 1989 and 1990, seven North American geographic organizations adopted the following resolution:

> WHEREAS, the earth is round with a coordinate system composed entirely of circles, and
>
> WHEREAS, flat world maps are more useful than globe maps, but flattening the globe surface necessarily greatly changes the appearance of Earth's features and coordinate systems, and
>
> WHEREAS, world maps have a powerful and lasting effect on people's impressions of the shapes and sizes of lands and seas, their arrangement, and the nature of the coordinate system, and
>
> WHEREAS, frequently seeing a greatly distorted map tends to make it "look right,"
>
> THEREFORE, we strongly urge book and map publishers, the media and government agencies to cease using rectangular world maps for gen-

eral purposes or artistic displays. Such maps promote serious, erroneous conceptions by severely distorting large sections of the world, by showing the round Earth as having straight edges and sharp corners, by representing most distances and direct routes incorrectly, and by portraying the circular coordinate system as a squared grid. The most widely displayed rectangular world map is the Mercator (in fact a navigational diagram devised for nautical charts), but other rectangular world maps proposed as replacements for the Mercator also display a greatly distorted image of the spherical Earth. (Arthur Robinson, "Rectangular World Maps—No!," *Professional Geographer* 42, no. 1 [1990]: 101)

61 Erwin Panofsky, *Perspective as Symbolic Form*, trans. Christopher S. Wood (New York: Zone Books, 1997), 27.

62 Svetlana Alpers, *The Art of Describing: Dutch Art in the Seventeenth Century* (Chicago: University of Chicago Press, 1983), 138.

63 Both Jonathan Crary and Panofsky dispute the idea of two different frameworks governing perspective—the northern (Dutch) perspective discussed by Alpers and the southern (Italian) perspective usually assumed under the designation "Renaissance perspective." Both claim an overriding epistemology associated with the camera obscura, on the part of Crary, and perspective, in the case of Panofsky. See Crary, *Techniques of the Observer*, 34–36. Panofsky argues that northern art emphasized the subjective aspect of perspective (the use of oblique views and the extension of the space of the painting to include that of the observer), while southern art foregrounded the objective, architectural "lawfulness" of the space. Although paradoxical, both are contained within the overriding logic of a perspective that produces a space that is homogeneous, continuous, and infinite. See Panofsky, *Perspective as Symbolic Form*, 68–70.

64 Ernst Cassirer, *Philosophy of Symbolic Forms*, vol. 2, *Mythical Thought*, trans. Ralph Manheim (New Haven, CT: Yale University Press, 1955), 83–84. The last phrase of this passage is a quote from Ernst Mach. Quoted in Panofsky, *Perspective as Symbolic Form*, 30.

65 Alberti, *On Painting*, 50.

66 Hubert Damisch, *The Origin of Perspective*, trans. John Goodman (Cambridge, MA: MIT Press, 1994), 28.

67 Jean-Louis Baudry, "Ideological Effects of the Basic Cinematographic Apparatus," in *Narrative, Apparatus, Ideology: A Film Theory Reader*, ed. Philip Rosen (New York: Columbia University Press, 1986), 286.

68 Metz, *The Imaginary Signifier*, 49.

69 Jean-Louis Comolli, "Machines of the Visible," in *The Cinematic Apparatus*, ed. Teresa de Lauretis and Stephen Heath (London: St. Martin's, 1980), 128.

70 Stephen Heath, "Narrative Space," in *Narrative, Apparatus, Ideology: A Film Theory Reader*, ed. Philip Rosen (New York: Columbia University Press, 1986), 389.

71 Crary, *Techniques of the Observer*, 117–36.

72 Cennino d'Andrea Cennini, *The Craftsman's Handbook*, trans. Daniel V. Thompson Jr. (New York: Dover, 1954), lxx. Also cited in Alpers, *The Art of Describing*, 223. Alpers comments, "To say an art is for women is to reiterate that it displays not measure or order, but rather a flood of observed, unmediated details drawn from nature. The lack of female order or proportion in a moral sense is a familiar sentiment from this time."

73 Erwin Panofsky, *The Life and Art of Albrecht Dürer* (Princeton, NJ: Princeton University Press, 1955), 61.

74 Svetlana Alpers, "Art History and Its Exclusions," in *Feminism and Art History: Questioning the Litany*, ed. Norma Broude and Mary D. Garrard (New York: Routledge, 2018), 187.

75 Lynda Nead, *The Female Nude: Art, Obscenity, and Sexuality* (London: Routledge, 2002), 11.

76 Panofsky, *The Life and Art of Albrecht Dürer*, 247.

77 Barbara Freedman, *Staging the Gaze: Postmodernism, Psychoanalysis, and Shakespearean Comedy* (Ithaca, NY: Cornell University Press, 1991), 2.

78 Damisch, *The Origin of Perspective*, 388.

79 Panofsky, *Perspective as Symbolic Form*, 61.

80 Brian Rotman, *Signifying Nothing: The Semiotics of Zero* (London: Macmillan, 1987), 17.

81 Rotman, *Signifying Nothing*, 19.

82 Linda Nochlin, *Courbet* (London: Thames and Hudson, 2007), 148–50.

83 Panofsky, *Perspective as Symbolic Form*, 66.

84 Panofsky, *Perspective as Symbolic Form*, 67.

85 Jean-François Lyotard, *Duchamp's TRANS/formers*, trans. Ian McLeod, ed. Herman Parret (Leuven: Leuven University Press, 2010), 172–73.

86 Lyotard, *Duchamp's TRANS/formers*, 173–74.

87 Damisch, *The Origin of Perspective*, 51.

88 Damisch, *The Origin of Perspective*, 388.

89 Damisch, *The Origin of Perspective*, 388–89.

90 For a more extensive discussion of this film, see Tom Gunning, "The Desire and the Pursuit of the Hole: Cinema's Obscure Object of Desire," in *Erotikon: Essays on Eros, Ancient and Modern*, ed. Shadi Bartsch and Thomas Bartscherer (Chicago: University of Chicago Press, 2005), 261–77.

91 Panofsky, *Perspective as Symbolic Form*, 30–31.

92 Hito Steyerl, "In Free Fall: A Thought Experiment on Vertical Perspective," in *The Wretched of the Screen*, ed. Julieta Aranda, Brian Kuan Wood, and Anton Vidokle (Berlin: Sternberg Press/e-flux journal, 2013), 12–30.

93 Steyerl, "In Free Fall," 14.

94 Laura Kurgan, *Close Up at a Distance: Mapping, Technology, and Politics* (New York: Zone Books, 2013), 9–11.

95   Kurgan, *Close Up at a Distance*, 11–12.
96   Kurgan, *Close Up at a Distance*, 12–13.
97   Kurgan, *Close Up at a Distance*, 14.
98   Kurgan, *Close Up at a Distance*, 20–21.
99   Peter Galison, *Einstein's Clocks and Poincaré's Maps: Empires of Time* (New York: W. W. Norton, 2003), 288.
100 Galison, *Einstein's Clocks*, 288.
101 Kurgan, *Close Up at a Distance*, 26.
102 Kurgan, *Close Up at a Distance*, 30.
103 This deindividualized individual is not the same as Gilles Deleuze's "dividual," which is a function of the current "control society" and counters the idea of the individual of mass culture as the smallest possible unit but also separate and separated from the others. The "dividual" is a fragmented subject dependent upon flows and transformations within a network and is a concept that is more intimately linked with the second type of subjectivity I discuss in the rest of the chapter. See Gilles Deleuze, "Postscript on the Societies of Control," *October*, no. 59 (Winter 1992): 5.

Chapter 6. The Concept of Immersion

Earlier versions of the first section of chapter 6 appeared in Portuguese in *Cinema Transversais*, ed. Patricia Moran (São Paulo: Editora Iluminuras Ltda., 2016); in Italian in *Filmidee*, no. 12 (October 7, 2014); and in *Ends of Cinema*, ed. Richard Grusin and Jocelyn Szczepaniak-Gillece (Minneapolis: University of Minnesota Press, 2020).

1   Roland Barthes, "Leaving the Movie Theater," in *The Rustle of Language*, trans. Richard Howard (Berkeley: University of California Press, 1989), 349.
2   C. C. Sullivan, "Chanel Ginza, Tokyo," *Architectural Lighting Magazine*, June 27, 2007, https://www.archlighting.com/projects/chanel-ginza-tokyo_o.
3   *Man Belongs to Earth*, accessed July 19, 2019, https://www.imax.com/movies/man-belongs-earth.
4   See Charles R. Acland, "IMAX Technology and the Tourist Gaze," *Cultural Studies* 12, no. 3 (July 1998): 429–45.
5   John Belton, *Widescreen Cinema* (Cambridge, MA: Harvard University Press, 1992), 197.
6   "Stories: True Experience," *Inland Empire*, directed by David Lynch (Absurdia and Studio Canal, 2006), special edition DVD, disc 2. At the end of this clip, Apple's logo appears, ironically proclaiming its status as an advertisement.
7   Haidee Wasson, "The Networked Screen: Moving Images, Materiality, and the Aesthetics of Size," in *Fluid Screens, Expanded Cinema*, ed. Janine Marchessault and Susan Lord (Toronto: University of Toronto Press, 2007), 84–85.

8 Acland, "IMAX Technology and the Tourist Gaze," 435.

9 Allan Stegeman, "The Large Screen Film: A Viable Entertainment Alternative to High Definition Television," *Journal of Film and Video* 36, no. 2 (Spring 1984): 24.

10 See Jacques Derrida, *The Truth in Painting*, trans. Geoff Bennington and Ian McLeod (Chicago: University of Chicago Press, 1987), 121–22.

11 See Longinus, *On Great Writing (On the Sublime)*, trans. G. M. A. Grube (Indianapolis: Hackett, 1991).

12 Edmund Burke, *A Philosophical Enquiry into the Origin of Our Ideas of the Sublime and Beautiful*, trans. Adam Phillips (Oxford: Oxford University Press, 1998), 113, Kindle version. This is true even though, for Burke, language retains its superiority over figurative painting, which is restricted by its mimeticism.

13 Burke, *A Philosophical Enquiry*, 128.

14 Burke, *A Philosophical Enquiry*, 121.

15 Burke, *A Philosophical Enquiry*, 124.

16 Paul Virilio, "Cataract Surgery: Cinema in the Year 2000," trans. Annie Fatet and Annette Kuhn, in *Alien Zone: Cultural Theory and Contemporary Science Fiction Cinema*, ed. Annette Kuhn (New York: Verso, 1990), 169–74.

17 Immanuel Kant, *Critique of Judgment*, ed. Nicholas Walker, trans. James Creed Meredith (Oxford: Oxford University Press, 2007), 89.

18 See Erwin Panofsky, *Perspective as Symbolic Form*, trans. Christopher S. Wood (New York: Zone Books, 1997).

19 For Brian Rotman in *Ad Infinitum*, writing in an attempt to analyze the semiotic and ideological implications of the mathematical concept of infinity, the infinite is a concept that is irredeemably theological and must be rejected. See Rotman, *Ad Infinitum—The Ghost in Turing's Machine: Taking God Out of Mathematics and Putting the Body Back In: An Essay in Corporeal Semiotics* (Stanford, CA: Stanford University Press, 1993).

20 Fredric Jameson, *Postmodernism, or, The Cultural Logic of Late Capitalism* (Durham, NC: Duke University Press, 1991), 9.

21 David Joselit, "Notes on Surface: Toward a Genealogy of Flatness," *Art History* 23, no. 1 (March 2000): 19–34.

22 Kant, *The Critique of Judgment*, 78, 85.

23 Allison Whitney argues strenuously that the spectator's body is very much involved in IMAX. She links this to a number of factors, including the fact that the heads of other spectators are continually visible, acting as a measure of scale and reminding the spectator of their own body's location in a theater. In the case of IMAX 3D, the space of the screen invades that of the spectator so that the only measure of scale becomes the spectator's own body. Finally, there is a kind of self-consciousness or self-awareness built into IMAX and IMAX 3D: "Just as the design of IMAX theaters asks you to contemplate your position and role as a spectator, the 3D film asks you to question the precise nature of your

binocular visual experience, and consider the extent to which your senses must work to render an intelligible image of the world. This notion of perceptual labor being part of the viewer's responsibility relates closely to IMAX's notion of the involved, active spectator." Whitney is insistent that the spectator is always aware of being both in the diegetic world and in the auditorium, "in the IMAX theater itself, where viewers are continually reminded of their roles and responsibilities in the production and reception of images." It strikes me as unlikely that spectators have any sense of "roles and responsibilities in the production and reception of images," and this and her invocation of an "involved, active spectator" are part of a larger strategy in the discipline to resist any notion of ideological positioning by the apparatus. I would argue, on the contrary, that whether or not the spectator is aware of being in an auditorium (and this is inarguable but not really what is at issue), the work of the film and of discourses about IMAX is to lure the spectator into another space, to delocalize them in the interests of an "absorbing" diegesis, not to provoke any critical analysis. It is interesting that while Whitney insists upon the spectator's continual awareness of their location in the theater, she speaks of the other "there" of the diegesis in much the same terms. She also treats 3D as though its effects were always "emergent," out of the screen rather than into it (for a discussion of both effects, see Kristen Whissel, "Parallax Effects: Epistemology, Affect and Digital 3D Cinema," *Journal of Visual Culture* 15, no. 2 [August 2016]: 232–49). Allison Whitney, "The Eye of Daedalus: A History and Theory of IMAX Cinema" (PhD diss., University of Chicago, 2005), 126, 133.

24 David E. Nye, *American Technological Sublime* (Cambridge, MA: MIT Press, 1994).

25 Interestingly, one of the descriptions of the experience of watching *Powers of Ten* echoes descriptions of the immersiveness of IMAX: "We fly through galaxies, solar systems, planets, are back in our park, back to the familiar and the comfortable. We want to stop here and recuperate in the warm sun, but the camera won't let us, it keeps galloping to smaller and smaller scales: to micro-scopic tissues, molecules, atoms, the interior of atoms, and we see the unknown grinning at us from this side as well. The unknown has surrounded us." Alan Lightman, "A Sense of the Mysterious," in *The Work of Charles and Ray Eames*, ed. Donald Albrecht (New York: Harry N. Abrams, 2005), 122–23.

26 "Powers of Ten and the Relative Size of Things in the Universe," Eames Official Site, accessed August 2, 2019, https://www.eamesoffice.com/the-work/powers -of-ten/.

27 For more on the role of the "geopolitically symbolic corporation" IBM and the Cold War context of the film, see Mark Dorrian, "Adventure on the Vertical," *Cabinet*, Winter 2011–12, accessed August 22, 2019, www.cabinetmagazine.org /issues/44/dorrian.php.

28 See Philip Morrison, Phylis Morrison, and the Office of Charles and Ray Eames, *Powers of Ten: About the Relative Size of Things in the Universe and the*

Effect of Adding Another Zero (New York: Scientific American Library, 1994), 128–44.

29   Morrison, Morrison, and the Office of Charles and Ray Eames, *Powers of Ten*, 145.

30   Zachary Horton, "Mediating Scale: From the Cosmic Zoom to Trans-scalar Ecology" (PhD diss., University of California, Santa Barbara, 2015), 166. Horton generates an incisive and provocative comparison of Kees Boeke's book, *Cosmic Zoom*, the Eames's first version, *Rough Sketch*, and the 1977 *Powers of Ten*, noting the disparities in their toleration of difference and heterogeneity of scales.

31   Steven Johnson, "The Long Zoom," *New York Times Magazine*, October 8, 2006, https://www.nytimes.com/2006/10/08/magazine/08games.html. In this article, Johnson is primarily interested in discussing the video game *Spore*: "The best way to come to terms with that feeling [the 'feeling of where do we fit in all of this'] is to explore those different scales of experience directly, to move from the near-invisible realm of microbes to the vast distances of galaxies. Of all the forms of culture available to us today, games may well be the most effective at conveying that elusive perspective, precisely because they are so immersive and participatory and because their design can be so open-ended."

32   Mark Dorrian, "On Google Earth," in *Seeing from Above: The Aerial View in Visual Culture*, ed. Mark Dorrian and Frédéric Pousin (London: I. B. Tauris, 2013), 298–99.

33   Hugh Hart, "Video: *Tree of Life* Visualizes the Cosmos without CGI," *Wired*, June 17, 2011, https://www.wired.com/2011/06/tree-of-life-douglas-trumbull/.

34   Jean-François Lyotard, "The Sublime and the Avant Garde," in *The Inhuman: Reflections on Time*, trans. Geoffrey Bennington and Rachel Bowlby (Stanford, CA: Stanford University Press, 1991), 99.

35   Lyotard, "The Sublime and the Avant Garde," 105–7.

36   Henri Lefebvre, *The Production of Space*, trans. Donald Nicholson-Smith (Malden, MA: Blackwell, 1991), 170.

37   Lefebvre, *The Production of Space*, 170.

38   Jean-Louis Baudry, "Ideological Effects of the Basic Cinematographic Apparatus," trans. Alan Williams, in *Narrative, Apparatus, Ideology: A Film Theory Reader*, ed. Philip Rosen (New York: Columbia University Press, 1986), 294.

39   Jean-Louis Baudry, "The Apparatus: Metapsychological Approaches to the Impression of Reality in the Cinema," trans. Jean Andrews and Bertrand Augst, in *Narrative, Apparatus, Ideology: A Film Theory Reader*, ed. Philip Rosen (New York: Columbia University Press, 1986), 300.

40   Christian Metz, "The Imaginary Signifier (Excerpts)," trans. Ben Brewster, in *Narrative, Apparatus, Ideology: A Film Theory Reader*, ed. Philip Rosen (New York: Columbia University Press, 1986), 253.

41   Hubert Damisch, *The Origin of Perspective*, trans. John Goodman (Cambridge, MA: MIT Press, 1994), 121.

42 Cited in Jonathan Sterne, *The Audible Past: Cultural Origins of Sound Repro-duction* (Durham, NC: Duke University Press, 2003), 151.

43 Sterne, *The Audible Past*, 151.

44 Thomas Elsaesser and Malte Hagener, *Film Theory: An Introduction through the Senses* (New York: Routledge, 2010), 130–31.

45 Michel Chion, *The Voice in Cinema*, trans. Claudia Gorbman (New York: Columbia University Press, 1999), 17.

46 See Rick Altman, "Sound Space," in *Sound Theory/Sound Practice*, ed. Rick Altman (New York: Routledge, 1992), 46–64.

47 James Lastra, *Sound Technology and the American Cinema: Perception, Representation, Modernity* (New York: Columbia University Press, 2000), 148.

48 Emily Thompson, *The Soundscape of Modernity: Architectural Acoustics and the Culture of Listening in America, 1900–1933* (Cambridge, MA: MIT Press, 2004), 284.

49 Thompson, *The Soundscape of Modernity*, 283.

50 Michel Chion, *Audio-Vision: Sound on Screen*, trans. Claudia Gorbman (New York: Columbia University Press, 1994), 100.

51 Chion, *Audio-Vision*, 150.

52 Chion, *Audio-Vision*, 151.

53 Mark Kerins, *Beyond Dolby (Stereo): Cinema in the Digital Sound Age* (Bloomington: Indiana University Press, 2010), 138.

54 Kerins, *Beyond Dolby (Stereo)*, 138 (my emphasis).

55 Kerins, *Beyond Dolby (Stereo)*, 130.

56 Dolby Atmos, "The Life of Pi Demo," accessed March 25, 2015, https://www.dolby.com/us/en/experience/dolby-atmos.html.

57 Bill Cribbs and Larry McCrigler, "The Spectrum of Immersive Sound," *Film Journal International* 117, no. 9 (September 2014): 65.

58 Cribbs and McCrigler, "The Spectrum of Immersive Sound," 62.

59 Dolby Atmos, accessed March 25, 2015, https://www.dolby.com/us/en/experience/dolby-atmos.html.

60 See Jonathan Crary, *Techniques of the Observer: On Vision and Modernity in the Nineteenth Century* (Cambridge, MA: MIT Press, 1992).

61 Elsaesser and Hagener, *Film Theory*, 145–46.

62 Pierre Hugues Routhier, "The Immersive Experience Classification System: A New Strategic Decision-Making Tool for Content Creators," *SMPTE Motion Imaging Journal* 127, no. 10 (November/December 2018): 46–54.

63 See Ozgur Oyman et al., "Virtual Reality Industry Forum's View on State of the Immersive Media Industry," *SMPTE Motion Imaging Journal*, vol. 128, no. 8 (September 2019): 91–96.

64 Routhier, "The Immersive Experience Classification System," 49.

65 Routhier, "The Immersive Experience Classification System," 53.

66 Britta Neitzel, "Facetten räumlicher Immersion in technischen Medien," in "Immersion," ed. Robin Curtis and Christiane Voss, special issue, *Montage A/V*, February 17, 2008, 147 (my translation).

67 Neitzel, "Facetten räumlicher Immersion in technischen Medien," 147.

68 Whitney, "The Eye of Daedalus," 94.

69 This is, of course, reminiscent of Bazin's essay on the idea of "total cinema."

70 Tim Recuber, "Immersion Cinema: The Rationalization and Reenchantment of Cinematic Space," *Space and Culture* 10, no. 3 (August 2007): 320.

71 Recuber, "Immersion Cinema," 323.

72 Recuber, "Immersion Cinema," 327.

73 Nigel Thrift, "Lifeworld Inc—and What to Do about It," *Environment and Planning D: Society and Space* 29, no. 1 (February 2011): 5–26.

74 Robin Curtis, "Immersion und Einfülung: Zwischen Repräsentationalität und Materialität bewegter Bilder," in "Immersion," ed. Robin Curtis and Christiane Voss, special issue, *Montage A/V* (February 17, 2008): 97 (my translation).

75 Marie-Laure Ryan, *Narrative as Virtual Reality 2: Revisiting Immersion and Interactivity in Literature and Electronic Media* (Baltimore: Johns Hopkins University Press, 2001), 9.

76 Alison Griffiths, *Shivers Down Your Spine: Cinema, Museums, and the Immersive View* (New York: Columbia University Press, 2008), 41.

77 Griffiths, *Shivers Down Your Spine*, 2.

78 Mark Andrejevic, "Theorizing Drones and Droning Theory," in *Drones and Unmanned Aerial Systems: Legal and Social Implications for Security and Surveillance*, ed. Aleš Završnik (New York: Springer International, 2016), 40.

79 Kristin Veel, "The Irreducibility of Space: Labyrinths, Cities, Cyberspace," *Diacritics* 33, no. 3/4 (Autumn–Winter 2003): 153.

80 Peter Sloterdijk, *In the World Interior of Capital: For a Philosophical Theory of Globalization*, trans. Wieland Hoban (Cambridge: Polity, 2013), 252.

81 Sloterdijk, *In the World Interior of Capital*, 254.

82 Sloterdijk, *In the World Interior of Capital*, 257.

83 Sloterdijk, *In the World Interior of Capital*, 263.

84 See Paul Virilio, *Open Sky*, trans. Julie Rose (New York: Verso, 2008), 40.

85 Dorrian, "On Google Earth," 291.

86 Dorrian, "On Google Earth," 294–95.

87 "What Does 'Scale the Business' Mean? How a Common Word Became a Staple of Business Jargon," Merriam-Webster, accessed July 27, 2019, https://www.merriam-webster.com/words-at-play/scale-the-business-meaning-origin.

Bibliography

Acland, Charles R. "IMAX Technology and the Tourist Gaze." *Cultural Studies* 12, no. 3 (July 1998): 429–45.

Agnew, Frances. *Motion Picture Acting*. New York: Reliance Newspaper Syndicate, 1913.

Alberti, Leon Battista. *On Painting*. Translated by Cecil Grayson. Introduction by Martin Kemp. London: Penguin, 2005.

Albrecht, Donald, ed. *The Work of Charles and Ray Eames: A Legacy of Invention*. New York: Harry N. Abrams, 1997.

Alpers, Svetlana. "Art History and Its Exclusions." In *Feminism and Art History: Questioning the Litany*, edited by Norma Broude and Mary D. Garrard, 183–200. New York: Routledge, 2018.

Alpers, Svetlana. *The Art of Describing: Dutch Art in the Seventeenth Century*. Chicago: University of Chicago Press, 1983.

Altman, Rick, ed. *Sound Theory/Sound Practice*. New York: Routledge, 1992.

Anderson, Joseph, and Barbara Anderson. "Motion Perception in Motion Pictures." In *The Cinematic Apparatus*, edited by Teresa de Lauretis and Stephen Heath, 76–95. London: Macmillan, 1980.

Andrejevic, Mark. "Theorizing Drones and Droning Theory." In *Drones and Unmanned Aerial Systems: Legal and Social Implications for Security and Surveillance*, edited by Aleš Završnik, 21–43. New York: Springer International, 2016.

Andrew, Geoff. "Abbas Kiarostami." Guardian Interviews at the BFI. *Guardian*, April 28, 2005. https://www.theguardian.com/film/2005/apr/28/hayfilmfestival2005.guardianhayfestival.

Arnheim, Rudolf. *Film as Art*. Berkeley: University of California Press, 1964.

"Artists Reveal and Reinterpret Captivating Imagery." *Artdaily.org*, July 16, 2005. https://artdaily.cc/news/14311/Artists-Reveal-and-Reinterpret-CaptivatingImagery#.XfAacy3My8o.

Augé, Marc. *Non-places: Introduction to an Anthropology of Supermodernity*. Translated by John Howe. New York: Verso, 1995.

Aumont, Jacques. *Du visage au cinéma*. Paris: Éditions de l'Etoile/Cahiers du cinéma, 1992.

Balázs, Béla. *Early Film Theory: Visible Man and the Spirit of Film*. Edited by Erica Carter. Translated by Rodney Livingstone. New York: Berghahn Books, 2010.

Balázs, Béla. *Theory of the Film: Character and Growth of a New Art*. Translated by Edith Bone. New York: Dover, 1970.

Balibar, Étienne. "Ambiguous Universality." *differences: A Journal of Feminist Cultural Studies* 7, no. 1 (Spring 1995): 48–74.

Ball, Joseph A. "Theory of Mechanical Miniatures in Cinematography." *Transactions of SMPE*, no. 18 (May 1924): 119–26.

Barad, Karen. *Meeting the Universe Halfway: Quantum Physics and the Entanglement of Matter and Meaning*. Durham, NC: Duke University Press, 2007.

Barlow, Tani E. *The Question of Women in Chinese Feminism*. Durham, NC: Duke University Press, 2004.

Barthes, Roland. *Camera Lucida: Reflections on Photography*. Translated by Richard Howard. New York: Hill and Wang, 1981.

Barthes, Roland. *Mythologies*. Translated by Annette Lavers. New York: Hill and Wang, 1972.

Barthes, Roland. *The Rustle of Language*. Translated by Richard Howard. Berkeley: University of California Press, 1989.

Barthes, Roland. *S/Z*. Translated by Richard Miller. New York: Hill and Wang, 1974.

Baudry, Jean-Louis. "The Apparatus: Metapsychological Approaches to the Impression of Reality in the Cinema." Translated by Jean Andrews and Bertrand Augst. In *Narrative, Apparatus, Ideology: A Film Theory Reader*, edited by Philip Rosen, 299–318. New York: Columbia University Press, 1986.

Baudry, Jean-Louis. "Ideological Effects of the Basic Cinematographic Apparatus." Translated by Alan Williams. In *Narrative, Apparatus, Ideology: A Film Theory Reader*, edited by Philip Rosen, 286–98. New York: Columbia University Press, 1986.

Bazin, André. "The Ontology of the Photographic Image." In *What Is Cinema?*, edited and translated by Hugh Gray, vol. 1, 9–16. Berkeley: University of California Press, 2005.

Bedding, Thomas. "The Modern Way in Moving Picture Making." *Moving Picture World* 4, no. 13 (March 27, 1909): 360.

Bell, Charles, Sir. *Essays on the Anatomy of Expression in Painting*. Birmingham: The Classics of Medicine Library, 1984. First published 1806 by Longman, Hurst, Rees, and Orme (London).

Belton, John. "The Bionic Eye: Zoom Esthetics." *Cinéaste* 11, no. 1 (Winter 1980–81): 20–27.

Belton, John. *Widescreen Cinema*. Cambridge, MA: Harvard University Press, 1992.

Benjamin, Walter. "On Some Motifs in Baudelaire." In *Illuminations*, translated by Harry Zohn and edited by Hannah Arendt, 155–200. New York: Schocken Books, 1969.

Benjamin, Walter. "A Small History of Photography." In *One-Way Street and Other Writings*, translated by Edmund Jephcott and Kingsley Shorter, 240–57. London: Verso, 1985.

Benjamin, Walter. "Theses on the Philosophy of History." In *Illuminations*, translated by Harry Zohn and edited by Hannah Arendt, 253–64. New York: Schocken Books, 1969.

Benjamin, Walter. "The Work of Art in the Age of Mechanical Reproduction." In *Illuminations*, translated by Harry Zohn and edited by Hannah Arendt, 217–52. New York: Schocken Books, 1969.

Bennett, Jane. *Vibrant Matter: A Political Ecology of Things*. Durham, NC: Duke University Press, 2010.

Bernique, Jean. *Motion Picture Acting for Professionals and Amateurs: A Technical Treatise on Make-Up, Costumes and Expression*. Chicago: Producers Service Company, 1916.

Bird, Robert. "How to Keep Communism Aloft: Labor, Energy, and the Model Cosmos in Soviet Cinema." *e-flux journal*, no. 88 (February 2018). https://www.e-flux.com /journal/88/172568/how-to-keep-communism-aloft-labor-energy-and-the-model -cosmos-in-soviet-cinema/.

Blanchot, Maurice. *The Gaze of Orpheus*. Edited by P. Adams Sitney. Translated by Lydia Davis. Barrytown, NY: Station Hill, 1981.

Blatter, Jeremy. "Constructing Scale." In *Paper Worlds: Printing Knowledge in Early Modern Europe*. Cambridge, MA: Collection of Historical Scientific Instruments, Houghton Library, Harvard University, 2010. Exhibition catalog.

Bonitzer, Pascal. *Le champ aveugle: Essais sur le cinéma*. Paris: Gallimard, 1982.

Bonitzer, Pascal. "Les dieux and les quarks." *Cahiers du cinéma*, no. 295 (December 1978): 4–9.

Bonitzer, Pascal. "Partial Vision: Film and the Labyrinth." Translated by Fabrice Ziolkowski. *Wide Angle* 4, no. 4 (1981): 56–63.

Bordwell, David. "The Movie Looks Back at Us." April 1, 2009. http://www .davidbordwell.net/blog/2009/04/01/the-movie-looks-back-at-us/.

Bordwell, David, and Kristen Thompson. *Film Art: An Introduction*. 5th ed. New York: McGraw-Hill, 1997.

Bordwell, David, and Kristen Thompson. *Film Art: An Introduction*. 7th ed. New York: McGraw Hill, 2004.

Borges, Jorge Luis. "Of Exactitude in Science." In *Jorge Luis Borges: Collected Fictions*, translated by Andrew Hurley, 325. New York: Penguin, 1999.

Bowser, Eileen. *The Transformation of Cinema*. Vol. 2, *1907–1915*. Berkeley: University of California Press, 1990.

Braun, Marta. *Picturing Time: The Work of Etienne-Jules Marey (1830–1904)*. Chicago: University of Chicago Press, 1992.

Brewster, Ben, and Lea Jacobs. *Theatre to Cinema: Stage Pictorialism and the Early Feature Film*. New York: Oxford University Press, 1997.

Brewster, Eugene V. "Expression of the Emotions." *Motion Picture Magazine*, July 1914, 107–14; August 1914, 101–9; September 1914, 97–102; October 1914, 113–19; December 1914, 111–14.

Brothers, Peter H. "Japan's Nuclear Nightmare: How the Bomb Became a Beast Called Godzilla." *Cineaste* 36, no. 3 (Summer 2011): 36–40.

Brown, Bill. *A Sense of Things: The Object Matter of American Literature*. Chicago: University of Chicago Press, 2004.

Brown, Bill. "Thing Theory." *Critical Inquiry* 28, no. 1 (Autumn 2001): 1–22.

Brown, Gillian. *Domestic Individualism: Imagining Self in Nineteenth-Century America*. Berkeley: University of California Press, 1992.

Bruno, Giuliana. "Film, Aesthetics, Science: Hugo Münsterberg's Laboratory of Moving Images." *Grey Room* 36 (Summer 2009): 88–113.

Bruno, Giuliana. *Surface: Matters of Aesthetics, Materiality, and Media*. Chicago: University of Chicago Press, 2014.

Burch, Noël. *Life to Those Shadows*. Berkeley: University of California Press, 1990.

Burch, Noël. *Theory of Film Practice*. Princeton, NJ: Princeton University Press, 1981.

Burke, Edmund. *On the Sublime and Beautiful*. 1756. Accessed August 30, 2019. https://ebooks.adelaide.edu.au/b/burke/edmund/sublime/index.html.

Burke, Edmund. *A Philosophical Enquiry into the Origin of Our Ideas of the Sublime and Beautiful*. Edited by Adam Phillips. Oxford: Oxford University Press, 1998. Kindle version.

Cahill, James. *Zoological Surrealism: The Nonhuman Cinema of Jean Painlevé*. Minneapolis: University of Minnesota Press, 2019.

Carcassonne, Philippe. "Les paradoxes du gros plan." *Cinématographe*, no. 24 (February 1977): 2–17.

Card, James. "The 'Intense Isolation' of Louise Brooks." *Sight and Sound* 27, no. 5 (Summer 1958): 240–44.

Carroll, Noël. "Film/Mind Analogies: The Case of Hugo Munsterberg." *Journal of Aesthetics and Art Criticism* 46, no. 4 (1988): 489–99.

Cassirer, Ernst. *Philosophy of Symbolic Forms*. Vol. 2, *Mythical Thought*. Translated by Ralph Manheim. New Haven, CT: Yale University Press, 1955.

Cennini, Cennino d'Andrea. *The Craftsman's Handbook*. Translated by Daniel V. Thompson Jr. New York: Dover, 1954.

Certeau, Michel de. *Heterologies: Discourse on the Other*. Translated by Brian Massumi. Minneapolis: University of Minnesota Press, 1986.

Chanan, Michael. *The Dream That Kicks: The Prehistory and Early Years of Cinema in Britain*. London: Routledge and Kegan Paul, 1980.

Chang, Michael. "The Good, the Bad, and the Beautiful: Movie Actresses and Public Discourse in Shanghai, 1920s–1930s." In *Cinema and Urban Culture in Shanghai, 1922–1943*, edited by Yingjin Zhang, 128–59. Stanford, CA: Stanford University Press, 1999.

Chion, Michel. *Audio-Vision: Sound on Screen*. Translated by Claudia Gorbman. New York: Columbia University Press, 1994.

Chion, Michel. *The Voice in Cinema*. Translated by Claudia Gorbman. New York: Columbia University Press, 1999.

Chou, Katherine Hui-ling. "Acting and Beyond: The Queer Stardom and Body Enactment of 'Leslie Cheung.'" Accessed August 29, 2020. http://www.airitilibrary.com/Publication/alDetailPrint?DocID=20702663-200901-201005250065-201005250065-217-248.

Chow, Rey. *Woman and Chinese Modernity: The Politics of Reading between West and East*. Minneapolis: University of Minnesota Press, 1991.

Clark, T. J. *The Painting of Modern Life: Paris in the Art of Manet and His Followers.* Princeton, NJ: Princeton University Press, 1999.

Colley, Jill Susan. "Unearthing the Close-Up: Spectatorship, Anxiety, and Abstraction in Early Cinema." PhD diss., State University of New York at Buffalo, 1998. ProQuest Dissertations Publishing (9905254).

Comolli, Jean-Louis. "Historical Fiction: A Body Too Much." *Screen* 19, no. 2 (Summer 1978): 41–53.

Comolli, Jean-Louis. "Machines of the Visible." In *The Cinematic Apparatus*, edited by Teresa de Lauretis and Stephen Heath, 121–42. London: St. Martin's, 1980.

Corrigan, Timothy. *A Short Guide to Writing about Film.* 5th ed. New York: Pearson Longman, 2004.

Crary, Jonathan. "Géricault, the Panorama, and Sites of Reality in the Early Nineteenth Century." *Grey Room* 9 (Fall 2002): 5–25.

Crary, Jonathan. *Techniques of the Observer: On Vision and Modernity in the Nineteenth Century.* Cambridge, MA: MIT Press, 1992.

Crary, Jonathan. *24/7: Late Capitalism and the Ends of Sleep.* New York: Verso, 2014.

Cribbs, Bill, and Larry McCrigler. "The Spectrum of Immersive Sound." *Film Journal International* 117, no. 9 (September 2014): 62–65.

Curtis, Robin. "Immersion und Einfülung: Zwischen Repräsentationalität und Materialität Bewegter Bilder." In "Immersion," edited by Robin Curtis and Christiane Voss. Special issue, *Montage A/V*, February 17, 2008, 89–107.

Damisch, Hubert. *The Origin of Perspective.* Translated by John Goodman. Cambridge, MA: MIT Press, 1994.

Daney, Serge. "The Forbidden Zoom." Translated by Ginette Vincendeau. *Framework: The Journal of Cinema and Media*, no. 32/33 (1986): 176–77.

Darwin, Charles. *The Expression of the Emotions in Man and Animals.* Edited by Joe Cain and Sharon Messenger. London: Penguin Classics, 2009.

Debord, Guy. *Society of the Spectacle.* Detroit: Black and Red 29, 1977.

Debord, Guy. *The Society of the Spectacle.* Translated by Donald Nicholson-Smith. New York: Zone Books, 1995.

deCordova, Richard. *Picture Personalities: The Emergence of the Star System in America.* Champaign: University of Illinois Press, 2001.

Deleuze, Gilles. *Cinema 1: The Movement Image.* Translated by Hugh Tomlinson and Barbara Habberjam. Minneapolis: University of Minnesota Press, 1986.

Deleuze, Gilles. "Postscript on the Societies of Control." *October*, no. 59 (Winter 1992): 3–7.

Deleuze, Gilles, and Félix Guattari. *A Thousand Plateaus: Capitalism and Schizophrenia.* Translated by Brian Massumi. Minneapolis: University of Minnesota Press, 1987.

Della Porta, Giambattista. *De humana physiognomonia libri IIII.* 1586. Public Domain Review. Accessed August 23, 2019. https://publicdomainreview.org/collections /giambattista-della-portas-de-humana-physiognomonia-libri-iiii-1586/.

Delluc, Louis. "Photogéne." In *Film Theory: Critical Concepts in Media and Cultural Studies*, edited by Philip Simpson, Andrew Utterson, and K. J. Sheperdson, vol. 1, 49–51. New York: Routledge, 2004.

Derrida, Jacques. *Of Grammatology*. Translated by Gayatri Chakravorty Spivak. Baltimore: Johns Hopkins University Press, 1997.

Derrida, Jacques. *The Truth in Painting*. Translated by Geoff Bennington and Ian McLeod. Chicago: University of Chicago Press, 1987.

Diamond, Hugh Welch. "Editorial." *Journal of the Photographic Society of London* 5, no. 70 (September 21, 1858): 21.

Didi-Huberman, Georges. "The Art of Not Describing: Vermeer—The Detail and the Patch." *History of the Human Sciences* 2, no. 2 (June 1, 1989): 135–69.

Didi-Huberman, Georges. "The Portrait, the Individual and the Singular: Remarks on the Legacy of Aby Warburg." In *The Image of the Individual: Portraits in the Renaissance*, edited by Nicholas Mann and Luke Syson, 165–88. London: British Museum Press, 1998.

Doane, Mary Ann. "The Close-Up: Scale and Detail in the Cinema." *differences: A Journal of Feminist Cultural Studies* 14, no. 3 (Fall 2003): 89–111.

Doane, Mary Ann. *The Emergence of Cinematic Time: Modernity, Contingency, the Archive*. Cambridge, MA: Harvard University Press, 2002.

Doane, Mary Ann. "Veiling Over Desire." In *Femmes Fatales*, 44–75. New York: Routledge, 1991.

Dolby Atmos. "The Life of Pi Demo." Accessed March 25, 2015. https://www.dolby.com /us/en/experience/dolby-atmos.html.

Dombois, Forian, and Julie Harboe, eds. *Too Big to Scale—On Scaling Space, Numbers, Time and Energy*. Zurich: Verlag Scheidegger & Spiess AG, 2017.

Dooling, Amy. *Women's Literary Feminism in Twentieth-Century China*. London: Palgrave Macmillan, 2005.

Dorrian, Mark. "Adventure on the Vertical." *Cabinet*, Winter 2011–12. http:// cabinetmagazine.org/issues/44/dorrian.php.

Dorrian, Mark. "On Google Earth." In *Seeing from Above: The Aerial View in Visual Culture*, edited by Mark Dorrian and Frédéric Pousin, 290–307. London: I. B. Tauris, 2013.

Dubois, Philippe. "Le gros plan primitive." *Revue belge du cinéma*, no. 10 (Winter 1984–85): 11–34.

Duchenne de Boulogne, G.-B. *The Mechanism of Human Facial Expression*. Edited and translated by R. Andrew Cuthbertson. Cambridge: Cambridge University Press, 1990.

Dyer, Richard. *White: Essays on Race and Culture*. New York: Routledge, 2013.

Dyer, Richard, and Paul McDonald. *Stars*. 2nd ed. London: British Film Institute, 2008.

Edgerton, Samuel Y. *The Renaissance Rediscovery of Linear Perspective*. New York: Basic Books, 1975.

Eisenstein, Sergei. *Au-delà des étoiles*. Translated from Russian into French by Jacques Aumont, Bernard Eisenschitz, Sylviane Mossé, André Robel, Luda Schnitzer, and Jean Schnitzer. Paris: Union Général d'Éditions, 1974.

Eisenstein, Sergei. "Béla Forgets the Scissors." In *The Film Factory: Russian and Soviet Cinema in Documents 1896–1939*, edited by Ian Christie and Richard Taylor, 145–48. New York: Routledge, 1994.

Eisenstein, Sergei. *Film Form: Essays in Film Theory.* Edited and translated by Jay Leyda. San Diego: Harcourt, 1949.

Eisenstein, Sergei. *Nonindifferent Nature: Film and the Structure of Things.* Translated by Herbert Marshall. Cambridge: Cambridge University Press, 1987.

Elam, Kimberly. *Geometry of Design: Studies in Proportion and Composition.* New York: Princeton Architectural Press, 2001.

Elsaesser, Thomas, and Malte Hagener. *Film Theory: An Introduction through the Senses.* New York: Routledge, 2010.

Epstein, Jean. "*Bonjour cinéma* and Other Writings." Translated by Tom Milne. *Afterimage* 10 (1981): 8–39.

Epstein, Jean. *Bonjour cinema: Collection des tracts.* Paris: Editions de la Sirene, 1921.

Epstein, Jean. "The Cinema Seen from Etna." Translated by Stuart Liebman. In *Jean Epstein: Critical Essays and New Translations*, edited by Sarah Keller and Jason N. Paul, 287–92. Amsterdam: Amsterdam University Press, 2012.

Epstein, Jean. "The Delirium of a Machine." Translated by Christophe Wall-Romana. In *Jean Epstein: Critical Essays and New Translations*, edited by Sarah Keller and Jason N. Paul, 372–80. Amsterdam: Amsterdam University Press, 2012.

Epstein, Jean. "Magnification and Other Writings." Translated by Stuart Liebman. *October*, no. 3 (Spring 1977): 9–25.

Epstein, Jean. "On Certain Characteristics of *Photogénie*." Translated by Stuart Liebman. In *Jean Epstein: Critical Essays and New Translations*, edited by Sarah Keller and Jason N. Paul, 292–96. Amsterdam: Amsterdam University Press, 2012.

Evans, Arthur B. "Optograms and Fiction: Photo in a Dead Man's Eye." *Science Fiction Studies* 20, no. 3 (November 1993): 341–61.

Evens, Aden. "Concerning the Digital." *differences: A Journal of Feminist Cultural Studies* 14, no. 2 (Summer 2003): 49–77.

"The Factor of Uniformity." *Moving Picture World* 5, no. 4 (July 24, 1909): 115–16.

Farrall, Lyndsay Andrew. *The Origins and Growth of the English Eugenics Movement 1865–1925.* Bloomington: Indiana University Press, 1969.

Field, Andrew D. "Selling Souls in Sin City: Shanghai Singing and Dancing Hostesses in Print, Film, and Politics, 1920–49." In *Cinema and Urban Culture in Shanghai, 1922–1943*, edited by Yingjin Zhang, 99–127. Stanford, CA: Stanford University Press, 1999.

Fielding, Raymond. *The Technique of Special Effects Cinematography.* 4th ed. London: Focal Press, 1985.

Fredericksen, Donald L. *The Aesthetic of Isolation in Film Theory: Hugo Münsterberg.* New York: Arno, 1977.

Freedman, Barbara. *Staging the Gaze: Postmodernism, Psychoanalysis, and Shakespearean Comedy.* Ithaca, NY: Cornell University Press, 1991.

Freud, Sigmund. "A Case of Paranoia Running Counter to the Psychoanalytical Theory of the Disease." 1915. In *The Standard Edition of the Complete Psychological Works of Sigmund Freud*, translated and edited by James Strachey, vol. 14, 261–72. London: Hogarth Press, 1953–74.

Freud, Sigmund. "The Interpretation of Dreams." 1900. In *The Standard Edition of the Complete Psychological Works of Sigmund Freud*, translated and edited by James Strachey, vol. 5, 489–90. London: Hogarth Press, 1953.

Freud, Sigmund. "Negation." 1925. In *The Standard Edition of the Complete Psychological Works of Sigmund Freud*, translated and edited by James Strachey, vol. 19, 235–42. London: Hogarth Press, 1953–74.

Freud, Sigmund. "Three Essays on the Theory of Sexuality." 1905. In *The Standard Edition of the Complete Psychological Works of Sigmund Freud*, translated and edited by James Strachey, vol. 7, 125–243. London: Hogarth Press, 1953–74.

Frow, John. *Character and Person*. Oxford: Oxford University Press, 2014.

Fuller, Kathryn H. "*Motion Picture Story Magazine* and the Gendered Construction of the Movie Fan." In *In the Eye of the Beholder: Critical Perspectives in Popular Film and Television*, edited by Gary Richard Edgerton, Michael T. Marsden, and Jack Nachbar, 97–112. Bowling Green, OH: Bowling Green State University Popular Press, 1997.

Furniss, Harry. "Those Awful Cinematograph Faces." *Motography*, May 3, 1913, 329–30.

Galison, Peter. *Einstein's Clocks and Poincaré's Maps: Empires of Time*. New York: W. W. Norton, 2003.

Gallagher, Catherine. *Nobody's Story: The Vanishing Acts of Women Writers in the Marketplace, 1670–1920*. Berkeley: University of California Press, 1994.

Galton, Francis, Sir. *Hereditary Genius*. New York: Appleton, 1883. First published 1869 by MacMillan and Co. (London).

Galton, Francis, Sir. *Inquiries into Human Faculty and Its Development*. London: J. M. Dent, 1911. First published 1883 by J. M. Dent & Company (London).

Galton, Francis, Sir. *Natural Inheritance*. London: Macmillan, 1889.

Gewertz, Ken. "A Bevy of Unknown Beauties." *Harvard University Gazette*, July 21, 2005. https://news.harvard.edu/gazette/story/2005/07/a-bevy-of-unknown-beauties/.

Giddens, Anthony. *The Constitution of Society: Outline of the Theory of Structuration*. Berkeley: University of California Press, 1984.

Giedion, Siegfried. *Space, Time and Architecture: The Growth of a New Tradition*. Cambridge, MA: Harvard University Press, 1941.

Gledhill, Christine, ed. *Stardom: Industry of Desire*. London: Routledge, 1991.

Goffman, Erving. "On Face-Work: An Analysis of Ritual Elements in Social Interaction." In *Interaction Ritual: Essays on Face-to-Face Behavior*. New York: Pantheon, 1967.

Gombrich, E. H. "Conditions of Illusion." In *Art and Illusion: A Study in the Psychology of Pictorial Representation*, 203–41. Princeton, NJ: Princeton University Press, 1969.

Gray, Richard T. *About Face: German Physiognomic Thought from Lavater to Auschwitz*. Detroit: Wayne State University Press, 2004.

"Great Artist Contest." *Motion Picture Magazine* 8, no. 7 (August 1914): 164–68.

Greenhood, David. *Mapping*. Chicago: University of Chicago Press, 2018.

Green-Lewis, Jennifer. *Framing the Victorians: Photography and the Culture of Realism*. Ithaca, NY: Cornell University Press, 1996.

Griffith, D. W. Advertisement. *New York Dramatic Mirror*, December 3, 1913, 36.

Griffiths, Alison. *Shivers Down Your Spine: Cinema, Museums, and the Immersive View*. New York: Columbia University Press, 2008.

Gunning, Tom. "The Cinema of Attractions: Early Film, Its Spectator and the Avant-Garde." In *Early Cinema: Space, Frame, Narrative*, edited by Thomas Elsaesser, 56–63. London: British Film Institute, 1990.

Gunning, Tom. "The Desire and the Pursuit of the Hole: Cinema's Obscure Object of Desire. In *Erotikon: Essays on Eros, Ancient and Modern*, edited by Shadi Bartsch and Thomas Bartscherer, 261–77. Chicago: University of Chicago Press, 2005.

Gunning, Tom. *D. W. Griffith and the Origins of American Narrative Film: The Early Years at Biograph*. Champaign: University of Illinois Press, 1994.

Gunning, Tom. "The Impossible Body of Early Film." In *Corporeality in Early Cinema*, edited by Marina Dahlquist, Doron Galili, Jan Olsson, and Valentine Robert, 13–24. Bloomington: Indiana University Press, 2018.

Gunning, Tom. "In Your Face: Physiognomy, Photography, and the Gnostic Mission of Early Film." *Modernism/Modernity* 4, no. 1 (January 1997): 1–29.

Gunning, Tom. "Phantasmagoria and the Manufacturing of Illusions and Wonder: Towards a Cultural Optics of the Cinematic Apparatus." In *The Cinema, a New Technology for the 20th Century*, edited by André Gaudreault, Catherine Russell, and Pierre Veronneau. Lausanne: Editions Payot Lausanne, 2004.

Hansen, Miriam Bratu. *Babel and Babylon: Spectatorship in American Film*. Cambridge, MA: Harvard University Press, 1991.

Hansen, Miriam Bratu. "Fallen Women, Rising Stars, New Horizons: Shanghai Silent Film as Vernacular Modernism." *Film Quarterly* 54, no. 1 (2000): 10–22.

Hansen, Miriam Bratu. "The Mass Production of the Senses: Classical Cinema as Vernacular Modernism." In *Reinventing Film Studies*, edited by Christine Gledhill and Linda Williams, 332–50. London: Arnold, 2000.

Hansen, Miriam Bratu. "Universal Language and Democratic Culture: Myths of Origin in Early American Cinema." In *Mythos und Aufklärung in der Amerikanischen Literatur/Myth and Enlightenment in American Literature: In Honor of Hans Joaching-Lang*, edited by Dieter Meindl and Friedrich W. Horlacher, 321–51. Erlangen: Universitätsbund Erlangen-Nürnberg, 1985.

Harrison, Louis Reeves. "Eyes and Lips." *Moving Picture World* 8, no. 7 (February 18, 1911): 348–49.

Hart, Hugh. "Video: *Tree of Life* Visualizes the Cosmos without CGI." *Wired*, June 17, 2011. https://www.wired.com/2011/06/tree-of-life-douglas-trumbull/.

Heath, Stephen. "Narrative Space." In *Narrative, Apparatus, Ideology: A Film Theory Reader*, edited by Philip Rosen, 379–420. New York: Columbia University Press, 1986.

Heath, Stephen. "Screen Images, Film Memory." *Edinburgh '76 Magazine* 1 (1976): 33–42.

Heidegger, Martin. *The Question Concerning Technology and Other Essays*. Translated by William Lovitt. New York: Harper and Row, 1977.

Hennefeld, Maggie. *Specters of Slapstick and Silent Film Comediennes*. New York: Columbia University Press, 2018.

Henry, Pierre. "Beautés photogéniques." *Cinéa-Ciné*, no. 17 (July 15, 1924): 18–19.

Higham, John. *Strangers in the Land: Patterns of American Nativism, 1860–1925*. New Brunswick, NJ: Rutgers University Press, 2002.

Hoffman, H. F. "Cutting Off the Feet." *Moving Picture World* 12, no. 1 (April 6, 1912): 53.

Holmberg, Jan. "Closing In: Telescopes, Early Cinema, and the Technological Conditions of De-distancing." In *Moving Images: From Edison to the Webcam*, edited by John Fullerton and Astrid Söderbergh Widding, 83–90. Sydney: John Libbey, 2000.

Holmberg, Jan. "Förtätade bilder: Filmens närbilder I historisk och teoretisk belysning." PhD diss., Stockholms Universitet (Sweden), 2000. ProQuest Dissertations Publishing (CA36980).

Holmes, Oliver Wendell. "The Stereoscope and the Stereograph." In *Classic Essays on Photography*, edited by Alan Trachtenberg, 71–82. New Haven, CT: Leete's Island Books, 1980.

Horton, Zachary. "Mediating Scale: From the Cosmic Zoom to Trans-scalar Ecology." PhD diss., University of California, Santa Barbara, 2015.

Huhtamo, Erkki. "Elements of Screenology: Toward an Archaeology of the Screen." *ICONICS* 7 (2000): 31–82.

Hutchins, G. F. "Dimensional Analysis as an Aid to Miniature Cinematography." *Journal of the Society of Motion Picture Engineers* 14, no. 4 (1930): 377–83.

Huyssen, Andreas. *After the Great Divide: Modernism, Mass Culture, Postmodernism*. Bloomington: Indiana University Press, 1986.

Jameson, Fredric. "Cognitive Mapping." In *Marxism and the Interpretation of Culture*, edited by Cary Nelson and Lawrence Grossberg, 347–57. Champaign: University of Illinois Press, 1988.

Jameson, Fredric. *Postmodernism, or, The Cultural Logic of Late Capitalism*. Durham, NC: Duke University Press, 1991.

Jameson, Fredric. *A Singular Modernity: Essay on the Ontology of the Present*. New York: Verso, 2002.

Jesionowski, Joyce E. *Thinking in Pictures: Dramatic Structure in D. W. Griffith's Biograph Films*. Berkeley: University of California Press, 1987.

Johnson, Steven. "The Long Zoom." *New York Times Magazine*, October 8, 2006. https://www.nytimes.com/2006/10/08/magazine/08games.html.

Joselit, David. "Notes on Surface: Toward a Genealogy of Flatness." *Art History* 23, no. 1 (March 2000): 19–34.

Kant, Immanuel. *Critique of Judgement*. Edited by Nicholas Walker. Translated by James Creed Meredith. Oxford: Oxford University Press, 2007.

Kee, Joan, and Emanuele Lugli. "Scale to Size: An Introduction." In *To Scale*, edited by Joan Kee and Emanuele Lugli, 8–25. West Sussex: Wiley Blackwell, 2015.

Kerins, Mark. *Beyond Dolby (Stereo): Cinema in the Digital Sound Age*. Bloomington: Indiana University Press, 2010.

Khodaei, Khatereh. "*Shirin* as Described by Kiarostami." *Offscreen.com* 13, no. 1 (January 2009). https://offscreen.com/view/shirin_kiarostami.

Kirby, Andrew. "Popular Culture, Academic Discourse, and the Incongruities of Scale." In *Geographies of Power: Placing Scale*, edited by Andrew Herod and Melissa W. Wright, 171–91. Malden, MA: Blackwell, 2002.

Kirtland, Katie. "The Cinema of the Kaleidoscope." In *Jean Epstein: Critical Essays and New Translations*, edited by Sarah Keller and Jason N. Paul, 93–114. Amsterdam: Amsterdam University Press, 2012.

Kittler, Friedrich. *Discourse Networks 1800/1900*. Translated by Michael Metteer with Chris Cullens. Stanford, CA: Stanford University Press, 1990.

Kittler, Friedrich. *Gramophone, Film, Typewriter*. Translated by Geoffrey Winthrop-Young and Michael Wutz. Stanford, CA: Stanford University Press, 1999.

Kittler, Friedrich. *Optical Media: Berlin Lectures 1999*. Translated by Anthony Enns. Cambridge: Polity, 2010.

Knabb, Ken, ed. and trans. *The Situationist International Anthology*. Rev. ed. Berkeley: Bureau of Public Secrets, 2006.

Koch, Gertrude. "Béla Balázs: The Physiognomy of Things." Translated by Miriam Hansen. *New German Critique*, no. 40 (1987): 167–77.

Kuhn, Annette, ed. *Alien Zone: Cultural Theory and Contemporary Science Fiction Cinema*. London: Verso, 1990.

Kurgan, Laura. *Close Up at a Distance: Mapping, Technology, and Politics*. New York: Zone Books, 2013.

Laplanche, Jean, and J. B. Pontalis. "Projection." In *The Language of Psychoanalysis*, translated by Donald Nicholson-Smith, with an introduction by Daniel Lagache, 349–56. New York: Norton, 1973.

Lastra, James. *Sound Technology and the American Cinema: Perception, Representation, Modernity*. New York: Columbia University Press, 2000.

Lavater, Johann Caspar. *Essays on Physiognomy: Designed to Promote the Knowledge and the Love of Mankind*. Translated by Thomas Holcroft. London: William Tegg and Co., 1850.

Lavater, Johann Caspar. *Essays on Physiognomy: For the Promotion of the Knowledge and the Love of Mankind*. Vols. 2 and 3. Translated by Thomas Holcroft. London: C. Wittingham, 1804.

Lavater, Johann Caspar. *Physiognomy; or, The Corresponding Analogy between the Conformation of the Features and the Ruling Passions of the Mind*. London: Cowie, Low, and Co. in the Poultry, 1826.

Le Corbusier. *The Modulor: A Harmonious Measure to the Human Scale Universally Applicable to Architecture and Mechanics*. Cambridge, MA: Harvard University Press, 1954.

Le Corbusier. *The New World of Space*. New York: Reynal and Hitchcock, 1948.

Le Corbusier. *Towards a New Architecture.* Translated by Frederick Etchells. New York: Dover, 1986.

Lee, Leo Ou-Fan. *Shanghai Modern: The Flowering of a New Urban Culture in China, 1930–1945.* Cambridge, MA: Harvard University Press, 2001.

Lefebvre, Henri. *The Production of Space.* Translated by Donald Nicholson-Smith. Malden, MA: Blackwell, 1991.

Levinas, Emmanuel. *Totality and Infinity: An Essay on Exteriority.* Translated by Alphonso Lingis. Pittsburgh: Duquesne University Press, 1969.

Lewin, Bertram D. "Reconsideration of the Dream Screen." *Psychoanalytic Quarterly* 22, no. 2 (1953): 174–99.

Lewin, Bertram D. "Sleep, the Mouth and the Dream Screen." *Psychoanalytic Quarterly* 15, no. 4 (1949): 419–34.

Lightman, Alan. "A Sense of the Mysterious." In *The Work of Charles and Ray Eames,* edited by Donald Albrecht, 118–23. New York: Harry N. Abrams, 2005.

Ling Long Women's Magazine, no. 129 (1934). http://wwwapp.cc.columbia.edu/ldpd /linglong/saxon?source=ling_mets/ling1934_129_mets.xml&style=styles/ling_xsl _33_1.xsl&clear-stylesheet-cache=yes.

Lippit, Akira Mizuta. *Atomic Light (Shadow Optics).* Minneapolis: University of Minnesota Press, 2005.

Loew, Katharina. "Magic Mirrors: The Schüfftan Process." In *Special Effects: New Histories/Theories/Contexts,* edited by Dan North, Bob Rehak, and Michael S. Duffy, 62–77. London: Palgrave, 2015.

Longinus. *On Great Writing (On the Sublime).* Translated by G. M. A. Grube. Indianapolis: Hackett, 1991.

Lugli, Emanuele. *The Making of Measure and the Promise of Sameness.* Chicago: University of Chicago Press, 2019.

Lukinbeal, Christopher. "Scale: An Unstable Representational Analogy." *Media Fields Journal,* no. 4 (2012): 1–13.

Lundemo, Trond. "A Temporal Perspective: Jean Epstein's Writings on Temporality and Subjectivity." In *Jean Epstein: Critical Essays and New Translations,* edited by Sarah Keller and Jason N. Paul, 207–20. Amsterdam: Amsterdam University Press, 2012.

Luria, A. R. *The Working Brain.* Translated by Basil Haigh. New York: Basic Books, 1973.

Lynch, Deirdre Shauna. *The Economy of Character: Novels, Market Culture, and the Business of Inner Meaning.* Chicago: University of Chicago Press, 1998.

Lyotard, Jean-François. *Duchamp's TRANS/formers.* Translated by Ian McLeod. Edited by Herman Parret. Leuven: Leuven University Press, 2010.

Lyotard, Jean-François. "The Sublime and the Avant Garde." In *The Inhuman: Reflections on Time,* translated by Geoffrey Bennington and Rachel Bowlby, 89–107. Stanford, CA: Stanford University Press, 1991.

"Man Belongs to Earth." November 23, 2015. https://www.imax.com/movies/man -belongs-earth.

Mannoni, Laurent. *The Great Art of Light and Shadow: Archaeology of the Cinema.* Translated and edited by Richard Crangle. Exeter: University of Exeter Press, 2000.

Mannoni, Laurent, Werner Nekes, and Marina Warner. *Eyes, Lies and Illusions: The Art of Perception.* London: Hayward Gallery, 2004.

Manovich, Lev. *The Language of New Media.* Cambridge, MA: MIT Press, 2001.

Marks, Laura. *The Skin of the Film: Intercultural Cinema, Embodiment, and the Senses.* Durham, NC: Duke University Press, 2000.

Marks, Laura. *Touch: Sensuous Theory and Multisensory Media.* Minneapolis: Minnesota University Press, 2002.

Marston, Sallie A. "The Social Construction of Scale." *Progress in Human Geography* 24, no. 2 (2000): 219–42.

Marston, Sallie A., and Neil Smith. "States, Scales, and Households: Limits to Scale Thinking?" *Progress in Human Geography* 25, no. 4 (2001): 615–19.

Marston, Sallie A., Keith Woodward, and John Paul Jones III. "Scale." In *The Dictionary of Human Geography,* edited by Derrek Gregory, Ron Johnston, Geraldine Pratt, Michael J. Watts, and Sarah Whatmore, 664–66. 5th ed. Malden, MA: Wiley-Blackwell, 2009.

McCall, Anthony. "*Line Describing a Cone* and Related Films." *October,* no. 103 (Winter 2003): 42–62.

McCall, Anthony, Malcolm Turvey, Hal Foster, Chrissie Iles, George Baker, and Matthew Buckingham. "Round Table: The Projected Image in Contemporary Art." *October,* no. 104 (Spring 2003): 71–96.

Metz, Christian. *Film Language: A Semiotics of the Cinema.* Translated by Michael Taylor. New York: Oxford University Press, 1974.

Metz, Christian. "The Imaginary Signifier (Excerpts)." Translated by Ben Brewster. In *Narrative, Apparatus, Ideology: A Film Theory Reader,* edited by Philip Rosen, 244–80. New York: Columbia University Press, 1986.

Metz, Christian. *The Imaginary Signifier: Psychoanalysis and the Cinema.* Translated by Celia Britton, Annwyl Williams, Ben Brewster, and Alfred Guzzetti. Bloomington: Indiana University Press, 1982.

Milutis, Joe. F2F. http://www.hyperrhiz.net/issue01/f2f/.

Mitry, Jean. *The Aesthetics and Psychology of the Cinema.* Translated by Christopher King. Bloomington: Indiana University Press, 1997.

Moholy-Nagy, László. *Painting, Photography, Film.* Translated by Janet Seligman. Cambridge, MA: MIT Press, 1969.

Morin, Edgar. *The Stars.* Translated by Richard Howard. Minneapolis: University of Minnesota Press, 2005.

Morris, Robert. "Notes on Sculpture." In *Minimal Art: A Critical Anthology,* edited by Gregory Battcock, 222–35. New York: E. P. Dutton, 1968.

Morrison, Philip, Phylis Morrison, Office of Charles and Ray Eames, ed. *Powers of Ten: A Book about the Relative Size of Things in the Universe and the Effect of Adding Another Zero.* New York: Scientific American Library, 1994.

Mulvey, Laura. "Visual Pleasure and Narrative Cinema." In *Narrative, Apparatus, Ideology: A Film Theory Reader*, edited by Philip Rosen, 198–209. New York: Columbia University Press, 1986.

Münsterberg, Hugo. *The Film: A Psychological Study*. New York: Dover, 1970.

Münsterberg, Hugo. *Hugo Münsterberg on Film: The Photoplay—A Psychological Study and Other Writings*. Edited by Allan Langdale. New York: Routledge, 2002.

Münsterberg, Hugo. *Psychology and Industrial Efficiency*. Cambridge: Cambridge University Press, 1913.

Musser, Charles. *Before the Nickelodeon: Edwin S. Porter and the Edison Manufacturing Company*. Berkeley: University of California Press, 1991.

Musser, Charles. *History of the American Cinema*. Vol. 1, *The Emergence of Cinema: The American Screen to 1907*. Berkeley: University of California Press, 1990.

Musser, Charles. "The May Irwin Kiss: Performance and the Beginnings of Cinema." In *Visual Delights—Two: Exhibition and Reception*, edited by Vanessa Toulmin and Simon Popple, 96–115. Eastleigh, UK: John Libbey, 2005.

Nead, Lynda. *The Female Nude: Art, Obscenity, and Sexuality*. London: Routledge, 2002.

Neitzel, Britta. "Facetten Räumlicher Immersion in Technischen Medien." Edited by Robin Curtis and Christiane Voss. *Montage A/V*, February 17, 2008, 145–58.

Nichols, Bill, and Susan J. Lederman. "Flicker and Motion in Film." In *The Cinematic Apparatus*, edited by Teresa de Lauretis and Stephen Heath, 96–105. London: Macmillan, 1980.

Nochlin, Linda. *Courbet*. London: Thames and Hudson, 2007.

"Notes." *The Chap-Book* 5 (July 15, 1896): 233–40.

Nye, David E. *American Technological Sublime*. Cambridge, MA: MIT Press, 1994.

Owusu, Kwame. "The New Godzilla Is 350 Feet Tall! Biggest Godzilla Ever!" *Movie Tribute*, February 28, 2014. https://www.movietribute.com/874/new-godzilla-is -350-feet-tall-biggest-godzilla-ever/.

Oyman, Ozgur, R. Koenen, P. Higgs, C. Johns, R. Mills, and M. O'Doherty. "Virtual Reality Industry Forum's View on State of the Immersive Media Industry." *SMPTE Motion Imaging Journal* 128, no. 8 (September 2019): 91–96.

Païni, Dominique. "Should We Put an End to Projection?" Translated by Rosalind Krauss. *October*, no. 110 (Fall 2004): 23–48.

Pang, Laikwan. *The Distorting Mirror: Visual Modernity in China*. Honolulu: University of Hawai'i Press, 2007.

Panofsky, Erwin. *The Life and Art of Albrecht Dürer*. Princeton, NJ: Princeton University Press, 1955.

Panofsky, Erwin. *Perspective as Symbolic Form*. Translated by Christopher S. Wood. New York: Zone Books, 1997.

Paris, Barry. *Louise Brooks: A Biography*. Minneapolis: University of Minnesota Press, 2000.

Pasolini, Pier Paolo. *Heretical Empiricism*. Edited by Louise K. Barnett. Translated by Ben Lawton and Louise K. Barnett. Bloomington: Indiana University Press, 1988.

Poe, Edgar Allan. "The Imp of the Perverse" (1850). In *Complete Stories and Poems of Edgar Allan Poe*, 271–75. Garden City, NY: Doubleday, 1966.

"Powers of Ten and the Relative Size of Things in the Universe." Eames Official Site, October 9, 2013. https://www.eamesoffice.com/the-work/powers-of-ten/.

Pratt, George C. *Spellbound in Darkness: A History of the Silent Film*. Greenwich, CT: New York Graphic Society, 1973.

"'The Pride of Jennico' Filmed." *Motion Picture News* 9, no. 8 (February 28, 1914): 27.

Ramsaye, Terry. *A Million and One Nights: A History of the Motion Picture through 1925*. New York: Simon and Schuster, 1986.

Recuber, Tim. "Immersion Cinema: The Rationalization and Reenchantment of Cinematic Space." *Space and Culture* 10, no. 3 (August 2007): 315–30.

Robinson, Arthur. "Rectangular World Maps—No!" *Professional Geographer* 42, no. 1 (1990): 101–4.

Rogers, Ariel. *Cinematic Appeals: The Experience of New Movie Technologies*. New York: Columbia University Press, 2013.

Rony, Fatimah Tobing. *The Third Eye: Race, Cinema, and Ethnographic Spectacle*. Durham, NC: Duke University Press, 1996.

Rosenbaum, Jonathan. "Shirin as Mirror." *Cinema Guild Home Video*. Accessed August 26, 2020. http://cinemaguild.com/homevideo/ess_shirin.htm.

Rotman, Brian. *Ad Infinitum—The Ghost in Turing's Machine: Taking God Out of Mathematics and Putting the Body Back In: An Essay in Corporeal Semiotics*. Stanford, CA: Stanford University Press, 1993.

Rotman, Brian. *Signifying Nothing: The Semiotics of Zero*. London: Macmillan, 1987.

Routhier, Pierre Hugues. "The Immersive Experience Classification System: A New Strategic Decision-Making Tool for Content Creators." *SMPTE Motion Imaging Journal* 127, no. 10 (November 2018): 46–54.

Ryan, Marie-Laure. *Narrative as Virtual Reality 2: Revisiting Immersion and Interactivity in Literature and Electronic Media*. Baltimore: Johns Hopkins University Press, 2001.

Ryfle, Steve. *Japan's Favorite Mon-Star: The Unauthorized Biography of the Big G*. Toronto: ECW Press, 1998.

Sadoul, Georges. *Histoire générale du cinéma*. Vol. 1. Paris: Denoel, 1948.

Schmitt, Charles B., and Dilwyn Knox, eds. *Pseudo-Aristoteles Latinus. A Guide to Latin Works Falsely Attributed to Aristotle before 1500*. London: Warburg Institute, 1985.

Schmölders, Claudia. *Hitler's Face: The Biography of an Image*. Translated by Adrian Daub. Philadelphia: University of Pennsylvania Press, 2009.

Schor, Naomi. *Reading in Detail: Aesthetics and the Feminine*. New York: Methuen, 1987.

Sekula, Alan. "The Body and the Archive." *October* 39 (Winter 1986): 3–64.

Siegrist, Christoph. "'Letters of the Divine Alphabet'—Lavater's Concept of Physiognomy." In *The Faces of Physiognomy: Interdisciplinary Approaches to Johann Caspar Lavater*, edited by Ellis Shookman, 25–39. Columbia, SC: Camden House, 1993.

Simmel, Georg. "The Aesthetic Significance of the Face." In *Georg Simmel: 1858–1918: A Collection of Essays*, edited by Kurt Wolff, translated by Lore Ferguson, 276–81. Columbus: Ohio State University Press, 1959.

Simmel, Georg. "The Metropolis and Mental Life." In *The Sociology of Georg Simmel*, translated and edited by Kurt H. Wolff, 409–24. London: Collier-Macmillan, 1950.

Simmel, Georg. "The Sociology of Space." In *Simmel on Culture: Selected Writings*, edited by David Frisby and Mike Featherstone, 137–69. London: Sage, 1997.

Simmel, Georg. "The Stranger." In *The Sociology of Georg Simmel*, translated and edited by Kurt H. Wolff, 402–8. London: Collier-Macmillan, 1950.

"The Size of the Picture." *Moving Picture World* 8, no. 10 (March 11, 1911): 527.

Sloterdijk, Peter. *In the World Interior of Capital: For a Philosophical Theory of Globalization*. Translated by Wieland Hoban. Cambridge: Polity, 2013.

Sloterdijk, Peter. *Spheres*. Vol. 2, *Globes, Macrospherology*. Translated by Wieland Hoban. South Pasadena, CA: Semiotext(e), 2014.

Smithson, Robert. "Cinematic Atopia." In *Robert Smithson, the Collected Writings*, edited by Jack Flam, 138–42. Berkeley: University of California Press, 1996.

Sobchack, Vivian. *Carnal Thoughts: Embodiment and Moving Image Culture*. Berkeley: University of California Press, 2004.

Spencer, Herbert. "Progress: Its Law and Cause." In *Select Works of Herbert Spencer: The Data of Ethics; Progress: Its Law and Cause; The Philosophy of Style. Essays*, 233–85. New York: John B. Alden, 1886.

Spengler, Oswald. *The Decline of the West*. Authorized translation and with notes by Charles Francis Atkinson. New York: Alfred A. Knopf, 1927.

Spitz, René A. "The Primal Cavity." *Psychoanalytic Study of the Child* 10, no. 1 (1955): 215–240.

Stafford, Barbara Maria, and Frances Terpak. *Devices of Wonder: From the World in a Box to Images on a Screen*. Los Angeles: Getty Research Institute, 2001.

Stegeman, Allan. "The Large Screen Film: A Viable Entertainment Alternative to High Definition Television." *Journal of Film and Video* 36, no. 2 (Spring 1984): 21–72.

Steimatsky, Noa. *The Face on Film*. New York: Oxford University Press, 2017.

Sterne, Jonathan. *The Audible Past: Cultural Origins of Sound Reproduction*. Durham, NC: Duke University Press, 2003.

Sterne, Jonathan. *MP3: The Meaning of a Format*. Durham, NC: Duke University Press, 2012.

Stewart, Susan. *On Longing: Narratives of the Miniature, the Gigantic, the Souvenir, the Collection*. Durham, NC: Duke University Press, 1993.

Steyerl, Hito. "In Free Fall: A Thought Experiment on Vertical Perspective." In *The Wretched of the Screen*, edited by Julieta Aranda, Brian Kuan Wood, and Anton Vidokle, 12–30. Berlin: Sternberg Press/e-flux journal, 2013.

Stiegler, Bernard. "Pharmacology of Desire: Drive-Based Capitalism and Libidinal Diseconomy." Translated by Daniel Ross. *New Formations* 72 (2011): 150–61.

Sullivan, C. C. "Chanel Ginza, Tokyo." *Architectural Lighting Magazine*, June 27, 2007. https://www.archlighting.com/projects/chanel-ginza-tokyo_o.

Tafuri, Manfredo. *Architecture and Utopia: Design and Capitalist Development*. Translated by Barbara Luigi La Penta. Cambridge, MA: MIT Press, 1976.

Taussig, Michael. *Defacement: Public Secrecy and the Labor of the Negative*. Stanford, CA: Stanford University Press, 1999.

Tavernor, Robert. *Smoot's Ear: The Measure of Humanity*. New Haven, CT: Yale University Press, 2007.

Thompson, Emily. *The Soundscape of Modernity: Architectural Acoustics and the Culture of Listening in America, 1900–1933*. Cambridge, MA: MIT Press, 2004.

Thrift, Nigel. "Lifeworld Inc—and What to Do about It." *Environment and Planning D: Society and Space* 29, no. 1 (February 2011): 5–26.

"Too Near the Camera." *Moving Picture World* 8, no. 12 (March 25, 1911): 633–34.

Tsivian, Yuri. *Early Cinema in Russia and Its Cultural Reception*. Chicago: University of Chicago Press, 1994.

Veel, Kristin. "The Irreducibility of Space: Labyrinths, Cities, Cyberspace." *Diacritics* 33, no. 3/4 (Autumn–Winter 2003): 151–72.

Vidler, Anthony. "Psychopathologies of Modern Space: Metropolitan Fear from Agoraphobia to Estrangement." In *Rediscovering History: Culture, Politics, and the Psyche*, edited by Michael Roth, 11–29. Stanford, CA: Stanford University Press, 1994.

Vidler, Anthony. *Warped Space: Art, Architecture, and Anxiety in Modern Culture*. Cambridge, MA: MIT Press, 2000.

Vinograd, Richard. *Boundaries of the Self: Chinese Portraits, 1600–1900*. New York: Cambridge University Press, 1992.

Virilio, Paul. "Cataract Surgery: Cinema in the Year 2000." Translated by Annie Fatet and Annette Kuhn. In *Alien Zone: Cultural Theory and Contemporary Science Fiction Cinema*, edited by Annette Kuhn, 169–74. New York: Verso, 1990.

Virilio, Paul. *Open Sky*. Translated by Julie Rose. New York: Verso, 2008.

von Helmholtz, Hermann. *Treatise on Physiological Optics*. Translated and edited by James P. C. Southall. Vol. 1. Menasha, WI: Optical Society of America, 1924.

Wagner, Anne. "Scale in Sculpture: The Sixties and Henry Moore: Rothenstein Lecture." In *Tate Papers*, no. 15 (Spring 2011). https://www.tate.org.uk/research/publications/tate-papers/15/scale-in-sculpture-the-sixties-and-henry-moore.

Walley, Jonathan. "The Material of Film and the Idea of Cinema: Contrasting Practices in Sixties and Seventies Avant-Garde Film." *October* 103 (Winter 2003): 15–30.

Waltenspül, Sarine. "The Camera as a Scaling Instrument: Focus on Cinematographic Modelling Techniques." Translated by Burke Barrett. In *Too Big to Scale—On Scaling Space, Numbers, Time and Energy*, edited by Forian Dombois and Julie Harboe, 33–48. Zurich: Verlag Scheidegger & Spiess AG, 2017.

Warner, Francis. *Physical Expression: Its Modes and Principles*. London: Kegan, Paul, Trench and Co., 1885.

Wasson, Haidee. "The Networked Screen: Moving Images, Materiality, and the Aesthetics of Size." In *Fluid Screens, Expanded Cinema*, edited by Janine Marchessault and Susan Lord, 74–95. Toronto: University of Toronto Press, 2007.

Wellbery, David E. *Lessing's Laocoon: Semiotics and Aesthetics in the Age of Reason*. Cambridge: Cambridge University Press, 1984.

Werneburg, Brigitte. "Ernst Jünger and the Transformed World." Translated by Christopher Phillips. *October* 62 (Autumn 1992): 42–64.

Whissel, Kristen. "Parallax Effects: Epistemology, Affect and Digital 3D Cinema." *Journal of Visual Culture* 15, no. 2 (August 2016): 232–49.

Whitney, Allison. "The Eye of Daedalus: A History and Theory of IMAX Cinema." PhD diss., University of Chicago, 2005.

Williams, Linda. "Film Bodies: Gender, Genre, and Excess." *Film Quarterly* 44, no. 4 (1991): 2–13.

Williams, Linda. *Screening Sex*. Durham, NC: Duke University Press, 2008.

Woods, Frank. "Spectator's Comments." *New York Dramatic Mirror*, March 22, 1911, 28.

Yhcam. "Cinematography (1912)." In *French Film Theory and Criticism: A History/Anthology, 1907–1939*, vol. 1, *1907–1929*, edited by Richard Abel, 67–77. Princeton, NJ: Princeton University Press, 1988.

Yonge, Charlotte M. *The History of Sir Thomas Thumb*. Edinburgh: Thomas Constable, 1856.

Yue, Genevieve. "The China Girl on the Margins of Film." *October*, no. 153 (Summer 2015): 96–116.

Zelle, Carsten. "Soul Semiology: On Lavater's Physiognomic Principles." In *The Faces of Physiognomy: Interdisciplinary Approaches to Johann Caspar Lavater*, edited by Ellis Shookman, 40–63. Columbia, SC: Camden House, 1993.

Zhang, Yingjin. *The City in Modern Chinese Literature and Film*. Stanford, CA: Stanford University Press, 1996.

Zhen, Zhang. *An Amorous History of the Silver Screen: Shanghai Cinema, 1896–1937*. Chicago: University of Chicago Press, 2005.

Index

reaction to close-ups, 120. *See also* Epstein, Jean, close-up theory

Epstein, Jean, close-up theory: autonomy, 48; celebratory nature, 1, 8, 32–33, 35–36, 290n49; faces, 33, 115, 118, 290n49; gazes, 44; nostalgic animism, 119; objects of desire, 293n33; *photogénie*, 32–33, 36; proximity to pain, 49; revolver example, 289n32; size, 33; temporality, 118

Esperanto, 14

Étant Donnés: 1. La Chute d'Eau, 2. Le Gaz d'Éclairage (Duchamp), 21, 229–30

Explosion of a Motor Car (Hepworth), 59

"Expression of the Emotions": overview, 92; deception problem, 95–96, 98; emotions lists, 94–95; illustrations, 95, 96, 97, 101, 106–7; individual-type tensions, 128; influences on, 92–93; physiognomic influences, 95, 101–2, 106–7, 300n27; as signs of interiority, 94–95; summary of arguments and claims, 93–94; universal language discourse, 115

facades, 170–71

face, 89, 121

face blindness, 168–70, 309n45

faces: Balázs, Béla, 103–6, 140, 301n46, 301n56; caricature, 68; centrality to cinema, 89–90; characterization, 19, 66–67, 277; cinema as, 120; contemporary focus on, 122–23; contradictions of, 123; crowds, 153; Deleuze and Guattari, 119–20, 304n93; and dream screens of breasts, 167–68; equivalency with close-ups, 38–39; Goffman, Erving, 120; intersubjectivity, 169; irrational-rational tensions, 128; legibility, 19–20, 39–40, 51, 90; *Letter to Jane*, 46–47, 164, 166; literary, 67–68; masks, 114–15; mask-window dialectic, 132; modernity, 121; mug shots, 110–11; politics, 45–46; as pure surface, 139–40; and representation, 39–40; roles of, 39; significance in cinematic history, 67; as signs, 120; Taussig, Michael, 131–32; theories of, 38–40; and transparency, 120. *See also* character

interiority, close-ups exposing; faces, close-ups of; facial expression; physiognomy; recognition; women's faces

faces, close-ups of: affect, 178; Balázs, Béla, 34–35, 38, 40–41, 71, 79, 115, 181; cinematic specificity, 90, 135; Deleuze, Gilles, 39; Epstein, Jean, 32–33; ethics, 169; gender differences, 138–39; as grotesque, 8, 19, 55, 59–62, 67, 138; impact of, 18, 37; individuals in modernity, 71; space and time separation, 34–35. *See also* facial expression; women's faces, close-ups of

facial expression: acting guides and manuals, 69, 70, 92; character interiority, 71; early journalistic discourses, 90–91; gender differences, 91; mediation, 130; method acting, 294n50; as natural language, 103; rationality, 128. *See also* "Expression of the Emotions"; facial expression films; facial expressions and universal language theory; physiognomy; women's faces

facial expression films: overview, 123; *Anna Held*, 55, 124, 125; defacement, 131; *Facial Expressions*, 55, 123–25; *Goo Goo Eyes*, 55, 124–25, 126; interiority access, 127; *The Old Maid in the Drawing Room*, 124; *Photographing a Female Crook*, 125–26, 128; physiognomy resistance, 125; *The Rose*, 55, 124, 127; *Sweets for the Sweet*, 124

Facial Expressions (Edison), 55, 123–25

facial expressions and universal language theory: overview, 90; Balázs, Béla, 103–6, 140, 301n46, 301n56; Brewster, Eugene V., 93; cinema's indexicality, 103; colonial contexts, 92, 102–3; modernity, 114, 121–22; physiognomy, 97, 102; racial problematics, 100; transparency, 102

feminism, 174–75, 179, 310n63. *See also* women

feminist criticisms of Dürer, Albrecht, 222–23

feminist film, 307n22

feminist film theory, 151, 307n22

fiction, category of, 69–70

"First Lady of the Screen" composite photograph, 112–14, 303n79

Pauletto, Sandra, 268

Pepper's Ghost, 11

persistence of vision theory, 197–98

perspective: overview, 21; Alberti's systems, 211–12, *214*, 215, 217, 234; in art history, 218–19; and cartography, 210–13, 215–16; cinematic images, 217; disorientation, 237–38; distance as relation to scale, 81; distortions, 231–32; in film theory, 81–82, 217–19, 230, 251–52; *Geography of the Body*, 231–32, *233*, 238, 280–81; homogeneous space, 215–16, 317n63; horizon, 234–35; infinity, 224–26, 230, 251–52; versus maps, 215–16; painter-viewer relations, 228; Panofsky, Erwin, 215, 219, 222, 225, 228–29, 234, 252, 317n63; and physiognomy, 108–10; realism, 233–34; Renaissance, 210–12, 215–16, 218, 224, 317n63; and spectators, 81–82, 217–18; as stabilizing system, 230; subject-object production, 228–29, 238; vanishing points, 81, 212, 222, 224–25, 227, 230; vertical, 21–22, 234–37; women, representations of, 220–30. *See also* Dürer, Albrecht

phantasmagoria, 11

phenakistoscopes, 197–98

photogénie: overview, 32; as cinephilia, 51–52; close-ups, 32–33, 45, 280; definitions of, 23, 288n9; Epstein, Jean, 23, 32–33, 118–19, 290n49; and the inarticulable, 51; movement, 118

Photographing a Female Crook (AM&B), 125–26, *128*

photography: "The Blue Marble," 235, 244; composite, 111–14, 303n79; forensic uses, 110–11; nonwhite skin, 141; and physiognomy, 109–10

physiognomy: overview, 91, 298n5; acting manual influence, 92; antimodernism in, 104–5; deception, 98; definitions, 96; evolutionary mythologies, 104; "Expression of the Emotions," 95, 101–2, 106–7, 300n27; faces in modernity, 114–15; forensic uses, 110; Gray, Richard T., 96, 107–8, 112, 115; Günther,

Hans F. K., 104, 302n66; historical contexts, 100, 102; individuals versus types, 112, 128; instinctive knowledge problem, 98; Kassner, Rudolf, 105, 112, 114–15, 301n55; linguistic analogies, 91–92; and perspective, 108–10; and photography, 109–10; popularity, 110; racism, 19, 100–2, 104, 106, 110, 130, 302n66; representational technology use, 106–7, 115; scientific aspirations, 96–98, 101; semiotics of, 98; Spengler, Oswald, 105; universal language theory, 97, 101–2; Werner, Heinz, 104. *See also* Lavater, Johann Caspar, physiognomic theory

Plateau, Joseph, 194, 197–98, 313n11

Pleynet, Marcelin, 217, 219

Pontalis, J. B., 207

pornography, 62–63

Porter, Edwin S., 35, 56

portraiture, 70, 178, 294n52

posthumanism, 23

Powers of Ten: About the Relative Size of Things in the Universe (Eames and Eames), 253–57, 321n25

Preminger, Otto: *Bunny Lake Is Missing*, 85, *86*, 231; *The Cardinal*, 222, *223*; *Whirlpool*, 231, *232*

projection: overviews, 21–22; in aesthetic theory, 204–5; and capitalism, 200–201; cartographic uses, 210–13; cinematic specificity, 20; experimental films, 162–63; geometric, 204, 210, 316n50; of motion, 199–200; optical toys, 198–99; in psychoanalysis, 21, 205–7; scalar effects, 20–21; scale, control over, 200, 209; term meanings, 204; the viewer's roles in, 205. *See also* avant-garde and projection; screens

prosopagnosia, 168–70, 309n45

psychoanalytic theory: breastfeeding, 167–68; categories, 168, 309n44; facades, 170–71; female paranoia, 206; projection, 21, 205–7; relationship between past and present, 191; screens, 167–68, 170

Ptolemy, 211–13

Sirk, Douglas, 76

Situationist International, 62, 294n37

size. *See* scale

Skladanowsky, Max, 192

Sleepwalkers (Aitken), 242–43

Sloterdijk, Peter, 13, 17, 25, 278–79

smartphones, 246–48

Smith, George Albert, 55, 59

Smithson, Robert, 1, 11

sound: dialogue intelligibility, 266–67; Dolby Atmos, 22, 269–70; editing rules, 270; film theory, 265; immersive, 269–71; mobility, 271; space, 266–68

sound perspective, 265–67

space: 180-degree rule, 268–69; abstract, 77, 87, 296n71; and the body, 74–75; coherency and fragmentation, 76–77, 79; contemporary contraction, 278–79; continuity editing, 77, 79, 209; diegetic, 77; disembodiment, 87; filmic organization, 78; frames, 76–79, 249, 260, 271; front-back relationships, 262–65; of globalization, 278; Hollywood cinema, 239; ineffable, 87; Lefebvre's theories, 74–77, 82–83, 86–87, 220, 262, 296n68, 296n71; modernity's impacts on, 87–88; off- versus on-screen, 239–40; organization at human scale, 83–84; pathologies, 170–71, 187–88; perspectival versus psychophysiological, 234; production, 75; rationalization, 74; reenchantment, 275; represented versus representational, 76, 296n68; sound, 266–68; spectator, 48, 77–78, 210, 264; stabilization and destabilization, 86–87; virtual real, 83. *See also* cartography; perspective; projection

special effects, 258–59, 284n23. *See also* scale models

spectacle, 48–49, 201

spectators: bodies, 84, 271; delocalization, 17; dreaming comparisons, 167; ideal positioning, 50; image origin knowledge, 200; IMAX, 248–49, 253, 320n23; immobility, 75, 262; location of, 26, 36; and perspective,

81–82, 217–18; scale models disorienting, 11–12; space, 48, 77–78, 102, 210, 264; and the turn, 263–64, 272. *See also* immersion

Spengler, Oswald, 105

Spitz, René, 167–68

Spivak, Gayatri, 123

stardom, 112

stars: China Girls (color calibration), 142; commodity capitalism, 71–72; composite photographs, 112–14, 303n79; "double body" phenomenon, 71, 182–83, 312n81; and the gigantic, 49; individual-type tensions, 112–14; modern faces, 114; repetition and recognition, 151; Shanghai, 182–84, 186

Stegeman, Allan, 249

Steimatsky, Noa, 290n49

stereoscopy, 219–20

Sternberg, Josef von, 185–86

Sterne, Jonathan, 264–65

Stewart, Susan, 26, 40, 48–49, 194–95, 200

Steyerl, Hito, 25–26, 234–35, 287n53

Stiegler, Bernard, 168, 309n44

Street Angel (Yuan), 180–81

sublime, 249–53, 259–61

sublime objects, 250, 253, 260, 320n12

Sullivan, C. C., 241

Sunrise (Murnau), 176

Sun Yu, 176, 181, *186*

superfields, sound, 267–68

surfaces, 139–40, 252. *See also* faces; screens

Sweet and Twenty (AM&B), 79, *82*

Sweets for the Sweet (AM&B), 124

Syrene, Egypt, 211–12, 316n54

Tafuri, Manfredo, 87

Talmadge, Norma, *96*

Tanteri, Matthew, 242

Taussig, Michael, 131–32

Tavernor, Robert, 7, 12

temporality: close-ups, 34–35, 41–42, 47, 118, 290n49; rationalization of, 74; relativistic, 236–37

theater design, 266–67

women's faces: in the avant-garde, 151–52, 162, 168; breastfeeding (psychoanalytic theory), 167–68; and cinematic apparatuses, 149; color-timing film leaders, 141, *144*; expressiveness beliefs, 91, 128; historical specificity, 162; ideal composites, 112–14; legibility, 152, 179; modernity, 168, 171; as pure surface, 139–40; screens protecting, 152–53, 307n29; standardization, 142; urbanity, 162, 181; white, 152, 162. *See also* women's faces, close-ups of

women's faces, close-ups of: Brooks, Louise, 135, *136*, 137; *Chelsea Girls*, 163, 308n33; del Río, Dolores, *138*; film theorist discourses, 135–38, 140, 148; Garbo, Greta, 135–37; *Goodbye, Dragon Inn*, 148; Hepburn, Audrey, 136–37; historical contexts, 138; Hu Die, *139*; *Ling Long Women's Magazine*, 139, 182; versus men's, 138; *The Passion of Joan of Arc*, 148, 164; reactions to other films, 143, 148; remembered, 41; Shanghai cinema, 178–84; *Shirin*, 143, *146–47*, 148–50; as soliciting viewing, 139, 148; universal language theory, 140; *Vivre sa vie*, 148, 164, *165*. *See also* facial expression films

Wong Kar-wai, 85–86, *87*

Woods, Frank, 102

Wrinkles Removed (AM&B), 55

Young, Clara, 91

Zelle, Carsten, 110

zero degree of scale, 8–9

zoom: in contemporary life, 256–57, 279; epistemology, 256–57; etymology, 257, 279; Google Earth, 256–57; *Powers of Ten*, 254, 256; and scale, 4–5; versus tracking shots, 4, 283n6